Through the eyes
of a child

Through the eyes of a child

New insights in theology
from a child's perspective

Edited by Anne Richards and Peter Privett

CHURCH HOUSE
PUBLISHING

Church House Publishing
Church House
Great Smith Street
London SW1P 3AZ

Tel: 020 7898 1451
Fax: 020 7898 1449

ISBN 978 0 7151 4088 8

Published 2009 by Church House Publishing

The opinions expressed in this book are those of the individual authors
and do not necessarily reflect the official policy of the General Synod
or The Archbishops' Council of the Church of England

Typeset in 9.5pt Stone Sans
by RefineCatch Limited, Bungay, Suffolk
Printed by MPG Books Ltd, Bodmin, Cornwall

Contents

Foreword by the Bishop of Oxford   vii

Acknowledgements   ix

About the contributors   xi

Prologue: The thirtieth anniversary of the International
Year of the Child   xv
Peter Privett

Introduction   xxi
Anne Richards

How to get more from this book   xxv

What is a child?   1
Nigel Asbridge

1   Nakedness and vulnerability   21
   Anne Richards

2   Creation   44
   Keith White

Activities   65

3   Spirituality   68
   Rebecca Nye

4   Word   85
   Joanna Collicutt

5   Play   101
   Peter Privett

Activities   125

6   Sin   128
   Emma Percy

7   Forgiveness   146
   Sandra Millar

8   Grace   165
   Angela Shier-Jones

9   Salvation   185
    John Pridmore

Activities   202

10 Death   205
    John Drane and Olive M. Fleming Drane

11 Judgement   223
    Paul Butler

12 Angels   247
    Howard Worsley

13 Heaven and Hell   269
    Philip Fryar

Activities   284

Resources   287

List of works cited in the text   289

Notes   303

General index   325

Index of biblical references   333

Foreword

One of the dangers of writing about children is that we oscillate between romanticizing childhood and being pretentious about it. There is, however, another way, and this book offers it.

Children may not come 'trailing clouds of glory' but they do at least suggest a model of spiritual simplicity that is both subversive and liberating. My recent experience of becoming a grandparent (extraordinary in one so young, I know!) has put me in touch afresh with the gift of seeing 'through the eyes of a child'.

The value of this volume is that it places the child as subject rather than as object. Here we have a diverse group of eminently qualified writers exploring big questions through a child's eyes. Children are not so much being 'written about' as 'written with'. Such a strategy makes us rethink every theological construct and revisit every spiritual cliché. Children are theological dynamite.

I can't remember who said, 'I like children, but I couldn't manage a whole one.' A whole child contains a whole world. We too easily analyse, package and store childhood according to adult criteria. This book sets its face against any such prescriptions. It attempts to let children be children and bring their own fresh insights to refurnish tired adult minds. Who knows where that may lead?

We are often called, rightly, to love our children unconditionally. A man once complained to his rabbi that his son had forsaken God. 'What shall I do, Rabbi?' he asked. 'Love him more than ever', replied the rabbi. However, I am also the recipient of that kind of unconditional love. I am the blessed recipient of my 6-month-old granddaughter's heart-melting smiles, which light me up inside. This love is mutual. It delights, surprises and energizes my experience of life. 'Through the eyes of a child' I see life dipped in God.

This fascinating book points us to the child-like vision that Jesus unerringly recognized as the key to entering the kingdom of God. The stakes are high. We have reason, therefore, to be deeply grateful to Anne Richards and Peter Privett for editing a timely, refreshing and disturbing volume in this UK Churches' Year of the Child. This is a book through which to see theology afresh. Inhabiting that world will hopefully change us.

After all, seeing is believing.

+ John Pritchard
January 2009

Acknowledgements

The editors and publisher would like to thank the following people for help with the writing of this book: Mary Hawes, Jenny Hyson, Diana Murrie, Doug Swanney.

The authors and publisher gratefully acknowledge permission to reproduce copyright material in this book. Every effort has been made to trace and contact copyright holders. If there are any inadvertent omissions we apologize to those concerned and will ensure that a suitable acknowledgement is made in all future editions.

Adrian Snell, 'A Little Child Shall Lead Them', taken from 'The Cry, A Requiem for the Lost Child', composed by Adrian Snell with Murray Watts, published by Serious Music UK Ltd. Reproduced by permission.

Extracts from Dylan Thomas, 'Fern Hill' in Dylan Thomas, *The Poems*, J. M. Dent. Reproduced by permission.

'Show me' from *My Fair Lady*, words by Alan Jay Lerner, music by Frederick Loewe © 1956 (Renewed) Alan Jay Lerner and Frederick Loewe, publication and allied rights assigned to Chappell & Co. All Rights Reserved. Used by permission of Alfred Publishing Co., Inc.

Associated Press for the photographs (p. 187) from *The Guardian*, 6 February 2007, and on p. 42, copyright © AP/PA Photos. Reproduced by permission.

Unless otherwise indicated, the Scripture quotations are from the New Revised Standard Version of the Bible, Anglicized Edition, copyright © 1989, 1995 by the Division of Christian Education of the National Council of the Churches of Christ in the United States of America, and are used by permission. All rights reserved.

About the contributors

Peter Privett is the Godly Play international regional training consultant for the UK, Europe and beyond. He is the author of *Living in a Fragile World: A Spiritual Exploration of Conservation and Citizenship Using the Methods of Godly Play*.

Anne Richards is national adviser for mission theology, alternative spiritualities and new religious movements in the Mission and Public Affairs Division of the Archbishops' Council of the Church of England. She is convener of the ecumenical Mission Theology Advisory Group and responsible for many publications looking at gospel and culture issues, including *Sense Making Faith: Body, Spirit, Journey*. She has been involved in a number of child-related resources from the Church of England, including *Children in the Midst*.

Nigel Asbridge is a former children's social worker who has been a parish priest in London for 15 years. He is now a director and chaplain missioner at the Church of England Children's Society which has been committed to securing social justice for children and young people for over 125 years.

Keith White is director of Mill Grove where, with his wife Ruth, he is responsible for the residential community, caring for children who have experienced separation and loss. He is former president of the UK Social Care Association and chair of the National Council of Voluntary Child Care Organizations. Currently, Keith is an associate lecturer at Spurgeon's College and visiting lecturer in child theology at the Malaysian Baptist Theological Seminary. He is chair of the Child Theology Movement and founder of the Christian Child Care Forum. He is the author of *The Growth of Love, Understanding the Five Essential Elements of Child Development*.

Rebecca Nye is a reader in education at Anglia Ruskin University. She was responsible for bringing Godly Play to the UK about ten years ago, helping to set up the first UK classroom at the University of Cambridge Divinity School and then directing a project on Godly Play and Children's Spirituality. Her

book publications include *The Spirit of the Child* with David Hay (second edition 2006) and *Psychology for Christian Ministry* (with Fraser Watts and Sara Savage). Rebecca is mother of three young children and also enjoys teaching for Cambridge Theological Federation and supervising postgraduate students researching children's spirituality.

Joanna Collicutt is senior lecturer in psychology and convener of the MA course in psychology of religion at Heythrop College, University of London. She is also associate tutor in psychology at Ripon College, Cuddesdon and a part-time curate in an Oxfordshire parish. Her background is in clinical psychology, and she has many years' experience working in the NHS. Her interests are wide ranging, reflected in publications in the area of cognitive behavioural therapy, brain and behaviour, psychological approaches to biblical exegesis, psychological responses to trauma, the spirituality of children and those with special needs, and medical ethics. She is a trustee of Godly Play UK.

Emma Percy is currently chaplain at Trinity College, Oxford. For seven years she was priest-in-charge and then vicar of Holy Trinity, Millhouses in Sheffield. The church had a lively involvement in children's work, especially with pre-school children and through close contact with the local infant school. Emma is the mother of two boys and is currently engaged in research into the practice of both ordained ministry and motherhood.

Sandra Millar is currently the children's adviser for the Diocese of Gloucester. She has many years' experience of working with children as a volunteer and her research interests include training of volunteers and adult learning. She has trained children's workers across the world – and has also managed to visit all six continents, including Antarctica! For fun, she reads books, talks to her dog and watches TV adverts.

Angela Shier-Jones is a Methodist minister who has held posts in the Bromley Circuit, Methodist tutor at the South East Institute for Theological Education and Director of Academic Programmes and Research at Wesley College, Bristol. She is the editor of *Children of God: Towards a Theology of Childhood*, published by Epworth Press. She is also the editor of the *Epworth Review*.

John Pridmore was for eleven years Rector of Hackney in the East End of London, before his retirement. Previously he was on the staff of St Martin-in-the-Fields. He has been a school chaplain and a religious studies teacher in England and in Tanzania. For four years he was chaplain of Ridley Hall, Cambridge, where he taught Christian Ethics and New Testament Greek. He has researched and published in the fields of the theology of childhood and

children's spirituality. His doctorate was awarded by the London Institute of Education. His recent book *Inner-City of God* is published by Canterbury Press.

John Drane is a bestselling writer and teacher, working in many areas, but especially in the fields of mission and spirituality. He is co-chair of the Mission Theological Advisory Group. He is the author of *The McDonaldization of the Church* and *After McDonaldization: Mission, Ministry and Christian Discipleship in an Age of Uncertainty*.

Olive M. Fleming Drane is particularly known for her work in Christian clowning and her work in spirituality. She is the author of *Spirituality to Go*, *Clowns, Storytellers, Disciples*, and, with John Drane, *Family Fortunes: Faith-full Caring for Today's Families*.

Paul Butler is Bishop of Southampton in the Anglican Diocese of Winchester. He has been involved in, and committed to, children's work throughout his ministry and was invited by the Archbishop of Canterbury to be an advocate for children within the College of Bishops of the Church of England, a role which he has pursued vigorously. He is particularly interested in how children outside the Church are engaged by the good news of Jesus Christ and how children are nurtured in discipleship.

Howard Worsley is director of education for the Anglican Diocese of Southwell and previously director of studies at St John's College, Nottingham. His doctorate was on *The Inner-Child as a Resource for Adult Faith Development*. He is the author of numerous booklets and articles on education matters and particularly on resourcing those who work with children in churches.

Philip Fryar lives in Essex and attended St Thomas of Canterbury RC Primary School and the Coopers' Company and Coborn School in Upminster. He is currently at Palmers College in Grays, Essex, studying for A levels. He is severely dyslexic and dictates what he writes to his computer. His hobbies are books, films, music and writing weird screenplays, because dyslexics love to multitask. He loves Philip Pullman's *Dark Materials* Trilogy and listening to new bands. His friends describe him as 'a cross-wearing maniac in a mosh pit'.

Prologue: The thirtieth anniversary of the International Year of the Child

Peter Privett

Thirty years ago the United Nations designated 1979 as the 'International Year of the Child'. This enabled various organizations that had children's needs on their agenda to give voice to the challenges of humanity's responsibilities to and for the world's children. To mark the thirtieth anniversary of the International Year of the Child, those who hold children's issues and child advocacy in the UK Churches have assigned 2009 as The Year of the Child.[1] This book is one contribution to that initiative.

This prologue offers an overview of developments in the 30 years since the International Year of the Child. How far have we come? One of the issues addressed during the International Year of the Child in 1979 was the plight of many children as they faced the trials of poverty, homelessness, war, hunger and disease. The promotion of the International Rights of the Child confronted the world's governments with their obligations and duties. Thirty years on, with increased globalization, open markets and global warming, we are still faced with the same issues of child labour, exploitation and deprivation. Children throughout the world are still hungry, still at the mercy of war and still dying unnecessarily because of disease.

The designated year also celebrated the contributions that children offer, their gifts and abilities, the ways in which their voices and experiences enriched the communities of which they were a part.

The child's voice

In succeeding years the theme of 'the child's voice' has been especially present in a variety of 'participation projects'. From the establishment and growth of school councils to various international consultancy conferences, children have been offered a place in which their views and opinions can enable possible changes in policy, strategy and action.

The creation of a space for the voice of the child has sometimes created an uncomfortable and challenging response for the adult world. One manifestation of this discomfort in the last 30 years has been most apparent in the issues associated with the emotional and physical abuse of children. The voices of children throughout the world have brought to light the betrayal that many of them feel when the safe boundaries they expect adults to hold, are broken by the very same adults in whom they have put their trust.

At the time of writing (May 2008), there are reports in the international news accusing members of the United Nations Peace Keeping Forces of incidents of child abuse. The adult world displays ambivalence to this voice of the child. The establishment of ChildLine and other agencies which seek to honour the child's voice is set against the still prevailing attitude in many adults which protests, 'How far can we trust children to tell the truth?'

Ambivalent attitudes to the child

The ambivalence is also apparent in popular culture where images of children are pushed to extremes: the innocent angel or evil demon. The growth of consumerism in the rich world has been quick to exploit the child pound potential and its associated choices, yet set against this is the increased restriction on play and freedom and the feelings of inhibition urged on by the adult voices warning against perceived, yet not necessarily corroborated, increases of risk and danger.

The ambivalence is even more apparent in the sweeping changes to the British education system during this period. The move from a Plowden[2] child-centred approach to a subject-orientated national curriculum, the change in language from 'education as service', to the language of 'product and consumer', the move from self-discovery to 'target and outcomes', and many more, are ones that have had far-reaching consequences. The educational reforms of the last years were introduced with a desire for a more equitable provision of education throughout the whole country, but the desire for more and more measurable outcomes has increased the pressures on children and adults working within the system. The vast revolution of cyber educational technology over the past 30 years has meant that our children are incredibly computer competent, yet according to a recent UNICEF report, Britain was ranked lowest among the countries for children's self-esteem and well-being.[3] The Church over the last 30 years has not been exempt from this ambivalent attitude.

The child and the Church

For the celebration of the International Year of the Child 1979, the World Council of Churches commissioned a leading theologian, Hans Ruedi Weber, to write a biblical study on the gospel texts of Jesus and the children. His insights from the Graeco-Roman and Jewish traditions and the gospel texts are still challenging and relevant today.[4]

They stand alongside a tradition of those who, over the past 30 years, have advocated the voice of the child in the Church, a voice that has at times been overwhelmed and marginalized. For example, the place and role of the child in the eucharistic community has been a long and protracted conversation in the Church of England, and although some progress has been made with the provision of guidelines on the admission of children to communion before confirmation, it is a discussion that is still going on in many places.

The last 30 years have seen important thinking about the Christian nurture of children and their place in the Christian community. The work of the, then, British Council of Churches in the publication of *The Child in the Church* in 1984 offered a major challenge to the Church to take its formal and informal provision of nurture seriously. It also offered the challenge of what we might learn *from* children.

The Church of England's *Children in the Way* (1989) and succeeding reports in the 1990s[5] focused on the image of the child as fellow pilgrim, the child as a member of an all-age community. Associated with this were the insights from James Fowler and John Westerhoff about faith development and the honouring of different stages of faith.[6] The identification of the different stage characteristics, the ways in which people believed rather than what they believed, offered the possibility of honouring the child's voice and experience alongside that of others.

As the twentieth century grew to a close, the growing perceived crisis of secularization gave rise to the issues of child evangelism and mission, and again there was the ambiguity of child as object of mission and evangelism set alongside the child as missionary and evangelist.[7]

Another factor in the equation was a renewed perception of a deep resource of innate spirituality that was being revealed in many places, especially at times of national crisis (for example, in the response to the death of Princess Diana in 1997).

Nurturing the spirituality of the child

The fact that religious education was still classed as a compulsory subject of the national curriculum and that schools were expected to address the issues of spirituality, resulted in an increasing interest in and development of these subjects in both faith and secular institutions.

The groundbreaking work of David Hay and Rebecca Nye in the area of children's spirituality has had far-reaching effects. Their concept of 'relational consciousness', of presenting the voice, the eyes, the experience of the child, in their advocacy for children's spirituality offers a challenge to the norms of adult perceptions.[8]

Her desire for meaningful methods of Christian nurture that might support the child has led to the current swell of interest in Godly Play. Based in the traditions of educators Maria Montessori and Sofia Cavalletti, and developed over the past 40 years by Jerome Berryman, Godly Play uses both religious symbols and words, verbal and non-verbal ways of knowing, to enable people to make meaning for themselves. The creation of a safe, child-friendly environment is key, as are the values of openness, process, play and exploration. The adult is seen as someone who supports the children in their learning and discovery, someone who is open to the voice of the child so that they might learn from the process as well. The languages of story and play are seen as those to which children naturally respond, and the use of natural materials that have been beautifully crafted gives the unspoken message of worth and appreciation.

The overall structure of a session that includes an intentional welcome and crossing of the threshold, a story followed by wondering, a time for individual play or response using a variety of materials ending with feast/prayers and dismissal/ blessing, is one that has been adopted and adapted by a variety of denominations and traditions. There has also been a great leaping of generational and institutional boundaries. What began as a model for the support of children's spirituality is now also being used by adults in a wide variety of settings, house groups, retreats, as well as care homes for the elderly and in some cases prison and hospital chaplaincy. Also, what was intended as a model of Christian church nurture for children has crossed over into the religious education world of schools and colleges.[9]

The child and theology

The stimulus for the growth of this movement has largely been due to a small band of people who have promoted the *theology of childhood*, the examination and recovery from the theological tradition of the theme of childhood.

Godly Play has been one model, among others, that has highlighted the strand of the *child as theologian*, children doing theology. Those of us who work alongside children have often been highly privileged and humbled by the theological insights offered by children as they grapple with the big existential questions of life.

Another recent strand remarked on in this book by John Pridmore in Chapter 9 and especially promoted by Keith White and others[10] is the ways in which the experience of childhood critiques theology. *Child theology* is the challenge of obeying the command of Jesus to place the child in the centre, to see what this does to our theology, our missiology, our pastoralia, and so on. The idea of this book began with a personal frustration. For over 50 years I've been involved with children's ministry. It began with a ministry 'to' children. Over the years, experience has shown me that the prepositions need to be changed. I now want to say a ministry 'with' and 'alongside' children.

I search British Christian bookshops for help with this journey and find material of varying quality (I've even written some myself!). Most give ideas and activities of what to do to children: there are the materials that outline a hundred ways of getting over a particular point of doctrine or ethical behaviour using drama, craft and games, there are the shelves of books of how pastorally to minister to children in bereavement situations, and even what to do with so called 'naughty' children, but when it comes to the *theology of childhood, children doing theology* or *child theology*, there is a dearth. The voice of the child in this sense seems to have been silenced. They are conspicuous by their absence. I've taken to asking booksellers, 'Where have the children gone?' Yet when I go to other countries there are books galore. When I came across David Jensen's *Graced Vulnerability*[11] in the bookshop at Washington Cathedral I utterly disgraced myself by shouting and whooping out loud with joy!

It was also a spur to action. I am deeply grateful to Anne Richards and to Tracey Messenger, commissioning editor at Church House Publishing, for their patience in allowing me to vent my spleen and allowing me to join them in the journey that invited adults to reflect on what children thought about some classic themes that have occupied theologians over the years.

This book is offered as an attempt to address the balance of the theological silence of children's voices. The themes of *the theology of childhood, children doing theology* and *child theology* are part of the warp and weft of the texts. It is an offering in remembrance of that made by Hans Ruedi Weber 30 years ago, and is one small contribution to the UK Churches' Year of the Child 2009.

Here is an invitation to look at some key theological themes *Through the Eyes of a Child*.

Introduction

Anne Richards

This is an unusual kind of theology book in that twelve of its thirteen chapters are written by adults, yet it is children who populate and animate each weighty topic – some of the most grave, difficult and beautiful topics in Christian theology. We hear the voices of those children and find them endlessly speaking to us of God. Those lucky ones, permitted to be purely themselves, explore the world as an adventure playground, bounce on the sofa and laugh with joy at the endless possibilities of the creation. These children tell us of love that endures, forgiveness that never runs out, a world that is good and above all, fun. Such children describe the world to us in a theological language reminding us that as adults we are amnesiac children, even twisted and ruined children, requiring us to remember and recall (sometimes painfully) how to play. Few of us, squinting through drizzle, as we transport young children late for school, would declare wonderingly that 'rain is what clouds do best'. And there are other children too, silent, rocking, hurt, deprived, whose voices and playful delight are denied them because our world is broken and damaged and because of the hurt adult power can bring into children's lives. Those children are here too, among these pages, indicting the adult world and our theological understanding with their pain and suffering, their absence, silence and death.

Looking through the eyes of a child is not a twee, cosy or easy experience. It can be unsettling, uncomfortable, edgy, especially as we can become shifted quite rapidly from our own particular Christian comfort zone. Children reveal the 'brilliance' of Jesus and are generous in a way that Christian teaching often is not. This means that it has been no easy task for the authors to produce the material in this book. The adult contributors have all tried to lessen their own impact on the material and present the children faithfully. This is not an easy intellectual or emotional exercise but takes a particular kind of discipline which is actually unknown in many other kinds of theological discourse. A certain kind of restraint has to be exercised which allows the children to express themselves without reinterpretation, explanation or dismissal of what apparently makes no sense. Even so, certain sorts of themes have emerged

between the chapters in this book. These include the omnipresent spirituality and relational aspects of children's lives and the importance of play as a way of manifesting God's presence in the world. Children subvert and challenge adults when they play and indict us when they cannot play, when we refuse to give them the space and blessing that was the gift of Christ.

The chapters tend to fall into two types: there are chapters which arise directly from research conducted among children and whose conclusions come directly from what they have to tell us. Those children are theologians reflecting back to us ideas and thoughts of God and are challenging precisely because those thoughts are not like ours. The other type of chapter reworks a theological theme through the eyes of a child, reformulating the easy comfortable theological world we often like to inhabit.

The material in this book shows clearly how children challenge our conventional readings of theology. We begin with an exploration of the very concept of 'child', demonstrating that we all have presuppositions and assumptions about children and childhood which are often very far from a God's-eye view of the child as one made in God's own image and worthy of vocation. This is followed by a chapter confronting some of the most difficult issues in our present society – the idea of the 'naked' child, at once vulnerable, demanding of our protection, and also a confrontational and emotive idea, opening up issues of possible abuse and exploitation. This first group of chapters is concluded by an examination of children in relation to creation, in which questions about freedom and the discovery of God at work in the world jostle uncomfortably with adult anxieties: should we let children (literally) play with fire?

The next group of chapters, on Spirituality, Word and Play go deeper into the heart of children's exploration of theological issues. Familiarity with Godly Play methods and insights is key in these chapters[1] and in each case adult theological viewpoints are shifted and disturbed. A thrown paper aeroplane is discovered not to be a bored child mucking about (as you might reasonably think), but unfolds into a vision of the crucified Christ making his way through Holy Saturday. A Godly Play exercise on the parable of the sower cuts deeply into received ideas about adult preaching and teaching and engagement with God's Word. Even more profoundly, but wonderfully, disturbing is the chapter on Play which almost proved impossible to write at all. How can you sit down and order words on a page which get at the myriad possibilities of creative play? Indeed, one child in this chapter engages most powerfully with the gospel by singing a spontaneous and creative song. How then can you

describe the theological possibilities of hiding behind a curtain, trying not to giggle, when you know the one you know you *really want* to find you is out there and will never stop looking for you, until you are found?

The next cluster of chapters consider Sin, Forgiveness, Grace and Salvation. The children in this section especially, challenge theories about children and childhood by refusing to fall into easy categorization.[2] For example, the chapters on Sin and Forgiveness interrogate each other and not only ask us to 'rethink' God in the light of children's insights and generosity towards sinners, but also highlight our own anxieties with paradox and contradiction with which children live so much more easily. The idea of 'good sin' which arises in these chapters is a kind of *felix culpa* which permeates the way the world is for children: a way of dealing with a fractured and imperfect world with an ability to see all kinds of possibility and opportunity instead of dead ends. Consequently, the chapter on Grace digs deeper into what children tell us about theological ideas of interdependence, community and relationship, which leads to gracious hospitality and sharing, while a powerful chapter on Salvation gathers up all these issues and focuses back on to those children who need saving, *now*, from the poverty and injustice in which they must live.

The final cluster of chapters concentrates on the traditional 'four last things' Death, Judgement, Heaven and Hell, together with research on children and Angels. In these eschatological chapters, adult concerns about death, dying and ultimate destiny are challenged by children engaging directly with loss and grief, and with the mysteries of Scripture in the parable of the sheep and the goats, and the protecting angel in Daniel's den of lions. Certainly, these children are often bound by their culture and their social situation (a number seeing the heavenly realm as populated by a kind of royalty, for example), but much of the language they use is conditioned by having to explain their insights to *us*. The drawings, which are vital to understanding the theological explorations in this section of this book, often challenge the narratives from which they are drawn, confronting us with thoughts and ideas which do not translate into mere words. Indeed, in the material on Judgement, one of the most unforthcoming children created an image of extraordinary thoughtfulness, richness and detail. The last word is given to a child on the edge of leaving childhood (as far as the world is concerned). It is close enough for him to look back and reflect on it, but enough of it has passed for him to look forward and see what it might mean for his spiritual development as an adult.

It is hoped that this book will be of value to all who work with children, teach children or engage with children liturgically. For this purpose, each chapter is

followed by questions for reflective engagement and each group of chapters has a number of activities related to it, to encourage ways of interacting with and learning from children. But more than this, the children whose voices are offered here challenge each one of us to re-examine our faith, our Christian lives and theological understanding. As the chapter on Salvation tells us, God's wisdom is seen playing in the street. We can see Spirit in every child, even those yet unborn about whom we can often say very little else. We need to strip away the romanticized notion of the child, the 'celebrity magazine' vision of the child, society's view of the child as both commodity and economic construct and see children as complete human beings who are also heralds and harbingers of the kingdom, testing us and often finding us wanting, yet willing to embrace us in all our imperfections, as God is.

How to get more from this book

Each chapter in this book is followed by some questions for reflection or discussion. It is possible for individual readers to choose particular questions for their own study or reflection, or some of the questions can be selected and used as an aid to group discussion. There are five different kinds of questions in each set:

- A 'concept' question, to encourage further engagement with the wider subject matter of the chapter;

- A question that looks at something specific offered by the chapter, perhaps to challenge or enable in-depth reflection;

- A question that offers a listing or drawing exercise for those who like to deal with questions in a practical way;

- A question that offers a biblical focus with suggested passages for study;

- A question that prompts readers and groups to look at using the ideas in the chapter to change ONE thing about their own situation.

This book also provides activities for groups of adults and children based on clusters of chapters. The activities are mainly designed for use with younger children, but in some cases older children could be involved in helping the adults with the younger ones. As with the questions, there are five kinds of activities:

 Game: The first type of activity encourages adults to be childlike and to play with children.

Create: The second type of activity encourages creative work, preferably along side children.

 Learn from: The third type of activity seeks to create a situation in which participants can learn more about or from children and may require adults to invite children to do something.

 Celebrate: The fourth activity encourages some form of celebration of or for children.

 Scripture: The final activity relates to Scripture and could then be followed through into worship, bringing participants back to being children of God together.

The activity section is designed not to be prescriptive but to enable reflection, contemplation and wondering. Some suggested Bible verses are included to aid this reflection if you find this helpful, but can be left out if not.

What is a child?

Nigel Asbridge

This opening discussion begins by questioning the presuppositions and assumptions concerning the word 'child'. This is because we all carry preconceptions about what a child is, based on our own experience of being a child, our relationships with children and the laws and regulations concerning children by which, in the United Kingdom, we are bound. Yet we do not very often stop to consider how difficult it is to pin down exactly what a child is and who we are talking about when we refer to them.

The discussion then looks at a number of contexts which surround the issue of 'child' and 'childhood' and uses a historical overview and statistical information to show how many of the assumptions we have inherited about children and young people are adult fictions which distract us from central questions about the experience of being a child. It is hoped that this approach will help readers engage open-mindedly with the children of the chapters in this book, whose voices and insights are at the heart of its theological enquiry.

What is a child?

We might think it is easy to tell what a child is, but actually, once we begin to think about it, it is fraught with difficulty.

One problem is that because all of us have been children, we assume that we know what the experience is of being a child – we imagine that we can remember. In fact, the business of remembering turns out to be extremely complex. Psychologists and cognitive scientists have revealed that our memories have a 'bias' that affects whether or not an incident will be remembered at all, how long it takes to recall a memory, and even the content of a reported memory. Typically we are more likely to remember occasions associated with the extremes of emotion, and to access those that are most important to our sense of self.[1] There is even a suggestion that we can acquire 'memories' – that is, we remember hearing others regularly recounting incidents from our childhood but recall them as if we remember the incidents themselves.[2] The result is that the memories of our childhood are not necessarily a reliable evidence base for what it is to be a child or, for that matter, what it was like for us to have been a child.

Coupled with this is the theory of childhood amnesia, which describes not the complete absence of early childhood memories but their relative scarcity. Psychologists explain this in terms of cognitive development: that children and adults experience the world in very different ways, within different frameworks and sets of relationships – some even suggest a different or absent sense of self in infancy – so that the adult mind no longer recognizes the cues left by the child to access those memories. The truth is that there are formative periods of our lives about which we simply have few or no reliable memories of our own, and while we may remember some incidents from our childhood these are selective, lacking in context and processed and reprocessed by a mind that functions very differently from that of a child.[3]

A second problem is that, while children are a necessary fact of human being, concepts of child and childhood (what a child is, what children do, their perceived capacities, appropriate relationships to the adult world, family and society and so on) vary culturally and historically and, indeed, have changed radically even, perhaps especially, in the past half century.

When is a child?

One way in which societies currently answer the question 'what is a child?' is by describing '*when* is a child': that is, they define children by age in years. Even here there is a lack of consistency and considerable variation within relatively recent history. One way in which we can look at this is by reference to those watershed ages which are characterized by laws and regulations. Many of these regulations relate to what people can legally do with, or to, their bodies. Under UK legislation at the time of writing a person can legally consume alcohol at the age of 5 but not purchase it until 18,[4] buy lottery tickets or a pet and leave school at 16. While people currently have to be 18 to get a tattoo without parental consent, there is no minimum age or similar requirement to have their bodies pierced, although some establishments impose their own age restrictions.

At 16 young people can also marry but require written consent from parents, at 18 they can do so with or without parental consent. In fact the minimum age for marriage in England and Wales changed only in 1929. Until then the age was 12 for girls and 14 for boys, with or without parental consent. The age of consent is another such watershed; currently this stands at 16 for both boys and girls, though the lowering of the age of consent for homosexual sex changed only in the last ten years. Globally, however, there remains considerable variation. In Mexico and the Philippines the age of consent is 12, in Spain and Japan 13, in Malta and Vietnam 18. Some national legal systems equate consent with marriage (e.g. 14 years in Pakistan and Saudi Arabia, where intercourse outside marriage remains illegal). Some countries continue to distinguish between the age of consent and the minimum age for marriage (e.g. Malaysia, 16 years for sexual consent, 21 years of age for marriage); still others distinguish between the sexes usually with a lower age, as much as four years, for females (Papua New Guinea being an exception).

The reasoning normally given for such regulation is the assumed need to protect *vulnerable* minors, it being a common belief in many contemporary societies that persons below a certain age lack the maturity or life experience to fully comprehend the ramifications of their actions. The age of consent to sexual acts is most often justified in these terms. In fact the history of the age of consent in the UK suggests different motives: set at 12 in 1275 in English law and therefore consistent with the legislation of marriage, the age was raised to 13 in 1875, and to 16 in 1885 not in an attempt to protect vulnerable young people but as part of a campaign to curb a growing sex industry affecting male adults.

What this shows is that the law assumes that there is some age range in which a person is 'a child' or which ranks as 'childhood'. During this period, children are not capable of informed decision making and to take advantage of such a person is a criminal act. But these statistics also show that the law is a blunt instrument in trying to decide 'when' is a child. This is because we have to face the question of whether young people's minds are sufficiently developed to make 'adult' decisions, or whether young people's bodies are sufficiently mature to be used in 'adult' ways. Yet maturity does not miraculously spring into being at watershed ages: growth and development in all human beings varies from person to person. The point at which adults feel their children should be treated as fellow adults is a matter of complex negotiation, which is often fraught with tension on both sides. Some parents treat their children as mature adults much earlier than the law would suggest was good for them. Others never ever treat their offspring as fellow adults.

We can also see that this leads to both mixed messages and confusion about what ages these criteria imply. Currently, a child under the age of 16 can consent to a potentially life-threatening and complex medical procedure if they are deemed to have 'sufficient maturity and judgement' and the ability to understand what is proposed, whereas a child is deemed 'criminally responsible' in English law at the age of ten without any requirement to assess their maturity or ability to comprehend the criminal nature or effects of their actions. In fact, from the fourteenth century children below the age of ten had been deemed *doli incapax* – incapable of guilt – and between the ages of 10 and 13 years could not be criminally responsible unless demonstrated otherwise. It was not until 1998 that this presumption was removed under Section 28 of the Crime and Disorder Act.

This cursory glance at the some of the legal parameters we set around childhood demonstrates the complexities that exist in defining what a child is. Here we see not only those cultural and historical differences but also some of the inconsistencies and ambiguities in our current thinking and attitudes towards children and young people. Moreover, in common with many of the other ways we think about and deal with children, there lies behind legislation a model based upon deficiency – that is, a child is defined in terms of a lack of capacity when compared to a normal or standard adult. Consequently, when we try to look through the eyes of children, at the kind of world in which they are growing and developing, we can see that the matter of self-definition is not only difficult but sometimes impossible to manage except by reference to external regulations. Teenagers flirt with the boundaries, making themselves look older to get into a 12, 15 or 18 rated film, or younger to qualify for cheaper rail fares or entrance tickets. There is clearly no easy answer to determining when being a child or childhood ends.

Whose is a child?

Another way of considering the question 'what is a child?' is by relationship. When a person becomes a parent, they have a child in perpetuity, whether the child is six, sixteen or sixty. Sometimes in obituaries the phrases 'leaves grown-up children' or, confusingly, 'leaves adult children' will be used. However, the norms for even these most basic of human relationships also vary historically and culturally. There is, for example, a widespread understanding that parents have some sort of authority over their children, but a variety of understandings about how far that authority extends. In some historical periods and cultures authority has been seen as absolute to the point of 'ownership', affording parents the right to give away a child for marriage or payment or even to abandon them. Meanwhile the debate in the UK about the parent's 'right' to smack their child is unresolved. Essentially, it is a question of the nature of the relationship between parent and child and what licence the particularity of that relationship permits.

The gender of both parent and child is often seen as determining the norms of relationship. Again, in terms of authority, in other cultures and times, it is typically the father who is identified as being the ultimate possessor of authority, but his authority over his daughter ceases when she becomes the property of her husband through marriage. While bonded and indentured labour is now illegal in most countries, it is considered permissible, even desirable in some circumstances, for a parent to relinquish their relationship with a child, for example giving their child 'up for adoption' or as part of a surrogacy arrangement. Since the first child protection legislation of 1889 the state has had the right to remove a child from its parents in certain circumstances and to assume parental responsibility. In these cases the parent–child relationship changes or is terminated. In other parts of the world, children are looked after by a cluster of (usually female) relatives such as aunts and grandmothers. There is, however, an important sense that a child should 'belong' to some person, family members, or a community. A child is to be located among some responsible adults. A lost child might therefore be asked the question, 'who do you belong to?'

What is a child *not*?

Perhaps the most obvious way of defining what a child is, is as an immature form of human being – a 'not-yet-adult' or an 'adult-to-be'. This form of definition requires us to have an understanding of what it means to be an adult and to differentiate children from that category. The problem then becomes that our model of human being becomes inherently hierarchical and inevitably we will begin to concentrate on the ways in which a child is deficient when compared to a mature adult, and in particular the adult male, who in earlier times was considered to be physically and mentally better developed than the female. Children are less physically strong, smaller, more prone to disease, weaker, mentally and linguistically less capable. The concept of human life stages, which can be found throughout secular and religious thought, becomes one of an ascent to adulthood and a subsequent decline into senility, and carries with it a hierarchy of human worth. For example, the table of redemption tariffs in Leviticus 27 values adults above children and males above females so that at the bottom of the scale, an infant girl is valued at 3 shekels and a male over 20 years at 50 shekels. Adults, put simply, are normative for human beings, and they are seen as being 'worth' more than children.

Human biology and childhood

This hierarchical picture of ascent and descent is not, however, necessarily mirrored in scientific understanding. Clearly, human beings grow and develop. Early life is often characterized by measurement and developmental checking. Bodies eventually become sexually mature. But bodies do not cease to change. Every human person experiences physical change as a result of increased age. Anthropologically, there have been some arguments about whether adults should actually ever be considered 'grown up' at all. Juvenile ape theory,[5] for example, suggests that the reason why we look, act and behave as we do is that we never actually mature into primate adults, but are somehow stuck in a juvenile form of primate life (neoteny[6]), sacrificing physical maturity for bigger brain size and thus making the transition between childhood and adulthood even more murky. In this perspective, adults are therefore either ruined children, or those who have passed out of 'early life' into a place called 'later life'.

On the other hand, the work of Freud, which through Erikson, Piaget and others continues to have great influence in child developmental and educational psychology, preserves the nineteenth-century dictum that *ontogeny recapitulates phylogeny*. To put it crudely, the triumph of Darwinist evolutionary theory led scientists to believe that, as any organism developed into its final mature physical and psychological form it went through a process that imitated the stages of the evolution of its entire species. For Freud then, children were not simply a less mature form of the adult human, they were also more primitive and prone to primal urges.[7] Mature or healthy adults are therefore children who have successfully evolved through a series of stages into complete human beings.

Darwinist exponents of the selfish gene theory,[8] however, would not argue that children are necessarily worth less than adults, or are incomplete in some way. In this view, offspring of any living things are valuable for the survival of parental genes and must therefore be protected and nurtured until they themselves are capable of reproducing and passing on the precious genes. 'Childhood', in this view, is merely the amount of 'investment' a parent needs to put into offspring in order to make it possible for the genes to survive.

Science, then, also gives us competing pictures of what we should expect to see when we consider a child.

A theological perspective

Theologically we would perhaps expect the picture to be clearer. After all, the Bible tells us that children are a gift from God. God addresses human beings as complete and whole individuals from before their birth and throughout their lives. Human personhood is not divided up into childhood or adulthood; it is merely personhood irrespective of age, social status or amount of learning, wisdom or experience. God calls each individual human being into a real relationship and to a real vocation, not a potential vocation somewhere in the future. Jeremiah protests, 'I am only a young person', but that is irrelevant to God. God calls Samuel, not the more experienced teacher and mentor. Baptism affords full not conditional or provisional membership of the Body of Christ. Yet Christian tradition and the internal life of our churches have often failed to reflect that children are active participants in the people of God who make independent contributions to the life of the Church rather than simply respond to the demands, instructions and interpretations of adult Christians. So when we look through the eyes of a child we look through the eyes of one who is regarded as a whole person before God, not an incomplete person or partial person, or adult-in-the-making.

Childhood

Concepts, even theological ones, are seldom unrelated to actuality, in that what is seen to be most true is generally that which is experienced as being true. However, while there has been a radical shift in the realities of lives of children and young people there has been no similar shift or discontinuity in our concept of childhood. That our concept of childhood no longer matches our experience of children may be one reason why the idea that we may be facing 'a crisis of childhood' has crept into popular awareness. The paradigmatic pictures of childhood that the Church has inherited from St Augustine, John Calvin, Matthew Arnold or even Karl Rahner simply will no longer do.[9] For the most part the only thing that the children they describe will have in common with ours is their age.

One of the striking things we come across when we start to look at how the ways in which the constructs of childhood have changed and developed over the centuries is how much attention is paid to children and childhood in the present day compared to in the past. We seem as a society to be preoccupied with the place of children in society, their families and friends, how they spend their time, their safety, educational progress, health and we are particularly fascinated by the crimes they commit and those committed against them. Alongside the academic disciplines that have traditionally focused on children, such as paediatrics and educational psychology, childhood itself has emerged as a legitimate subject for study and often those who do so have found that contemporary childhood is 'under threat',[10] 'toxic'[11] or 'disappearing'.[12]

When we look at earlier historical literature we find that, although children formed a significant proportion of the population and had a much more active role in society and the economy, they are almost invisible. Literature about children is rare; rarer is literature for children and, rarer still, literature by children that might offer us some insight into the experience of the child. With some notable exceptions, children are usually only mentioned in terms of inheritance or property or as subsets of a household or in instructional manuals directed towards parents on appropriate child rearing and education. The few accounts devoted to children do not offer us much in the way of answers to the questions we may naturally wish to pose from the twenty-first-century perspective on childhood. Moreover, what accounts do exist are usually written by adult males who are members of the wealthier, literate classes. They are normally writing about their own children or children from their own class and more often than not they concern themselves with sons (sons as heirs) rather than daughters. We therefore know less about how 'girlhood' was conceptualized and still less about the lives of the vast majority of children from outside that small elite class.

Living and dying in childhood

Added to this is what was one of the most pressing realities of childhood until very recent history – infant and child mortality. Throughout most of human history mortality rates among children under twelve years have ranged from about 20 to 30 per cent, with still higher rates in times of social distress. In the United Kingdom child mortality only entered a consistent but gradually accelerating decline towards the close of the eighteenth century. Remember too that the number of children as a proportion of the total population has and continues to decline significantly, which means that the death of a child was formerly a far more common event. To give a context: of all deaths in London in 1751, half were of children aged under ten. None of these figures include stillbirths, which were not considered sufficiently significant or abnormal to be worthy of being recorded in England and Wales until 1928.[13]

Childhood and the business of reproduction were as much about death as life. The child was not therefore simply an 'adult-to-be' but a 'may-be-adult' and even, in a society where to be an adult is to represent the fullness of human being, no more than a potential human being. Childhood became not only a life stage marked by deficiency but also one marked by mortal and therefore moral danger. The childhood of former times was a sickness to be recovered from and a hazardous period to be passed through as quickly as possible.

This posed a problem for theologians and moral philosophers alike. Jews and Christians understood that according to their biblical tradition children and life itself were a gift from God and a sign of his blessing of them as his people, part of his covenant to Abraham. Death was a curse, the price of sin or disobedience, as was childlessness. Children seemed to embody both blessing and curse and thus the models of child oscillated between the child as a 'holy innocent' and the child as demon.

It was the model of the child as depraved, however, which came to dominate Christian thought. For philosophers of other faiths such as Hammurabi, Aristotle, Cicero and Cassius Dio, children were likewise gifts of Providence or the gods, but both were fickle and none of them the one supreme God who held sway over creation. For them the death of a child was about Fate, a curse, witchcraft, a lack of favour with a god or the result of some divine spat between gods. For Christians and their Jewish forebears, however, God was faithful and constant. If the wages of sin were death and children died, children must be sinful. Being apparently incapable of sinning themselves, sin was seen to be derived from conception, through which babies shared in original sin. Scripture told them that humans were 'evil from youth' (Genesis 8.21) and that 'I was born guilty, a sinner when my mother conceived me' (Psalm 51.5). The disobedience of the young threatened to bring disaster on the whole community and therefore the urgent task of parenting and child rearing became one of disciplining and training children from an early age, including the use of corporal punishment (Proverbs 13.24; 22.15; Sirach 7.23), be it in the Law for the Jewish people (Deuteronomy 6.7; 11.18-19; 31.12-13) or from the Reformation onwards through more formal forms of education. Biblical and Christian texts all stress the accountability of parents for any lack of spiritual or social discipline in their children (Sirach 30.1-13, *The Apostolic Constitutions*, Jerome, Chrysostom, Erasmus, etc.). Thus, for Calvin, children are born with 'the seeds of sin' which during their natural development yield 'the fruits' of sin. Parenting becomes a process of disciplining children away from this natural sinful state by 'ruling' or 'overwhelming them'.[14]

A remodelling of childhood

This model of childhood dominated Christian thought, and thereby the wider understanding of childhood, up until the end of the eighteenth century, when in common with many of the accepted types, the Romantics recast childhood. Just as the natural world, which had been identified with an absence of divine and human order (hence 'pagan' and 'heathen') was now seen to stand for primal good untouched by human destructiveness and sin, and the increasingly industrialized urban world to be one of godlessness, evil and chaos, the child came to be seen as innocent and unsullied, and childhood as a period of innocence and carefree living. The nineteenth-century theologian Schleiermacher described children as 'innocent gifts of God' and 'pure revelations of the divine from which no conversion is necessary'.[15] Because childhood is an ideal time, child rearing also becomes about safeguarding the child's innocence as much as the child itself, and protecting and prolonging childhood. As Schleiermacher had it, the duty of parents is 'to remove anything whereby love can be disturbed and open simplicity may be wounded'.

Ironically, by the time the Romantic ideal of childhood had captured the Victorian imagination in the middle of the nineteenth century, more than half of the work force was aged under 14 years.

More disturbingly, the concept of the 'child-as-innocent' also coincides with the emergence the child as an object of sexual desire. A new industry evolves from the mid-nineteenth century onwards based around the sexual exploitation of children in the form of child pornography and brothels. That there is a relationship between the two, 'child-as-innocent' and 'child-as-sex-object' is suggested by the expression of this adult male preoccupation in terms of 'defloration'. In other words, the sexual fantasy was (and perhaps is) based upon possessing and destroying innocence.

The problem with the predominance of the model of the child-as-innocent is that an 'innocent child' is a person without agency, a 'non-person'. Modern thought inherits an awkward mix of these contradictory ideas. Parents remain the principal focus of responsibility for the conduct and especially failures of their children while wider society is largely able to abrogate its own, but also the responsibility to protect their children's innocence in a society that sexualizes them for the very fact that they are perceived to be asexual.

Where do children belong? Children and families

In order to think more clearly about child and childhood, we must also consider where children are located and their significant relationships. The association between children and families is also a constant throughout theology and secular thought, based on the fact that that is where most children seem to be or, perhaps, that that is where we would like them to be. The association is so close that most often 'child' is treated as a subset of 'family'. The family continues to be thought of as defining the set of a child's principal relationships, and is promoted as the basis of social cohesion and as a necessity for the sort of 'successful' childhoods that yield 'successful adults'. We often make this association without recognizing that family forms and their relationships to the wider society have shifted significantly. Once more, the radical changes in how families are currently formed and their social function are features of recent history.

In non-industrialized societies family can be regarded as approximating society. A person has being, identity and social status through membership of family; ownership is hereditary, power and hierarchy for the most part dynastic. Families tend to be large and not just extended but also complex (e.g. married siblings and their children, Levirate wives, the membership of bondsmen/women, adopted and fostered children, multiple sequential or concurrent marriages, concubinage, etc.). It is estimated that households in feudal England, for example, tended to have an average membership of around 20. A rural community, that is, most communities before industrialization, may have comprised of no more than one or two such families. The family was both social and economic unit although subdivided often on gender and age grounds into various functions in which children had a significant part to play. They were a significant source of labour and a tradable commodity but also provided social stability both in terms of the continuity of the family/social and economic unit and as social security – they were the future carers and breadwinners when the current adult generation were no longer able to provide for themselves.

Children were therefore a necessity but producing and rearing children was a costly business. The average woman would have been pregnant an average of 20 times in her lifetime (this compares with an average of 2.1 in modern Britain[16]) and therefore much of her time was dedicated to this single function. Complications during or following childbirth were the single most common cause of death among women and remain so in poorer countries – the cause of death in an estimated 1 in 5 women.[17]

In Europe the first changes to this norm of extended and complex families came with the ending of the feudal system and the evolution of new socio-economic patterns that coincided with the Reformation, essentially halving the size of the average household. As with child mortality rates, the maternal mortality rate began to decline from the end of the eighteenth century but stabilized in the 1850s, being the cause of death for 1 in 8 women.[18] At this period the average woman gave birth to around 6 live children, although more than a third of women gave birth to 8 or more. The processes of enclosure and the drift towards urbanization and industrialization continued the gradual change in the nature of the family from the place where economic activity took place to a place that its members, including children, left to 'go out to work'.

Chosen children

Once more the most radical changes are the most recent. Maternal mortality continued at the same rate from the 1850s at 1 maternal death in every 100 live births until the late 1930s when the rate began to decline to current levels of around 1 maternal death in every 3,800 live births.[19] Maternal death in childbirth became an event that was comparatively rare so that it is no longer widely perceived as one of the risks associated with pregnancy and childbirth. The legalization of abortion and availability of effective contraception in the 1960s introduced the notion of 'choice' to childbirth. The ability to choose not to have a child, while still being sexually active, seems to imply, however erroneously, that a woman or couple can also 'choose to have a child'. This, coupled with the changing economic function of the family, means that children are no longer seen as social necessity but rather as an individual's 'lifestyle' choice. The child is therefore no longer seen as a gift from God, Providence or nature but an adult's right. Medical science has invested heavily in affording a parent or parents that right, and alongside these developments in fertility techniques and a growing knowledge of genetics, the right to have a child has developed into the right to choose the child we have, if only under current legislation, in terms of discarding the ones we do not want.

The availability of contraception and abortion has had significant effects on family. People, it seems, have always been sexually active outside the confines of marriage; indeed, marriage was in part one remedy for those for whom sexual activity had resulted in pregnancy. Although the illegitimacy rates across Britain varied significantly from region to region in the nineteenth century, the national rate remained at around 9.5 per cent throughout. Amendments to the Poor Laws, which relieved unmarried fathers of responsibility for the upkeep of their children, led to large numbers of children becoming 'foundlings'. The 1851 census shows that 13,265 such were placed in workhouses or orphanages and categorized 19 per cent of under-twelves as 'urchins'. Again, there are geographical variations, but children were born in 20–30 per cent of recorded marriages within the first eight months. One of the effects of contraception is that fewer sexual partners 'have to get married'; indeed the proportion of those choosing to continues to fall even when there is a pregnancy. The proportion of married couple families continues to decrease from 76 per cent in 1996 to 71 per cent in 2006 whereas over the same period the proportion of cohabiting couple families has risen from 9 to 14 per cent. In the 2001 Census 1 in 4 dependent children lived in a lone-parent family up from 1 in 14 in 1971.

The second effect is that there are simply fewer children as a proportion of the population. In 1901 children under 14 represented 34 per cent of the population. By 2001 that figure had halved to 17.2 per cent (11 million). Only 30 per cent of UK households now contain children, the same proportion as single occupancy households. Families themselves have shrunk. At the end of the nineteenth century the completed family size averaged 5.2 children, in 1901 3.5 children, in 1971 2.4 children, in 2001 1.7. Moreover, a disproportionate number of those children (34.5 per cent) are born into the poorest 10 per cent of households, with half of them being born into households where no adult is working.[20]

We continue to associate child with family and to identify family as the place where the child has its primary relationships. However, there are now fewer children in fewer families and increasingly those families are occurring in the poorest sections of the population. The child's place and function within the family has shifted from one of an essential contributor to a passive recipient or commodity. The family itself has ceased to be a social agent, becoming instead a private place removed from economic activity and identified as a place of safety and recreation. The family has also reduced in size and scope with the effect that within the family the potential for a multiplicity of relationships between the child and other children and adults is diminished and, outside the home, children's relationships, including those with their peers, are increasingly mediated by adults.

What do children do? Children and society

The next question we have to consider is one of even wider context: what does the child in today's world have to offer to our society? One way we can trace this is in relation to government policy regarding children.

The first time that English legislation turns its attention to the welfare of children is as part of the Elizabethan Poor Laws from 1563 onwards. Those same economic forces which reshaped the family – urbanization, enclosure and the final death throes of the feudal system, growing population and a series of famines – also led to the displacement and disintegration of many families. The state found itself dealing with children in and separated from families. Poverty had become seen to be a moral issue, and with the era's emphasis upon individual responsibility, it was the poor that were seen to be those who were morally responsible for their own poverty. The poor were categorized for the first time into the 'deserving poor' (i.e. those who were entitled to social support because they were incapable of working) and the 'undeserving poor' (i.e. those were not entitled to social support because although capable they had no employment or were beggars or petty criminals), who were to be treated harshly to punish them for their immorality and encourage them to reform. Infants were categorized as deserving poor and entitled to parish relief while children over seven were considered capable of supporting themselves and were boarded out as labourers. Those over 14 and unmarried became 'parish apprentices' (as distinct from the contemporary guild apprenticeships) to provide labour for up to seven years as the parish saw fit. Many of them, including girls, were sent to feed the demand for labour in the growing cities and in early industrial processes such as mining and copper industries.

There is a framework to childhood implicit here, and one common to Aristotle, Aquinas and the medieval world that passes into English Law at this point: 1 to 7 years is infancy, 7 to 14 childhood. At 14 a child becomes an adolescent (a young adult rather than old child and so, for example, a 14-year-old male can marry) and at 21 the adolescent becomes an adult. While some allowance is made for infants, children over seven were seen as capable of being economically self-sufficient and therefore contributors to the wider economy.

The Reformation, with its emphasis on the responsibility of the individual, also heightened the importance of formal education. However, although the number of schools increased, the education of children remained a haphazard affair and confined in the main to children from the wealthier classes and particularly boys. The predominant contribution of children to society continued to be their labour for the next three centuries. The 1861 census showed that 38 per cent of the population was aged under 14 years but that 51 per cent of the workforce was aged between 7 and 14. Further, 51 per cent of girls and 67 per cent of boys under the age of ten were in full-time employment. Education remained largely a private affair, despite the 1833 Factories Act, which introduced two hours' compulsory schooling for under-tens. The Education Acts of 1839 onwards began to allot public funds for the education of poor children and by the middle of the century around 80 per cent of children were receiving some form of formal education but only for an average period of two years. Subsequent Acts made schooling compulsory from the ages of 5 to 13 with exemptions (for example, if the child's wage was necessary to support the family or there was no school within a mile) and gradually raised the minimum school leaving age to 14 by 1900. This coincided with the development of mechanization in factories and agriculture that meant the demand for child labour was declining.

Twentieth-century changes

The twentieth century saw complete removal of children from employment and into education in Britain and other post-industrialized countries, moving from being significant contributors to public wealth to a private benefit at public cost. We should not forget that children remain essential sources of cheap, expendable labour in the current global system of industrial production, including in the extraction of raw materials and production of completed goods for western consumption. It is estimated that globally there are 281 million 5- to 17-year-olds (9 per cent of all children; 158 million aged 5 to 14) engaged in such activity, predominantly in Africa and Asia.[21] In short, child labour has simply moved to other parts of the world along with the industrial production base. Since 1972 the period for compulsory education in Britain has remained between the ages of 5 and 16 years. However, an increasing proportion of young people have continued in full-time education or training after the minimum school leaving age. In 1951 only 9 per cent of students continued in education or training after the minimum leaving age. By 2001 this figure had risen to 76 per cent, with 11 per cent neither in education nor employment. A similar trend can be seen in pre-school education with 21 per cent of 3- to 4-year-olds in full-time preschool in 1971 rising to 66 per cent in 2006.[22]

This move from employment to education as the primary occupation of children is of course in many ways laudable. There remain questions as to just how much time children and young people need to be in full-time education. It remains government policy to raise the compulsory school leaving age to 18 by 2013, and to extend the school day with the extended schools agenda. In the UNICEF Innocenti report the well-being of children in the United Kingdom and the USA was shown to be the lowest among the 22 wealthiest nations, with the highest rates of mental ill-health, teenage pregnancy, drug and juvenile offending, and so on. Both nations have a significantly higher number of hours spent at school, longer periods of compulsory schooling and yet no concomitant higher level of academic achievement. At very least this demonstrates that schooling as we have defined it does not of itself deliver well-being, indeed the evidence gathered from children and young people in various studies points to the probability that the education system with its tests, standard values and achievement measures may actually be detrimental to children's well-being.

The shifts in patterns of compulsory education have also had the effect of extending infancy to adulthood. The ancient framework of childhood, although there are many aspects of it we would challenge, at least recognized the changing and growing capacities of the child and reflected this in an expanding set of rights and responsibilities in the social arena. As it is, our children may have more rights but far less agency, and are seen to belong in the home–school, adult-controlled environment. Moreover, in a post-industrial society that measures the value of its members less by what they produce than by what they spend, children's only function is as a route to their parents' purses including the 'pester pound'. Childhood has not been commercialized, parenthood has.

Contemporary childhood

Contemporary models of childhood can be seen to have inherited an awkward mix of many of these often contradictory ideas. While we use the vocabulary of 'innocence' sparingly the concept continues to dominate our understanding of childhood. We see children primarily as recipients rather than agents in their own rights and choices, and in need of protection or safeguarding. Notorious cases such as the death of Victoria Climbié and the revelation of a series of abuses of children in care in the 1990s, although they have led to significant improvements in child protection for the most vulnerable, may also have led us to be overcautious and had a detrimental effect on the relationships between adults and children and young people. Furthermore, the emphasis on 'stranger danger' often leads us to ignore that the vast majority of child

maltreatment continues to occur within the home and that significant factors
in its occurrence are deprivation, social and familial fragmentation and
inequalities in wealth which, given emergent social trends, are likely to
affect more children.[23]

Alongside this fear for children there coexists a fear of children, perhaps best
illustrated by the newspaper headlines such as 'Let us tame these feral children
now' (*Independent*, 29 April 2002), 'A generation of young savages' (*Mail on
Sunday*, 17 April 2005) or 'Yobs are laughing off their ASBOS' (*Daily Mail*,
14 January 2006). Dispersal Orders permitted under the Antisocial Behaviour
Act (2003) have been used by a number of local authorities to effectively
enforce blanket bans on young people from town centres and public
transport, and some 3,500 'Mosquito Teen Deterrent' sonic devices are in
operation in public spaces.[24]

Although we have dispensed for the most part with the concept of original sin,
some still seem to assume, like Calvin, that there is some innate proclivity
among children that means that without discipline ('good parenting') and
training (often identified with schooling) a child will inevitably become
deviant.

Childhood as experienced

So far, these observations tell us what adults think of children rather than how
children experience childhood. As one part of the Good Childhood Inquiry, in
2005 the Children's Society commissioned a national survey of a representative
sample of over 11,000 young people aged between 14 and 16 years. More
than 5,000 younger children also took part throughout 2007 in the 'my life'
postcard survey. Both survey questionnaires centred upon the same two
open-ended questions: what do children and young people think makes
for a good life for them, and what are the things that stop them having a
good life?

Detailed responses to these questions together with recommendations can be
found in the various publications of the Good Childhood Inquiry and the
report itself.[25] However, what emerged from the early stages of analysis was
that the responses of children and young people and the associations they
made between various aspects of their lives fell naturally into three broad
groupings, which can loosely be thought of as 'relationships', 'environment'
and 'self'. Furthermore, the ways in which children experience childhood do
not fit neatly into the frameworks that adults routinely apply and seem

therefore to suggest a distinctive concept of contemporary childhood among those who are living it.

'Relationships' was the most significant cross-cutting theme in each of the areas interrogated by the Inquiry and had four sub-themes: love, support, fairness and respect. Love was an aspect that was particularly emphasized and most often associated particularly but not exclusively with 'family' (itself a broader concept than the adult parents and siblings, family-friends and for younger children, their pets). 'Support' (a listening ear, source of practical solutions/encouragement) was derived both from family and from friends as well as from significant adults, teachers being the most often identified. 'Fairness' was both about justice (being treated fairly, equality of opportunity, diversity) but also associated with rights of agency (being allowed to choose, freedom of movement) and, closely related to this, the theme of 'respect' describes positive mutual relationships and regard.

'Environment' defines the areas in which children and young people operate and therefore encompasses the material (the child's own wealth, family wealth, relative wealth/inequality), the home, school, the local area/outdoors (safety, freedom, bullying, poverty) and the wider national and global arenas. The third grouping is around 'self'. Important sub-themes include 'health' (physical, mental and emotional) but also 'lifestyle' (leisure time, fun, balance of time, school pressure, getting into trouble), 'values and attitudes' (faith, morality, spirituality), 'happiness', sense of 'identity', learning and growing, and aspirations.

'Safety' and 'freedom' were also important sub-themes, but for children these were feature of both 'relationships' and 'environment'. Education, meanwhile, does not fit neatly into any one category, being the location of certain positive 'relationships', an 'environment' in which a child operates and associated with 'health' – an aspect of learning and growing, and lifestyle.

Looking at childhood *through the eyes of a child* we see a model of the child as a complete person ('self'), although still learning and growing. They see themselves as active participants in relationships with adults (as well as their peers) in a variety of environments. They have a sense of self, values and an understanding of their relationship to the environment and others that is not necessarily dependent upon the instruction, interpretation or mediation of adults.

Why does this matter to the Church?

This changing picture of childhood matters on two counts. The first is very practical. If the Church is to continue its long history of a ministry to children it needs to take account of the realities of children's lives, who and what children are. At a very basic level, there are fewer of them and, if trends continue, what children there are will for the most part not be from the traditional groupings with which the Church has traditionally worked. Just as *Mission-shaped Church*[26] sought to find fresh expressions of church in a changing context, so we need understand the changing context of children and childhood to find new and appropriate ways of being church for and with them. We need to be able to see through the eyes of the child, because the child is best placed to inform us about what some of those fresh expressions may be.

The second is more fundamental. Of all the biblical pictures of childhood none is unique to Christianity except Jesus' teaching recorded in the Synoptic Gospels (Mark 9.35-37; 10.13-16; Matthew 18.1-14; 19.13-15; Luke 9.46-48; 18.15-17), in which he appears to turn contemporary concepts of the child on their heads: the child is the model for greatness, children are possessors of the kingdom, examples for adults to follow, valuable of themselves and to be identified with him. Often the ways in which we have interpreted this teaching have owed more to secular constructs of childhood rather than the internal evidence of the Gospels. For example, we have often interpreted the instruction to 'be like a child' in order to enter the kingdom in terms of adopting a purported childlike innocence or unquestioning acceptance, neither of which characteristics feature in the concept of child of the first century where a child was considered to be wicked, sinful and lacking in the capacity to comprehend. In fact Jesus' teaching about children is entirely consistent with the remainder of his teaching about the kingdom of God, in which context these accounts appear. In the sermons of the Plain and the Mount, Jesus tells us that the kingdom belongs to the 'poor' or 'poor in spirit'. Later in Matthew's Gospel he makes the same sort of identification of himself with the hungry, the thirsty, the naked, the stranger, the sick and the imprisoned. In short, Jesus places children among the group of objects of social justice. In this way, the instruction to change and become like a child is not to adopt some childlike quality, but adopt their lowly status and therefore akin to his instruction to the rich man, which follows this account in Mark 10, to give up his possessions. To explore what it is to be a child is therefore not simply to understand an immature phase of human being but to explore a paradigm of citizenship in a society modelled on Christian values.

This challenges us not simply to change how we see children but how we conceive of our social world, how we model childhood, how we model our churches. Without the participation of children, not simply their presence, the Church, and society as a whole, is as incomplete as when it excludes the poor or the sick. Theology needs to be challenged by the vision, perspective and experience of children. Theology is often a very adult discipline composed of a sophisticated language about God. Much theology is that of the white, male, western adult and carries prejudices and preconceptions from those genres. Today traditional Christian theology is enhanced and challenged by many different voices and perspectives: from liberation theology, feminist and womanist theology, Korean Minjung theology, and other liberation and third world theologies. Yet even so, the theological insights of children do not intrude. Theology remains the province of adults talking to and about other adults about the nature of the supreme adult who is God.

Yet children have much to tell us about God, for God calls them from their earliest beginnings and walks with children down the years. This experience of God informs children's spirituality and prompts its growth even if this process later becomes part of our forgetting. The spirituality of our early years, in whatever form it develops, makes us into the believers (or not) we will become. If we would understand ourselves as adult Christians then, the theological perspective of the child can add insight and flavour to our lifetime experience of God.

Questions

1. What thoughts, ideas and images does the word 'child' evoke for you?

2. Karl Rahner talks about childhood being an 'abiding reality'. Spend some time reflecting on any important transitions in your childhood. Was there ever a time when you felt that you were no longer a child? If so, why?

3. Make a list in two columns under 'child' and 'adult'. What kinds of attributes (young/old?), events (school/work?) or ideas (naive/wise?) belong in each column, including church matters?

4. Using this chapter as a background, why do you think the disciples were so unhappy about children coming close to Jesus (Mark 10.13-16)?

5. What kinds of activity in your church are aimed at children? What ONE thing could be changed to include children and young people more?

1

Nakedness and vulnerability

Anne Richards

Few things can stir human emotions as much as the idea of the preciousness and vulnerability of children. Our instincts, as human beings, are to care for and nurture children, and we become quickly distressed at the idea of children being hurt or harmed. Yet key theological concepts about our origins, human growth and ultimate destiny are also opened up by reflecting on the vulnerability of children, including the child Jesus. In this chapter I use the concept of 'the naked child' to open up a number of these key theological concepts. This concept is not without its difficulties, as I shall show, as the phrase 'the naked child' is itself a confrontational and emotive form of words in today's society. It is precisely because the idea of 'the naked child' is often so difficult in our society that I want to explore it in detail and also to begin to try to understand what it is like to *be* a vulnerable and naked child in the twenty-first century.

The chapter falls into two parts: in the first, the emphasis is on what the naked child tells us about God's purposes and what looking 'through the eyes of a child' does to enlighten us; in the second, the emphasis is on how adults view the naked child in our society with all the difficulties and challenges that that presents.

The first section explores the human birth experience and how looking at that theologically asks us to consider what we learn if we look through the eyes of the unborn child. These questions require us to look again at theological issues surrounding the incarnation of God in Jesus and what ideas about the Holy Family do to pictures of the 'innocent' or 'good' child. What does it mean to be 'born again' and how do matters of vulnerability and trust relate to life after death? These are things which can be illuminated by looking through the eyes of the naked child. The second section deals with adult sexuality and shame and how these matters become tangled up with issues surrounding the naked child. Although the naked child can offer prime theological insights, these can be lost or beyond reach in a society which sadly sometimes sees the image of the naked child as an opportunity for evil. Yet, the naked child can also tell us much more about the real presence of evil in the world, things that we really do need to know about. How can we look upon such a child and respond appropriately?

Part 1: Birth

> She was so perfect, the most perfect thing in the world. I counted all her fingers and toes. Nothing so truly good had ever happened until she was in my arms and I was stroking her dark, wet hair. I was crying and saying 'thank you, thank you'.
>
> (Drea Lopez, first-time mother)

The majority of adults are most strongly confronted by the naked child at the moment of their own child's birth. In developed countries, where food, medicine and care are taken for granted, and childbirth is prepared for, many parents report seeing their child entering the world for the first time as a powerfully uplifting spiritual experience. For some, the emotional and spiritual elements get woven into the many rituals and preparations which are now seen as *de rigueur* for impending parenthood, involving elaborate preparation of the birthing room, choice of music, scent, warm-water baths and pools, photography and the question of whether to have an elective caesarean section rather than vaginal delivery.[1] Such issues, discussed at length in some mother and baby magazines, place an emphasis on making the experience of childbirth a positive and memorable time and a distraction (if one is lucky) from pain, effort, fear, suffering and blood. For some other parents, living in extreme poverty or deprivation, the naked child may also come to them with joy and delight but the experience can also be coloured by challenge, fear, resignation or even dread. The naked child at the moment of birth therefore confronts all of us with evidence of who we are and how we live: whether it be in spoiled, pampered luxury or desperate poverty, yet theologians do not necessarily spend time on what the significance of the moment of birth adds to our understanding of what it is to be human.

Birth and blessing

Whatever the surroundings, in normal circumstances we look upon the child in childbirth, checking that it has been delivered safely, that the child is healthy and to see (if we do not already know) whether the child is a boy or girl. In some cultures this last question is of profound importance, indicating to the parents whether or not they have been 'blessed' with a child of the desired sex (usually a boy). So childbirth is not just a powerfully emotional event, but one which can have extraordinary spiritual implications, including the sense that the child is a gift from a heavenly power. For many people, what God has granted them in the naked child is an inheritor, having economic and cultural significance for the family. That child may be looked upon from the start as worker, servant, provider of grandchildren, means of alliance with other families, fashion accessory, or person to guarantee help in the parents' old age.

Birth and relationship

Childbirth is also a time when the maternal human body has to work extremely hard and requires the skill and care of midwives and obstetric staff whose purpose is focused on the delivery. The object of the whole process is the safe birthing of the child. It is a point at which love relationships elsewhere in the family can be severely tested, especially if there are a number of different vested interests in the child. It is also an event in which a rite of passage is being enacted and which concludes with family members assuming new or extended roles: mother, father, grandparents, brother, sister, aunt, uncle. So the child can teach us something we may have never considered before – about new life, love, creation, relationship, mystery suddenly made real. It also teaches us about our own birth, that we were once just as naked and vulnerable, helpless and waiting to be loved and nurtured.

Birth and memory

Being born as naked children does not remain in our memories, although a number of new religions, practices and therapies in western society suggest that not only do we retain such memories but they have to be dealt with and perhaps cleansed of their traumatic components. Astrologers and other diviners would have us believe that the child is open to all kinds of external influences from the nakedness and openness of the birth moment and that these can be detected, charted and used to perceive a person's future. Our birth is therefore mysterious to us, but an important and significant event when we first became independent individuals living on our own: our birthday. It is significant enough in our culture to be remembered with presents and cards. If all kinds of religious and spiritual practice see the birth moment as important and would have us reflect on it, what does Christian faith have to say about the intimacy and intensity of the birth experience of the naked child?

Birth and death

The book of Ecclesiastes 5.15 declares that, 'As they come from their mother's womb, so shall they go again, naked as they came; they shall take nothing for their toil, which they may carry away with their hands', and similarly Job 1.21 says, 'Naked I came from my mother's womb, and naked shall I return there; the Lord gave and the Lord has taken away; blessed be the name of the Lord.' At birth and death, then, we see most clearly what God intends for the human condition, what it means to be an embodied creature and what it means to be incarnate. At the moment of birth, nothing of this can be hidden or disguised, so the child faces us with the ontological reality that we are creatures of flesh who will live and who will die. Moreover, even in today's world, the space between these two conditions can be very brief. The naked child challenges us to create a world in which birth offers the best chance of a long healthy life lived to the full. The statistics concerning child mortality in underdeveloped countries therefore are often the basis for television advertisements by charities asking for aid.

So the naked child at the moment of birth also comes to us in new, perfect flesh, unsullied and untried by the experience of living. As in the example of Drea, above, new parents are often amazed by the softness and colour of newborn skin, the fineness and silkiness of baby hair, the miniature perfection of nails, the smell of a newly minted human being. Other advertisements often play on the softness and sweetness of naked baby bodies, urging us to buy products which remind us of the joy and pleasure of children, and what it was like to be a child.[2] Naked children are beautiful and remind adults forcibly of how far we have travelled along life's pathway towards the nakedness of death. Naked children teach us about the cost of experience and how it forces us into forgetfulness. For, as we grow and acquire more memories and experiences for good or ill, the freshness and emotions of our first impressions change. Intense emotional experiences, such as the pleasure (or trauma) of the first day at school, may remain relatively untouched, but day-to-day experiences are gradually overwritten and remembered differently. If we flourish, just manage, or if we just struggle to survive, our scars overlay the memory of the untouched flesh.

Growth and learning

Further, as we grow, acquired knowledge usually overlays unfettered imagination:

> The dinosaurs are in a circle. They are having a fight. Raaaaaaarrgh! Then they go over here and talk about their toys.
>
> (Jude, aged 3, playing with toy dinosaurs)

Knowing nothing about dinosaurs, Jude is free to have them play fight, wander about and talk about their toys. The dinosaurs do what he is in the act of doing, so he is one of them and they are part of his present experience. Imagination fills in the gaps and provides a wonderful vista of possibilities. However, inevitably adults begin to close the gaps. On this occasion Jude was told the names of the various dinosaurs and their relationships to one another: this one is a meat eater; this one eats plants. As the child learns, the dinosaurs begin to occupy an agreed picture of prehistory; distant from the child, they no longer chat about their toys. Learning therefore also accompanies a forgetting, but being in the midst of children can remind us forcibly of how much we have forgotten.

The unborn child

> It was before I started to do This Living, when I was in my perfect Red Sea. Everything went soft and slow back then, and I was always warm and glowing.[3]

The experience of the unborn child in the womb might be considered as close as we can get to the original Edenic experience, or the experience of being in perfect communion and interrelationship with God. In Scripture the unborn child is seen as especially responsive to God, and already in a loving and knowing relationship with him. We can see specific examples of this in Scripture (including Job 10.8-11,18; Jeremiah 1.4,5; and Luke 1.41-5). Theologically, we tend to overlook the experience of the child in the womb, because we have no memory of it and because we assume that such children have no impact on the world. In fact, however, we may be overlooking experiences of being human which have a great deal to teach us about how incarnation in the context of eternity works. Our time in the womb, through the eyes of a child, teaches us something about our ultimate destiny. Before we are born, we have a unique existence, being embodied, but enclosed within a body; receiving from that body what we need, but being allowed by that body to become what we are meant to be. As Christians we need to pay more attention not only to embryology but also to the *experience* of the unborn child and what it offers to us, since this is often left out of debates on abortion or on the responsibility of pregnant mothers not to harm their babies. We often treat such debates in terms of adult human ethical issues, and do not, in talking about the sanctity of the life of an unborn child, spend much time asking ourselves what God is saying to us through the experience of being an unborn child that *all* of us carry. That experience is not simply of passive existence. Pregnant women feel their children kicking, turning, grasping, touching and reacting to sounds, and will become anxious if the child grows unusually still or if the pattern of activity suddenly changes. Ultrasound and the complex imaging techniques, now available, teach us more about the unborn child's extraordinary journey of development and active exploratory life. Yet we do not often look carefully at what such technology offers to us in terms of theological ideas. The naked child that is in the process of becoming in the womb is first a model to us of how actively to *be*, before becoming later free to explore, to use her senses, to react to noises, to suck, twist and kick and to become equipped for another kind of life altogether.

Prematurity and experience

Rosemary Kay's *Saul*, quoted above, is the story of her own premature 23-week baby, who struggled for life in hospital for months before succumbing to meningitis shortly before the actual date on which he was due to be born. He is an unborn child forced to live in the world he is not ready for. What is both shocking and moving about the account, told from Saul's point of view, is the way the treatment of Saul's naked body constitutes his entire view of the world and his feelings about it. Through empathy with her child and what he went through, Rosemary Kay requires us to consider how the naked child learns through touch experience and decides about the world:

> I could feel my skin. It was warm where I was lying on it and cold against the air. I could feel them breathing, their breath freezing wind on my face. It was dry skin now, so thin I felt the stabbing deep inside.

> My ankle stung where they left something in, and my arm throbbed and my belly button hurt and all the feelings got sucked up into the rest of me.

> 'Right, umbilical line's secure . . . arterial one in his ankle . . . and how's the long-line in his arm?'

They think I'm asleep, but I'm just lying still, feeling it all, learning about living.[4]

This narrative sharply reminds us that the unborn and the newborn naked body is the conduit for intense experience of the world and that adults often forget the significance of comfort and pain to the small child. The voices of the doctors and nurses show that they are thinking about the procedures for keeping the child alive, but not what that experience of living might mean and especially not in a child who is barely alive anyway. The spirituality of that child cannot even be imagined. As parents we may react quickly to a child's cry of distress, but we may forget that what seems a mere discomfort to us may disturb the child's entire perception of the world. How can we say that there are not spiritual ramifications to those experiences or not take them into account? What happens to our naked bodies as infants, the experience of warmth and comfort against our skin, the pain of nappy rash or cold, may affect how we handle other experiences in the future, whether it be our naked bodies undergoing surgery in hospital or the way we choose clothes to cover our skin. These initial experiences may therefore feed into the foundations of our perceptions of God and our spiritual journeys.

Incarnation

The baby Jesus got no clothes on, daddy.
(Dominic, aged 3, looking at the Christmas crib)[5]

The naked child in our midst, and the experience of birth, is inextricably related theologically to the incarnation of Jesus. One way in which this comes across to us is in painting, whether we are familiar with the actual works, or have seen the images in books or on Christmas cards. Although early nativities often stylized the Madonna and child so that both had similar features and clothing, from the Renaissance onwards, artists, notably in nativity scenes and other images of the Virgin and child, typically revealed the child as naked and vulnerable among the clothed adults, even though, as Scripture mentions, the practice was immediately to swaddle children in tight wrappings (Luke 2.7).

In some examples, this was done because the artists sought to draw out a naturalism from the depiction of the naked child Christ at one with this, his own created world. In Fra Filippo Lippi's *Madonna in a Wood*, for example, the Christ child lies on the ground, sucking his finger. In other examples, such as in Gentile da Fabbriano's *Adoration of the Magi*, the adults are richly clothed and the painting is awash with colour and the brilliance of fabric. In such a setting the naked Christ stands out, intensely vulnerable, completely human, yet set apart, both by his nakedness and by the fact of his being tiny and a child. In Raphael's painting of the *Madonna with the Christ Child Blessing and St Jerome and St Francis* [6] we see the infant Christ sitting supported on his mother's knee. Christ blesses the viewer, but is not capable of mastering his own body. He cannot act towards human beings without the nurture and care of his parents. The tradition of such painting also focuses the viewer's attention on the Christ child: the power of such art and its theological message is concentrated in the smallest person as the centre of the painting around whom the larger, clothed adults bend themselves, sometimes womb-like, protecting his vulnerability. The paintings evoke wonder: God made himself this small, this delicate, this vulnerable.

In addition, the tradition of such paintings teaches us something about humans in relation to God through their attitudes towards the naked child. In paintings of the adoration, the magi offer their gifts on their knees, often while the child blesses them. Typical adult–child relations are reversed. Power and glory, wisdom or honours have no special place or meaning before this naked child, what matters is the pledge of love and steadfastness. So many of the statuary altarpieces of Renaissance Italy also show the clothed Madonna carrying the naked child, reminding the worshipper directly of the precious cost of incarnation and also challenging the human social world of adult-to-adult relations which ignores or tries to reinterpret the world seen through the eyes of a child. Such Christian artists remind us through the naked Christ child, that the child's view is truth, God's truth. If it were not so, then God would not have been born as a helpless babe.

The humanity and divinity of Christ

Such paintings and statues tell us more theological truth. In his nakedness, we see that Jesus is fully human as well as fully divine. He is also a complete human being, created male, not a hybrid creature or manufactured in the form of a human. In a number of famous examples of Christian art we see human infant dependence reflected in the Christ child nursing at the breast. [7] We can be sure, in the presence of this naked child that incarnation is a complete experience and that God has truly come to live as one of us. Since this Christ is dependent on his mother for food, comfort, warmth and security and cannot grow to fulfil his Father's will without it, each naked child who is entrusted to us reminds us that God calls each one of us to be co-creators of his purpose and intention. God requires our skills and gifts, love and care, to build a kingdom. The naked child is a constant reminder of our calling and God's desire for us and this is reiterated in birth images in Scripture. For example, Romans 8.22 says, 'We know that the whole creation has been groaning in labour pains until now'.

In seeing God among us as a naked child, we are faced immediately with the risk God took to send Jesus incarnate among us. This is especially clear in a context where children were dying or being killed. Scripture reminds us of the vulnerability of the naked child, and the story of the Incarnation is told in just such a context: in the Gospel of Matthew Herod orders the slaughter of the firstborn which Jesus must escape:

> When Herod saw that he had been tricked by the wise men, he was infuriated, and he sent and killed all the children in and around Bethlehem who were two years old or under, according to the time that he had learned from the wise men. Then was fulfilled what had been spoken through the prophet Jeremiah:
>
> > A voice was heard in Ramah,
> > wailing and loud lamentation,
> > Rachel weeping for her children;
> > she refused to be consoled,
> > because they are no more.
>
> (Matthew 2.16-18)

These ideas are enshrined not only in Christian art, but also in medieval hymnology. The 'Coventry Carol', for example, reminds the singer of the 'little tiny child' who is being lulled to sleep, while outside the raging Herod, the adult consumed by fear of losing power, is after his blood. Indeed the naked child is present in many Christmas hymns and carols. The Lord and creator of the universe has become a helpless babe: 'lo within a manger lies/ he who built the starry skies',[8] 'this very Lord he made alle thing',[9] 'for that child, so dear and gentle/Is our Lord in heaven above'.[10] The naked child in painting and in music asks our imagination to blend with our experience, so that the fact that we have all been naked children teaches us powerfully that God submitted his Son, the Lord of all, to an embryological becoming in Mary's womb that carried with it every risk and hope. The newborn Christ is subject to all the danger and difficulty which human birth and infancy is heir to. The naked child teaches us something about God's risk and intention to begin Jesus' experience of the human condition without precondition or expectation.

'Innocence'

> I shall then show forth Thy praise,
> Serve Thee all my happy days;
> Then the world shall always see
> Christ, the Holy Child, in me.[11]

Christmas carols also tell us that the Holy Child is the pattern for human childhood: 'For he is our childhood's pattern/Day by day like us he grew/He was little, weak and helpless/Tears and smiles like us he knew'.[12] There are some problems with this, in that the true humanity of the nakedness and vulnerability of the infant Christ is translated into passivity, quietness and 'goodness'. In this view, the Christ child does not trouble the adult world; he is seen and not heard. In fact he remains a quiet obedient child until he turns suddenly into the stroppy kid who goes missing on a journey and has to be looked for by anxious parents.[13] Paralleling the Holy Child with expectations for our own children therefore carries tremendous burdens and can influence the way adults have expectations of 'good' children. Children are not necessarily 'meek and mild', but some Christian adults become upset if children are not quiet and respectful in church and may even designate children as 'bad' or disruptive if they fail to live up to the Christ child's pattern ('no crying *he* makes'), the one who is God. In depictions in art and music, the Christ child, though human, is far too involved with his God-given destiny (hence the acts of blessing, or graciously receiving) to scream blue murder or whine incessantly, and this instinctive gravitas, goodness and holiness gets tangled up with other ideas of innocence and sinlessness.

Sin and sinlessness

Theological ideas of the sinlessness of Christ, the one born of a virgin and uncontaminated by human original sin, link with the scriptural idea of the naked child as one who reminds us of that state of innocence before experience and the inevitable Fall into both sexuality and sin. Innocence is a difficult and sometimes bogus concept when it is applied to children, but theological understandings of what it means to the human condition can be more rigorous. Scripture is clear that human beings have passed from a state of naked unknowingness to a sexual maturity in which nakedness is shameful (e.g. Isaiah 47.3). However, there are several layers to this 'innocence' and the resultant loss of this state. The concept includes human physical maturity, but also knowledge of oneself and others, and also a changing relationship with

God. Innocence in this sense is an environment where God is continually present, an Edenic and heavenly state of being. In Scripture this inherent sinfulness of our condition manifests itself once the ability to be naked without shame is lost; the primal beauty and mirror of God's image is marred and cannot be recovered. The transition and its relation to our knowledge of God are related in the book of Genesis. Adam and Eve as primordially created humans 'were both naked, and were not ashamed' (Genesis 2.25). Once they become aware of themselves as sexual beings, 'they sewed fig leaves together and made loincloths for themselves' (3.6-8). God's questioning of Adam confirms that the humans are naked children no longer and therefore can no longer exist in a state of perfect relationship of giving and taking with the parent who is God. That 'innocence' is lost. From this point, the humans are subject to time and experience and must fend for themselves. The expulsion from the garden is in itself a birthing experience, removing the humans from a place where nurture is provided without thought, to a dangerous and difficult environment in which they must learn how to care for themselves. There is no way back to the garden of Eden, just as a person cannot be born again from a mother's womb. Instead, sexuality makes it possible for them to replicate the creative experience and the primal act of God in the garden, 'Adam knew his wife Eve, and she conceived and bore Cain, saying, "I have produced a man with the help of the Lord"' (4.1). On this understanding, 'innocence' is not something irretrievably lost to the human condition but can be sought after through human love and having children, as a picture, emotional experience or foretaste of the restoration of oneness with God made available to us in Christ for all eternity.

Jesus as second Adam

There is therefore a tremendous amount of theological significance invested in the naked body of the newborn Holy Child. The history of orthodox Christian tradition, as well as the various strands of heretical thought, shows theologians trying to make sense of what this naked child might mean. Jesus is born as we all are born, in the Incarnation he becomes one of us, yet by virtue of his virgin birth, by the special circumstances of his conception and incarnation as God's Son, fully human and fully divine, he is also a child like no other. When we say the creed in church or look on the doll in the Christmas crib, it can be difficult to imagine the long history of thought, prayer and faith that has been invested in what this particular naked child might mean, but perhaps one particular strand is readily identified in a well-known hymn of John Henry Newman:

O loving wisdom of our God!
When all was sin and shame,
a second Adam to the fight
and to the rescue came.

O wisest love! that flesh and blood,
which did in Adam fail,
should strive afresh against the foe,
should strive, and should prevail.[14]

By means of this virgin birth, the Holy Child is understood not to inherit the effects of the Fall and can restore the relationship between God and humankind, making him a new or second Adam (e.g. Romans 5.12; 1 Corinthians 15.22).

This idea in turn required solutions to the complex theological problems of Mary's own status as regards original sin[15] and fourteenth- and fifteenth-century imagery of Jesus' conception and birth as taking place without disturbing Mary's virginity. For example, one image offers the idea that Jesus was both conceived and came into the world like sunlight passing through glass.[16] Clearly, however, what this teaching and imagining of the Nativity does *not* do, is imagine the birth of Jesus through the eyes of the child Jesus. Thus the incontrovertible fact of the naked Christ child as alive and aware remains a challenge to our theological thinking about how Christ came into the world, born of a virgin, which is at the heart of the creeds. The lack of this perspective leads to further complications: the Holy Child becomes invested with all kinds of ideas about Edenic innocence as opposed to the human birth experience, purity as opposed to human inherent sinfulness and what it means to be a 'good' or 'perfect' child. Yet the idea of the naked child as 'innocent' and pure, however, persists in our society and has a powerful hold on the adult mind. For example, in one advertisement for spring water, images of naked babies pass in front of the viewers' eyes as they are told how pure and good the water is.

Born again

He don't look happy. Is he going back inside my mummy?
(Paige, aged 2, on meeting her newborn brother Calum)

Moreover, the inability to see the naked Christ child through Christ's own eyes extends to the circumcision. In Jewish tradition, as in so many other cultures still today, circumcision carries symbolic community initiation, closeness to

God, healthiness or cleanliness, and a transition, still understood in some tribal communities, from 'wet' to 'dry' and from 'offensive' to 'beautiful'. Anthropologists have also pointed to the fact that in some societies, late circumcision marks the point at which the naked male child passes (or is reborn) into adulthood. In Jewish tradition it had spiritual, social and cultural connotations as part of the becoming or journey of a person dedicated to live in God's way (as in Genesis 17.10ff.). Jesus was himself circumcized according to the tradition and this was part of his experience of being a child, yet we seem to spend no time theologically on what this meant to his later explanations of God's relation to human beings, even though it becomes a topic of considerable debate among his followers, where the central question is whether the uncircumcised Gentiles can have the same access to Christian salvation (see Romans 4).

It is no surprise then that Jesus talks to Nicodemus about being born again (born from above). Jesus would be perfectly aware of the physical facts of birth and the ritual uncleanness requiring purification for females which attended birth in Jewish tradition (Leviticus 12), as well as the covenantal initiation experienced by the male child in circumcision. Against this background, Jesus indicates that actual birth is not replicated but the powerful experience and fresh start with which the naked child faces us can be gained in a spiritual form which fits us for heaven. Just as there are human initiations, rituals and processes which recover the naked child in perfect relationship with God, so there is a spiritual birth through the power of the Holy Spirit which makes possible reconciliation between human beings and God. We can say that Jesus' own experience of being incarnate in the Spirit is behind this explanation, but so is his human experience of being born and circumcised as a Jewish child. What happened to his naked body has significance for his *whole* life and teaching, not just what happened to it at his life's end. Without seeing through the eyes of Jesus as a child, we will not notice the importance of 'humans can reproduce only human life' in this important passage:

> Jesus replied, 'I assure you, unless you are born again, you can never see the Kingdom of God.' 'What do you mean?' exclaimed Nicodemus. 'How can an old man go back into his mother's womb and be born again?' Jesus replied, 'The truth is, no one can enter the Kingdom of God without being born of water and the Spirit. Humans can reproduce only human life, but the Holy Spirit gives new life from heaven. So don't be surprised at my statement that you must be born again. Just as you can hear the wind but can't tell where it comes from

or where it is going, so you can't explain how people are born of the Spirit.'

(John 3.3-8, New Living Translation)

Baptism

It has been suggested by some scholars that some baptismal rituals in the time of Jesus required the person to be naked and then reclothed as a symbolic re-enactment of birth as a naked child. Jesus is depicted in Christian art as being baptized naked in the Jordan by John.[17] The naked child is at the centre of baptism, as baptism recovers the naked child in the person and presents them new and pure to the community of God. Baptism, including the baptism of adults, is therefore a sacrament that refers to and integrates the experience of being a child. So it is that Jesus argues that children must not be forgotten, ignored or overlooked; rather adults must privilege the child's experience and insight and become like them in order to enter the world where God lives.

Soul

We can see the link between the naked child as a mirror of the unspoiled image of God in us when we consider the depiction of the soul in various ways as itself a naked child. Again, in Christian art, there are many depictions of souls as both small and naked, such as in the painting of the crucifixion by the Master of the Death of St Nicholas of Munster, in which the souls of the two thieves crucified with Jesus are caught by an angel and a demon as they emerge.

> But I have calmed and quieted my soul,
> like a weaned child with its mother;
> like a weaned child is my soul within me.
>
> (Psalm 131.2)

The soul is seen as a child, because God is the parent. The soul longs to be returned to its origin in the parent, so the psalmist calls the soul a weaned child because for the time we are on earth we are separated from God. Unsurprisingly, the soul has often been envisioned by writers and artists as a naked child. In the final instalment of the *Harry Potter* series, J. K. Rowling talks about Voldemort, the evil nemesis of Harry Potter, as a person who trusts no one, forms no relationships and desires never to die. He becomes the antithesis of a human being. Yet stripped from his body, Harry Potter encounters the essential Voldemort as a naked child, but one that is monstrous, deformed, pitiful and lost: 'It had the form of a small, naked child, curled on the ground, its skin raw and rough, flayed-looking, and it lay shuddering under a seat where it had been left, unwanted, stuffed out of sight, struggling for breath.'[18]

The naked child therefore also stands for the essential part of us and reminds us of how we are connected to God, where we have our origins and where we have our home. We hope to come as children before God, to be recognized as his children and to be born, through death, into eternal life with him.[19]

Trust

> If I got lost, my dad would come and find me. He would go in a taxi and it would cost *loads* of money.
>
> (Kofi, aged 5)

As the soul trusts in God, its origin, so the naked child, experiencing the world, yet intensely vulnerable, teaches us a great deal about the concept and experience of trust. The naked child only has the confidence to go out and encounter the world, to play in it, to have fun in it and to risk the danger of it, if the child knows that the adults in his/her life stand behind to protect and to help in case of difficulty. Like Kofi's dad, no matter what the cost, we would move heaven and earth to find our missing child.[20] If the naked child's vulnerability is breached, if she experiences hurt or fear, confidence is restored by the loving arms of the parent, carer or other loving adult. However if children learn that trust is misplaced, that there is no one to protect or who will help if their vulnerability is breached, that is the end of trust and the child is damaged.

This matter of trust is of powerful theological significance. The ability of the naked and vulnerable child to be sure of the protection and care of the adult, even if the adult is out of sight or somewhere else, teaches us about the importance of trust in our spiritual growth. So it is that Jesus teaches us to call God 'Father' and establishes the importance of relationship. Parables also teach us about the love God has for each person, the God whom we can trust as we trust adults as children. Learning to trust as naked and vulnerable children prepares us therefore for our death and what lies beyond it. Jesus says that we must enter heaven as little children, and so we must learn from them about unconditional love and trust. When we die, we are as naked children, waiting for the love and unfailing steadfastness of the parent from whom we took our being to gather us up: 'underneath are the everlasting arms'. When Jesus heals Jairus' daughter, this is a mirror of the way we die trusting in God's promises through Christ and are saved by God as a parent who cares for the needs of the child. Jesus calls the child from her death (or death-like state) and immediately instructs the adults to feed and care for her (Mark 5.35-43).The words of Jesus, 'the child is not dead, but sleeping' are echoed in sentiments on many gravestones and often the laying out of the dead and choice of a coffin have a symbolic significance of returning the dead person to a womb-like state ready for rebirth. Death rituals in many cultures involved giving the dead person food, clothing and useful artefacts to care for and equip that person in the afterlife and some cultures buried their dead in a foetal curl. The trust of the naked and vulnerable child in us therefore teaches and reminds us of our own need to trust God and to prepare to be as a child again.

Exploration

> Her favourite thing to wear is . . . nothing.
>
> (Advertisement for Huggies nappies)

Furthermore, a consequence of having trust in the essential goodness and care of people around means the naked child is free to explore and use her body to experience the world to its fullest extent. Parents will know that small children often resist being clothed, or having to get dressed again after a bath, and like playing naked on the beach or running round the garden. Small children experience the world holistically, the feeling of sun, water and air on skin is delicious, extraordinary, and allows children to learn about their bodies and their place in the environment. We know that young children often hate the confining feelings of their clothes and enjoy jumping in the paddling pool or the sea, or rolling in the grass. To refuse them this pleasure, refuses them something about their identity as human beings, as part of the natural world, and condemns them forever to a grown-up world where nakedness is shame and clothing equals responsibility. The nakedness of childhood has a spiritual element, which we both envy and refuse to allow. We take away many of those experiences from them when we (as our western society requires) put them in clothes.

The naked child in non-western cultures

Redmond O'Hanlon comments on visiting the Yanomami people in South America that a child living in that environment experiences an extraordinary closeness with his mother. He observes one family where the child experiences constantly the reassuring touch of skin-to-skin contact at all times.[21] This can be the natural state of affairs in cultures where it is not necessary to cover up the body. Pictures of the Madonna, even stylized ones, often show the infant feeding, flesh is in contact with flesh, which teaches us something about the closeness and interaction of God's own person. Yet in our society, babies are immediately wrapped and dressed, even swaddled, and have often been removed from the mother to the nursery. Only in recent years has it been deemed that this is good for neither mother nor child and that childbirth practices should allow the naked child to be placed on the mother's skin as soon as possible and for that physical contact to be part of the child's initial experience.

It is interesting that in our own society obsessed with fashion and clothes, people often turn to spiritual, healing experiences, or practices to promote well-being, which require the removal of clothes and the experience of touch. Many people enjoy saunas, massage, immersion in water at blood heat and other therapies which involve their skin being touched. Perhaps this is precisely because we want (or have missed) the child's experience of being naked in the environment and experiencing touch sensations which add to a sense of being close to God.

Part 2: Adulthood as loss and the coming of shame

One matter which is not often explored is that when we become sexually mature and become adults we do not gain something but actually experience loss. Once we become capable of making more of ourselves, the way in which as naked children we feel the world belongs to us has to be relinquished. In the *His Dark Materials* trilogy, the writer Philip Pullman explores this notion.[22] At adulthood, humans become visible to murderous spectres who previously would not have harmed them; the children's inner selves become fixed and adults are so jealous and hateful of the freedom and love children enjoy they seek to trap them, experiment on them and ultimately kill them. Many 'classics' of children's literature privilege the world of the child but with the sense that the adult world is hovering around the edges ready to pour cold water, interfere with the magic and wonder or simply dismiss the child's experience, and demand, like Zebedee, that the adventure is over and that it is time for bed.

The book of Genesis indicates, as we have seen, that the path to adulthood includes a transition from innocent nakedness to a correlation between nakedness and shame. Thereafter are many references to nakedness/shame and the need to clothe the naked and end their shame as an act of compassion. Revelation 3.18 says: 'I counsel you to buy from me gold refined by fire so that you may be rich; and white robes to clothe you and to keep the shame of your nakedness from being seen; and salve to anoint your eyes, so that you may see', and similarly, Revelation 16.15: 'See, I am coming like a thief! Blessed is the one who stays awake and is clothed, not going about naked and exposed to shame.'

Sexualization of children

In a society obsessed with sexuality this shame also gets read backwards until it despoils the way we might otherwise see children. We may shake our heads with incomprehension when some paedophiles insist that children are aware of their sexual potential from the earliest age and want to explore it fully with other children and with adults, but our western society as a whole is responsible for a sexualizing of children. This means that such a society often refuses to make space for the experience of children and will not look through the eyes of a child. Instead, such experiences are covered up or obliterated by adult power. In particular, high street shops are full of designer clothing (e.g. Little Labels) and accessories specifically aimed at presenting mini-adults. Children can also end up wearing clothes such as jackets and T-shirts covered in titillating or ambiguous messages: 'sexy lady' 'I need spanking', 'tiny totty', 'naughty girl', 'super stud', etc. Children are offered copies of underwear, make-up and other attire worn by sexually mature adults and encouraged to become imitations of people with adult bodies and desires.

The double standards of our society are exposed in the film *Little Miss Sunshine* in which seven-year-old Olive longs to take part in a beauty pageant and display her dance routine. When (after many mishaps, including a collection of pornographic magazines [sexually available females] discovered and then coveted by the policeman who stops the family), they arrive at the pageant, Olive finds herself in the company of a collection of mini models, wearing skimpy swimsuits, covered in make-up and standing in alluring poses to impress the judges. Olive, with her ponytail, podgy body, gap teeth and glasses, is horrified and dismayed that she cannot compete with these prepubescent paragons of female beauty. But there is a twist, Olive comes out to do her dance routine, having been taught by her crazy grandfather 'who taught me all the easy moves', and begins what is immediately recognized by the audience as a strip tease. The adults, who have been enthusiastic about the swimsuit parade and all the pouting lips, now fall into embarrassed silence as Olive peels off her scarf. Suddenly, with the stakes being upped from implied sexual titillation to frank exposure of it, everyone is disapproving. The day is saved by the family getting up on stage with Olive and dancing normally with her, having fun. Needless to say, she doesn't win.

We therefore make it possible for the naked child to clothe herself in a way that is sexy and sassy, but give the same child no warning what to do if others act on the signals being sent out, or even what such signals might mean. We say that it is part of a person's human rights and personal autonomy to do with the naked body as we will and not expect it to have consequences. One result of this is that we live in a society that is now terrified of misinterpreted behaviour towards children. Cases make the newspapers when adults end up in court for having sex with minors, but who then argue that they were unable to tell that the child in question was anything other than a consenting adult because of the way they looked and acted. Outraged people then counter, 'But *why couldn't they tell* it was a ten-year-old child?' These difficult and distressing questions eat into the issue of trust and of right behaviour between children and adults and make it more difficult to look through the eyes of a child into the worlds they are being offered in the media, through peer groups, through the Internet, through magazines and through advertising.

As a consequence of all these things, there comes about a perception that adults are terribly dangerous towards naked children and we ourselves have made naked children incredibly dangerous. We feel extremely strongly about hurt perpetrated upon children. The naked *dead* child is felt within our psyche in the western world as the worst of human horrors. Stories in which adults abuse the trust that children place in them and cause children terrible injury and suffering outrage us and make us demand both retribution and stronger protections, such as with the Victoria Climbié case, or with the deaths of Jessica Chapman and Holly Wells. The fear of paedophiles, traffickers and child abductors and the damage they do to children, especially when children are kidnapped, tortured and murdered, leads to public outcry and demands to know where sex offenders are at all times.[23] We increasingly hear stories of predatory adults posing as children on the Internet to befriend children or young people and groom them for sex. People who have committed crimes against children, especially sexual crimes, have to be segregated in prisons for their own safety. We say we are appalled by the proliferation of child pornography on the Internet and unable to understand the people who download and use such material. All of these things show the adult world penetrating into and damaging the world and the experience of the child, making children powerless and ultimately silent. Yet these crimes are only part of a general trend in our society refusing the freedom and truth of the child's experience and this is therefore of theological significance, since, a world where the child is not heard and is transformed into some*thing* for use by adults, is a world which refuses the vision of what God wants for us.

The way we feel about the vulnerability of children requires us, rightly, to put laws and guidelines in place to ensure child protection. Yet in a society like ours, such intense and complex protections, while designed properly to create safe spaces for children, may also of necessity become associated with some loss of happiness and freedoms associated with being a child. Adults in positions of responsibility, adults whom the children should trust, may often not feel they are permitted to touch or comfort children or to reach out to restrain them, lest it be interpreted as assault or crossing of a boundary we have imposed on the idea of the naked child. So situations occur where it is assumed that adults *always* intend the worst. This can lead to situations such as when a member of the clergy who publicly kissed a child on the cheek for winning a prize was arrested for assault. People who have taken pictures of their children enjoying themselves in the garden or the bath have been reported to the police as having sinister purpose and intent. Yet this in itself exposes another double standard prevalent in our society, since there are any number of celebrity 'mother and child' portraits by fashionable photographers in which either the child or both the mother and the child are naked. Moreover, the naked child can be referenced as a particular kind of image or statement. Indeed, one of the most iconic photographs of the twentieth century, Annie Leibowitz's photograph of John Lennon and Yoko Ono, portrays Lennon as curled against Ono in a childlike pose, naked, clinging, embracing. Such 'artistic' fashion photography, published widely in magazines and other media, send us the message that the naked child is to be admired, appreciated and adored. Yet private photography is suspicious and to be viewed with concern. Our society says it is impossible to feel innocent pleasure in seeing a child enjoying being naked, because our own inherent nastiness inevitably gets in the way.

What therefore we do not ask is what it is like to live in such a society through the eyes of a child. If a child is hurt and needs comfort and help but cannot have it, what message does it send back to the child? Does the child learn that all adults are to be feared in some way, or likely mean them harm? What kind of message does a child receive if he or she perceives that they need protection from all these others? If this is ever the case, then it is more difficult to offer the idea of a loving Father God who watches and waits for eternity, waiting to take in his arms and kiss the beloved. Frank Furedi, writing in the *New Statesman*, 26 June 2008, argues that some of the protections we have put in place actually run the risk of preventing good, motivated and trustworthy adults from watching out for children:

> During the course of our discussions with people working in the voluntary sector, it became evident that applying formal procedures to the conduct of human relations also threatens to deskill adults. Many adults often feel at a loss about how they should relate to youngsters who are not their children. When formal rules replace compassion and initiative, adults become discouraged from developing the kind of skills that help them relate to and interact and socialize with children. This process of deskilling the exercise of adult authority may have the unfortunate consequence of diminishing the sense of responsibility that adults bear for the socialization of the younger generation. Individuals who talked to us about the 'hassle of paperwork' also hinted that they were not sure that working with kids was 'worth the effort'. And if adults are not trusted to be near children, is it any surprise that at least some of them draw the conclusion that they are really not expected to take responsibility for the well-being of children in their community?[24]

The naked child is therefore simultaneously the figure of untouched purity but also of dread of exposure of human wickedness. The more small children are encouraged to become sexualized, the more paranoid society becomes. For example, Northumbria police removed a photo called *Klara and Edda bellydancing* by Nan Goldin from an art exhibition. In the photograph two small children are having fun dancing together. One of them is naked and lies on the floor facing the camera. The photograph generated a great deal of negative publicity, including towards the photograph's owner, Sir Elton John. The CPS decided that the photograph was not indecent, but for others, the photograph raised heated questions about where the line could be drawn between pornography, indecency, offensive images and fine art. One commentator argued that the photo might not be seen as indecent by some people, but the fact that it *could* be used by evil people for their own gratification was enough reason for it not to be shown.[25] Maybe a test of purity of heart might be to look upon the image of the naked child and feel nothing but wonder and joy in God's creation. It is noticeable that in all the controversy over the photo, few commentators had anything to say beyond the fact of the child's nakedness, and nothing about the joy and pleasure of seeing children dancing, laughing and having fun.

The suffering of the naked child: a challenge

Yet there is no doubt that the image of the naked child can also testify to the horror and evil we can perpetrate on others through human actions. For many people, the idea of poverty and suffering in the undeveloped countries comes with the television images of starving naked children with swollen bellies and stick-thin limbs. Most appeals for money and help come with pictures of such suffering children. Indeed, one of the most famous photographs of the twentieth century is a gut-wrenching image of a naked child.[26]

A nine-year-old girl, Kim Phuc, runs screaming straight at the camera. Behind her, are adults in their army uniforms and helmets, carrying guns, but these protectors are running away too. Behind them, clouds of darkness and destruction boil up. Everyone in the photograph has clothes, except for the central figure who holds out her arms as she flees. To the viewer her posture has an echo of crucifixion, or of desperate supplication, but in fact she is holding her arms out because she is suffering from napalm burns. She emerges from the nightmare of the bombing of her village in Vietnam bearing on her naked body the marks of human destruction and damage. The photograph is shocking and arresting, but is more than just a record of the horror that is war.

The child is running at us, the viewers, her nakedness cannot be ignored or covered up; she demands something of us, some act of response or care. The naked child confronts us and shames us. She is coming for us; she is going to run straight into our arms. What will we do then?

The answers to that question are complex and often troubling. The naked child in our midst evokes many feelings and desires. We live in a society which promotes the safeguarding and care of vulnerable and hurt children, but at the same time we live in a culture which exploits and exposes them. The theological importance of the naked child in our midst is therefore paramount for the kind of society we should aim to achieve, and the message of love we should promote.

Above all we need to listen to the message of the naked child. The naked child who is happy and exploring, confident in the protection and love of adults affords us a glimpse of God's desire for us to be joyful and complete in his eternal presence. Yet the naked child who runs away screaming from adult war and destruction, who sits in a corner afraid lest she incur the wrath of a parent, who is looked on with lustful eyes, is a picture for us of ourselves cut off from God's love, the hell we would all rather avoid. The naked child, in her vulnerability and her potential is a picture for us of our ultimate destiny and we must choose and strive for the life for her which we would wish for all of us.

Questions

1.   What kinds of feelings and emotions does the word 'birth' evoke in you?

2.   This chapter talks about the necessary provision of safe spaces for children. In what ways are your own church facilities and provisions safe for children? Can you identify any drawbacks in making these provisions? Looking through the eyes of the children you know, what is *like* to feel safe?

3.   In two columns list the ways you think children are vulnerable in today's society and what kinds of measures or actions keep them safe.

4.   Revisit the creation stories in Genesis. What does Scripture more generally tell us about our bodies and what we should do with them?

5.   Make a list of all the ways your church celebrates baptism, confirmation, youth activities, etc. What ONE thing could be changed to add to the celebration of children in your church?

2

Creation

Keith White

This is a very tentative, pioneering journey into what for me is largely unknown, and certainly uncharted territory, and what I have written is offered in that light. I would like to think that some of the exploration here will provoke discussion as well as identify gaps in current theological thinking and reflection about children and creation.

What I argue in the chapter is that a thoroughgoing doctrine of creation necessitates some encounter with the whole of theology, notably eschatology and the kingdom of heaven.

In attempting something of this scope, and taking my cue from the actions and teaching of Jesus, children and the image of child have been considered as invaluable resources. Yet children have been absent from most doctrines and theological reflections on creation, both as objects of inquiry and as the subjects of reflection. I suggest that this neglect, which is counter to biblical models and injunctions, may have deprived adults individually and collectively of one of the key resources in this area. One of the images that they bring with them is that of 'play', and I wonder whether this might provide not only some insights into the heart of creation and the creator, but also at the same time help to alleviate some of the scholasticism and heaviness that characterizes much theological work on creation.

The world as an adventure playground

We have two oak trees that I climb.
They are huge.
There is a pond nearby in a field
and it leads to a waterfall
which crashes into a stream.

Home is by the waterfall

because of the splash.
When I have a fight with my brother, the crashing and splashing
of the water makes you calm
It washes it all away.[1]

The extended family of which I am a part is based in East London, but we are
blessed with a holiday home in North Wales. In addition to my own biological
family of five generations, there are others who have lived with us over the past
century because they could not live with their own kith and kin.[2] Not long ago
some of these young people were camping with me in the Rhinog Mountains
in North Wales (geologically part of the Harlech Dome). We had pitched our
tents by a small lake (*llyn*) and one of the boys had been scrambling over the
surrounding uniquely rugged outcrops, often frequented by wild goats, before
the morning mists had evaporated. As he rushed towards us, spurred in part by
the smell of a cooked breakfast, he shouted out his discovery: 'This is one big
adventure playground!'[3]

The more I have come to know of the nooks and crannies, the cracks and slabs,
the waterfalls and pools, of this rocky area of North Wales with and alongside
children and young people, the more accurate his conclusion has seemed. We
have found perfect slate 'slides'; see-saws in the branches of living trees; white
water and waves; ledges ideal for jumping or diving into mountain rockpools;
beaches with various textures of sand inviting us to dig and build features of
our choosing without fear of ridicule or the risk that what we created might be
permanent and labelled; and of course every sort of mountain terrain with its
own particular rock, flora and fauna.

Of course we would not have been able to experience Eryri (Snowdonia) in this
way if we did not know it well, and have appropriate knowledge, experience,
training and equipment. The mountains, rivers, lakes and sea can be very
dangerous places, and even when the weather is fine there are still the risks of
hurting yourself (for example, cutting your hand on slate or falling on uneven
rock), of getting lost (either by yourself, or as part of a group that loses its way
in the evening darkness), or of being scared by the sheer scale of ridges,
mountainsides or waves.

We are able to explore and have real adventures in this grand expanse of the
natural world because the children and young people are safe in the
knowledge that we would never lead them into unnecessary danger, that if
they were to become lost we would search until we found them, and that if
they are hurt we will take care of them. It is challenging terrain and water, but
we feel able to engage with it so fully, because we start from a secure base.[4]

That said, and acknowledging that Snowdonia is a very special place, perhaps we can still take the young person's words one stage further and enquire whether the whole created world, natural and human, personal and social, historical and contemporary, from a child's perspective might be experienced and enjoyed as 'one big adventure playground'.[5] If so, any theology of creation must be a journey of adventure too.

Doctrines of creation

As it happens I began work on this chapter while I was lecturing in Nepal, within sight of the Himalayas, mountains that I had read about since 1953 when I first saw the film of the conquest of Everest by a British-led team. While I was sitting on the rooftop of a home for Tibetan refugee children the clouds lifted for the first time during my trip, and I will now always carry with me imposing images of some of the towering, though geologically compared to much of Snowdonia, young, peaks and ridges of creation. I was travelling light in terms of theological resource material, and so it seemed sensible to use to the full the books that I had with me. One of these was a summary of Christian doctrine, *Theology for the Community of God*, by an American theologian and former colleague, Stanley Grenz.[6] It is not necessarily typical and inclusive of every shade of Christian doctrine, but we can let it stand as an example of how one recent theologian has approached the subject of creation, *inter alia*, in the West.

His work, like the genre in which he worked, is characterized by categories and headings (put very simply, it is not narrative or poetry) and he begins with an exploration of 'God as the creator of the world' considering how the Trinity, Father, Son and Holy Spirit play complementary roles in what he describes as the free and loving act of creation. The Father fulfils the primary role, the Son is the principle of creation, and the Spirit is the divine power active in creating the universe. After a brief discussion of God's sovereignty in relation to creation and history, he looks at past and future dimensions of creation. He refers to the suggestion of the German Old Testament theologian, Gerhard von Rad that the Priestly writers intended the sixth day of creation to symbolize the present (history), and the seventh day as the future completion of God's creative activity.[7]

Grenz argues that this means that the paradigm of 'essential human nature' should be seen, not in the pristine primal pair, but in the resurrected humankind in the coming kingdom of God. He concludes with the description of how God's purpose in creation is Community. (He is careful to pursue the theme suggested in the title of his work right through, including this particular doctrine.)

The style and content of Grenz's book is thus typical of much traditional western theology: seeking to wrestle with a range of well-known theological and philosophical questions in order to provide some coherence, both within the selected topic, and also between this doctrine and the rest of the treatise. With the memories of exploring Snowdonia with children, behind me on the one hand, and the glimpses of the sheer scale of the Himalayas visible in the early morning on the other, the chapter by Grenz seemed noticeably lacking in its reflection of the colours, textures and sounds of creation. What is more, human beings in general don't really seem to be an integral part of this treatment of the doctrine of creation and must wait for their treatment in a later chapter entitled 'Anthropology'. And children are almost completely ignored, not only in the chapter on creation, but throughout the work. It seems strange to focus so specifically on the human species within creation, while almost tuning out children altogether. We might venture to conclude that this represents a theological blind spot.

Yet, sadly, most western systematic theology shares this blind spot: it is generally pursued with children invisible or marginalized,[8] so their absence in this particular work may not be thought surprising. However, because Grenz gives prominence in this work to the theme of community, one might be tempted to think that the absence of children is rather atypical both of historical and sociological evidence of human communities, and also the stuff of the biblical narratives. Their invisibility is therefore doubly puzzling. And their absence means that if creation is the theatre of God's glory, as Calvin suggested, then it seems a rather limited drama that is being played out. It lacks some of the most important characters in creation. And there is little hint that the scene sets symbolize a big adventure playground!

The scope of 'creation'

Grenz shows he is aware how challenging it is to decide upon the scope or boundaries of the doctrine of creation. The question is whether it is restricted to the creation/formation of the natural universe, first things and first principles, or is more properly speaking about everything, embracing in one way or another every theological doctrine. For ease of reference we may choose to see creation as about the first things, and eschatology as about the last things, with the rest of theology either somewhere in between, or enfolding them both. But the more we delve into the essence and implications of creation the more we find ourselves drawn into the rest of the theological enterprise, and into the places where children are present but usually overlooked, playing by themselves.

Creation itself for Christians is inescapably christological. For example, we read in John 1.2: 'All things came into being through him, and without him not one thing came into being'; Colossians 1.16-17: 'for in him all things in heaven and on earth were created, things visible and invisible, whether thrones or dominions or rulers or powers – all things have been created through him and for him. He himself is before all things, and in him all things hold together.' And in him creation and eschatology come together. Thus in Revelation 21.6: 'I am Alpha and Omega, the beginning and the end.' There is no way of dealing adequately with the biblical witness without a Trinitarian understanding of creation. We inescapably find ourselves deep within the doctrine of God. Yet if the doctrine of creation is of its nature christological then it should be profoundly respectful of the one who placed a little child in the midst of his disciples as a sign of himself, the one who sent him, and the kingdom of heaven.

We also find that redemption and salvation, if they are to be adequately dealt with, must be set within an understanding of creation, God's nature, his providence and his relationship with creation. One of the books that provides a useful overview of the theology of creation is a collection of papers edited by Colin Gunton, *The Doctrine of Creation*.[9] It argues that the way the doctrine has been dealt with over the centuries has been unduly limited and partial, overly concerned with scientific formulations and questions. I have also found Dietrich Bonhoeffer's *Creation and Fall* a welcome companion while working on this chapter.[10] Although neither book refers specifically to children, both were written with an openness that resembled in some way the freshness of a child's encounters with creation.

If we are to draw the main body of Scripture within the ambit of creation/redemption/eschatology then perhaps one of the key concepts is the kingdom of God. If creation begins and ends in God, from eternity to eternity, then how can we best describe the period, however great or small a time in historical terms, in which human beings occupy planet Earth (and perhaps other planets in the future)? Theologically speaking, God is ceaselessly at work through creation, his Spirit and his Son, and reconciling the world to himself. However dark the shadows thrown on life by nothingness and sin, the light still shines, and from the stump of Jesse there is a shoot that blossoms. And whatever earthly kingdoms may come and go, God's way of doing things (the kingdom of God) is still in evidence to the eyes of faith. Empires tumble and are ground into the dust, but his kingdom is quietly and unobtrusively advancing with children somewhere near its heart.

Birth and creation

We can see this immediately in biblical language. An image that recurs at different points of Scripture is that of birth pangs and birth itself. In Isaiah the final chapter links creation (Isaiah 66.2: 'All these things my hand has made and so all these things are mine') with the last things (the new Jerusalem) using the extended symbol of birth (Isaiah 66.7ff.: 'Before she was in labour, she gave birth . . . Shall I open the womb and not deliver? . . . As a mother comforts her child so I will comfort you.') Paul uses just this image in Romans 8.22: 'We know that the whole creation has been groaning in labour pains . . .' to relate the things of human history to what is being revealed of the Christian hope for the future.

The new creation will not appear effortlessly, as if it were a carbon copy of the original or primary creation: it involves suffering, patience, endurance, mercy, love and grace. We might venture to say then that creation cannot be described without reference to other doctrines, and that creation, kingdom of heaven and eschatology may be described and related by a symbol of birth. There is no sentimental or romantic idea here: rather one that recognizes the risk and the pain of real human birth. In this way, complex theological issues are made easier to understand if we think analogically to our own experience of children coming into the world. In addition, because in both the Old and New Testaments children have a special place in revealing aspects of the kingdom of heaven, we can argue that children have a vital role in the theology of creation.

Without lapsing into allegory we can imagine how the natural world (universe) in creation is like the birth of a child; how through history there are the growing pains; and how eschatology attends to the future of the child in maturity. A baby is both complete and born to develop; there is potential and that which is still to be realized. So it is with creation and the kingdom of heaven. They are both 'now' and 'not yet' theologically speaking. So the way we look upon newborn and young children, celebrating everything they do day by day, but thinking about their future, making provision for it and working for their happiness and realization of their potential, gives us a way of understanding how the kingdom can be here among us and yet still to be realized.[11]

The birth of a child can be a difficult and messy business. It is not just that childbirth involves pain and blood, but that a baby is a mysterious creation. It is both complete as a being and also incomplete in that there is unrealized potential, just as in the blossom or the apple pip. The completeness of the baby challenges notions of outcomes and achievements. It simply is, and defies much analysis once you get beyond weighing and measuring the tiny form. Is this tiny baby indicative of the nature of the kingdom of heaven? Can this squalling creature really be ordained to silence the enemy and the avenger (Psalm 8.2)? We may ask similar questions of the kingdom of heaven, when it is compared to earthly kingdoms and powers. Perhaps the best that we want for our children, that desire born of love and hope, is like what God wants for the creation and the focus of his reconciling work.

We can see this in the book of Job where the relation of God and creation is explored in some depth: 'Has the rain a father, or who has begotten the drops of dew? From whose womb did the ice come forth, or who has given birth to the hoar-frost of heaven?' (Job 38.28-29). Creation is the result of God's parenthood and is cherished and nurtured and sustained by him. There is also imagery consonant with this reading of Job in Proverbs, for example, 3.19-20.

If the purpose of God's providence and grace in a person's life is that she might be reborn (born again) is not the whole of creation to be conceived (!) in this way?[12] Thus Revelation 21 depicting the new heaven and new earth could be seen as the birth of a new creation 'making all things new', with the process of growing up implicit in the process: rather than the new creation being instantly and finally formed.

Bringing the theology of creation to life

In my teaching around the world I have found that Asian theologies can help fill out, fill in and clothe many of the words and concepts of western theologies of creation. What follows are quotations from the work of a Taiwanese theologian, Choan-Seng Song. It seems to me when I share his work with students that it is as if we have invited children, their laughter and play into the lecture room:[13]

> Perhaps a poet can tell us how we should go about theology. Look out of the window of your workroom and imbibe the colours with which God has adorned nature! Then there will be more colour in your theology. Listen to dogs bark, birds sing and insects hum outside your workroom. Then your theology will become audible as well as legible.

Can sun, moon and stars praise God? Of course they can. Theologians must regain the ability to hear them sing and praise God . . .

God seems especially patient in Asia. Space is vast. History is long. Culture is rich. Persons are numerous. The heart nourished by such culture embraces deep emotion . . .

Is it that the passion shown in the birth of a child gives us a glimpse into the passion of God giving birth to creation?

Here we find a very different theological approach to creation. It involves listening to real sounds, observing real colours, being open to particular cultures and, not least, considerable patience. For this reason it may serve as a bridge to the experience and world of children as they interact with and enjoy creation. There is a place for imagination, exploration, inner experiences such as wonder, and the recognition that head knowledge is not an adequate vehicle for the encounter between a human being and the many-splendoured natural world. This brings us closer to the richness and texture of the Psalms (for example Psalms 65, 93, 96, 98, 104 and 148). We could also turn to the art of humankind in its many different forms, for reflections of the primary creation and imaginings of how things really are, what they mean and how they might be. Where do children speak of creation if not in drawings, writings and play? This is where we look for the nearest approximation to what we think of as theology.

Suppose we were to stop and listen for children's voices. What might we hear? Looking out at the breathtaking beauty of the Himalayas, what might the Tibetan children have said and still be saying about beautiful and mysterious sights in creation as well as brokenness and the damage humans can do to the world of nature as well as to their homeland? One resource I always have with me in Asia, which, despite dating from 1991, always seems to resonate with all my Asian theology students, male and female, is *Children's Letters to God*, which we may set beside the contemporary voices of the children around us today.

Children's Letters to God

I always take this gem of a collection with me when lecturing in theology. *Children's Letters to God* [14] is particularly dear to me and what struck me on re-reading the letters with this chapter in mind was how nearly all of them related to some aspect of creation.

I sometimes leave them around so that the children in our household can read them, and from what I can detect they seem to scratch where the itch of modern children is. They are full of the colours and shapes of the created world, and although none of them is what you might term christological, they delve into many theological realms where angels fear to tread, in a very direct and spontaneous way.

Going back before Grenz's starting premises, one child asks the very acute and perceptive question: 'How did you know you were God?'(2) But the children are not stuck with such profound philosophical and psychological questions: for them they want to explore the interface between their experience of the real world, and what they understand of God. Time is an important issue to children: 'My grandpa says you were around when he was a little boy. How far back do you go?'(22) It is not just about the eternity of God, but the source of all human beings: 'I know all about where babies come from, I think. From inside mummies and daddies put them there. Where were they before that? Do you have them in heaven? How do they get down here? Do you have to take care of them all first?'(23) (One wonders whether Susan, who wrote this letter, knew the carol, 'Once in Royal David's City', with its line 'He came down to earth from Heaven.')

Another wrestles with *deus absconditus* in creation: 'Are you really invisible, or is that just a trick?'(5) And then a question for us all from Richard Dawkins to Creationists: 'Did you mean for giraffe to look like that, or was it an accident?'(7) And with that in mind, there is the question, 'How come you didn't invent any new animals lately? We still have just the old ones.'(26) While thinking about old animals, here's a thought: 'If you let the dinosaur not extinct we would not have a country. You did the right thing.'(54) And here is a thought about the first of God's created things: 'We read Thos. Edison made light. But in Sunday school they said you did it. So I bet he stoled your idea.'(53)

The place of death in creation is a common concern: 'Instead of letting people die and having to make new ones, why don't you just keep the ones you got now?'(8) 'I love you because you give us what we need to live. But I wish you would tell me why you made it so we have to die.'(55) And this ties in with 'I would like to live 900 years like the guy in the Bible.'(50)

'Do animals use you or is there somebody else for them?'(10) raises thoughts on the place of the animal kingdom in the whole of God's creative purposes: something that Grenz does not seem to consider of importance. Looking back, 'When you made the first man did he work as good as we do now?'(21) (This has been a constant theme of adult observation in history.)

How sin fits into God's creative plan is near the source of several letters: 'I wish there wasn't no such thing of sin. I wish that there was not no such thing of war.'(37) 'Maybe Cain and Abel would not kill each so much if they had their own rooms. It works with my brother.'(38)

We conclude with some thoughts of children as they ponder creation: 'It is great the way you always get the stars in the right places.' 'I didn't think orange went with purple until I saw the sunset you made on Tuesday. That was *cool*.'(59)

There is no thought of theological categories here, but rich ideas about nature, time, history, relationships and death. If the children think they are doing something more serious than playing, then we might still characterize their attitudes very often as playful. That is their metier and their gift to us.

Getting to grips with the natural world

The role of play in the development of every aspect of human development was one of the great insights of Friedrich Froebel.[15] He saw the natural world with its sounds, colours, rhythms, textures all combined in some form of movement as the ideal context in which little children grow and develop holistically. What I have learned through my own work with children confirms Froebel's insights.

Of all the times when I have been privileged to explore the natural world with children and young people, two immediately came to mind when I was working on this chapter. On both occasions I was holding a baby in my arms at night-time: once in India, the other time in Wales. Both night skies were remarkably clear, to the extent that the Milky Way was visible to the naked eye. On both occasions the little child was totally absorbed by the stars. And they both pointed continuously to what they saw. What they made of the sight and experience I cannot of course say, even though as an adult I was tempted to impute to them an element of wonder.

What cannot be ruled out is the possibility that the two babies were at one with creation in ways that can never be recreated by the adult imagination, however vivid. If we dare to try to look through the eyes of those children, is it possible that they were at one with creation to the point where their souls and the universe itself were interwoven, where their pulses and the pulse-beat of the stars were in tune and in time? With questions such as these we stand in the presence of impenetrable mysteries, but the fact that they are asked is significant. Something was going on in the experiences of the babies in my arms that will not let me forget such remarkable possibilities and intimations.

Children interacting with creation

I have also observed older children from a range of different backgrounds and cultures directly encountering the physical world in North Wales. Their relationship with it is so predominantly tactile and active that it challenges adults to look at, and reflect upon, the created world differently.

For example, on the beach they instinctively scrape, burrow and reshape the *sand*. Very often they choose to leave their mark, often their name. (In this way their actions may be seen as symbolic of human history.) This is not always intentional or conscious: they will sift the sand through hands, and stroke it with their feet while having a meal or talking, for example. Their 'knowledge' of the earth comes to them from a range of touch experiences and reminds us that biblically God is said to shape us from earth with his hands, and that we return to dust (Genesis 2.7; 3.19; cf. Isaiah 64.8).

The *wind* plays its part in shaping the sand dunes on 'our beach', and the appearance and experience of the sea, and kites are one of the ways in which we encounter air. The wind at sea level and on the mountain ridges is sometimes a source of incredulity. And when fortunate enough on the Carneddau Range to watch chough going through their manoeuvres, I have watched children's faces light up with admiration like the words of the psalmist: 'By the streams the birds of the air have their habitation; they sing among the branches. From your lofty abode you water the mountains; the earth is satisfied with the fruit of your work' (Psalm 104.12-13).

And holidays, whether on the beach or in the mountains, would not be complete without barbecues, and here we come to the experience of *fire*. No child can sit and watch a fire without wanting to feel it in some way, usually with a lighted stick. Cooking on the fire, roasting marshmallows and sitting singing around the embers are part of the process of enjoying the heat and warmth but also the riskiness of fire. As adults perhaps we forget that fire can be symbolic of God and is also at the heart of traditional sacrifice. The children's fascination with fire at a barbecue can take us back to those times when people felt especially close to God and saw his nature in the fire.

Water play is infinitely varied: from the discovery of temperature with the very first dip of a toe into the sea or stream, to splashing, swimming, rowing and sailing. And the sounds are as integral to the experience as the feel of being in the water. Playing with gullies of water scraped in the sand with the incoming tide and tide-fights are part of the pattern of the encounter. There are hints of the primal 'deep', the Flood, the crossing of the Red Sea and baptism.

In every one of these experiences there is a degree of risk and danger: that is inherent in the very nature of the created world. To eliminate risk from the lives of children would be to deny them the very contact with the world for which they strive, and are created.

All these things, earth, air, water and fire, interact with each other: they are interconnected and form part of a dynamic and integrated whole into which the children fit and which they encounter holistically. I guess that if we were seeking to describe the common denominator here, it is play. Children feel no qualms about playing with what adults may view as the glories and grandeur of nature, but which they experience as earth, water, air and fire. My sense is that the children's desire to play in and with nature is a sign to adults of how our heavenly Father desires that we interact with his creation, and with him. However what comes to me from the privileged position of being able to observe this play over a period of more than 40 years, is that although as adults we might sometimes think in terms of the 'sublime' (here I am using the word in Ruskin's sense of 'the effect of greatness upon the feelings'), children and young people are taking creation for granted rather more than they used to. Or, if that is not an accurate description, then they are interacting with it without undue reverence or deference. It is not sacred or hallowed. Adults might sing 'O Lord my God, when I in awesome wonder consider all the works thy hand hath made . . .', but young children seem to want to scramble on the mountains and climb the trees rather than to consider them with anything like awe or wonder. What does sometimes emerge is a sense of regret, among older children, for the way we behave towards the creation:

> I lived next door to a field.
> I liked to look out and
> see the baby lambs
> I can't do that now
> as the field has
> been turned
> into a building site
> for new houses.
> I feel very upset about this.[16]

Children and sensory experience

Dr Sofia Cavalletti, the former Hebrew scholar who later concentrated on communicating the essential elements of the Christian message to children using the philosophy and methods of Maria Montessori, has paid great attention to the role of all five senses in the ways in which children express their spirituality: if theology leads churches to stress thought rather than direct experiences it may well not only stifle the development and expression of children's discoveries of spirituality, but also deprive adults of their wonder and joy as mediators of some things within nature.

Because the four elements play such an important role in philosophy and religion worldwide one might have assumed that any theology of creation would refer to them as a matter of course. Biblical theology would find in them a very rich vein. But western theology seems to be focused on a rational approach to the philosophical questions posed by creation, rather than direct encounters with the created order.

The more I have pondered my memories of being with children in the mountains of North Wales, the more I have come to see that abstract reflection on, or analysis of creation is not typical of the way that children explore and encounter nature. Adults have long (though not always) had some notion of that which is rude, wonderful, terrible and sublime when considering this area of the United Kingdom. And it is easy to assume that children bring the same categories to their experience of it, and that they have or identify with these feelings. My sense is that such feelings come at the earliest with puberty. As far as I can recollect things that is how it was with me. I wrote about nature in diaries and essays and it was only as a teenager when writing about the intense feelings I had associated with a sunset on the north coast of Cornwall that any Romantic sense of nature was in evidence.

So what can we say about the relationship between young children and the elements of nature? I think it is more like this. They are developing a grasp of their own capabilities, senses, movement, control, and their bodies are the key factor in creation. However much we might like to think otherwise, it seems to me that encounters with earth, air, water and fire serve to further this process of self-discovery rather than to explore the geography, geology, chemistry, physics and botany of the creation. What I mean is that they are not only not stepping back to reflect on what it might mean, but in fact doing the very opposite: they are not thinking about things in this quasi philosophical or Romantic way, and that is the crucial and essential point.

They are part of nature interacting with other parts of nature and it is the sensations of the breeze in their hair, and on their faces; the splashing of the water between their toes; the feel of grains of sand sifting through their fingers; the sparks of the fire arcing through the darkness; the moonlight on the water right up to their feet that are the very essence of how they experience creation. They do not have or seek a philosophy or theology of creation: things are nearly all about tactile experiences of it. I venture to suggest that this is also characteristic of their relationships with animals. This is true also of unpleasant experiences, the messiness and 'gunge' of the natural world as this example shows:

> I have to get up each morning and take the chickens out of the shed
>   and feed them.
> I really like helping at lambing,
> pulling lambs.
> Sometimes when you're pulling a lamb comes out dead.
> I was pulling once and the leg came off because it had died inside.
> Our dog started to eat it.
> There's loads of gunge and mess.[17]

The common thread to all this experience would best be described as play or drama: a give and take between the child and the elements.

Identification with creation

When thinking of the essential mystery of the natural world Ludwig Wittgenstein commented: 'It is not *how* things are in the world that is mystical, but *that* it is.'[18] It seems to me that children are relating to the world at the level of ontology rather than epistemology, and it is this that is a constituent of the wonder and awe that adults may feel when we are privileged to be with them in this exploration. But there is another dimension to this encounter. Byron spoke of the mountains, waves and skies being part of him and he of them: some fusion between the individual and the natural world through the imagination. And I wonder whether children reveal something of this mysterious process. Gabriel Marcel argued that, 'Mysteries are not truths that lie beyond us: they are truths that comprehend us.'[19] We cannot separate ourselves from mystery. And that is what the encounter between child and nature exemplifies: the little child cannot and does not separate out self and other, me and that: they are in some way intertwined, not by means of reflection and analysis, but by experience. 'This is me: this is not me' will only become clear later. For now the sand sifting through the fingers, the shafts of sunlight reflected from the ripples in the water disturbed by the feet, seem an extension of the hand and foot. So in this example, a child describing the natural world makes a shape with her body to tell adults about her identification with a loved tree:

My special place is an oak tree.
It's quite near my home in the garden. All the birds sing in it.
The branches are like this.

*(She held her arms
in the shape of a V)*

I can sit there.
I get a little wooden red chair
and use it to climb up.
I specially like being there
when it's sunny.[20]

Although I would not dare to claim to know what children are feeling or experiencing in their encounters and play in, and with, the natural world, nothing I have observed can be used as evidence against the possibility that, in the words of William Blake, it might be they represent a way of connecting with creation through minute actions and interactions:

To see a World in a grain of Sand
And a Heaven in a Wild Flower,
Hold Infinity in the palm of your hand
And Eternity in an hour.

Of course, Blake is reflecting in the way that very gifted adults do, whereas my contention is that little children do not think like this at all. All the same, their spontaneous experience may not be so far removed from what Blake describes, for when a child holds a stone, a plant, a flower, it is all that matters in the whole wide world at this precise moment. It has become everything, not by conscious reflection, but because nothing else matters. It is not about an illustration of a theme, part of a lesson, a stage on a journey, but the whole point in and of itself. So often when it seems as if little children are on a walk, or in the middle of a game, as if they are reaching a new plane of consciousness, and making connections, I notice that they surprise adults by stopping the walk or the game by focusing on a single object. Blake therefore could be said to portray the kind of concentrated attention and insight that this child shows:

I love it when the sun breaks through the clouds and the sun shines
   through and the rays are shining on the hills and the rain is
   glistening . . .
And everything looks as if it is covered in diamonds . . .
And the spiders' webs glisten . . .[21]

But I must add a note of realistic caution at this point: this interaction with the natural world has been bought and protected only with great cost and care. The pressures of the global media would seek to entrap children and young people in a virtual world in which tactile and direct experiences are replaced by electronic impulses. We have no television or electronic devices in North Wales, at the same time that the world of childhood is moving in exactly the opposite direction (in leisure, home and classroom). Perhaps this is not so far removed from the way in which theology has been abstracted from the real world? Do we owe it to our children to give them the chance to be amazed by spider webs rather than just by Spiderman?

The secondary creation

Another gap in the traditional doctrinal treatment of creation concerns what J. R. R. Tolkien called the 'secondary creation': that which artists, poets, musicians, sculptors, dramatists and so on, make. If art and artistic endeavours do not sit somewhere in this doctrine, where do they fit in the overall theological scheme of things? Presumably it might be within anthropology.

We are not here just thinking about a one-way process in which we find somewhere to reflect upon such human endeavour in the canon of theology, but also a process which learns from such human activity. Art can provide windows onto creation, and it may be that the artistic process can function as a symbol of God's relation to creation. Secondary creation can be seen as seeking to do things God's way (in humility and going with the grain of nature) and therefore as potentially an agent of the kingdom of heaven. It echoes the primary creation, and creates symbols of possibility and infinity. It goes beyond a representation of the world as it is, and imagines how things might be.

But there is a risk all through that we may take a solely adult view or perspective on creation and assume that secondary creations are thought out and reflective. What if they are much closer to the primary creation, and if the play of children with the elements is not near to the essence of such secondary creation?

If this is so then we would do well to pay careful attention to the playful interactions of children with creation: their movement of hands and feet through water, of what they shape in the sand, what they scratch on slate and so on. Not because it is 'high art', but because it is a window into the primary creation. In such play is there any distinction between creation and re-creation? If not then we may have a valuable clue in our theology: perhaps this is one of the ways in which God's pre- and post-lapsarian creation are connected.

We have come close to the concept of pure art ('Art pour l'Art': art for art's sake). It embodies its own meaning and does not require reference to another framework or metanarrative. The play of children with creation is not in the service of another process, but is sufficient in and of itself. But this is not a form of art that is abstracted in some way from primary creation, but dependent on and part of it. There are some modern artists like Richard Long who make art in nature by making patterns with stones, or patterns in sand, to be eroded and destroyed by natural forces. Is this a return to a childlike way of doing art, like making snow angels or snowmen?

This is not the time or place to try to develop a theory of art as secondary creation seen through the actions of children, but I sense that such a theory may be possible, and that it could yield valuable insights into the nature of creation. If the kingdom of heaven is to be seen as 'God's way of doing things' (and this is how I prefer to describe it), then a child playing in and with creation may be a sign of this kingdom. When the time and place are ripe for this, then the doctrine of the Incarnation will be one of the crucial ways into, and frameworks for a fresh understanding of creation.

Children and creation in the Bible

In the book of Proverbs Wisdom is the first act of God's creation. She is birthed by God. She bears witness to God's creation and is intimately familiar with the workings of the cosmos. But Wisdom was not born fully formed as an adult, but as a growing child. Although the usual translation of Proverbs 8.30 is about Wisdom being 'filled with delight and rejoicing', a more accurate translation of the Hebrew would be: 'when he carved the foundations of the earth, I was beside him growing up and I was his delight day by day, playing before him always, playing in his inhabited world'.[22] William Brown points out that traditional translations and interpretations of this text assume that Wisdom portrayed as a child playing is incongruent with Wisdom's primacy. But he argues that play may be primary when it comes to the development of Wisdom! The translators seem to have been embarrassed by the association of Wisdom as a playing child, not least in the context of the act of creation. Why should that be so? What if playing with the natural world is natural and instinctive: does that in some way belittle its grandeur and deface its essence?

The thought of Wisdom playing beside the creator God day by day as creation unfolded is consonant with the argument of the German theologian, Jürgen Moltmann in his book *God in Creation* where he develops the metaphor of creation as play.[23] Could we re-read the accounts of creation in Genesis alongside watching children at play and so learn more about the nature and purposes of God?

And if we ask what connects the origins of creation with its fulfilment and final realization at the end of the age, we could argue that it is 'God's way of doing things'. As indicated above, this is my preferred dynamic equivalent for 'the kingdom of heaven'. In and through the natural world, and throughout human history, enfolding the whole universe, God the creator continues his loving and gracious purposes in drawing all things to their full potential in him. And the chosen symbol of this loving process is the child placed beside Jesus. Similarly, the visions of this new age and realm in the Old Testament prophets have a unique role for the child, notably Isaiah 11. Here the child is playing in the world God intends.

And if we ask whether it is scientists and those who make a formal study of the natural world who see into its heart, Jesus reminds us that such things are hidden from the wise and educated, and revealed to little children. In a unique expression of feeling he says 'Yes, Father, for such was your gracious will!' (Matthew 11.26).

Children taking the lead

This begs the question of how adults help children into deeper relationships with and understandings of the natural world. Few would argue that there should be a Rousseau-like space given to a child to develop this relationship for herself. On the other hand, the way in which children are connected with creation raises a profound issue of whether formal education can undermine that relatedness. There has to be some integration of these perspectives, and the closest I have come to this is in a poem by Jane Clements, a teacher in the Bruderhof Schools, that captures the implications of this for the teacher–child relationship:

> Child, though I take your hand
> and walk in the snow;
> though we follow the track of the mouse together,
> though we try to unlock together the mystery
> of the printed word, and slowly discover

> why two and three makes five
> always, in an uncertain world –
>
> child, though I am meant to teach you much,
>
> what is it, in the end,
> except that together we are
> meant to be children
> of the same Father
>
> and I must unlearn
> all the adult structure
> and the cumbering years
>
> and you must teach me
> to look at the earth and the heaven
> with your fresh wonder.[24]

The force of the word 'unlearn' suggests that knowledge and acquired skills can equip us for adult occupation and living, but at the same time serve to cut us off from a powerful source of finding out about God. If we will let them, children teach us, educating us in things we have forgotten or displaced about how God is active in creation.

Children and the global future

Whereas the traditional theological reflections on creation have tended to consider the origins and nature of the universe as depicted in the Scriptures, or to look towards the endgame and completion of the process God initiated, a whole new dimension has been thrust on us by our growing awareness of the fragility of the earth's ecosystems. Humans no longer live in a world of inexhaustible resources irrespective of the way we live. We are having a profound impact on the whole climate, and hence the future of planet Earth. In this context creation and eschatology come together: understanding the nature of creation in order to work together to preserve and nurture what is yet to be.

Part of the doctrine of creation concerns human relationships with and within it. Stewardship is one of the metaphors deriving from the Genesis accounts. And this is not about an abstracted individual stewardship (how should an individual act responsibly in the natural world), but about the role of the whole human race. Child theology (that is, an emerging form of doing theology summarized in the documents of the Child Theology Movement[25]) requires us to consider all this with the following three prophetic aspects in view.

Children's growing awareness of global issues

Perhaps there are different aspects of the Christian story (doctrines) that resonate with particular groups at particular times in history. This has been true of eschatology and millenarian movements, with church, with salvation, with Holy Spirit, for example. If so, it would not be surprising if the doctrine of creation became of special significance to our children and their children. There is much current discussion of the origins of human life and of the universe itself, and equally a growing concern for the future of the planet. Christian young people will therefore be trying to understand their theological bearings within such a context. If, for adults who were growing up post-1910 the slogan of the 'World for Christ in the next generation' generated by the Edinburgh conference of world mission in that year was a predominant framework, it may well be that now it is the environment. The Lambeth Conference of 1988 designated a fifth mark of mission to the four established around proclamation, nurture, service and challenge to injustice. It states: 'to respect the integrity of creation and to sustain and renew the earth'. For our children, this important 'mark' of mission may rise to the top of the agenda.

So when the biblical narrative and stories are recounted, children and young people may well be reading them in this evolving metanarrative. And the primal myths in which chaos and order, dark and light, monsters and the heroes contend for supremacy will have a contemporary relevance. It is the future of life as we know it that is really in the balance.

Children's agency in the stewardship of the world

The combination of increasing global awareness and a sense of the unfolding agency of children and young people may create an environment in which we see children increasingly lead (take care of) the process of caring for planet Earth. In this way the prophecy of Isaiah 11 may find some practical expression in our own times. Perhaps reflection on this process will mean that more theological work is done by children, or at least is initiated by their concerns and activities. Further, if adult priorities continue to be dominated by short-term parochialism, tribalism and warfare/defence, then it may be that children will be the ones who challenge these priorities with those of their own.

Children's futures: the way we are living today is our legacy to them

At the same time it may well be that children living in all parts of the world are increasingly critical of the way adults are currently living. Their contributions may be vital theologically. In the Old Testament it is the questions of children that provide the context for a rehearsal of doctrine and tradition.[26] Perhaps the global questions of children today and tomorrow will open up new horizons in theology.

But, is it is possible that the electronic communication that is dominating the lives of children as never before in human history will prove to be an opiate, separating them from the real world, and dulling their senses? If so it may be the children of the poorer parts of the world, who are daily and dramatically in contact with creation, who may lead the way. Their voices will provide a moral imperative for action to cooperate with the creator in caring for a world that humans have marred and scarred so deeply.

Questions

1. What kinds of experience might help us to see 'a world in a grain of sand'?

2. Look at some holiday photos or travel brochures and try to imagine what you see as an 'adventure playground'. What hidden potentials for play and exploration do you think the pictures might have?

3. List all the risks you're worried about in relation to children in two columns, 'worth taking' and 'not worth taking'.

4. Have a look at Psalm 8. What are the babes and sucklings doing in the psalmist's wonder at the magnificence of creation? How does this relate to Keith's story of holding the child in his arms under the stars?

5. In what ways is God's creation celebrated in your church? What ONE thing could be enhanced by encouraging children to participate and contribute more to it?

Activities

What is a child? / Nakedness and Vulnerability / Creation

1. **Game**

You will need pencils or crayons, paper, Post-it™ notes. You can play this game by yourself or with children.

Draw a simple stick figure on a piece of paper. On Post-it™ notes begin to list or draw any items, people, qualities or factors that create a sense of protection for a child. Be specific. You can use both concrete and abstract words, e.g. clothing, arms of embrace, smile, affirmation, safety. Place the notes in a series of concentric circles around the figure starting with the most basic needs. When you have built up the layers of protection notice your feelings and thoughts. Begin then slowly to remove one note at a time and reflect on the implications of their removal. A meditative verse for this activity might be, 'she wrapped him in bands of cloth, and laid him in a manger' (Luke 2.7).

2. **Create**

You will need some creative materials, paints and paper, old cardboard boxes, clay, etc.

Create something together with a child or a group of children. It could be a simple scribble picture, a sculpture from junk boxes, or clay modelling. Let the children choose what to make and go along with them. Be aware of the processes rather than the product. What are you, the adult, learning about this particular act of creation? Use the insights to reflect on verses from the beginning of Genesis such as 'God saw everything that he had made, and indeed, it was very good' (Genesis 1.31).

3. **Learn from**

You will need a comfortable place to sit or lie down.

If possible spend some time paying attention to how your child or a group of children sits, runs and plays. Now become aware of your own body. Sit comfortably but alert and be aware of your breathing, your body posture, the complex interactions of biological processes – the blood coursing through your veins, the intricate connections of the nervous system. Compare the way you move and hold yourself with your observations of children. What do you learn?

You can use the words of Psalm 139.13 as a quiet meditation, 'For it was you who formed my inward parts; you knit me together in my mother's womb.'

4. **Celebrate**

Pay special attention to children's responses to the elements in nature. For example:

- Water – on a visit to a pond, river, stream, the sea; at bath-time; water play; washing up; a swimming lesson; a walk in the rain;

- Fire – lighting a candle; making a bonfire; fireworks; barbeques, cooking, etc.;

- Earth – playing in a sand tray; digging in the garden; making mud-pies; working with clay;

- Air – running in the wind; kite flying; throwing paper aeroplanes; playing with balloons; blowing bubbles.

What do you notice? What are the similarities and differences between your responses and those of the child? In what ways does this inform or challenge your theology of creation? You can use this verse for reflection, 'Their young ones become strong, they grow up in the open; they go forth, and do not return to them' (Job 39.4).

5.  **Scripture**

Begin by compiling some biblical images of children and childhood, such as Genesis 1.27; Genesis 21.1-20; Deuteronomy 14.28,29; Proverbs 22.15; Isaiah 38.19; Matthew 18.2-5. What other texts could you add to increase this complex picture? What picture of childhood is created here by extending the range of the biblical references?

3

Spirituality

Rebecca Nye

With my mind and with my eyes [is how I see God].

Sometimes I feel . . . um . . . I am in a place with God in heaven and I'm talking to Him . . .

And um there's room for us all in God.

He's . . . God . . . well, He's in all of us . . . He's everything that's around us.

He's that microphone . . . He's that book. He's even . . . He's sticks. He's paint . . .

He's everything around us. And, inside our heart. Heaven.

By the way, have you seen *Indiana Jones and the Temple of Doom*?

('John', aged 6[1])

Overview

The last two decades have witnessed seismic changes in the way children's spirituality is thought about. At the centre of this change has been the importance of seeing spirituality through the eyes of children, on *their* terms. Accompanying this has been a sense of revelation for adults too, not only touching their understanding of and work among children, but also affecting their own, adult, spiritual life. This area is therefore a live example of the two-pronged vision set out by this book: about providing a more sensitive understanding of the reality of children's lives, and also stimulating broader debates in practice and theology inspired by the perspectives of childhood.

Choosing an illustration of this is not easy, since this dual effect is such a constant in my own experience. Each time I glimpse more of the landscape of children's spirituality, my *own* spiritual horizons are altered and challenged too. It's possible I am just a slow learner, but I suspect it also has to do with a deeper truth: that to 'enter the kingdom of heaven' we do, continually, need to reconnect with childhood and children in the most radical (and yet often ridiculously simple) ways.

Spiritual aeroplanes

Here's one example. In our church 'children's group', *Sunday after Sunday*, a few of the boys would always make paper aeroplanes. This happened during the brief time available after the 'lesson' (usually a Godly Play story) and the discussion ('wondering') we'd had as a group, in which their engagement had usually been enthusiastic and full of questions. While others in the group then choose to paint, draw, write or work with the story materials to 'explore some more how it made them feel', these particular boys just 'opted out' and made aeroplanes – every week. Some people in the congregation began to hear of this and mutter complaints. This was surely not Christian spiritual education? But two things happened which taught me, yet again, the value of setting aside the adult 'norms' of spiritual evidence – the 'lovely children's prayers', 'the neatly drawn picture of the story' – looking instead at these children's responses on *their* terms, and in so doing, finding my own spiritual understanding refreshed and reconfigured.

The first thing happened in conversation with two of the boys as they gave their aeroplanes test flights. I asked, perhaps pointedly under the circumstances, if they thought there was really any point in having a time at church for 'children's group'? Though they were apparently just mucking about by now, they were adamant it mattered, saying, 'you need a time and place to just rest and be yourself'. As I considered those words (and saw past the aeroplanes), I realized this was possibly the most genuine understanding of Sabbath I'd heard in a long while. And I wondered how many of the adults (including myself) came even close to an authentic peace and presence in church. The aeroplanes suddenly seemed crucial to this – they were the safe, familiar, relaxing way of 'being' here. This was an offering of 'themselves', a response freely chosen by them, not coerced or offered to impress me or the congregation.

The second thing happened some weeks later when I was clearing up after most of the group had gone back into church. I picked up yet another paper aeroplane from the edge of the table, though this was a high-tech model, made from card and with art straws on one side down the length and across the wings – for balance maybe, or as undercarriage, I thought. It was also white on one side, black on the other – perhaps they'd not had time to finish making the whole thing black, like those stealth bombers they sometimes talked about. I sighed and asked my son if he knew who this aeroplane belonged to, knowing that he and the other boys had been busy together in their usual manner. He gave me a puzzled look, the one that says, 'Mum, don't you understand *anything*?' He explained that 'aeroplane' was Jack's 'Risen Christ' and he pointed out the side with Jesus' body hanging from the dark cross, and the empty cross on the other in brilliant shiny white card. Who can judge what spiritual development might look like? Certainly *I* got a sharp push forward that day. But perhaps the Sabbath function of making aeroplanes for those boys had leapt that week into a different set of possibilities, finding that the religious language and symbolism offered week by week could be used to make meaning, at a moment, and in a way that was so right for them. And just the right lesson for me!

Children's spirituality today: current understandings

When once there was almost no reference to 'spirituality' in the same breath as 'children', now there are numerous books, research projects, conferences and even a journal about children's spirituality.[2] This change has mostly occurred in the last 15 years. So, although the findings, or the emerging 'stories' are compelling, this is an area still in relatively early development. It is therefore easy, and necessary, to be critical of what is said in general about children's spirituality, in terms of what still needs to be addressed to understand how cultural, religious, social and gender differences modulate this phenomenon.

In the UK, interest in children's spirituality came initially from the school education sector, not the Churches, as teachers and education inspectors grappled with the implications of the 1988 Education Act. This stated that as well as moral, cultural, mental and physical development, education should 'promote the spiritual development of pupils in school and of society',[3] and it became clear that this was a generic task, not restricted to the provision made by religious education. This required a broader, more open, examination of what 'spiritual' might mean, and a realization that while adults might try to agree on this, it would be foolish to overlook the contribution of children's experience and evidence. Arguably, the empirical evidence, observations of children themselves, has been the most important factor shaping the current views, making this area and change in thinking also interesting politically. And though the Churches did not instigate the interest in this area (though more so, as one would expect, in the USA), they have played a vital role in helping the interest develop and sharpen.[4]

Crucially, the discovery of an existing, empirically researched approach to both *thinking* about and practically *doing* something about children's spirituality – Berryman's Godly Play[5] – has provided churches with a much needed 'piggy back' into this area. And as if in return for the initial favour of getting the ball rolling, the ways Godly Play's philosophy and practices support children's spirituality have been welcomed by the school sector too.[6]

The key features of the 'new' understanding of children's spirituality, gleaned mostly from studies of children themselves, are just summarized here.[7] Even reading, in full, the accounts from which these are drawn gives merely useful pointers towards insights about the full nature of children's spiritual lives. Perhaps that is a key feature itself – this is an area only partially glimpsed by adults, possibly also partial to children themselves. And there is no substitute for learning about this area in the company of children and the process of self-reflection this can stimulate too.

Key features

First, it is now thought that children's spirituality is not exclusively about extraordinary experiences, or a few extraordinary children. Rather it is as much

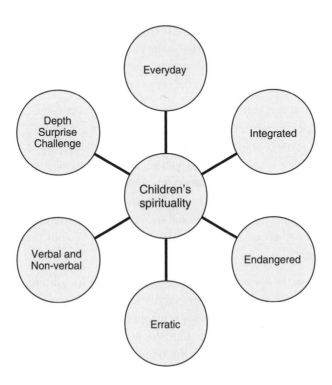

evident in very ordinary, *everyday* aspects of children's lives, and very probably a reality for *every child* – regardless of their religious or other factors in their upbringing.

So, the challenge is whether adults are able to see or hear this spirituality when it may be expressed in such ordinary verbal and non-verbal forms. One way in which adults might learn to look through the eyes of a child might therefore be to pay more attention to the language of spirituality as part of ordinary discourse among children. Imagine the scene: a group of ten-year-old girls sit chatting in their playground at break. They talk about the greenness of the green grass, and then about the sky and about water, and briefly one of them wonders about what clouds are made of. These are things which delight and amaze them. They are curious that they each have a different favourite thing that 'does that' for them.

Overhearing this conversation, one might find it hard to ascertain if this has much to do with their spirituality. But, later on her own, one of the girls explained, in a language we are more attuned to, that this chat had been about 'what was holy', and how it's weird that it's different for her friends, because it's so clear to her that the sky is holy. The question about 'what clouds are made of' seems to clinch this – they represent such mystery for her, a sense that such knowledge is impossible knowledge, a realm beyond knowing, certainly not answered by physical facts about water vaporization. Ordinary schoolgirls, chatting about everyday features of their environment find rich spiritual inspiration and can explore core spiritual themes – what is sacred, what is mystery and the intimation of transcendence this suggests.

A second strand in current thinking about children's spirituality is their capacity for *depth* and to take adults by *surprise*. Some of that has to do with the previous context of low expectations, which the latter part of this chapter will explore. But it is also a genuine feature of their spirituality to speak out, to be prophetic, to articulate (not necessarily through words alone) the need for a change or to offer a new way of seeing things. Children are blessed by greater degrees of freedom from conventional lines of thought and response: their spiritual perception can take in a greater range of colour than our 'trained' vision.

For example, in the eyes of a seven-year-old child, the fraught questions about admissions policies at Church schools (and the charge of indirectly favouring middle-class families) could be easily resolved using his spiritual framework. He argued that the Church should be there for everyone, and especially for those in need. Church schools should be the same. So provide enough for everyone who wants to go, and meanwhile have an entry selection test. This test would identify the children who were most 'in need', educationally and in terms of the broader provision the school hoped to offer – children already doing 'well' should go elsewhere as they were less vulnerable. He even proposed expelling children from Church schools once they reached a certain level of achievement and well-being, to make room for others! In recent adult debates on this matter it's much less common to hear spiritual, Christ-like principles being invoked.

Other key features of childhood spirituality include its *integration* and its *erratic course*. Children do not separate out 'spiritual' from other aspects of their lives, as adults are prone to do. The quote which opened this chapter is an example of that – the boy spoke in the same breath about his sense of God's presence and about an exciting film he'd seen on television. Often children also find a way to integrate or link these apparently disconnected pieces too. Nor is there an inevitable course of 'development'. Children can leap to profound abstract spiritual insights from within a clearly literal mindset one day, and the next find the same literal style of thinking fairly inhibiting. John Hull's *God Talk with Young Children*[8] provides an excellent, evidenced-based, essay on this.

Perhaps another way of reading this 'erratic' quality is as the work of grace, or the spirit, something neither in the child's control nor the educator's control. Acknowledging this challenges how to support and promote spiritual growth. It questions the basis of working through prescribed stage-based schemes of work, or following too closely the prescriptions of faith development theories. For example, children's spirituality does not always obediently focus on 'belonging' issues in advance of 'believing' issues, as Westerhoff might imply about faith, but can skip wildly from one to the other, even apparently 'regressing' to the style of an even earlier stage yet sometimes reaching just as profound conclusions via that route.

It is obvious that spirituality at any age, but most of all in childhood, exists on *both verbal and non-verbal* planes. Nevertheless, there is a strong tendency to overlook the rich qualities of the non-verbal as a stimulus, a way of processing and as a means of expression for children's spirituality. It can be *so* tempting to value verbal over non-verbal, or non-verbal only to the extent that we can hear it put into words. One consequence of this temptation is that the spiritual life of less verbal (often younger) children is overlooked and that their journey begins with the negative lesson that a central core of their spiritual engagement is both invisible to others and presumably of lesser value.

Although the following event does illustrate the non-verbal channels of children's spiritual engagement and response, it also falls into the temptation to be 'really' convincing when the non-verbal takes on additional strength through words – when the child adds verbal explanation.

One Sunday we began to tell the story of Jesus' life, beginning with the infancy narrative using the Godly Play lesson 'The Faces of Easter'. In this lesson, the children are invited, one at a time, to bring something (wordlessly), indeed anything, to put beside the picture of Mary, Joseph and the Christ child which has been the focus during the storytelling. This 'action wondering' replaces the more usual *verbal* wondering common in other lessons, where the group in invited to comment aloud on the story in a variety of ways. The first child (aged 8) noticed a shaft of sunlight on the floor and insisted that we moved the picture and ourselves around it, so that she could bring the sun to the story. Another child (aged 7) noticed a church banner, showing Mary, in the corner of the room. It was too big to move and 'bring' to the picture, so she enacted her contribution by standing with outstretched arms, one reaching up to Mary on the banner, the other reaching down towards the picture in our midst, and remained in this position for the next ten minutes. There were a number of younger children (aged 3–5), some of whom brought figures from the nativity set displayed prominently, some who just sat.

I wondered if the oldest boy, aged 12, would want to play along at all in this rather young group. I looked up at him for his 'go' and he went to the windowsill and brought down a clay duck hidden behind a withered plant. Internally I supposed this was his way of playing along with the younger children, bringing a 'toy' for the baby. We sat quietly for a few moments to give all their offerings and actions a little time to be present altogether. Then some of the children chose to add words to this visual and action-based spiritual response. The older 'duck' boy explained he had brought the duck as a symbol of *conflict*, the conflict which accompanied Jesus from the moment of his birth to his death and even his Resurrection. He explained that he associated the duck with 'Christian' conflict, having heard adults in our church heatedly debating where to place this rather ugly ornament someone had given to the church, and he'd been amused to note that they'd tried to solve the problem by hiding it behind the plant in the parish room!

There seemed so many levels represented by this choice of the duck – a statement about the meaning of Jesus' life as a whole, not just the part of the story we had focused on that day, a statement about Christian communities and their difficulty with conflict, a statement about knowing things that no one has 'told' you, about making religious meaning with everyday stuff and much more. This was fully *in* his action of bringing the duck down from the windowsill, and in *his* heart and mind; all his verbal explanation did was open his spiritual perceptions up for the rest of us to see too. I was stunned and thankful to be privy, through his words, to what this duck represented for him, and corrected from my simplistic thinking that it was meant as a bath toy for the baby Jesus. But this experience was more important as a lesson for me about children's powerful relationship to *non-verbal* communication and meaning making. For all we know, similarly multilayered, profound feelings and provoking thoughts surround the non-verbal offerings (items brought, actions taken, moments of stillness, etc.) of any child in our groups. For the girl who brought the sunshine, or the three-year-old who brought the donkey from the nativity scene, a child who chose not to get anything at all – equally profound, perhaps ineffable, spiritual processing may have been taking place. Indeed challenging children to turn these into words may be detrimental, diluting the power of the non-verbal to represent spiritual complexity.

Studying children's spirituality in the mid-1990s, David Hay and I found a consistent feature of children's spirituality was that it seemed to be an *endangered* species, moving towards extinction.[9] This was not so much *our* conclusion, but the feeling of the children themselves. Despite relishing the chance to share various aspects of their spiritual lives as research participants – their experiences, their views, their questions and their fantasies – most of the children felt this area had no value in the eyes of others, and little future as they concentrated on growing up. In other words, spirituality felt like something 'to grow out of', and this message seemed to come from the world, and adults, around them. This impression included the 'messages' they received from religious sources; the children felt sure that this area (of personal spirituality) was dismissed as much by ministers of religion and RE teachers as by others. Arguably, since then schools make greater efforts to promote and support children's spirituality, lending a different view, that this is *not* something embarrassing, childish or of little value. Equally, it is possible that in some contexts, religious influences are able to lay more positive foundations, and build two-way bridges between the child's spiritual insights and the traditional spiritual language of the church, temple or mosque.

Children's spirituality: helping adults to see *themselves* through new eyes?

Without wanting to distract attention from the difficult task of nurturing children's spirituality (especially in view of its tendency to become endangered as children approach their early teens), the features of spirituality in childhood shed an interesting light on some characteristics of *adult* spiritual life too.

The themes of so many spiritual 'guidebooks' include addressing the problems we encounter if our spiritual categories become too reified and our spiritual practice rather compartmentalized. We tend to exclude the ordinary and everyday – a hallmark of childlike spirituality.

In spiritual direction adults often seek to be connected with something deeper, sensing a void in terms of challenge or uncertainty about change. As if their spiritual life has succumbed to being rather superficial and predictable, adults seek permission to see or do things really differently, yet this was a natural feature of childlike spirituality.

So being more aware of strengths and weaknesses of childhood spirituality may offer a way to face the problems of the adult spiritual journey too. For example, taking 'refuge' in a non-verbal way of wrestling with issues may be both childlike but also a route to the more complex layers of meaning and feeling that words can sometimes keep at bay. Similarly, an erratic course of 'development' is probably not only true in childhood. It would be a more helpful expectation to apply to all spiritual life. Far too much adult angst seems to flow from a sense of 'not keeping up' with the high point or peak spiritual experience (conversion, confirmation, or when I was at *that* church, etc.). Learning from children, and of course reconnecting with our own spiritual lives *as* children if possible, could help to reassure adults that the dynamics of spirituality do not necessarily follow logical, western, criteria where verbal 'beats' non-verbal, and 'good' religious development is linear and unidirectional. However, being persuaded of this, and the benefit for adults, may depend on how seriously children's spirituality is taken in the first place. For example, in *The Shape of Living*, Professor David Ford talks about his experience of the L'Arche community. Jean Vanier, founder of L'Arche, told him that the parents of dying children are often alone, but at L'Arche in the eucharistic community, they can be held. David Ford speaks about Antonio, whose experience particularly affected him and of whom Jean Vanier said, 'It is beautiful but dangerous to live with him: he demands a lot of presence.' David Ford found in Antonio's experience, albeit an experience of disability and finally death, 'the awaited beauty'.[10] Similarly, the Anglican bishop of Rochester, the Rt Revd Dr Michael Nazir-Ali, has spoken of profound experience in confirming young people with Down's Syndrome.

The crucial question facing this area now is whether we can now just more easily list features of children's spirituality, or whether this shifts the paradigm more radically, calling for a new understanding of what being a child means, and who we all might be in the light of that starting point.

Lessons from the past: blind spots and children's spirituality

So far this chapter has offered an account of how children's spirituality is seen in current thought, and reflects some trends in current practice too. But as this still feels to many people to be a *new* way of thinking about children, the danger is that unless we properly understand the historical context in which this emerged as 'news', the older, established ways of thinking may regain dominance.

The current determination to recognize children's spirituality has been both important in terms of appreciating their spiritual life per se, but it has also been an important factor in taking children and children's voices more seriously in general, on their own terms, especially in the Churches. To lose ground because we failed to understand the inheritance of views out of which this all emerged, would therefore be a twofold disaster.

Two patterns of thought

Until the recent changes in thinking, arising partly from new research and some new models of practice, there have been essentially two patterns of thought about children's spirituality. One traditional pattern of thought has been the tendency to hold up adult models and criteria of spirituality as 'the' models,[11] at least implicitly, and interpreted the task of children's spiritual nurture as helping children aspire to matching those, adult, criteria. The other pattern has been to pay almost no attention whatsoever to the spiritual qualities and needs of children, focusing instead on other things. These have included developing children's religious knowledge, behaviour or the formation of positive attitudes towards their religious identity. Spirituality was deemed a matter for later development, perhaps subsequent to sufficient foundations in these other areas.

These two negative patterns of thought were rarely explicitly articulated as the official views on the subject, which is perhaps why they persisted unchallenged for so long. A notable exception was Ronald Goldman, whose Piagetian-based work on the development of children's religious understanding has influenced decades of age-based Christian resources for children. He *did* make his negative assumption about children's spiritual potential clear:

> In short, sin, death, frustration, enmity, lack of purpose, weakness, must
> have been known in some measure first hand if anyone is to feel the
> need to be saved from them . . . we need to have lived long enough to
> have experienced the real problems of the human condition before we
> see the point of what religion offers.[12]

He also stated categorically that spiritual experience was, compared to
adulthood, 'rarer in adolescence and practically unknown in childhood'.[13]

Probably most people choosing resources that were inspired by Goldman's
views (i.e. that children's mental capacities restrict their depth and grasp of
religious material) have not been *conscious* of the negative position about
children's spirituality these contain. Nonetheless, the low expectations many
adults have about the spiritual in childhood have been unconsciously formed
through their immersion in resources emerging from such thinking. For some,
this may have been the root cause of their exasperation or burn out in their
ministry with children – a realization that no matter how well tailored to the
child's cognitive or social developmental stage, the task of Christian nurture
was missing something fundamental.

It is also important to consider the other casualties of the Goldman legacy.
There must be many *children* subject to resources and church programmes
informed by this negative mindset about spirituality in childhood. Both as
children, and the adults they have grown up into since, their spiritual threshold
has no doubt been anaesthetized by the treatment sanctioned by such
thinking and the practices this sponsored.

So, without 'meaning to', these two patterns of thought (that adult spirituality
sets the model and that childhood is not much of a site for spiritual work) have
operated at an *implicit*, insidious, level evident in practice and post hoc
justifications of practice. Additionally, a dearth of a priori theological thinking
about the nature of childhood, and a lack of careful, open, observation of
children, has also lent support, by default, to these assumptions that children's
lives are seldom or ordinarily the site of valid spiritual experience, spiritual
imagination, spiritual needs or questions.

Voices in the wilderness years (*c.* AD 32–1988!)

There were important, more positive, influential voices in the past, though less
commonly from a religious quarter. While poets such as Traherne, Blake and
Wordsworth made compelling claims about the spiritual riches and
ordinariness of childhood, the thinking and practice apparent in conventional

religious circles usually suggested children's spiritual resources were deficient in comparison with those of adults – until they had learnt and internalized the prayers, the practices and the beliefs of the tradition.

Interestingly, over the centuries, there have been a number of isolated voices challenging these ways of thinking, but somehow their challenges did not find a foothold sufficient to change the direction of the received views about childhood and its spirituality. For example, Marcia Bunge's collection of studies[14] about what Christian thinkers have said about childhood picks up some potentially significant advocates for taking a positive view of children's spirituality, including Bushnell in the nineteenth century and Rahner in the twentieth. Even earlier, a generous reading of *parts* of Luther's and Wesley's work could have formed a basis for a different direction for children's spirituality, though one reason for this not happening may have been a lack of sufficient sustained thought about children to establish a coherent and influential view across their work – a problem we still need to be very conscious of today. There are still almost no theologians who focus predominantly on childhood.

Pierre Ranwez,[15] a French Roman Catholic writing at the same time as Goldman, also offered a promising, but apparently ignored, positive case for spirituality in childhood. This was motivated by essentially Catholic concerns about how one might judge that a child is spiritually ready to begin taking the sacraments, and specifically examining 'the workings of grace in a child'. However, his exploration of this subject has astonishing resonance, both in thought and method, with contemporary scholarship.

For example, he draws on both *theological and psychological* reasoning to create a case that children have a positive capacity for personal religious life. By virtue of his or her creation (and salvation) a child is necessarily spiritually alive ('impregnated with grace'),[16] but the development of consciousness affords the opportunity to choose how this creaturehood is exercised. In this Ranwez was remarkably radical, ahead of his time. He argued that a child who freely and consciously chooses a course of action (however mundane), and who is motivated by his or her age-appropriate sense of morality and response to another, may be said to be acting 'religiously'. In other words, the child's very first free act – that which is not simply instinctive – is potentially a religious act in Ranwez's view. This brings perception of children's spiritual life right down to infancy, and into the everyday. In fact, he gives as an example a baby's intentional smile in response to their mother's love. Perhaps these kinds of perceptions would be helpful in learning not only to look through the eyes of a child but also in matters such as baptism preparation, where sometimes the parents are unable to connect with the preparation material. Ranwez's approach would make such preparation begin from the innate spirituality and religious response of the child.

Examining his own claims further, he notes that mastery of consciousness and the free will to act in an intentional manner is a gradually acquired skill, experienced initially in rather fleeting bursts (which find echo in the 'erratic' feature discussed above). He also is aware that in the early years a child is 'imperfectly conscious' in the sense that reflection on their acts and motives is limited. Nevertheless, he comes to the conclusion that while these limits may prevent a child from relating experience easily to others, or even to themselves, 'the child is conscious in the depth of his soul, and can express this is a certain way'.[17] He presented a case for locating the spiritual within children's earliest everyday experiences and on their own developmental and spiritual terms, not bootstrapped by adult religious and moral codes. Indeed Ranwez warned against reading too much into the child's use of religious language as a genuine sign of childhood spirituality, preferring instead a naturalistic, observational method focusing on the child in interpersonal settings. He also encountered the problem well known to contemporary researchers, namely that such signs of spirituality are fundamentally ambiguous, in isolation, and so need to be observed over a period of time as one gets to know the child more intimately, as well as reflected upon in terms of one's own spiritual tradition. His observational method also included child-led dialogue, drawing and picture prompts – foreshadowing the significance of the non-verbal as a means of expression for children's spirituality.

Had Ranwez's (ignored) ideas become the reference point instead of Goldman's, our insight into children's spirituality could have been far more developed by now. It is hard to pinpoint exactly what accounts for one voice being heard, and another ignored. Recently, what seems to have made a difference is the attention to the *voices of children*, and the will of others to make those heard. This direct kind of evidence has been able to controvert the old thinking. However, it will be the challenge of the next revolution to move beyond voices and learn more about spirituality from who and how children are, that is, their non-verbal 'being' in counterpoint to our adult preoccupation with 'doing'.

Children's spirituality: finding its place in the wider politics and flow of spirituality

If you search the index of any 'comprehensive' work on Christian spirituality, it is extremely rare to find even a mention of childhood. Although so much of the language around spiritual life concerns development, growth and nurture, as a subject for study it has been traditionally dealt with exclusively as an adult matter. A recent exception is *The New SCM Dictionary of Christian Spirituality*,[18] in which this author provides entries about childhood and about adolescent spirituality.

This is then a particular point in history, almost a birth, when eyes are opening to the reality (and challenges) of children's spirituality. A similar search in any comprehensive text on child psychology traditionally found nothing on 'spirituality' either, but at least one major textbook has just broken that silence too.[19] As children's spirituality tries to take its place in these contexts, it may be interesting to consider how (and why) it will fit in now.

Taking the long view, Dupré[20] makes the interesting point that the conceptualization of spirituality took an important new (and long-lasting) turn following the Reformation. He observes it moved away from the ordinary, communal, rhythm of life towards being a much more private, inner and therefore reified phenomenon. It makes 'sense' that this turn of direction supported the exclusion of children from the remit covered by such a conceptualization of spiritual life. In our shorthand thinking, adults are granted a private life, but children more often are seen to 'belong' to the public (group) world, as pupils or as aspects of their family: children are less autonomous, accorded less private life. Indeed, writing about the place of spirituality in religious education in 1991 (before the seismic changes), Copley and colleagues suggested that because spirituality lay outside the 'public' domain, teachers (among others) dealing with children's religious nurture could not, and should not, attempt to grapple with spirituality as this trespassed into 'issues which may be seen as "private" or not the business of the teacher'.[21]

In the early Reformation period when spiritual life took on this new aura of something private, an inner life, there was clearly a struggle when children manifested unmissable spiritual features.[22] The view of what a child was, conflicted with what spirituality was taken to be. Attention focused on *how like an adult* the child was behaving, that is, how contrary to the natural state of being a child. In fact, the interpretation often turned away from treating the child as having any real part in the situation, but instead regarded him or her as a merely passive channel for the divine. As spirituality became reified as something more private, actively worked on and sought by an individual, rather than something given, ordinary, common to all/communal and a matter of grace, it was incomprehensible that children could experience this.

However, there's also a more auspicious pattern, for our purposes, noted in Dupré's long view of the history of spirituality since the Reformation. He observes that transformative, new spiritual movements have often arisen from the margins, to some degree in reaction to the mainstream, traditional or authoritative patterns of religious thinking. In other words, they are responses to the need for 'seeing something more to this', a new kind of vision, through new eyes. Emergent movements in spirituality therefore often have the quality of the lone, marginal or new voices, addressing the limitations of the old 'wisdom'.

The current climate of excitement surrounding the 'discovery' that children's spirituality may be a rich, challenging and possibly radically transforming reality for the Churches seems to fit exactly this pattern – coming from the margins and refreshing those parts of traditional thought which have begun to feel stale or neglected. Certainly in most of the literature about children in the Churches, and about those who are called to minister among them, there is agreement that marginalization is a key characteristic.[23] The seismic changes in the view of children's spirituality as something valid, to pay attention to, suggests we may be in the midst of an emerging new spiritual movement or force.

The way ahead?

There are in fact at least two major 'ways ahead' on this new road.

Clearly, one is to continue to pursue the reality of children's spirituality, their insight and outward vision. This requires consideration of the child in her own right, and requires hearing and observing children in new ways. Our mindset about spirituality and about children needs to be radically open to do that, at least critical of the inherited mindset that focuses on what children cannot do or lack.

Already this has begun to reveal how much we've been missing. It suggests that it has not just been our *thinking* about children that's needed an overhaul, towards basing that on a closer engagement with how they see things. But also it has major implications for practice. This challenges us to transform radically what we do with and how we are with children, both in formal religious nurture and perhaps just as crucially, in the 'ordinary' time too.

But the other important way forward concerns the manner in which the corollaries for adult spiritual insight are dealt with. This chapter has put forward a number of arguments for children's spirituality potential to inform and change the way we conceptualize adult spirituality. The extreme would be to reverse the pattern – to hold children's spirituality up as a model and argue that the task for the spiritual nurture of adults is to aspire to match that, recapturing the spiritual qualities set out by childhood.

On the one hand, this *is* extreme and problematic. There's a real danger endorsing an artificial 'childishness' in adult spiritual life, that throws out reasoning, accumulated knowledge as well as the wider realms of experience usually privileged to adult life, such as sexual relationships, work and aging. There is also the danger of placing children on a pedestal when 'their spirituality' is set up as some kind of ideal exemplar. Looking through the eyes of a child is not the same as copying children or mimicking them. Children's spirituality is no more uniform than anyone else's; variety and individual difference are, if anything, more likely in the early period of our lives before a certain amount of conformity, perhaps through common spiritual language and practice, lends some shape to our spiritual lives. So, to set up an exemplar model of 'children's spirituality' is both artificial and will impact dangerously for real children who will inevitably deviate from this, in other words, can only fall from the pedestal we create.

On the other hand, the idea that adult spirituality might be informed and complemented by insights from children's spirituality is *not* so ridiculous, though perhaps it always needs to contain a hint of the radical to have its effect. Passages in the gospels have Jesus make repeated references to the need for adults to attend to childhood as a model for their spiritual growth and transformation. And some theologians have explored this theme, *for adults*, such as Rahner's examination of childhood as an 'abiding reality' and the task of spiritual growth as one of growing towards 'infinite openness'.[24] Interestingly, many more theologians down the centuries seem to have ignored or reinterpreted these passages as merely allegorical provocations, that is, not really a challenge to consider children's spiritual lives in any detail or with serious intention. There is a fork in the way ahead for a new branch of theology too, fuelled partly by the attention to children's spirituality.

Questions

1. What do you think is involved in Christian spirituality? Do you think children's spiritual insights are different from those of adults and if so, why?

2. This chapter talks about children 'growing out of spirituality'. What do you think this looks like and in what ways can we help to nurture children's spirituality?

3. Make a timeline of events and occasions which are important to your spiritual journey to date. How many of these belong to your childhood and how did they contribute to later important events?

4. How does the story of the call of Samuel (1 Samuel 3.1-21) give us insight into how God interacts with children and young people?

5. Thinking about the worship in your church, identify ONE thing which might be enhanced by including children's own spiritual insights.

4

Word

Joanna Collicutt

Introduction

Children pose a challenge to adult ways of engaging with stories and texts, perhaps especially sacred stories and texts. They can provide a radically different, if not frankly superior, way of approaching the Bible. This is for several reasons. First, children are fresh (or at least fresher than their adult counterparts). They have not had time to become inured to or to develop defences against the strangeness of the biblical text – something referred to by Paul Ricoeur as its *alterity*.[1] They do not need to cultivate Ricoeur's prized *second naivité* because they are already naive.[2] Secondly, children have a great capacity for playfulness. This frees them to respond to the playful invitation offered by the biblical text to intimate engagement unencumbered by excessive deference. Thirdly, children are used to situations in which their ignorance and limitation are manifest. They can tolerate the fact that they are not masters of the text.

At a more fundamental affective level children are poised to hear the message of the Christian gospel. The yearning to be secure and grounded in a loving relationship is high on their agenda, and so they can with relative ease tune into the heartbeat of the Christian stories and texts which assures, 'Things are OK because I AM here.'

Children have also helped me to reflect on the sharing of the word of God through using the biblical text in preaching. In this chapter I will share something of what I have learnt from them.

An afternoon of wondering

I told the following story to a group of children one Wednesday afternoon as part of a Godly Play session:

> The kingdom of heaven is like when a sower, someone who scatters seeds, goes out and scatters seed along the path. As the sower sowed

seeds along the path, the birds of the air came and ate the seeds. The sower also sowed seeds among the stones. When the seeds tried to push their little roots down among the stones they could not push their way into the ground. When the sun came out it scorched the seeds and they died. The sower also sowed seeds among the thorns. When the seeds tried to push their little roots down among the thorns, they could push them part way in, but the thorns choked them, and they died. The sower also sowed seeds in the good earth. When the seeds pushed their little roots down into the good earth, they could go all the way in. They grew and grew. When they were all grown up they were ripe for the harvest. Then they were cut off and gathered up. The harvest was thirty, sixty and one hundred bushels.

Now, I wonder if the person had a name? I wonder who the person could really be? I wonder if the person was happy when the birds came and ate the seeds? I wonder if the birds were happy when they saw the sower? I wonder if the birds have names? I wonder what the person was doing when the little seeds could not get their roots in among the stones? I wonder what the person was doing when the little seeds were choked by the thorns? I wonder what the person was doing when the little seeds were growing in the good earth? I wonder what the harvest could really be? Was it like this or perhaps like this? I wonder what the sower used for seed? I wonder what the sower sold? I wonder what the sower kept for food? I wonder if the sower was surprised by the harvest? I wonder what surprised the sower most?[3]

There is an unusually large number of wondering questions in this presentation, and I was unsure how well the children would respond to them. As usual, I need not have worried. Their responses exceeded my expectations, and made me think again about the whole enterprise of preaching the word of God.

The children's wondering went something like this:

Why did the person bother to sow on the ground that he knew wasn't going to bear fruit? Was he careless – or did he decide to take a risk? Perhaps he couldn't tell which ground the thorns were going to come up in.

Was the harvest all or none – or was it that the different sorts of soils produced varying amounts of harvest – with some seed in poor soil surviving against the odds?

Was the sower waiting and watching for the harvest or did she go off and make a cup of tea and come back later, or leave it for someone else to gather?

Why did she scatter the seed so widely – isn't it better to put seed where you can see it and can control it? Why didn't she cultivate the ground?

This Godly Play session brought together two themes which I shall use as organizing motifs in this chapter. The first is Jesus' story of the sower (Mark 4.1-9 and parallels). The second is the concept of play.

The place of preaching the word in the Church

The letter to the Ephesians describes the church as people cooperatively growing up into Christ, who express this process in holiness of life (Ephesians 4.15-17). Growing up into Christ happens right across the lifespan and is dependent on adequate and appropriate nurture. Both the shared bread of the Eucharist and the shared word of Bible reading and sermon can be seen as nurture (see, for example, Jerome).[4] The word of God is compared to bread by Jesus during his temptation (Matthew 4.3-4; Luke 4.3-4; Deuteronomy 8.3). In John's Gospel Jesus is described as the eternal *Logos* in whom is life (John 1.4), and also as the bread of life (John 6.25-40). For adequate nurture to occur the eucharistic bread must be presented, broken, shared and eaten; likewise the word must be presented, opened up, shared and apprehended. In both of these human speech-acts Christ is made present to the faithful participants through the gracious action of God.

The relationship between the bread of the Eucharist and the living bread that is Christ is mysterious. Christ is encountered by the believing community in the Eucharist, and the Church then has the task of making sense of this experience.[5] Nevertheless, the breaking of the bread and the pouring out of wine have a clear physical analogical connection to the historical circumstances of Jesus' death, and are thus partly mnemonics. In addition, eating and drinking enact the mutual indwelling of Christ and the believer and affirm the nourishing quality of the encounter in highly literal terms.

In a similar way, while the potential of the biblical text to nourish has been asserted by many,[6] the relationship between this text and the living Word that is Christ remains mysterious. Christ is encountered by the believing community in the text[7] – the text thus authenticates itself[8] – and, again, the Church has the task of making sense of this experience. The human words of both text and preacher have, in their form, a clear analogical connection to the

Logos. Hearing the text read and expounded enacts the divine speech-acts of creation (Genesis 1; John 1.1-3) and redemption (John 1.14; Hebrews 1.2-3). Furthermore, through the medium of remembered story the words of both text and preacher have, like the bread and wine, the capacity to bring the hearer close to the Jesus of history.[9]

There is a profound irony here. In many Anglican congregations children who bring so much and who need so much are welcomed and present for the first and last parts of the Eucharist – the Gathering and the Dismissal only. They are very often absent or non-participants in the two parts that offer bread to the people of God – the liturgy of the Word and the liturgy of the Sacrament. Bible and sermon are construed as too-solid food on which children may choke, but the alternative offered them is frequently sickly sweet junk-food which is in its own way equally indigestible. The fact that children may themselves be bearers and interpreters of the word to adults (Matthew 21.15-16) is rarely acknowledged, and may in some cases be actively resisted.

The nature of the word

In many ways bread is a good metaphor for the word of God. It is particularly powerful in communicating the way that the word is experienced by the believer: as something or someone who is substantial, satisfying deep hunger (John 6.35), that must be fully ingested if health and strength are to be sustained.

Nevertheless, alternative metaphors may be more apt when considering the word from other perspectives, for instance that of the person who witnesses to the word or shares it with others. The image chosen by Jesus in this context is that of the seed (Mark 4.14). The writer to the Ephesians invokes a related image to remind us that the results of Christian growth in response to nurture are best understood not so much in terms of gaining inches around the waist, but in terms of the bearing of good fruit (Ephesians 5.9. See also Galatians 5.22-23).

This image of the seed tells us much about the properties of the word of God, his speech-acts of creation and redemption. First, a seed is small and easily overlooked (1 Kings 19.12). Secondly, it has enormous potential disproportionate to its size (Mark 4.30-32). Thirdly, all that is necessary for it to reach its potential is contained within it. Fourthly, it nevertheless requires sufficient appropriate local conditions if this potential is to be realized. Fifthly, there may be a substantial period of time between the planting of the seed and its subsequent germination and growth. Sixthly the process of growth, of the emergence and development of the plant, is a mysterious, wonderful, and yet quite natural process of transformation (Mark 4.26-29). Indeed this final property is an image that has been directly applied to the death and resurrection of Jesus (John 12.23-24).

The children's responses to the story of the sower can help us engage more deeply with the dilemmas faced by those whose task is to share the word of God. First, 'Why did she scatter the seed so widely – isn't it better to put seed where you can see it and control it?'

The Church has come to understand that the word represented by the seed is in some sense present in, or borne witness to in a special way by the biblical text. Christ himself is encountered through engagement with the biblical text. Nevertheless, the eternal *Logos* is not identical with the words of the text. And, while the text is a verbal medium, there is nothing essentially verbal about what it conveys. God graciously inhabits the human words of the text, much as he inhabits the human products of bread and wine, and is found in both by the believer, but he is not constrained by their form. Nevertheless, there are some characteristics of the biblical text which seem to be homologous with the Word to which it bears witness. These include its polyvalence, strangeness, incongruity and elusiveness, characteristics which cry out, 'Come play with me!'

Engagement with the biblical text has a sacramental quality, and in this sense the text can be considered sacred. But, in the words of Walter Brueggemann, 'the inherent Word of God in the biblical text is . . . refracted through many authors',[10] and some work is required if it is to be drawn out. There is a range of opinions (which reflect the children's wondering question about controlled sowing) as to how much work is actually required, of how transparent the text actually is with respect to the Word, the degree of effort that needs to be employed in sowing the seed, and indeed what this work actually involves. For instance, what method does one employ in deciding whether a particular text 'has succeeded or not succeeded in being truthful and faithful witness [to the Word]'?[11]

Nevertheless, because the word itself is a healthy, potentially life-giving seed, it does not require any genetic modification. This is the rationale behind Karl Barth's approach to preaching. In his view the word essentially speaks for itself, and the task of the preacher is to proclaim or announce it with clarity and accessibility, but definitely not to modify it. Indeed the preacher is only a human being, and is not actually capable of modifying the word in any meaningful way.[12] The preacher is thus best thought of as the servant of the word, or perhaps its 'midwife'.[13]

Barth's high view of the word that is entrusted to the preacher rightly acknowledges that it is God who speaks, that it is God to whom the text bears witness, that it is God who created the seed. This is at once frightening and reassuring, because it both makes the sacred nature of the task of preaching very apparent and yet stresses that God's word can be trusted to work on its own behalf (Isaiah 55.11). The sower does not need to mess with the seed – she only needs to sow it. It may flourish despite her weakness or the unpromising character of her hearers. In the words of the children, 'Perhaps [the sower] couldn't tell which ground the thorns were going to come up in . . . [could] some seed in poor soil survive against the odds?'

There are, of course, significant questions raised in connection with this sort of analysis. In the words of the children, when does glorious risk taking become simple carelessness? How can one tell the difference between messing with the word of God and proclaiming it with clarity, accessibility and relevance? Exactly how does one act as a servant to the word rather than its master? Is Barth correct to insist that the preacher is really just an announcer or broadcaster, a kind of bystander in an exclusively divine enterprise? Surely he has some responsibility to ensure that local conditions are optimal for the word to take root, grow and to bear fruit? If it is true that the preacher should not be engaged in genetic modification it does not necessarily follow that he should not be cultivating the soil (Luke 13.8-9).

The reception of the word

A lot rests on what one understands the reception of the word to involve. For Barth the reception, like the proclamation, is essentially a divine act.[14] The believer receives through faith, but this faith is divine in origin and supernatural in character. There is nothing human about it because human beings are part of a natural order that is fallen and corrupt, and they cannot receive the gift of God through their own activity. God not only created the seed, he also waters the soil (Isaiah 55.10). Barth is therefore suspicious of any attempt through preaching to change the attitude of the hearer. This is because he understands attitudes to be 'psychological' and therefore fallen, human and natural, bearing no relation to faith.[15] He sets the psychological against the spiritual.

Barth's view, though influential in some quarters, is not representative of the majority of contemporary approaches to preaching, which share the children's unease at the idea of broadcasting the seed without cultivating the soil. Nevertheless, because this chapter draws heavily on psychological theory, it requires some further consideration and criticism.

From a *theological perspective* there are alternative approaches that give greater weight to the human response to divine revelation, which have an equal claim to orthodoxy and conform better to biblical anthropology.[16] These approaches place greater emphasis on the creation of humanity in *imago dei* rather than on the Fall. From a *philosophical perspective* it can be argued that Barth's dualistic position is nonsensical. If the human psyche is, as it were, a bystander rather than a participant in the process of revelation through the reception and transmission of the word, then the word has not been revealed to it at all.[17]

From a *practical perspective* Barth's position is confused. Activities that are clearly psychological in nature are inconsistently treated as fallen and natural (e.g. trying to inculcate an attitude in the hearer) or sacred and spiritual (e.g. reading the text and consulting commentaries). This inconsistency arises from the fact that all human activities are psychological, and indeed physically embodied, so the enterprise of delineating some as non-psychological is both arbitrary and meaningless. On the other hand, it is important to identify some sort of method that distinguishes treating the text with respect from using it as the servant of one's own agenda. Among others, Karl Rahner and Walter Brueggemann have written helpfully on this theme.[18]

The biblical concepts of faith, hope and love conform well to the technical psychological concept of 'attitude',[19] though of course an exclusively psychological description does not do them full justice. From a *psychological perspective* Barth's account of the passive nature of preacher and hearer is implausible. It is obvious that preaching is psychologically active; it is also well established in contemporary cognitive psychology that hearing and understanding are psychologically active.[20]

Finally, from a *biblical perspective*, it is clear that the biblical writers took the psychological nature and social context of their audiences into account.[21] Paul in particular is explicit about the way that he does this in evangelistic preaching (1 Corinthians 9.20-23), and also crucially assumes that cultivating the soil in which the seed is planted is a legitimate, even desirable, human activity, which in no way detracts from the sovereignty of God (1 Corinthians 3.6-7).

So, while the essential requirement of the preacher is to proclaim the word, it is both permissible and desirable that something is also done towards increasing the likelihood that it will take root, flourish and bear fruit in the life of the hearer. The children's reflection on the story of the sower prompts a number of considerations: it is worthwhile scattering fairly widely, it is not always apparent what constitutes good soil, and seed may perhaps flourish even in bad soil, but it is only sensible to do what one can to make the soil receptive. The story of the sower can stand on its own, and in the Godly Play version it is presented with few embellishments. It is the subsequent wondering that works the soil, that makes a deeper reception more likely.

The wondering of these children helps us to see the issues raised in the sharing and receiving of the word 'through the eyes of a child'. And we find that we are not 'dumbing down' to the child's level, but instead are shown how both the linear and paradigmatic aspects of the story of the sower can be held in creative tension.

The parables of Jesus have a linear narrative plot within which events happen, but they also have deep paradigmatic structures embedded within them. These hold stable spiritual truths ('It's OK because I AM here') alongside highly subversive elements ('The way I AM here is not as you expect'). Adults are not attuned to the way these interact, with the paradigmatic structures interrupting and fracturing the narrative in ways that can be shocking. In contrast, children seem to be attuned to, and indeed to enjoy, the fractures, responding with wonder and playful daydream. The brilliance of Jesus' stories may sometimes *only* be revealed by the responses of children.

We see this in the children's responses to the story of the sower. For example, 'Was he careless . . . or did he decide to take a risk?' is a question that literally 'unearths' the connection with the divine creator and his world. We are confronted with an edgy and difficult question: does God really care about all that fails to flourish, suffers and dies, or does he risk a different kind of relationship with human beings in which our response really matters?

If children have this particular facility, which seems to have been lost by adults, where does it come from, and how can adults best learn from them? In the remainder of this chapter I will develop this analogy – looking particularly at how cognitive and developmental psychology may offer us tools for dealing with the birds of the air, the thorns and the stones, and considering especially that the notion of play can show us a way in which the soil may be enriched and fertilized.

Cognitive development across the lifespan

The developmental psychologist Jean Piaget argued that the mind can be understood as a network of schemas (a schema is a deep enduring cognitive structure, something like a mental map, which may have an affective aspect and is expressed in habitual ways of perceiving and acting on the world). According to his theory, the cognitive development of children is not just the continuous accumulation of knowledge about the world, but is instead a process of active schema construction. Provisional hypothetical models, initially highly sensorimotor in character, later more abstract, are constructed, refined and developed, or replaced by models that fit the child's widening experience better. Cognition is seen as enactive, and much of the child's behaviour is understood as experimentation.[22]

Piaget argues that it is through the challenge to existing schemas posed by real-world incongruities that cognitive abilities advance in young children. The development of schemas occurs through the interplay of two complementary processes. The first of these is assimilation. This is where an existing mental schema is applied to a real-world situation, and the situation is made to fit the schema. The second is accommodation. This is where the mental schema changes in response to the situation. Too much assimilation makes for a kind of rigid mental imperialism over the world; too much accommodation makes for mental insecurity and the risk of being overwhelmed by each new experience. (Both extremes, in their respective forms of paranoid delusions and loosened mental associations can be seen in severe mental illness.)[23]

Here is an example from early childhood in the sensorimotor domain. The infant has established a simple schema: 'All things that roll are balls.' Experience 1: An orange rolls. Assimilation → 'An orange is a type of ball.' Experience 2: Parent peels the orange and gives the infant a segment to suck. Accommodation → 'Not all things that roll are balls.' Conflict: Reorganization → 'Some things that roll are good to eat, and that is their main use – but you can also play with them.' Experience 3+: Rolling spherical fruit around, dropping it to see if it will bounce. Trying to roll a banana, or a sausage, what about a chocolate mini-roll? → Expansion of new schema through play. We can see here the foundation for the kind of more sophisticated exploration and wondering that opens up story.

In the process of development, not only are individual schemas refined, but a whole network of relationships between schemas is established. Schemas stand in meaningful relationship to one another. (For instance, a 'world as dangerous' schema is likely to be related to a 'self as vulnerable' schema. A 'sphere' schema is likely to be related to a 'cylinder' schema.)

Childhood and adolescence are the times of most rapid and dramatic psychological development. For children many experiences are new, and every day can be an adventure. As adulthood is reached and organizing principles with which to interact with the world have been laid down, the opportunity for cognitive development through major schema reorganization in response to anomalous, strange or intriguing experience in everyday life is reduced. One reason for this is that developed schemas influence the attention mechanism, so that information that fits with them is selectively attended to and recalled, and information that does not fit is not noticed or forgotten. In this way life becomes less exciting but more predictable and secure. Much can be done on 'automatic pilot', and therefore much is done that way.

The downside of this is that adults tend to lose precisely the kind of ability to wonder, dream and play that offers insights into the word and work of God. Indeed adults may *depend on* children to help them rediscover these abilities, or at least to share the insights that such abilities bring. (For a biblical example, see 1 Samuel 3.) So it makes little sense to exclude children from those points of Christian life and worship where their skills of creative wondering are sorely needed.

Nevertheless, psychological change and development can and do take place in adults, especially if they are able by temperament or training to keep the open mind and alertness to anomaly that is characteristic of creative artists, research scientists or children. (This perhaps sheds some light on Mark 10.15.) These are characteristics that allow the biblical text to be appropriated as an open living story of God's dealings with his people rather than as a closed summary statement of theological orthodoxy.

In adult life, just as in childhood, psychological growth occurs when new information results in schema change that involves the interplay of assimilation and accommodation so that schemas become more differentiated, nuanced or expansive. This process may involve the radical shattering and reconstitution of schemas,[24] or it may be a more leisurely and gentle affair.[25] In any case the schema that emerges will have a clear place in relation to other schemas. It will be embedded in semantic memory, linked by associative networks organized in terms of narrative, logic or temporal contiguity.[26] Along with this goes emotion ranging from 'burning hearts' (Luke 24.32) to a sense of warm satisfaction or peace.

What is play?

In humans and higher mammals novelty, strangeness and incongruity evoke fear, exploration and play. (Which of these responses occurs is dependent on other setting conditions.) In the biblical accounts the normative response to an encounter with God is fear, and this is in turn often answered by a divine instruction not to be afraid, and an invitation to explore and even to play. The biblical text too can evoke disquiet because of its strangeness but, as we have seen, this very strangeness also invites play. It is possible to resist the invitation. Walter Brueggemann points out that both literal and liberal readings of the text can be psychological defences against its 'potentially dangerous, upsetting, and subversive power'.[27] We can also see this defensive process at work in the temptation to avoid 'difficult' texts in preaching or Bible study, and in the way that adults give formulaic or closed answers to children who ask open, playful or challenging questions arising from the text.

Play and exploration are closely associated. The distinctive aspects of play have been identified as flexible behaviour patterns, positive affect and non-literal thinking – 'as if' imagination.[28] In a less technical and more theologically driven account Jerome Berryman also notes the fun and imagination involved in play, but in addition he emphasizes its creative nature, the fact that it involves wonder and laughter, is absorbing, can help problem solving, is often social, and is one way in which human beings encounter their creator.[29]

In terms of Piaget's theory, play is behaviour that is dominated by assimilation.[30] A child who uses a stick as a gun, then as a walking-aid, then as a brush, then as a sword, then as a tent pole, then to stir a mud pie is stretching and expanding the 'stick' schema by acting on the environment, seeing the environment primarily as a foil for the stick. By the use of imagination in fantasy play the child's schemas for a while dominate reality, and developing skills can be practised.

Berryman's Godly Play approach to religious education is heavily influenced by Piagetian theory, particularly in its acknowledgement of the embodied and enactive nature of cognition, and the necessity of establishing a coherent and accessible network within which schema development can take place. The active wondering that takes place in Godly Play sessions may include a good deal of assimilative play. However, there is also space for 'pure wonder'. This sort of wonder, and the related phenomenon of awe, are dominated by accommodation.[31] The child is for a while the servant of his environment rather than its master, engaging with the disquiet caused by its strangeness, understanding the limitations of his schemas, rather than attempting to dominate and impose his schemas upon it. In Piagetian terms this is not play at all. Nevertheless, this chapter follows Berryman in treating both active wondering and pure wonder as different aspects of play.

You cannot play if you are worried or insecure, so play is a sign that you have appropriated the divine command 'Do not be afraid!' and the gospel message 'Things are OK because I AM here.' Play is a sign that a place of light and safety has been found in a universe that is deeply dark and dangerous. Play is a means both of accepting and enacting the transformation of the universe, of embracing blessing. Trevor Dennis's retelling of the story of the Fall as a loss of the ability to play is enlightening in this respect.[32]

Playing with the biblical text

Play is a response to novelty, incongruity and strangeness. The biblical text catches the attention as something new, incongruous and strange.[33] The text is itself playful. Within it we find models of assimilative play (active wondering). For instance, the reapplication of images to new situations with a consequent enrichment and refinement of the image itself is a feature of much Old Testament prophecy, and is also a characteristic of the teaching of Jesus (e.g. Ezekiel 34 and Luke 15.3-7). It has been argued that this 'generative' quality is a distinctive feature of Scripture.[34] In the New Testament both John and Paul use word play to good effect (for instance, John's use of 'lifted up' and Paul's play with the concept of 'law').[35] We also find pure 'observed wonder'[36] in the text, through the presentation of miraculous and awe-inspiring signs.

The text also invites the reader or hearer to play. Assimilative play (active wondering) is evoked by the polyvalent nature of the text,[37] in particular the parables of Jesus.[38] Pure wonder is evoked by the incongruity that first catches the attention, and its duration extended through the use of paradox, so that the initial shock continues to be held in consciousness.[39]

The table below summarizes psychological responses to novelty, incongruity and challenge, together with illustrative biblical examples. These include both assimilative play (active wonder) and pure wonder, which result in schema change, together with simple connection that embeds a schema more securely in semantic memory. All of these responses are relevant to the reception of the word.

Paul is a particularly playful writer. The example given in the table is his play with the concept of circumcision, which he uses as a cipher for the law; as

	Cognitive process	Task requires	Feeling of	Cognitive outcome	Biblical example
Assimilative play (active wondering)	Assimilation dominates	Imagination	Fun	Schema expanded	Paul plays with circumcision (Galatians 5.3,4,12)
Pure wonder	Accommodation dominates	Engagement and absorption	Disquiet	Schema more nuanced and differentiated	Jesus asks a wondering question (Mark 2.18-22)
Use of metaphor	Connection	Coherence	Peace	Schema embedded in semantic memory	Sewing up John the Baptist (John 1.21,23)

something that involves physical flesh and can therefore be linked verbally with his flesh–spirit dualism; as something that with one slip could become castration and therefore effect impotence and infertility; as something that involves cutting and can be made to stand for separation and alienation from Christ. Paul is angry as he writes to the Galatians, but he is also having fun as he explores and expands this imagery. Crucially, Paul is able to be 'playful' with people he knows, members of a church he founded, something that is not open to him in his relationship with the church at Rome.

Jesus is answering a wondering question in the example from Mark's Gospel given in the table. His activity has caused disquiet because it does not fit with existing expectations of how a holy man should behave. His answer requires some engagement on the part of the reader. It can be paraphrased – 'You are right to detect incongruity in my actions. Your existing schemas cannot do justice to me or to the eschatological moment which I proclaim. If you merely try to assimilate, the schemas will break. You need to develop new or more nuanced schemas.'

The human need to make connections is illustrated in the example from John's Gospel given in the table. John is a new and mysterious figure. His questioners are trying to work out how he relates to their network of existing schemas. If John can be made to fit, or at least to connect, his questioners will have a better sense of what they are dealing with, and some confidence or peace of mind. In fact his answer raises more questions.

Using play and wonder in sharing the word with children and adults

In considering the implications for preaching and similar ways of sharing the word, such as biblical storytelling, I shall return to the story of the sower and make some connections with the psychological analysis presented above.

The first thing to do is trust. We need to trust that the seed is good, present the word, start with the word. Preaching needs to be an exposition of the biblical text and people – both children and adults – can be trusted with it. The exposition needs to be clear and accessible, and where it is relevant to an ethical theme or real situation in the life of the congregation this should be drawn out. But the text should not be used to answer set ethical or theological questions.

The second task is to catch the attention of the listeners. We mustn't let the birds of the air eat the seed because the hearers have 'tuned out' through over-familiarity or boredom. Jesus was a master of this through his use of parable and incongruous wisdom teaching, designed to 'tease [the mind] into active thought'.[40] It is important to make it clear that what is being said is sufficiently new to require engagement. The perceived significance of the word is also enhanced if the person sharing it communicates authority, authenticity or 'presence' so that it is less likely to be summarily dismissed. This authority may reside in scholastic expertise relating to the text, or in authentic personal experience that connects with the text – a living witness. Sharing personal experience of wrestling with the text also demonstrates its relevance and provides a model for engaging with it. It gives permission for both children and adults to find the text difficult, a source of difficult or even unanswerable questions.

It is also vital to connect with where the hearer is in terms of life situation, culture, generation, education, and so on. We need to break up the stony ground so that the roots can go deep by providing a way that the developed schema can fit with an existing network of assumptions. Using metaphor (and even quite young children can cope with simple analogies), speaking of the unfamiliar in terms that are suggestive of the familiar allows the hearer to feel fundamentally safe.[41] It is particularly important if the novelty of the text is to be pushed to the limits to allow it to evoke wonder and indeed awe, and thus keep back the assimilative thorns in the mind of the hearer. Her disquiet needs to be 'held' as she tries to accommodate to this novelty, and one way that this can be done is through clear respect for her existing base assumptions.

As a reorganized schema emerges it will be enriched and strengthened if it is playfully applied to new areas – this feeds and waters the soil. It helps to remember that the hearer has a limited span of attention and capacity to process information,[42] so on any occasion of sharing the word keeping to a single main organizing theme, to which sub-themes can be clearly connected, is important. Play with the text can be quite ranging and should stretch the hearer, but it is the role of the preacher or leader to guide it and set some limits determined by doctrinal orthodoxy, and by factual historical and textual considerations. The emotional state of the hearer(s) also needs to be considered.

The overall aim of this sort of approach is to leave the hearer with the seed planted in ground that has been cleared, weeded, fed and watered, trusting the seed and respecting the hearer. There should be sufficient tension left unresolved for wonder, sufficient new insight for play, and a basic sense of security so that these activities can be constructive rather than destructive. Nevertheless, sharing the word with both adults and children involves risk, not least because the hearer has some responsibility for reception of the word. This model of preaching is not one of filling the listener with historical facts, literary theories or doctrines. Rather, these may form a context within which wondering occurs and which can prescribe its limits. The hearer is not an empty vessel to be filled, or a vessel full of errors to be corrected, but an active listener with whom to connect, whose own wisdom and insights can be drawn out and built upon. The model is not one of free play, but of play guided in conformity with the explicit agenda of participation in the kingdom of God. The preacher or storyteller, like the parent, is not the expert, but a fellow-wonderer, a playmate, who is perhaps further along the road in some respects, but who is also travelling.

Questions

1.   Think about your own knowledge of the Bible. In what ways has your depth of understanding God's word increased over time? Do you think you have to have spent a long time in study and reflection to appreciate the fullness of God's word?

2.   How do you think looking 'through the eyes of a child' might affect the theory and practice of preaching?

3.   On a piece of paper draw a horizontal and a vertical line. On the horizontal line list the main events in a short biblical story or parable, for

example Abraham entertaining his three visitors (Genesis 18.1-15), or the parable of the prodigal son (Luke 15.11-32). On the vertical line, list all the themes, ideas and images which emerge from the story. How does preaching and teaching in your church relate to the material on these two lines? Is one axis more important than the other?

4. Reflect on the children's perceptions of the parable of the sower (Matthew 13.1-23). In what ways do these confirm or challenge your reading of this parable?

5. Does the preaching and teaching in your church consider the responses of children and/or young people? Can you think of ONE way or ONE occasion in which preaching and teaching could be enhanced by reference to children's thoughts and ideas?

5

Play

Peter Privett

Problems and a health warning

This chapter presents a real dilemma. It's a dilemma of the integrity of integrating the method and the message. If I'm honest I have to admit that the following could be dismissed on those terms.

Play, for children, is of supreme importance and I hope to illustrate that this can also be true for adults. The problem arises out of the method in which this adult book has chosen to operate. The problem is particularly highlighted in a chapter about *play*. Most play for children operates in the non-logical, non-verbal realms of language. Many of the illustrations here are not necessarily about what children say, but what they do, and the ways in which they do it. The real difficulty is in the translation process, in the interpretation from one language to another. It's the problem of being 'lost in translation'. Adults usually prefer to operate in the logical world, the world of words and ideas. Original visions can vanish, in the telling, in the adult-eration.

I am not exempt from this and admit freely that the experience of these children makes me reflect on things that perhaps the original experience didn't intend. The only excuse I make is that their playfulness awakens a sense of playful association in me.

The other dilemma is based upon the very characteristics of play. By definition play is very elusive, it defies capturing and if caught ceases to be play. It's the same problem with God. How can you define mystery? Words just won't do.

But we are creatures of language and words are part of our meaning-making system. I'm perhaps over-egging the pudding here, but want to make these words provisional and unbinding. Please play with them. Don't take them too seriously.

The best person at playing with words is James Joyce, by refusing language conventions he comes up with new vocabulary that gets at all sorts of other meaning, like 'cropse' which suggests both death (corpse) and rebirth (crop), and his description of Noah in *Finnegans Wake* as a 'zoolous patriark'. This always reminds me of the way children get words, idiom or sentence structure 'wrong' as they start to learn the 'rules' of language, but often in ways that get at the heart of what's really meant. For example, one child, wondering about splashes of rain on a car window, commented: 'rain is what clouds do best'.

What is offered here is a collage of different thoughts; there could be others of course, this is not a systematic or exhaustive study of the subject. In fact the writing of this piece has shown me that here is just the tip of the iceberg.

Bouncing with bric-a-brac

David Miller has written extensively about play and in a paper given to a group of academics on the subject he uses the word *bricolage*.[1] The *bricoleur* is a person who works with their hands, in contrast to an expert craftsperson, someone who does the best with what is lying around. The following *bricolage* is what was to hand.

Here are some ordinary experiences that I have been privileged to have with children at play, some bric-a-brac that might be set alongside one another. As the cart travels along the highway the different objects bounce alongside each other producing happy connections, a wall of meaning from just ordinary stuff. Here is a place where a ball can be bounced against a collection of bricks. Here is an invitation to play the game of bouncing some thoughts and connections from the experiences of children at play, the disciplines of practical theology and the theory of play.

I am indebted to a serendipitous Internet search where I came across an article by Fraser Brown and Sophie Webb outlining their play work with Romanian orphans.[2] Fraser Brown, with a PhD in the topic of play, is currently on the staff of Leeds Metropolitan University. His reflections on play-work theory for me had enormous resonances and similarities with those of practical theology.

The definition of play is extremely slippery. It can mean many things to many people, but this chapter does offer some generally accepted values and characteristics.

It is perhaps important to distinguish between what play is and what isn't play.

The key themes of complex flexibility, openness and relationship are also mentioned.

Through play we can begin to discover our own identity and our place on and in the world. Finally, play challenges our ethical behaviour, our choices of how we act in the world. It bounces along with Isaiah, Jeremiah and the rest of the prophetic tradition of the Old Testament. Play offers opportunities to see other realities.

And what of our experience of God? Well bouncing along with the above are sin, creation, salvation, emptying, blessing, to name but a few.

What this chapter doesn't do is critique the various ideas. That is a job for another time. For example, I've concentrated on some of the positive aspects of Jürgen Moltmann's insights with the awareness that sometimes his argument can turn play into something functional and therefore it becomes 'not play'. In his own words, 'Don't turn play into an ideology. Don't be a kill joy.'[3]

Towards the end of this chapter is the story of a toddler who can't stop laying hands on people and objects. His uncontrolled blessing of the world is crucial for this chapter. To bless is to call out the good!

While writing this I kept wanting more room to lay out the books, the articles, the illegible scraps of paper with unfinished sentences, and in the end it became a constant process of moving and juggling the different aspects to see the different associations.

Here is no systematic argument, many things are left unsaid and many are assumed.

Undergirding everything is the playful dance of Trinitarian relationship, the threefold processes of creation, redemption and sustenance. These are implied but not coherently or tidily expounded. They can't be, as they always escape neat pigeonholing. This is especially true of the experience of children's play.

So let's begin the bouncing with a child's paradise song of play.

Here is an opportunity to be bounced into another world.

Songs of paradise?

> What I really, really, really, really, really want would be paradise . . . everyone to play with.

> It's like you're brought up inside a child's playpen.
> It's a huge one of those.

> Imagine this huge playpen of a town
> You bounce off the sides and never get out![4]

These two comments come from rural children living on the borderlands of England and Wales, the first was Alice aged 9, the second Jamie, a little older, aged 14. The first comment was spoken in a rather quiet dreaming voice after an animated conversation with a small group about freedom, independence and lack of restriction.

The second comment came in the context of the frustrations of living in a small market town, the lack of facilities, the lack of opportunities. They were part of in-depth conversations at the beginning of the century, unlocking people's dreams and visions for the present and the future.

At the dawn of the twenty-first century we find ourselves living in a global village coping with the climate of plurality and diversity. The children in their comments face us with crucial questions as to how we might coexist in the world that has difference and diversity as key features. Do we build up the walls of the playpens and shoot each other from behind the enclosures and retreat to encampments? It is interesting to note that one of the original meanings of the word 'community' comes from *communitas* – a place where weapons were stored, a place of retreat when under attack from the enemy. Or might we begin to celebrate and encourage diversity, and see in difference a hope of paradise where there is endless opportunity for playful interrelationship?

But it might depend on what sort of play we're talking about, on how we might understand the word. So let's look at some definitions.

Play – what is it?

My Oxford English Dictionary definition of 'play' runs to nearly two pages of rich and ambiguous associations. Play is linked to ecstasy, creativity, exploration and joy as well as deception, exhaustion, triviality and irresponsibility. The derivatives have incarnational overtones that connect to our physicality, to the language of the flesh. They are embodied meanings, kinaesthetic understandings: Old English *plegian* – to exercise, *plega* – brisk movement, and middle Dutch *pleien* – to leap for joy, to dance. These bodily descriptions connect us to the child who throws her whole body into the activity, to remind us of the enfleshed, incarnational activity of God, who throws the divine self into the world.

The historian Johan Huizinga in the seminal study of play, *Homo Ludens*, understands this mysterious illusive ambiguity: 'Play is a function of the living, but it is not susceptible of exact definition either logically, biologically, or aesthetically.'[5] So it would seem that play is a slippery, changing, shifting commodity. It can mean many things to many people.

In a variety of writings and reflections (e.g. by Aristotle, Schiller, Freud), it has been seen as the release of excess energy, a means of catharsis, a safety valve for the emotions, a flow of creative energy, a resolve for psychic conflict, an activity for its own sake and many more.

The purpose of the chapters in this book is to see if the world of the child might throw some light on our understandings. What might children's experience of play show us? What happens when we place a child at the centre and see the world through their eyes?

The child psychologist Jean Piaget believed that, for children, play was about the pleasure of the activity and it was done for its own sake.[6] It's like this child's experience of dancing in the rain, of getting thoroughly soaked. The words were spoken with animation and excitement:

> Once I was in my T-shirt and shorts and I was running about in the thunderstorm outside. I was struck by lightning . . . I was tingling all over.

There followed a long discussion with the other children about whether he was really struck by lightning. What really happened wasn't the issue. It was evident in the tone and the way he spoke that the experience was elemental and of deep significance. There was no outcome except joy and abandonment in the experience.

The psychologist Catherine Garvey[7] identifies five commonly accepted features of play: it's pleasurable and enjoyable; its motive is intrinsic; it's spontaneous and freely chosen; it involves active engagement; and it works non-literally. All five are involved in Ian's short description mentioned above.

Pseudo-play?

Jerome Berryman explores the opposite of Garvey's qualities, and for him the opposite of play is *emptiness*, a draining of life and energy.[8] On the surface it may appear as play but in reality it is what he describes as 'pseudo-play'. The characteristics here include numbness, a hollow simulation of life; a parasitic draining of energy from others to maintain survival; a detachment which appears involved; an exploitative nurturing creativity in order to take it from others. Here, there is a disconnection between the verbal and non-verbal signals. The words might issue an invitation to play but the reality of the situation shows that mutuality, spontaneity and the other characteristics outlined by Garvey are absent. It may appear to be attractive, but the transaction becomes a one-way process, one of manipulation, a power struggle, a compulsive activity. He uses the example of the two main characters in William Golding's *Lord of the Flies*:

> Jack is Ralph's opposite. His play is not for the sake of play, but is calculated to attract followers . . . He opposes Ralph's reasoned and cooperative approach to leadership by an exercise of power . . . he compels others to follow him and tries to disguise what they are doing as play.[9]

The consequence of this pseudo-play has drastic effects. What was fun and play and laughter leads to a dreadful deathly climax.

Huizinga, writing in response to the Nazi influence in Europe, calls this process the bastardization of play, or 'puerilism'. He sees that much that was claimed as play was in fact superficial, crude, sensationalist and intolerant. 'The spectacle of a society rapidly goose stepping into helotry is for some the dawn of a new millennium. We believe them to be in error.'[10]

Play was being perverted into totalitarian ends and therefore ceased to be play. To compound the problem those who were perverting it still saw it as play. Huizinga raises some important issues as to the quantitative and qualitative nature of play. How do we know what play is? What judgements are brought to our discernments? It also raises ethical issues as to how we play together, how we organize our life together, which will explored later in this chapter.

The corruption and perversion of play has resonances in the story of Jesus' conflict with the scribes from Jerusalem in Mark 3.20-30. In this story, Jesus is accused of being possessed by evil. The previous stories in Mark's Gospel have dealt with Jesus' work of healing and restoration. The crowds have been amazed and have glorified God. The scribes want to call this evil. Jesus seems to suggest that when a society calls obviously good, health-giving actions bad, and vice versa, then there is a sense that the point of spiritual destruction has been reached. It is unforgivable. Life has been disconnected.

A similar struggle about identifying the inner motives is found in Paul's letter to the people of Rome as he describes the experience and nature of sin:

> I do not understand my own actions. For I do not do what I want, but I do the very thing I hate . . . I can will what is right, but I cannot

do it. For I do not do the good I want, but the evil I do not want is
what I do.

(Romans 7.15-20)

For Paul, when faced with this dilemma, it was important to return to the
foundations of faith, to fundamental principles. The perversion of play is
countered similarly, a return to some of the principles and qualities identified
at the beginning of this chapter.

Synergy

A return to play may bring salvation. One of the characteristics of play is that
when it happens there are feelings of connection with the physical materials
involved and connection with the inner world of the self and others. Berryman
uses the word 'synergy' to describe the experience of playful connection.
He connects this to the writings of Mihaly Csikszentmihalyi and the concept
of *flow*, which is described as a state of joy, creativity and total involvement,
in which problems disappear and there is an exhilarating feeling of
transcendence.[11] We shall return to this later. For Csikszentmihalyi the opposite
of flow is *psychic entropy*, which he describes as an impairment of
effectiveness, a disorganization, a weakening of the self, and a loss of
motivation and being. The emptiness and disconnection that both Berryman
and Csikszentmihalyi describe is often found in children who have been
deprived of basic care and love, children who expend what little energy they
have in the basic fight for survival. Children in this situation find it almost
impossible to play.

Fraser Brown and Sophie Webb in their play project with Romanian orphans
give a powerful description of the emptiness which they encountered at the
beginning of their research:

> *The silence*. Every room was full of children in cots, but it was so quiet.
> Even when we entered the room there was no sound from the children.
> They just looked at us. The smell of urine in every room was almost
> unbearable. *The emptiness*. Each room had just the cots with plastic
> mattresses. The children were dirty and wearing clothes that were too
> big for them. Some were wearing jumpers as trousers, and none of
> them were wearing shoes. There were rags around their waists, which I
> later found out were ripped up sheets tied to keep the nappies in place.
> These rags were also used to tie the children to the cots. Most children
> were sitting rocking and others were standing up banging the sides of

their cots against the walls. Giving the children a cuddle was strange as they either held on too tightly, or they remained stiff and unfeeling.[12]

'Disconnection', 'alienation' and 'abandonment' are all theological words with theological connotations in describing the experience and condition of sin and evil.

The contributors to a study of Constructive Theology,[13] which seeks to bring together diverse and conflicting theological views, begin with two models of sin and evil that have predominated in western thinking. The first is based in the familiar biblical story of Adam, where sin can be interpreted as a result of individual action, a personal responsibility for rebellion. In this example, evil is created by the perpetrators: those who treated the Romanian orphans so badly. The second model has its roots in ancient myth, especially Greek, where sin is rooted in human experience. It's not about human action but the complex interaction of misfortune, the impersonal forces of circumstance. It's notable in the effect it has upon the victims. This model allows a sense-making framework for where the orphans have ended up and pushes us to ask what human beings can do to alleviate the situation.

Constructive Theology and compound flexibility

Too often in classic arguments about doctrine and theology the believer has been forced to accept an either/or choice – orthodoxy or heresy. However the Constructive Theologians would not us let rest on too easy a choice. For they argue that even in the thought of classic theologians, in both Paul and Augustine, you can trace developments of both models. As the chapter on sin in the Jones and Lakeland book progresses, it becomes more complex and more flexible to include a rich variety of viewpoints such as personal, corporate, postcolonial and post-structuralist insights. The point here is not the detail of the arguments, but the use of a theological process that seeks to enrich the discussion from a simplistic either/or approach to a more complex, multidimensional viewpoint.

The world as seen through the eyes of these orphans, shrunk to their rag bonds and their cots, challenges us to leave such distinctions aside in the face of the needs of children who cannot play. Who *cares* where the sin is, when they have not been allowed this varied and diverse experience of existence. The refusal to allow the children the space, freedom and emotional resources to play denies their humanity and creates for us, the adult onlookers, a clear understanding of the evil of their condition.

Salvation comes with the play project outlined by Brown and Webb, which involves a wide range of elements from basic care to complex therapeutic play. They echo the Constructive Theology approach, when they claim that it is the enrichment of an environment that holds greater potential for the development of the child. Emptiness, disconnection, psychic entropy are countered by the offering of a rich and varied diet of different elements.

For Brown the enrichment of an environment is undergirded with the idea of *compound flexibility*. In play work this is not just about the flexibility and adaptability of toys and play objects, but the ways in which these affect the flexibility of the child. 'The play process not only enables the acquisition of information about the world, but also encourages the development of flexibility and may even perform the function of enabling the brain to retain plasticity.'[14] Linked to this is the idea that inventiveness and creativity are related to the proportion of variables provided.

A small example of this can be seen in Alex aged five as he responds to a Godly Play story about the beginning and end of Jesus' ministry. The story has been told with two wooden models, one of a synagogue, the other of an upper room. There are small replicas of a reading desk, a scroll, a table and a simple abstract human figure. The sides of the models can be removed and the two buildings can be joined together to create the basic shape of a parish church. The story is told simply, with space for individual imagination. Open questions follow, which encourage flexible reactions. There is then time for free response. Alex chose to work with the models and spent nearly a quarter of an hour absorbed in all the possible permutations. Furniture was arranged in different combinations, the wooden sides were constantly shifting to create new buildings and arrangements. Alex was completely undistracted by the variety of other activity around him. He gave total attention to his constant regroupings.

His attention was then taken by the human figure which he danced to the wooden models and it prompted a creative song . . .

Do de do de do
Here comes Jesus, Jesus
Do de do de do
Here comes Jesus
He's going to turn it all upside down and inside out again.
Do de do de do . . .

Alex understands the concept of plasticity, of compound flexibility and sees that the Jesus figure constantly offers alternatives, different viewpoints. By right, he joins the ranks of Constructive Theologians.

David Jensen, another of their number, similarly sees the person of Jesus as enabling us to encounter and celebrate difference.[15] The scandalous insights of faith and theology have at their heart an understanding of compound difference.

The Risen Christ's appearance in Mark 16.6-7 is in Galilee, the threshold of the Gentile world, a world where cultural difference exists. Difference is also offered to us in the human person of Jesus – his birth, teaching and death – in the particularity of a Jew from first-century Palestine. But the vision of faith also offers us the mysterious Christ who is God's enfleshed, God's revelation in vulnerability. 'The God of the incarnation reveals Godself not in suffocating sameness, but in the varied.'[16]

Jensen sees the gospel as a radical alternative to the present status quo of the dominance of globalization and marketplace economies, where everything is easily homogenized and reduced to the realms of commodity and consumer. Christians are given the opportunity to sing the rearranging song of Alex, to proclaim hopes for a playful paradise, and to speak out with the rural young person at the beginning of this chapter against that which builds up the sides of the playpen:

> To proclaim Christ is not only to say 'yes' to a world of difference but to say 'no' to those powers in the world such as racism, anti-Semitism, sexism, consumerism, and militarism that would destroy difference under a religious banner.[17]

Rebecca Nye[18] in her groundbreaking research into children's spirituality also stresses the importance of playful flexibility. She observed that when children described spiritual experiences or stories they significantly used language that was both playful and flexible, and it allowed them to use the familiar language systems that were part of their everyday lives. 'In contemplating matters of mystery, un-intelligibility or exceptional magnitude they had adopted a system of expression that allowed them to be silly and experimental to be wrong and to be creative.'[19] Nye, like Alex, deconstructs the familiar model of adult spirituality, often based in the extra-ordinary, and offers us the challenge of the child's natural playful paradoxical adaptability. It is the same challenge that Jesus offers: 'whoever does not receive the kingdom of God as a little child will never enter it' (Mark 10.15).

Negative capability

Here is Alex again. It's another Godly Play story. This time the parable of the Good Shepherd has been told. The material consists of a gold box in which there is a large piece of green felt, a small piece of blue felt, some pieces of dark felt, and some strips of brown felt There are also painted figures of a shepherd, some sheep and a wolf. The story has blended together elements from the twenty-third psalm, the parable of the lost sheep from Luke 15, and elements of the Good Shepherd discourse from John 10. Alex is once again absorbed in free play with the materials. He seems particularly interested in hiding each of the sheep under pieces of felt and wanting the shepherd to find them. He explores more and more different hiding places and then discovers that his large multicoloured tie is dangling into the materials. This becomes another hiding place for the sheep which are individually rolled up into his tie. An adult then interrupts the play and tells him to take them out as he is spoiling his nice new clothes. At that point he loses interest in the play.

Most adults when they come into contact with children often bring their own needs and desires and agenda. Most children quickly learn that the priorities of adults are the ones that rule the day. Insights from the Marches Chronicles, a project that charted the lives of children and adults in the borderlands of Hereford and Shropshire at the beginning of the twenty-first century, offers a litany that was unsolicited and repeated by every child with which we entered into conversation:

> Adults never listen
> or take us seriously.
> If they do listen, then they usually laugh.[20]

The breaking of this pattern is often noticed and appreciated as this story from an older woman shows:

When I was walking past the kids in the square, I said 'Good evening' to them, and they replied, 'Good evening.'

As I walked on, one of them ran after me,

'Thank you for saying good evening to us,' he said, 'hardly anyone ever does.'[21]

Here is someone who offers a different way of being with children and young people; she offers an alternative, a change of behaviour.

One of the key features in the theory of play work is the idea of negative capability. It involves the suspension of judgement and prejudice where the play-worker tries to go with the flow of the children's needs and tastes. It's a letting go of the usual power systems. It is similar to systems of counselling where the counsellor is not there to control or offer advice, but to listen first and then perhaps offer resources for the client to work out their own solutions.

The idea of emptiness was explored in a previous section with its association with alienation and sin. Here the idea of emptiness is seen as something positive and akin to the classical language of the mystics, where the ability to let go of the ego and usual power structures is a means of creating a space in which something new can happen. Associated with this is Csikszentmihalyi's writing about the flow of energy. This forgetting of the self, this letting go, so that one forgets that one is immersed in the process, is central to the creative process and is one that many artists and musicians will describe. But it is not just about traditional creative experiences, as it can be experienced in the everyday world of work. He tells the story of a young woman who in her job as a lawyer while chasing references or outlining possible courses of action for her senior partners has the intense feeling of being lost in the work when every piece of information and research seems to fit.[22]

Stephen Verney's study of St John[23] makes free play with this idea as Jesus is presented as the one who offers an alternative to egocentric activity. He is one who empties himself to offer connectional love, expressed in the new commandment of corporate service. 'I give you a new commandment, that you love one another. Just as I have loved you, you also should love one another' (John 13.34).

This negative capability, explored by Jensen this time, in his study of the theology of childhood[24] calls for a place of vulnerability in the adult, and is a quality that brings us close to the nature of God. 'By becoming vulnerable with children in our midst, we not only stake a claim with their lives, we understand more fully what it means to be created in God's image and what it means to be church.'[25]

Vulnerability includes the possibility of relationship, the recognition of co-dependent need, the connection with an other. Once again the idea of difference is entwined here. For Jensen the two ideas are stitched together in a reflection on the nature of the Old Testament understanding of covenant. God decides to enter into close relationship with the people of Israel, human beings who are not God. It is a covenant based on risk, as the Old Testament story describes a relationship of brokenness and failure as well as intimacy and mutual concern. Within the divine nature there has to be emptying for covenant to happen. 'The divine life is not a mystery enclosed in itself, but embraces those who are not God.'[26]

The emptying of adult baggage is essential to the play relationship with the child, especially in a therapeutic setting, and Brown and Webb quote the dangers of adults who bring their own neuroses into the setting and do more harm than good. Rowan Williams[27] has highlighted the dangerous tendency in everyday modern life where adults express a jealous, competitive relationship with children. The result is the creation of chaotic and often dangerous interactions and spaces, where there is a confusion of roles and responsibilities. The task for the adult in these settings is to let go of their egocentric needs and meet the needs of the child by holding and creating safe boundaries so that the child can have a place to be the child. It is one of the lessons that is continually being learnt by adults as they develop skills and practice in the art of Godly Play. The ability to sit back, to allow people to discover their own learning, to learn the art of sitting comfortably with silence and non-action is hard, but productive.

Alison Summerskills is a skilled church children's worker and has had much experience in the traditional methods of Sunday school. Five years ago she came across Godly Play and since that time has attended Accredited Training sessions, and has immersed herself in the theory and practice, but: 'the slow process of transforming my practice from deeply rooted beliefs about the nature of a teacher, still like yeast in a bowl of flour, continues to work in me'.[28]

She describes the inner tensions of telling a story, to a group of 10- to 11-year-olds, about the Exile and the Return to Jerusalem, of wanting to tell the children of the connections that she made to their lives:

> With exile I could see the life application – moving on from primary school, a hot topic for some of them. Surely they would connect. We wondered together. I wondered, which bit of the story is for them? Silence, thoughtful silence – but still silence.

Previously she has talked about her disappointment when the children are silent. She has a worry that they might not make connections. In a Godly Play session children are not offered a previously planned activity or craft. Children choose their own response, be it craft, sitting, playing, reading, or whatever. The adult is available if the child wants, but otherwise sits still and doesn't interfere.

> Afterwards a child came to me and said: 'It's a bit like when my best friend and me quarrel – and I know how it feels when we make up again.'

> It was a salutary reminder that I, the wise adult, cannot give children meaning – only get out of the way and allow them space to make their own connections. Paradoxically too, it was only some time later when I stopped worrying about the silence that greeted my wondering questions, that the children were set free to wonder aloud.[29]

Maria Harris[30] in her theological reflections on the art of teaching offers a different model to that which is usually promoted. Although her subject matter is teaching, what she says can be applied to this aspect of play. She counters the usual assumptions of concentration on methodology, content, skill, techniques, and so on, with the idea of majesty and mystery. Comparison is made to the attitudes with which we might experience a work of art. The task is to see what is there, to let it speak. For her, *contemplation* is the important first part of the process. It is important to be still, to attend, to respect and revere the people and space. You don't begin with the material, the subject matter. Instead what is important is an uncluttered appreciation of what exists already, free of preoccupation, preconception and interruption. The teacher is called first to be at the disposal of and to be present for the other person.

The dynamic of I–Thou

This disposal to the other is seen as a dynamic process. It is not done in isolation. It is a relationship involving others. For Harris the idea of engagement is important, and the idea that subject matter not only includes the content of the activity, but also refers to the people engaged in the activity. The subject is the complex interrelationship of content, process and people. Play is not an *I–it* activity but *I–thou*.

Contemplation becomes not a just a means of retreat, of standing back to look at the world, but it is also a self-reflecting process of looking at how we look at the world. Engagement raises the dilemma of withdrawal. For some play-workers the task will be the task of preparation then withdrawal. The content and intent of play belongs to the child. The starting point is the child's agenda. In the child's daily life, play is a key place where they are in control of events. The adult is encouraged in the process of un-adult-erated play. The issue then becomes one about the quality of the engagement, the conditions which nurture the child's agenda.

Maxine Green and Chandu Christian use the concept of and the processes associated with 'accompanying'.[31] One of their images is from Indian music where a tabla player creates basic drum rhythms providing a space and framework for the improvisations of the musician who plays the sitar.

In play-work theory, the adult enables the space and framework so that the child's agenda is the starting point. Intervention is tentative, hesitant, extremely cautious and in some cases non-existent. Harris highlights the importance of emergence, where the teacher, the adult, and in this argument, the play-worker is seen as a midwife enabling new life to happen. The agenda is the play of the child. She illustrates this with the story of Zorba the Greek,[32] who comes across a cocoon and tries to hurry the process by opening the insect case and in so doing kills the potential beauty. Too much pressure too soon violates the law of nature. The creature needs its own time to grow and develop. Patience and time are needed by the nurturer. There are no guarantees. The agenda is the subject matter of the subject. The qualities she promotes are ones of non-violence, waiting, the setting aside of power, the reliance on unpredictability. They echo the thoughts about vulnerability that have been previously explored.

There is, of course, enormous ambiguity within the biblical narrative about the nature of God but one strand highlights the engaged vulnerability of the divine. Creation is seen as a divine playground in which creatures, human and other, are invited to play and enjoy the delights of the cosmos. Sabbath is especially a time not just for rest but for that playful delight and enjoyment. God is part of the *I–Thou* relationship, not set apart from creation. The stories tell of a God of emotions who is not unaffected by the ordinary affairs of the world. For example:

> I have observed the misery of my people who are in Egypt; I have heard their cry on account of their taskmasters. Indeed, I know their sufferings, and I have come down to deliver them from the Egyptians.
>
> (Exodus 3.7-8)

God can be seen as a co-player in the world, one who signals engagement in worldly experiences and situations that often have disengagement as their theme. The engagement of God is seen as a response to the agendas that we humans offer. This sometimes delightful, and sometimes difficult, play relationship is based in a God who is willing to become as vulnerable as a child, to become one with the human agenda of bodily living. God joins in the game of carnality of being enfleshed, the game called incarnation.

The playing of the incarnational game is also a process of incarnation. It is *in* the playing of the game that incarnation happens. Not only this, but *I–Thou* is also given birth. It is in the game of *me* and *you* that the understanding of *we* develops.

Empathy and attunement – I AM

In the theory of play-work the ideas of empathy, affective attunement and mimesis are important. The adult can't make someone play, they can only invite, and this is most successfully communicated through the non-verbal language systems: smiles, eye widening, gestures, and so on. Engagement in play will depend upon appropriate responses.

Two weeks ago I [Peter] was asked by a friend to look after her 9-year-old son for the day. It was a unique experience and afterwards it felt like playing the game of surrogate grandfather. Our day was taken up with watching Harry Potter videos, making bread together and a time of creativity with silk paints in my studio where we made a 'designer' painted cushion. But it was the end of day, when I was feeling rather tired, that the real play started.

'Can we play hide and seek, you count and I'll hide,' said Ben.

This was fine, but our house is rather small and the opportunities for hiding places are rather limited. After pretending to search in unlikely places I then discovered him. Thinking the game was over I didn't expect the comment of 'It's now your turn you hide and I'll count . . .'

Trying to squeeze my adult shape into small corners behind curtains, etc. was ungainly and ridiculous. This reciprocal game went on for over an hour, with neither of us getting tired or bored.

There was mutuality here, a desire to enter into a reciprocal relationship of play. What stimulated this shared silly play wasn't the spoken invitation, but the giggles, the holding of breath, the screwing up of the eyes, the sing-song call of 'com . . . ing', the laughter of being found.

Research has shown that there seems to be an inbuilt human desire to empathize with others. Newborn babies are not passive beings but primarily interested in human beings rather than objects. Play becomes one of the means by which this human connection can be expressed. One of the characteristics is *mimesis*:

> Mimesis rests on the ability to produce conscious, self-initiated, representational acts . . . thus mimesis is fundamentally different from imitation and mimicry in that it involves the invention of intentional representations. When there is an audience to interpret the action, mimesis also serves the purpose of social communication.[33]

The game of hide and seek was a means of our mutual communication. Ben's initiative enabled me to enter the game and our continued enjoyment fed the other. When appropriate playful constructive relationships occur, that have the qualities of empathy and attunement, then it is very likely that they will contribute to the development of the child's self-esteem. Children love adults who are willing to play.

Roberts has identified that different children may well have different preferred ways of playing.[34] Although she focuses on the world of the pre-school child her ideas may have some general application as well. Different categories of trajectory, enclosing, connecting play may well be supported by the young child's cognitive development. When a play-worker introduces some bats and balls into the experience of a 'trajectory child' (one who repeatedly enjoys throwing objects in their play) who continually throws stones, a multilayered message is being conveyed.

There is first an unspoken acknowledgement that the worker has understood the nature of the child's preferred style. She is also offering an opportunity to develop the preferred skill and diffuse possible injury or damage without resorting to disciplinary behaviour. Inherent is also the feeling of respect that this matters to the child and that the consequence may well be a development of esteem.

The consequence of the adult entering fully and playing the game of hide and seek had ramifications. The honouring of the game and becoming at one had consequences. A phone call from Ben's mother in the evening revealed that he couldn't stop talking about both the game and the day we spent together. It had given him delight and joy. He went to bed on top of the world.

I'd like to return to the verb *to be*. The game of incarnation might be more than an experience of immersion, of absorption. It can also have powerful implications as well as empowering outcomes. The one who understands the nature of I AM and enters into the relationship of WE ARE is also enabling the game of I AM for those involved. This has enormous consequences for *us*. What appears to be innocuous and trivial, 'after all, it's just play', takes on ethical dimensions.

In the science fiction novel *The Player of Games*, Iain M. Banks[35] has a character who is a professional game player who is tricked into cheating just so he can get the best and most beautiful result out of a game. He is sent to an alien species whose whole culture depends on a game: Azad. Everyone plays and where you are ranked in the game determines your status and your job. So people gang up on each other, do deals, and form alliances to climb up the ladder. The winner becomes emperor. But the hero (who doesn't really care, he's an alien and he's told that the media will be manipulated to say he lost) begins to play in earnest when he finds out about the dark underside of the people's culture. He sees pornography, abuse, victimization, violence, appalling, grotesque and vicious crime. Then he begins to play to win. He wants to win now, so that his moral beliefs in the good, the liberal, the egalitarian and so on will be victorious. What he doesn't know, is that he himself is a pawn in a bigger political game . . . So game playing carries powerful moral impulses and ideas and we can't 'play nicely' unless we have respect for others and their roles in the game. Game play to cheat, hurt, dominate or subdue others is not true play. True game playing as 'play' requires equality of opportunity, taking turns, graciousness and magnanimity in winning or losing and the giving and receiving of pleasure. Game rituals include trash talk but also shaking hands after a game.

Pat Kane's *Play Ethic*[36] also identifies the importance of the ethical dimensions of play. He places the right to play alongside the obligation to care:

> The right to play with the state, the market and the third sector supporting our desires to compose a richly satisfying and value creating life – is counterbalanced by the obligation to care: the same institutions expecting that the inevitable fragility of human beings be directly addressed by players.[37]

This twofold understanding of rights and obligations is very much present in the everyday games that people play. One of the ancient understandings of play involved not only the freedom of play but also the lessons learned from the darker side of failing and losing. Kane stresses the importance of both aspects. In many games there are winners and losers and one of the important lessons we learn as a child is the ability to handle loss, defeat and failure, and in facing this, the possibility of forgiveness and restoration.

Delia Smith in a short interview on BBC Radio 2 spoke passionately about the beautiful game of football and her connection with the Norwich 'canaries'.[38] She talked about the importance of children attending matches, of how through the shared experience of the game it was one way in which they began to understand the nature of community living. The game was also about being initiated into the customs, the rules, the constraints and boundaries of behaviour. The communal sharing of exultant joys with a home win and the despairing pain of the lost game are fundamental building blocks for our communal understandings. The same issues are attached to other game playing: Twister, Pictionary, cards, arcade games, quizzes, and so on.

Delia Smith's comments were undergirded by a deep belief in mutual communal responsibility, echoing Kane's challenge of balancing rights and obligations. The acknowledgement of our common human fragility enables the difficult learning of loss, of failure and defeat. The ability to embrace vulnerability may well also be an important ethical demand and challenge.

Don't speak of love – show me

Play leads us to ask questions about how we might live and organize our corporate life together. What values and choices will we make as we seek to create the common good?

James, aged three, attends church with his elder sister. Mum sings in the choir.

At home he spends a great deal of time going around placing his hands on objects and people's heads and muttering as he does it.

The adults are puzzled by his behaviour, and then they discover that he is blessing them.

Two children were playing in a paddling pool on a hot day. Their friend came round to play. A few minutes later the friend (still fully clothed) appeared in the kitchen completely soaked. As he

> was dried off he explained that his two friends had blessed and
> baptized him . . .

One meaning of the word *bless* is 'to speak well' of something or somebody. Berryman defines the word *blessing* in terms of calling out the good in a person or situation. 'A blessing affirms a person and yet calls forth the best in him or her.'[39] His study of the millstones texts in the Gospels and their use of extreme and violent language highlights the extreme life and death nature of blessing (see, e.g. Matthew 18.6-9; Mark 9.42-8; Luke 17.1,2). It is also echoed in the indignation shown to the disciples when they prevent the children from receiving a blessing (Mark 10.13-16). Human survival is entirely dependent upon blessing, not the opposite.

As James goes about laying hands on people and muttering he reminds us of the intrinsic nature of God. It is summed up in the continued and repetitious work, divine action and words of blessing, of the cosmic reverberation of '*That's Good*'. To bless something or somebody is not primarily about the words. The most powerful expression is the action, the behaviour, the process, the experience of blessing.

Eliza Doolittle towards the end of the musical *My Fair Lady* is exasperated by the plethora of fancy words from Freddie. She has had enough of being told to get the words right from Henry Higgins and feels used and abused:

> Words, words, words
> I'm so sick of words
> I get words all day through
> First from him, now from you
> Is that all you blighters can do
> Don't talk of love – SHOW ME.[40]

The words of James's blessing are not the intelligible part, it is his touching and laying on of hands, his actions that speak of blessing.

The issues surrounding child abuse highlight the importance of the right sort of touching. Not any touching and action will do. The intention of the touch is crucial. But it's more than this. The way in which the touch is perceived and received is also crucial. Berryman sees that blessing involves a complex interaction of relationship. 'Blessing involves all three aspects of the moral event. It includes motive, act and result. You cannot subtract any of these aspects of the moral situation and still have blessing.'[41] James's laying on of hands has connotations of healing and Berryman highlights this connection, where Jesus' action of blessing is often linked with the restoration of health.

In the gospel this is more than a magical sign of power, but is often a sign of the in-breaking of the messianic kingdom, a sign of the completion of, and wholeness of all things.

Hans Ruedi Weber, in his book celebrating the 1979 International Year of the Child, sees the blessing and embrace of the children by Jesus in Mark 9.36 as deeply significant.[42] He links Jesus' action to popular rabbinic teaching where the resurrection of the people of Israel will happen 'when God embraces them, presses them to his heart and kisses them; thus bringing them into the life of the world to come'.[43] This blessing is not the same as the liturgical pat on the head at the communion rail. It's so much more profound, it is a deep sign of the messianic kingdom.

Alternative realities

James's act of blessing is even more. It sings along with the hope for a playful paradise quoted at the beginning of this chapter. We are presented with songs of hope for a different order of things. They are the words and actions of a prophetic ministry, the anticipations of alternative realities.

One of the features of play is the ability to enter the world of *as if*, of *what might be*.

Play offers an opportunity to suspend disbelief to enter time and space to make belief. No this isn't a typing error; make believe may well lead to the creation of new possibilities. Play is a not only a creative opportunity it is a prophetic opening, a *kairos* moment of new beginning. 'The songs of our playful children are an invitation to the adult world to suspend judgement and enter wholeheartedly into this imaginary world.'[44]

Time and reality for a brief moment can be suspended to create a moment of now, which is not measured in the quantity of outcomes. One of Garvey's descriptors of play claims its intrinsic nature, the delight in process not the product.

I [Peter] was outside one of Europe's great cathedrals watching the tourists enjoy the summer sun and noticed two adults with two young children. The adults were keen to point out to their children the beauties of the building. An older girl played the

> game, her younger sister, in the presence of such grandeur,
> preferred to give her whole attention to a small puddle on the
> ground, and the rainbow smears of engine oil that were creating
> patterns in the dark water. The parents were annoyed that her
> attention was not being given to the real world. Or perhaps it
> was . . .

This is beginning to sound challenging and dangerous to a world preoccupied with consumerism and the market economy. Play could lead to revolution. Sam Keen and Jürgen Moltmann certainly thought so. For Keen the revolution involved a recovery of the Dancing God.[45] Man the Worker through play could become Man the Graceful – *homo faber* to *homo tempestiuus*.[46] Play offers a freedom to admire rather than possess, to enjoy rather than exploit, to accept rather than grasp.[47]

For Moltmann, play has, as well as its deep theological aspects, also a highly political function. In the principalities where freedom is rare, in the dominions of oppression, play and laughter are silenced and almost non-existent. One can only laugh into freedom. The inauthentic play of superficiality, the pseudo-play that does little more than provide a suspension of the status quo or stabilize a political system, is of no use.

It was the questions that children often ask that influenced Moltmann. Why did God make the world? Why did God become human? His response was that God played meaningfully and freely with God's own possibilities without the need of reason or product. God is. I AM.

The other insight is that this play is a gratuitous gift, a demonstration of joy and pleasure. Jesus corresponds to God's deep freedom of love and the laughter of Easter reveals deep play.

> So the purpose is . . .
> So the point is . . .
>
> Well the point is that there is no point.
> The ultimate purpose of history is similarly playful.
> When we play authentically we usher in the future.
> We are given a foretaste of *glory*.

Moltmann's song and the song of the child at the beginning of this piece create a harmony together:

> It is totally without purpose, as a hymn of praise for unending joy, as an

ever varying round dance of the redeemed in the Trinitarian fullness of God – and as the complete harmony of body and soul.[48]

What I really, really, really want,
would be paradise
everyone to play with . . .

Epilogue

Jerome Berryman points to the fact that much writing about the theology of play was done in the 1970s with an outpouring of playful theological contributions, but since then there has been a severe paucity, a drought, a 30-year lack of significant input. Perhaps it is time for a resurgence. The popularity and growth of Godly Play not only in the UK but also in Europe and elsewhere is perhaps a sign of the times where the shoots are beginning to spring again.

Another shoot, or giant plant, is Pat Kane's *Manifesto for a Different Way of Living*, where he argues forcibly for the spirit of play to enter all aspects of our life. Moltmann and Kane highlight the problem, that for humans the Puritan work ethic always seems to want to strangle the ethic of play. Could this be a description of the world at the beginning of the twenty-first century?

For Moltmann, another problem was associated with the lack of clarity in the theology, the elusiveness of the definition. This chapter at the beginning noted play can mean all things to all people. Theology likes definitions. It loves boundaries. But this elusiveness is precisely the point. Play will not be contained within a strong castle or bound with chains.

It will quickly escape, transpose into something else. Plasticity has been named as a characteristic of play. If the realms of formal theology are too strong and defining then it will escape and transfer to the less defining. Its presence will appear unannounced in other disciplines. It seems to bounce into other categories that officially might not be defined as play, but when you enter the doors a playground is clearly visible. Play transcends the definitions of whether it is secular or sacred, it makes no distinctions. It's like a young child who sees the divine in the ordinary, in the everyday. Like the ambiguity of parables, those who have ears to hear and eyes to see might be the ones to whom play is revealed.

Like the Johannine Spirit it involves a rebirth, a blustering wind-filled re-naissance.

Like the Spirit, like a wind, it involves a coiling, a twisting, an encircling wrap around engagement. 'The wind blows where it chooses, and you hear the sound of it, but you do not know where it comes from or where it goes. So it is with everyone who is born of the Spirit' (John 3.8).

Do de do de do
Here comes Jesus, Jesus
Do de do de do
Here comes Jesus
He's going to turn it all upside down and inside out again.
Do de do de do . . .

Questions

1. What do you imagine when you hear the word 'play'?

2. This chapter describes 'blessing' as calling out the good in people. What occasions for blessing adults and children in your church could be re-examined for their capacity to call out and celebrate the good?

3. Make a list of words you associate with play, using this chapter if it helps. How many of these words would you associate with the Father (Creator), the Son (Redeemer) or the Holy Spirit (Sustainer) and in what way? How many of these words would you associate with 'Church'?

4. Choose any suitable parable (e.g. the lost sheep in Luke 15.3-7) and spend some time wondering and dreaming about what is happening in it. Note down any fresh insights which come to you and any difficulties you might have with using this 'playful' means of Bible study.

5. What kinds of event at your church allow adults to play? Can you imagine ONE more occasion which could include the opportunity to play?

Activities

Spirituality / Word / Play

1. **Game**

You will need some paper, paints, crayons, pencils, pens and Post-its™.

Draw an image of something regarded as religious, such as a church, cross, chalice, Bible, etc. Invite some children to colour and decorate it. With the children, begin to make a story about the image – what is it doing, what is its history, who looks after it, etc. As the story develops, write or draw the main points, names of people, places or events on the Post-its™ and stick them around the image. When you have quite a few Post-its™, separate them and begin new stories starting with the people or the events. When everyone has had enough of the never-ending story reflect on how far you have journeyed from the religious starting point, either by 'unwinding' the story through the post-its, or reflecting on the image which was the point of origin. You can use the verse, 'the stone that the builders rejected has become the chief cornerstone' (Psalm 118.22; Acts 4.11) to focus your meditation if you wish.

2. **Create**

You will need some plastic cups or pots containing different soils (sandy, stony, wet, rich, etc.) and a packet of cress or other fast-germinating seeds.

Reflect on the children's perceptions of the parable of the sower in the 'Word' chapter. In what ways do these confirm or challenge your reading of this parable? Work with a group of children to sow seeds in different soils and water them. Keep the pots in different environments (light, dark, dry, wet, etc.) What happens? Note what comments the children make about the seeds and how they prosper. What else might you learn about the parable of the sower from this exercise?

3. **Learn from**

You will need to set up a simple play experience indoors or outdoors.

Set up a play experience for a child or a group of children, then sit back. Pay attention to your feelings and reactions as you watch the children. How hard is it to not interfere? When is it right to step in? Would you like to get involved yourself? Are you laughing or feeling anxious? When the play experience is over, note down your thoughts and feelings. Reflect on what you have learnt about yourself, the child. You can use the verse, 'If you, then, who are evil, know how to give good gifts to your children, how much more will the heavenly Father give the Holy Spirit to those who ask him!' (Luke 11.13) as a focus of meditation if you wish.

4. **Celebrate**

You will need sheets of paper, pencils, crayons, paints, glitter, etc.

With a group of children, show them how to make a paper aeroplane if they don't know how to do it. Now colour some sheets or paper with drawings or paints and glitter. Add some messages, prayers, texts or reflections. Hang them as a mobile, pin them on a board for prayer requests or throw them to be picked up and read by other people in a group or a worship session. Make sure the aeroplanes are cleared up if not all are recovered. You can reflect on the verse, 'so shall my word be that goes out from my mouth; it shall not return to me empty, but it shall accomplish that which I purpose, and succeed in the thing for which I sent it' (Isaiah 55.11) if you wish.

5.  **Scripture**

Look for some 'playful' texts in Scripture. What stories come to mind which could reflect the human experience of play or the playfulness of God? Look at, for example, Zechariah 8.5; John 3.8; Jonah 4.6-11.

6

Sin

Emma Percy

A Catholic priest was talking to a class of seven- and eight-year-olds, and asked 'What must you do to be forgiven?' There was a quick response from one eight-year-old boy: 'You must sin!' Central to the Christian theology of forgiveness and salvation is an understanding of sin. The Church teaches the universality of sin; as St Paul puts it, 'all have sinned and fall short of the glory of God' (Romans 3.23). In different periods of the Church's history, and within its many and varied traditions, the focus on human sinfulness is relatively constant. Sometimes human depravity and sinfulness is a major focus of Christian teaching; and at other times the essential goodness of the created order has, while not denying human sinfulness, shifted the focus away from indebtedness to one of blessing.

Yet while one can be reasonably clear about the teachings of the Church throughout the ages (variable though they may have been), much less is known about how notions of sin have been constructed and understood in the pews and the wider public sphere. Society has been lenient on some issues that the Church has taken a tough line on and vice versa. What might have been condemned as a vice by some has been condoned by others. The language of sin has been used beyond the Church to convey behaviour that ranges from evil to promiscuous or naughty. It has been used to express moral outrage and at the other extreme to promote chocolate snacks. A recent launch of luxury range of choc ices was named after the seven deadly sins.[1]

The Church traditions offer definitions of sin; there are ten commandments, seven deadly sins and more besides. But it is fair to say that constructions and foci of sin are contested within ecclesial communities. Some will stress personal sin (including sexuality), while others place an emphasis on the collective (e.g. political, social and environmental). Social and cultural contexts inevitably shape the local church's attitudes to particular sins and what was once roundly condemned by all, for instance usury, is now accepted behaviour.[2] There is an accommodation between society and the evolving Christian understanding of what the faith teaches in Scripture and tradition about the outworking of sinful behaviour.

In this chapter, I have been asked to look at one particular group's attitude to sin. The aim is to reflect on sin through the eyes of children. Let me say at the outset that, given the space available, the essay can be no more than a sketch. The children consulted are drawn from a limited sample, and I don't in any way claim to be offering a definitive or general account of children's views of sin, based on the evidence gathered. However, the insights gleaned are nonetheless useful. In the light of this, the reflections, insights and observations that follow have some weight – but a more detailed survey would be required for a fuller picture.

I interviewed about 20 different children, mostly in family or friendship groups. I spoke to most of the children using a small tape recorder and encouraged a general discussion around the topic, asking a number of specific questions. Some of the interviews were in the children's own homes; all were in places that were familiar to them. In most of the interviews I was the only adult present, with the parents' consent. In two, the mother of the children was present for the entire discussion. I would have liked to have used some more creative ways of exploring the topic but time and circumstance prevented that. In previous parish experience I have used games such as ball throwing at a target or pictures from newspapers to explore different ways of understanding sin. The samples were all drawn from the local area. This means that due to the demographics of where I live, they are white and from articulate families. Some of the children have been brought up in consciously Christian families; others are fairly regular or occasional churchgoers. Others are from non-churchgoing families in the village. They attend a mixture of schools, with all the local primary schools having Church affiliations, and others attending nearby private schools, including a Cathedral school. So this sample, although limited (i.e. it is quite rich in Christian culture), is still potentially insightful. In talking with the children, I tried to explore in a broad and open way their concept of sin. It was important for me not to try to put definitions into their minds, but rather allow the conversations to be shaped by them. These were merely prompted by a short set of questions about what they thought sin was, who sinned and how sin related to God. All the children were interviewed in groups, which were a deliberate device to enable the children to talk to one another, and allow the conversations to be built up among the children, so that their insights were driven by each other rather than by me.

Sin as being bad

The word 'sin' is familiar to any regular churchgoer, and would certainly have some meaning to adults beyond the Church. In the wider public sphere, sin has an ambivalent quality: it carries negative connotations, but also a sense of 'naughtiness' and indulgence. In the beginnings of my interviews with groups of children, I asked them whether they recognized the word, and what they thought it meant. The children ranged in age from three to thirteen years old. Interestingly, none of the children under the age of seven claimed to know the word, or what it meant.

I found this intriguing, as a number of these children were regular churchgoers, and had attended Sunday school and other church-based children's activities. Granted, this is a very small and possibly unrepresentative sample, but it is interesting to note that even children from church families did not appear to recognize a word that they must have heard used regularly in the liturgy. This indicates that words used in church liturgy, but not used outside that context, probably do not 'connect' with children in the way that their parents imagine. It is not that the children haven't heard the word, as such; but that it hasn't been used in enough contexts for them to process it. Put another way, the 'currency' of the word has not achieved significant recognition to enable it to have appropriate value. In turn, this suggests that there may be other words or concepts contained within liturgy that children hear and repeat, but do not comprehend – largely because they are not used outside the context of worship.

This raised a further question. Is the word 'sin' deliberately not used in Christian education with younger children? One suspects that patterns vary across traditions and denominations. It is probably the case that different traditions feel more comfortable talking explicitly to children about sin. Certainly in the Roman Catholic Church, children being prepared for their first communion at seven would also be prepared for confession, and therefore deliberately taught about sin. I sense, however, that in other traditions there is a dislike of thinking about children as sinners. I was recently involved in preparing two nine-year-old girls for baptism, and their mother reading the order of service questioned me at length about whether I was implying her girls were intrinsically sinful. The language, to her, was 'negative' and 'undermining'. I am aware that clergy have mixed feelings about the language in the *Common Worship* Baptism service. The previous questions in *The Alternative Service Book* asked, 'Do you repent of your sins? Do you renounce evil?' The new questions are:

'Do you reject the devil and all rebellion against God? Do you renounce the deceit and corruption of evil? Do you repent of the sins that separate us from God and neighbour?' The language is strong but in all the questions, especially the last, we find an understanding of sin that fits the children's relational understanding: sin is to do with fractures in relationship. In preaching at infant baptism I have often made the clear distinction between a position that sees children as intrinsically sinful and in need of purification, and a theology that accepts that part of the human condition is to sin. The former implies that we are sinful in essence; the latter position accepts that our sinfulness comes from how we live as human beings, with others, in the world.

In her book *Let the Children Come*, Bonnie Miller-McLemore comments on our confusion about children and sin:

> We automatically react negatively to the idea of children as sinful or depraved, but the history of the 'depraved adultish-child' of premodern times and the 'innocent childish-child' of modern times has shown the limits of both views. The reign of the cherished, romanticised child created its own set of problems every bit as troubling as belief in the sinful, corrupt child had done. Both are inventions or social constructions in need of fresh reconsideration.[3]

Her summary of the changing attitude to children, and the need to revisit how we understand their sinfulness, correlates with my own sense that though parents and church leaders feel wary of talking about sin to children, all the children I spoke to were quite clear that everyone, including children, sins.

The older children in my survey all recognized the word, and when asked, told me that they learnt about sin in church, school – through RE lessons and assemblies – and from parents. The family as a repository of knowledge and reflection only came up in consciously Christian households. Those who attended church fairly regularly, rather than week-by-week, did not know the word from home at all. They were all clear that sin meant doing or being bad. 'Bad' was the most common word used to define sin, and occasionally the phrase 'doing wrong'; interestingly they did not use the word 'naughty'. One group talked about it as 'disobeying people who were more important', such as parents, teachers and other leaders. A few talked about 'disobeying God'. By disobedience they clearly meant doing things contrary to what they had been told. Older children talked of not doing things they had been asked to do by parents, such as tidying up their room or helping around the house. Younger children used more social examples. The youngest child, whom I spoke to with his two older sisters, informed me that being bad was 'biting' and being good was 'playing nicely'; and being really bad was 'bouncing on the sofa with your shoes on'. There was a clear sense in all the children that I spoke with about the concepts of doing bad things or doing wrong things.

When I asked the children what kind of people sinned, I was able to note how often the younger children referred to burglars or robbers, and even on one occasion, pirates. My assumption is that this image of the burglar as a bad person comes from children's books and television. My memory of reading children's books to my own children in their infant years is that burglars do turn up quite often as a recognizable 'baddy'. They are dressed in clothes that conventionally depict a burglar, and are usually caught by the end of the story. Pirates are also recognizable 'baddies' in books and films, yet at one level these literary and screen depictions are usually relatively safe, offering children an image of a bad person designed not to create fear. The idea of the burglar did not seem to connect to any actual events a child knew by experience, but to a conceptualized bad person they had encountered in the stories they had been told. This notion of someone who invades the safe place and breaks in might also say something about parental fears that children pick up on.

This raised further questions: how do we talk to children about sin and wrongdoing? When I was a parish priest taking services for pre-school children, I did use secular books about naughty children to explore the idea of doing things wrong. These books dwelt on naughtiness; even I wasn't comfortable with discussing categories that might be considered really bad. There is a tension in wanting to shield children from the darker side of life, though traditionally fairy stories have engaged with concepts of wickedness. So one wonders what kind of stories might be useful in exploring the darker side of humanity with today's children. What kind of story connects the concept of sin into their lives? Are there Bible stories that we don't tell because they convey images of God's wrath rather than love and mercy? Noah's flood becomes a story about animals rather than judgement on the wicked. None of the children, even the children from Christian homes, suggested any biblical stories that might connect to sin or wrongdoing. This also related to comments from some of the older children about how church always focused on the positives. As Christians, I suspect, we are deeply influenced by the cultural ideas of children's innocence, such that we often fail to help them explore the sinfulness of themselves and the wider world.

Everyone sins, no one is perfect

Among the older children in the survey, there were a few who connected sinful people with wider public events. One child mentioned whoever had 'kidnapped' Madeleine McCann, the young child abducted in Portugal, as a bad person. Another child talked about Hitler or Al-Qaida as examples of bad people. Though very quickly, almost all the children concluded that everyone sins. One five-year-old girl very firmly told me that children sin, and all agreed that from a very young age being bad was part of human nature. The children didn't seem to question the reality of this or to wonder why this was, but simply stated the reality they encountered that all people did things wrong. No one was perfect. Most of the children felt that babies didn't sin, but some were less sure about this. This raises the question of whether it is simply the baby's inability to act independently that meant it was not seen as capable of sin or whether the baby was not yet able to participate in a social relationship. However, all were very clear that sinning started early, and was a part of human life. They all seemed very comfortable with the notion of universal sinfulness, and were particularly clear that it started very early. For most of them, sin started with the possibility of independent conscious action; though they obviously didn't quite put it like that. It may well be that their understanding of sin was deeply connected to their experience of being told off. Mobility brings with it the possibility of overstepping boundaries, of literally and metaphorically going too far.

The children all admitted that they did things wrong, apart from one eight-year-old who wasn't going to admit to anything that might incriminate him. He was the middle child in the family, and his mother was present for the interview. I think his default position was to not own up to anything he didn't have to! He and his five-year-old sister had a heated exchange about this, with her insistence that he, she and all children were guilty of fighting. The children would not use the word 'sinner', but they volunteered that they were not perfect. In fact, they stated that nobody was perfect. Their examples tended to depict sin as a fracturing of good relationships. Thus, young children talked about fighting and hitting, and all talked about hurting people. The older children were clearly able to see that hurting could be more than physical; there were both emotional ways of hurting people and the concept of disappointing adults by their bad behaviour.

Sin as a fracturing of social relationships

Children, by the fact of their dependency, live in social communities with rules. Through the experience of home and school they are constantly being told what is acceptable and what is unacceptable behaviour. One child, aged five, was clear that she knew what was right and what was wrong – in terms of behaviour – because she went to school. She was coming to the end of her first year at school, and had had to learn how to cooperate in a class of 30 children, listen to the teacher and conform to accepted behaviour. This had taught her a conscious awareness about doing the right thing. In the home, her older sister said that the younger children learnt by doing things and being told off for the things that were wrong; and also by observing what other people were told off for. In this, she was like the other children I spoke to: learning about good behaviour through family life, school and peer groups.

A key part of a child's development is the way children learn to behave alongside others. They learn through a mixture of taught rules, modelled behaviour, and trial and error – to behave in a way that is acceptable to those around them. It is hardly surprising, then, that young children are relatively clear that they get things wrong. They are told that, often. This telling is not on the whole a negative experience, but if handled correctly, is a tool for development. Children gain from understanding the boundaries. All the younger children offered examples of hitting, biting or fighting as bad behaviour, and playing nicely as good behaviour: a message no doubt reinforced at home and school. Children live in a world where it is considered normal and acceptable to comment on good and bad behaviour. They have a sense that good behaviour is rewarding, and bad behaviour will in some way be punished. The combination of home and school makes it very easy to talk about what is good and bad, especially in the way they treat others.

In this way, children's experience of everyday life differs from that of adults, where we rarely correct each other's bad behaviour unless it is extreme. Reflecting on this made me wonder whether we could be more prescriptive with children in terms of good spiritual behaviour – helping them to learn good habits of spiritual life. Our culture arguably struggles with concepts of obligation and duty, preferring ideas of gratification and fulfilment. Yet these are valuable tools in developing a religious discipline. Children live in a world where they are constantly obliged to conform to actions and behaviours, because they are told to rather than because the behaviours gratify them; and perhaps Christians need to be clearer about religious duties and obligations. I admit that my own children have been explicitly taught that attending church is a Sunday *duty*, which might not always be enjoyable, but is nonetheless a means of a healthy spiritual life. One does not attend for short-term gratification (though it is lovely when you get that), but because it is the right thing to do. There is of course a danger in this position if duty becomes connected with things that are unpleasant. There are many adults whose childhood experience of Christianity has left negative feelings about the Church. What is important is to help children reflect on the cumulative effects of being part of a church community, to encourage them to find experiences that are gratifying, but to learn that it is about long-term relationships not short-term entertainment. It is also important for them to learn how their involvement in the congregation gives hope and pleasure to others. In an individualistic world it is valuable to inculcate habits of community.

In the light of the importance of sociality and community I note that the older children also used social language to talk about their understanding of sin. The issue of bullying was offered as an example of bad behaviour, and the idea that you could hurt people by saying things was expressed. The problem of bullying and the need to live well together in community is a strong part of most schools' personal and social education (PSHE), and children clearly articulate the principles of respecting others as a central aspect of behaving well. The language improves, but the principle of playing nicely continues to be keenly felt as good behaviour. Our schools are increasingly confident about teaching children how to behave in ways that value and respect others. They may not use the language of sin, but they do encourage children to understand that actions have consequences, and that people can be hurt both by those who act unkindly and by those who stand by and let it happen. Again, I wonder if the Church takes seriously the possibility of connecting this language to our inherited language of sin and its role in fracturing relationships.

The children were also happy to explore the reasons why people do wrong or sin. One of the oldest boys I interviewed simply said of himself: 'If I knew why I sinned, then I wouldn't sin any more.' The younger children offered very simple explanations. You hit back when you've been hit; or you overreact to something that you don't like. You hurt other people because you don't like them. Clearly there was a sense that children had been taught to manage their feelings and to learn that simply reciprocating hurt for hurt leads to escalation of the problem not a resolution. I may well have received very different answers in communities where adults bring children up to give as good as they get. As they got older, the reasoning became more sophisticated. Thus, children discussed how you might end up hurting other people in order to fit in with a crowd, or to prove yourself. As one older boy put it, 'People sin to draw attention to themselves or because they have something wrong with them.' An older group of girls aged 10 to 12 expressed the belief that happy, joyful people won't sin as much, as they will be less likely to feel the need to 'put their hurt onto other people' – a phrase they used about people who had had a hard childhood and might therefore act out their own pain by inflicting it on others. They also made a very interesting observation: that sometimes people sinned, but others were ultimately responsible. They gave the example of soldiers fighting in a war killing people, but the people in government being responsible for the decision being guilty of a greater sin than the ones actually hurting people.

Again, the children's discussion of why people sin showed a strong sense of social relationships. They seem to understand life lived with other people, and are aware of the influence of others. You might sin to impress your crowd, or show off or because others have deliberately led you astray. So a mixed group of 7- to 11-year-olds talked about how people could deliberately tell you to do things that they knew were bad, and you didn't. You could therefore sin in a sense, through ignorance, though presumably those leading you astray were also guilty of sinning. Most of the children were relatively comfortable at grading the bad things, and saw deliberate, premeditated bad behaviour as the worst. It was interesting that they graded things on the intention of the sinner rather than on the act. As one child said, 'The worst sin is where you know how sad it will make people, and do it anyway.' They also projected their experience onto others, so saw the really bad people in the news as people who had probably been hurt or damaged to make them behave badly. This kind of 'therapeutic' language again pointed to a relational understanding of sin. In their understanding people who had been damaged by the sin of others may well go on to sin badly. This didn't make it right in their eyes but offered some kind of explanation. They didn't use the language of evil, or in any way mention the devil or Satan.

The regular Confession used in the Church of England Communion service talks about sinning 'through negligence, weakness or our own deliberate fault'; or in another version, 'ignorance, weakness and our own deliberate fault.' It was clear that although the children did not use these terms, their explanations pointed to them. Thus, they talked about sinning through ignorance, especially when you were young or where you didn't know the full consequences. This was still doing wrong things, but was not as bad as other wrongdoing, especially if you learnt from your mistakes. Even babies could sin through ignorance, according to some of the children. Weakness was also understood as a reason for sinning. This was about an inability to stand out from the crowd; a sense of past hurt, or even, as one child of seven expressed it, 'Sometimes you just get so angry that you can't control what you do.' The older girls talked about drugs and the way people did things that they thought they would like, but that were wrong. This was the closest anyone came to a concept that sin might be in some sense done for pleasure. They quickly commented on the fact that people would learn that it wasn't good for them. There was a clear sense that deliberately doing things wrong was part of their own experience, and their observed experience of others.

The children predominantly thought of sin as action: doing things to hurt others. The older children were conscious of sinning in word and deed, but interestingly only a few of them talked about sin as thinking wrong things. This is perhaps not surprising when we take note of the social aspect of the children's understanding of sin. Thoughts are personal, and if not expressed, can appear to have no impact on other people. However, a couple of the children talked about how bad thoughts about people had a negative impact on themselves, making them feel guilty. And one ten-year-old child expressed a clear sense that God knows your thoughts, and will make you feel guilty for unkind ones. The link between knowing that something was wrong because of its consequences was quite strong in the children's understanding of what was wrong, even if the consequence was simply being told off by an adult.

There certainly seemed to be a sense that things were wrong whether you got caught or not. The experience of being told off was about understanding the boundaries and learning where behaviour was unacceptable. It is clear that the sample of children I spoke to all come from households where concepts of fairness and consistency were part of the adult reaction to bad behaviour. It would be very interesting to know how concepts of wrongdoing would be expressed by children growing up in households with very inconsistent adult behaviour. This is also true of ideas about how sin is dealt with. For most of these children an expression of sorrow was the first step of winning back adult approval. Some actions might lead to consequences of being grounded or foregoing certain privileges, but none of them lived in households where they feared that bad behaviour would alter their status as loved children. This parental attitude to wrongdoing thus correlated to religious ideas about God, to whom you said sorry for not always being good, while continuing to trust in his love for his children. This is a very different model to earlier Christian emphasis on the wrath and judgement of God.

Since the children were focused on sin as action, I asked them whether you could sin by not doing something. The wonderful confession in Cranmer's Daily Office speaks of what we have done and what we have 'left undone'. The children all agreed that you could sin by omission. One wise child answered this with an example: 'If my neighbour asks me to look after their cat and I don't, the cat could die and then my not doing something will have killed the cat.' They were, on the whole, clear that not doing things you had been asked to do could be a form of wrongdoing. Again, this usually connected to deliberately disobeying instructions given by adults, parents or teachers. This further emphasizes the understanding of sin as having something to do with social relationships. Wrongdoing is about hurting people, disobeying people and letting people down. It is strongly relational in character. These children came from loving homes and they were well aware that misbehaving fractured the home or school atmosphere. They were conscious of this through their own behaviour and through the behaviour of others towards them. Again, I think the issue of consistency in adult attitudes has shaped the understanding of these children and it raises interesting theological questions about how much our understanding of God is influenced by our experience of parental behaviour.

God's attitude to sin

This became even more interesting when the children were asked what God thought about sin. Some of the children had mentioned God when we first began talking about sin. One ten-year-old boy said that sin was 'doing things against Jesus and against God'; and one eight-year-old girl talked about sin as 'breaking the Ten Commandments', and thought that people who didn't believe in God were sinners. The rest of the children didn't really talk about sin relating to God until I specifically asked them. The children quickly asserted that God loved them whether they were good or bad. The older children also stressed God's forgiveness and mercy. Obviously, this was a message that had been impressed upon them through church and home. In fact, one of the older girls commented on her experience – that church tended to focus on the positive aspects of faith. She said, they tell you 'Jesus has died . . . but very quickly. It is all right: he is risen!'

I was interested in what this tells us about different ways of connecting children to the Christian story. In my own role as vicar of a parish in Sheffield we always organized both a children's workshop on Maundy Thursday and a family service on Good Friday. At both of these events we would engage with the idea of the cross as connecting to human sinfulness. At the workshop we did various activities over the years, making crosses out of nails, or using tacks to nail a simple figure on to a wooden cross. One year we painted pieces of broken pottery so that our church Easter Garden could be full of dark broken bits for Good Friday, representing the hurtful unhappy things in life, and the pieces turned over on Easter Day to show colourful, cheerful signs of new life coming out of brokenness. For a number of years we made a giant banner with a cross of dark stones for Good Friday which could all be turned over to reveal a sparkling, colourful cross on Easter Day.

At the Good Friday service we would sometimes ask children and adults to choose newspaper images of the world's suffering to nail literally on to a large wooden cross. One year we used dried rose petals to throw on a large black cardboard cross on the floor, thinking of all the bad things in our life that we wanted to be rid of. The children then helped to throw the rest of the petals on the cross to represent the wider sinfulness of the world. As we sung a hymn we lifted up the cardboard cross and the petals became a beautiful outline of a perfect empty cross space on the floor. These visual rituals helped to focus something of the idea of Christ bearing our sins on the cross. I also found that children responded well to the idea of sin as falling short when they were asked to throw soft balls to try to reach a line. Some fall short, some go too far, reminding us of sin as our failure to live up to what is expected and our ability to trespass and go too far. Most of the children I interviewed here did not have these kinds of ritual memories of connecting their understanding of sin to the cross. It made me aware that our key penitential occasions are often not on Sundays, but, for instance, Ash Wednesday and Good Friday. These can be easily missed, even by regular churchgoers, who move from Jesus entering Jerusalem with palms, to the joy of the Resurrection, without pausing at the cross.

Reflecting on the children's comments about God and sin, it became clearer that they understood God to be sad about sin, because it made people sad and unhappy, but they also wanted to emphasize quickly that he forgives sin. This was all explained by the strong belief that God wants people to be happy. A ten-year-old boy referred to the way God could forgive someone; but that the politicians or lawmaker could still execute the individual wrongdoer. The older girls expressed a sense of unease with the fact that God forgave sins, and yet there was so much suffering, chaos and evil around in the world. One said that, in a way, God was selfish because he pushed sin away, but the people still had to live with the mess. There was a sense that God could sort out his relationship with people, but the sinfulness of humans continued to affect the state of the world we live in. There was little sense that sin offended God, or that God was angry; though one child talked about God being disappointed at our sins. There was absolutely no expression of God's wrath.

It is clear that these are children who have grown up in different families and different churches, and have all been given a vision of a loving, forgiving God. This is very different from earlier models, where a fear of God's wrath might have been used as a tool for encouraging right behaviour. One wonders whether this is a theological shift or a cultural one. I expect that, in some sense, it is a mixture of the two. Understandings about child psychology have encouraged us to believe that children develop best through security and being loved. Education has moved away from physical punishment, and has attempted, rather, to reward good behaviour and encourage aspirations to be good. Punishments are still a part of home and school, but the atmosphere in recommended behaviour has moved from 'do this, or else' to 'do this, because it pleases people when you are good, and everyone will be happier'. Punishments are about 'time out' or being 'grounded', providing time to reflect and acknowledge wrongdoing rather than suffering painful consequences.

Emphasizing God's love and forgiveness establishes a secure sense in the children of being loved. Nevertheless, there could be a danger that churches underplay God's sense of justice, and fail to offer an account of the world's suffering. Churches may also fail to offer an image of God's anger at sin. I wouldn't want to return to an image of an ever-vigilant God looking to punish sinful children. But are we, as parents and church leaders, too wary of touching on the darker side of human nature and the cost of forgiveness? Some of the children talked about God just pushing sin away, and forgetting it, without a real sense of this affecting God.

The problem of human sinfulness and the chaos of the world did arise when the children talked about the fact that nobody was perfect. One ten-year-old boy said that God didn't control us, because if he did then we wouldn't sin. He expressed a basic understanding of human freedom and the need for a choice to make our behaviour free. He thought that people were half-evil and half-good, and that there was freedom of choice to act either way. This was the same child who talked about God being disappointed when we sinned, implying an understanding that we could choose the good.

The older girls also explored something of this free choice, but took it in quite a different direction by suggesting that a perfect life in which someone never did anything wrong would be boring. 'If you didn't sin once, it would be extremely difficult and it would be boring.' As they explored this idea, they talked about how you sometimes learn from the things that you do wrong. 'If you never fell off your bike, you wouldn't know it hurt.' At a very simple level, they were exploring the idea that pain and suffering are part of the experience that enriches life and helps you to appreciate the good things as well as the bad. They mentioned Adam and Eve, and said that perhaps it had been a good thing that the apple had been taken. They also talked about the way the small things that you did wrong helped to teach you not to do bigger things. Again we should note that these children experienced being hurt with being comforted and consoled. They did not come from homes where pain and suffering were linked to neglect, nor were they told that it was in some sense good for them.

The girls' notion that sin is a part of the necessary process of human development has resonances with the theology of Irenaeus. Writing in the second century, he believed that Adam and Eve were created immature, and that the Fall was a necessary part of human development, leading to a world where the pain and sorrows help humans to mature. Life was by necessity a 'veil of tears', and it was through the suffering of life that human beings learn to be good. This sense of maturation through the experience of a sinful world had definite resonance in the children's understanding. They expressed, in different ways, the view that it was through experiencing or witnessing the consequences of wrongdoing that you learnt to do better. Being good was a process of learning, which happened through the experience of getting it wrong as well as getting it right. The worst sin, the older girls agreed, was where you really knew all the consequences of an action, knew how much it would hurt others, and then deliberately did it. There was a sense in which sin was seen as both bad, and yet in some way a necessity of life. Perfection wasn't possible, or even, in one sense, desirable, as it was not human.

One child did express a sense of God's disappointment when we get it wrong, and the imagery of God tended to be parental; of God being like a parent urging us to be our best, and disappointed when we don't live up to expectations. Yet alongside this was the idea that God could recognize when you were trying. God could see the thought process behind actions, and would be sympathetic to the attempt to improve. Therefore, at times, God would be more understanding than a parent who might just see the consequences and not understand the thought process. Intentions were seen to be important, but it was also clear that when you got things wrong, at one level, it didn't matter whether you meant it or not, the consequences could still be the same for others.

There was little sense of how God forgave us our sins. One older child mentioned Jesus' dying in connection with this, but only in passing. Another of the children talked about God cleansing sin: a sense that God could wash it away. All of them gave the impression that God's forgiving of sins was relatively automatic, and simply part of what God did. They also had a strong impression that although God might get a bit weary of forgiving the same people the same things, he continued to forgive and didn't reach a point where he said 'enough was enough'. Again, I was left to wonder how we express the cost of God's forgiveness, or whether that is something children should come to understand as they mature. Attending a children's service at a recent Good Friday, I was struck with how quickly the leaders moved from the cross to focusing on the Resurrection: almost as if they felt that the sadness and pain of Good Friday was not suitable for children to dwell upon.

Inevitably, the children's understanding of wrongdoing and sinfulness was tied to their own experience. When they were asked about wider world issues, pollution and climate change were the most frequently mentioned subjects. This is now a key topic in school and in the media, so perhaps it was not surprising. But I was interested that there was little mention of war or terrorism. Pollution and climate change were discussed as ways people have treated the world wrongly, and were about collective sinfulness. It was clear that this was something we were collectively involved in, and it was interesting to see how clearly that sense of collective responsibility for pollution was understood. Children could make connections between their own actions and the wider consequences as these had been pointed out.

For the children to make sense of other kinds of structural sin, similar connections would need to be made. They have no sense of connection to decisions made by politicians or corporate business. In a sense this is fair, as they do not vote and have limited purchasing power. However, it would not be difficult to have a discussion about whether buying trainers made by underpaid children was a bad thing, and I think discussions like this would enable children to see the connections between the choices we make in life and the consequences for others. As they themselves said, it is about making the connections and seeing the consequences.

Conclusion

The conversations I had were with a small group of children who all come from relatively secure backgrounds – where good behaviour is acknowledged and expected – and bad behaviour is commented on and may lead to punishment.

They were all either in school or nursery education, where again good behaviour would be rewarded and bad behaviour noted and possibly punished. They live in a world where people in authority are constantly telling them what to do. In talking to the older girls about the word 'trespasses' they all started to laugh when we said that it might mean crossing the line. That is what parents say, they said, 'You have crossed the line, go to your room' or 'You have gone too far this time.' Even the young children repeated instructions, so the three-year-old told me that bouncing on the sofa was very bad, although his sister modified this to say only with your shoes on. Clearly this is a strong house rule, reinforced by parents and siblings.

The children's concept of sin was shaped by their personal experience of living in relationships. Their home lives functioned on household norms of good behaviour, and specific roles that were meant to protect them or the furniture. Their educational lives functioned around rules imposed to keep order in the classroom, and the more complex issues of peer relationships. Clearly, the issue of hurting others arises out of their interaction with peers. This meant that young children talked about hitting, fighting and hurting others as being bad, while older children broadened this out to include name calling, bitching about people and bullying. Living within this reality it is hardly surprising that the children had a strong sense of universal sinfulness! All at times have experienced being hurt and hurting others, intentionally or accidentally. All knew something about disobedience and how a wrong intention could lead to bad consequences.

There was a strong sense of the cumulative nature of sin. Feeling hurt oneself could lead to hurting others. Feeling sad could lead to doing wrong; and feeling angry could lead to loss of control. There was also an understanding that doing small things wrong could lead to bigger things. This was why, as one girl said, parents were always saying, 'Well you shouldn't have been there in the first place!' There was a clear belief that those who were really bad had probably had difficult childhoods, or a lack of love, or genuine harm done to them. The idea that hurt can multiply the ability to hurt others was commented upon by most of the groups. There was, though, a surprising lack of judgementalism, which perhaps says something about our therapeutic culture. Bad people have probably become bad in these children's language, rather than simply being bad. One child expressed the belief that we were all a mixture of evil and good, and we had to learn how to act out of the good rather than the bad.

Clearly, children are influenced by the prevailing ideas in their homes and schools. In a different culture they might well use a very different language to talk about sin and see it as a product of evil. These children had a relatively benevolent view of the world. Their experiences of life contained failure, wrongdoing, tellings off and consequences, but all couched in loving forgiving language and this translated into their theology. These children are developing concepts of right and wrong through the relationships around them. It seems that modern understandings of infant brain development would stress the fundamental importance of good social relationships for developing the capacity for emotional intelligence. Sue Gerhardt in her book *Why Love Matters*[4] looks at the way very young children's brains develop in the early years through their social relationships, especially with primary caregivers. We are not born good or bad but our earliest experience of how we are loved and valued, or not, impacts on our capacity to negotiate the social relationships in our world. As humans we are created to be social beings, we are born into relationships and these help to shape our capacity for relating well to others and to God. Sin is the behaviour and thought patterns that fracture these relationships. Much of what these children understood as sin was simply boundary testing. As they grow older they will experience a world in which sin is not simply personal but is about what the Bible calls the powers and principalities (Ephesians 6.12, RSV), the structures and cultural patterns of behaviour that are part of our daily living and are much harder to counteract.

It is not possible to draw any major conclusions from such a limited sample of conversations. But the predominant thoughts that I am left with are these. First, children are more comfortable in talking about sin than adults are about discussing the idea of children and sin. These children clearly understand concepts of right and wrong, but also know that it is not humanly possible always to get it right. They expressed interesting ideas about how we learn from the wrong we do, and how repeated suffering can lead to more sin and suffering. Second, the children in our survey were mainly from Christian homes, yet they had very underdeveloped concepts of the cost of sin in the drama of salvation. They were deeply reassured of God's love and forgiveness, but were almost too blasé about God's ability to dismiss sin. Third, the language and concepts of sin that were used, although obviously naive and nascent, seem to flow out of a culture that is conditioned by positive affirmation rather than corrective criticism. That same culture is the one that forms parental values, which is centred on choice and freedom, and the addressing of our needs and desires. It does not dwell on the darker side of human nature, except in extreme cases. Fourth, and consequently, the ideas of sin that children have are posited mainly in behavioural examples or in particular exemplars (e.g. pirates, burglars). But these 'roles' are somewhat remote from experience, and remove the concept from any deep and immediate relationship with a person. Fifth, and finally, the children interviewed clearly live in a world where right and wrong are regularly articulated. But those who work with them in church, and other areas of Christian development, may need to relearn a more robust language of sinfulness – to help them to explore the darker aspects of life as imperfect humans in a fallen world.

Questions

1. What do you understand by the word 'sin'?

2. This chapter suggests that as a Church we do not dwell on the darker side of human nature or the cost of forgiveness. How do you think these matters might be explored appropriately with children?

3. Choose one of the Ten Commandments or the seven deadly sins (lust, gluttony, greed, wrath, sloth, envy, pride) and put it at the centre of a spider diagram. Fill the diagram with possible consequences of transgressing (who gets hurt, what relationships are broken, etc.). Add to the diagram in a different colour what actions or processes could mend or heal the fractured relationships. How many of these are already identified by the children in this chapter. What *can't* be healed or mended?

4. Choose a suitable biblical passage concerning sin, for example Genesis 18.16-33; John 8.3-11; Romans 6.7-23. How do the children's thoughts on sin help to open up this passage?

5. What kinds of occasions in your church allow reflection on sin, repentance and the possibility of new life? Can you think of ONE way in which such an occasion could be enhanced by children's reflections on these issues?

7

Forgiveness

Sandra Millar

Introduction

A few years ago I was making a Simnel cake with my seven-year-old nephew. He watched carefully as I placed eleven marzipan balls round the edge. 'But there were twelve disciples', he said. So I explained that only eleven go on the cake because of Judas who betrayed Jesus. 'Didn't he know that Jesus would forgive him?' he asked incredulously.

This short exchange reveals both the naivety of children's responses and also their profound and challenging thinking. On the one hand, Ben had no idea of the way in which the Church has utterly condemned Judas from Scripture through tradition, but on the other, he opens up all kind of issues about the nature of forgiveness.

Forgiveness is one of those concepts that is both deceptively simple and agonizingly difficult. For Christians, forgiveness takes central stage as part of the Lord's Prayer, said daily by billions of people worldwide, 'Forgive us our trespasses as we forgive those who trespass against us.' For adults, it becomes a complex issue at many levels – emotionally, socially and theologically. But in the same way that feminist theology challenged some of our basic understandings of God and our relationship to him and to one another, so child theology can have the same impact. Children's understanding is simultaneously straightforward and profound. They grasp complex nuanced truths and yet are also deeply fundamentalist, expressing absolute opinions with firm conviction. Forgiveness is part of their everyday reality, and in this chapter I will explore how a child's theology of forgiveness unfolds, and how that affirms and challenges some of our traditional understandings.

Getting children talking

Much of the work for this chapter was done in a series of group discussions with children from two different communities. The children were drawn from a variety of economic, social and educational backgrounds and although none of them were regular churchgoers, all had contact with church and Christianity through school, one group attending a Church school, the other a community school with strong church links. They ranged in age from 5 to 11 years old, a mixture of boys and girls. Perhaps surprisingly, there were few identifiable differences in their understanding across age, background or gender. The discussions began by asking the children to choose from a wide range of images a picture that they linked with happiness and one that made them think about sadness. This allowed them to begin talking about abstract ideas very quickly, and some of them used the chosen images later on as a reference during the discussion. The choice of images and the language used to describe them began to reveal some of the elements that inform the development of a theological framework in childhood. Immediately the children connected 'people' with happiness:

> I like this picture. They're having a laugh.
>
> > (aged 11, giggling ballet dancers)

> These two people are smiling – that's happy.
>
> > (aged 5)

In contrast, the choices about sadness were often about space and absence:

> This is sad – there's no one in it. Perhaps someone has fallen off the cliff and died.
>
> > (aged 5, a seaside scene)

> This is a sad lady. She's on her own and maybe her husband has died.
>
> > (aged 6)

> This is so sad. It makes me feel trapped and horrible.
>
> > (aged 10, picture of the fence at Birkenau)

A theological framework

In these opening moments of conversation the children were reflecting their own lives and interests (for example, choosing pictures of animals ' 'cos I love dogs'), but were also revealing the paramount importance of experience. Recent theological frameworks, such as feminist, black, liberation and other theologies, have emphasized the place of experience as a starting point, and it provides the basis for developing child theology. Children form their understanding from the particular events and everyday circumstances that they encounter, and in an even more accentuated way than is found in feminist theology they first draw upon their experience of relationships and particularly family frameworks to shape their ideology and theology. Children's worlds are bounded by the people around them from the moment of birth (even conception). Slowly over the first few months and years the network of relationships expands, but always from the base reference point of home, however good or bad that experience might be. Christian and secular observers of family and childhood all note the importance of early relationships in forming children's moral, emotional and spiritual awareness.[1]

Secondly, children's theology is intuitive, reaching beyond the limits of the language and knowledge they have been given to explore moral and spiritual concepts that adults all too easily assume are beyond their scope. As the children chose pictures and started to talk about them they began to go beyond what was visible in the pictures to explore other possibilities and implications drawn from the images:

> This woman is poor and is being punished because she is lazy.
>
> (aged 9)

> They might have played a joke or a trick on their Mum.
>
> (Picture of children rolling about laughing)

This intuitive or imaginative response can begin with what we might expect, using the frame of reference from their social world or from the world of story, whether books or other media. But it is sometimes surprising, as children approach subjects in a lateral or tangential way, demonstrating 'out of the box' thinking as they look at the world around them. It is this intuitive response that makes their theology fascinating.

Cavalletti writes at some length about the mystery of children's intuition, suggesting that the ease and spontaneity of a child's religious response emerges from the depths of a child's being in a wholly natural way. As those who work closely with children invariably discover, children know things that no one has told them. Cavalletti goes on to argue that this innate response to God grows from the child's need and capacity for love:

> Therefore it is not in search for compensation that the child turns to God, but from a profound exigence within the child's nature. The child needs an infinite, global love, such as no human being is able to give . . .

In the contact with God the child finds the nourishment the child needs in order to grow in harmony.[2]

The language that children use to describe this instinctive awareness of something Other is often archetypal, drawing on images of light, dark, growth and flourishing.

Berryman[3] suggests that this reflects the very earliest experiences of absence and presence in infancy. One of the basic games that children play from the age of around 4–6 months is the game of 'peek-a-boo'. A key part of the game is the relationship between dark and hiding and light and awareness, thus reinforcing the essential idea that dark equates with 'bad' and light with 'good'. As facility and confidence with language increase over the years children, then adults, become more concerned with describing evidence and facts rather than relying on their instinct and intuition. This develops into some of the mismatch between adults and children in the area of spirituality, and the possibility for adults to be surprised out of their frameworks by the insights offered by children.

Thirdly, their framework is mystical. Children draw on imagination and creativity to reach beyond the boundaries set by their known world. They apply known concepts and vocabulary in new and unusual ways as their talk about sin and forgiveness reveals. The results are not uniform, as children may reach very different conclusions from the same input. (We will see that clearly in the response to the story of Judas: whereas Ben was mystified by Judas's failure to know a forgiving God, other children are equally adamant that he deserved punishment.) In ways that are frequently surprising to adults they use symbolic and metaphoric language to describe abstract notions of good and evil, bringing together intuition and experience as they explore spiritual concepts.

First the sin . . .

Although this chapter is primarily concerned with forgiveness, the discussions began with sin – for unless there is an awareness of wrongdoing there is no need for forgiveness, and for children their understanding of sin begins with their experience – and wrongdoing is very much part of their world! Initially, sin was described in concrete terms in relation to sibling, parents and friends:

> I don't know about sin, but being naughty is like when I play my Mum up like last night. I know it's naughty because my Mum got cross with me. I was shouted at and that makes me feel horrible inside.
>
> (aged 5)

> Sin is what's in you. Sin might be not finishing your work or not making your bed. It might be something like doing work and then scribbling it out.
>
> (aged 10)

> Biting, pushing over or saying nasty words are sins. Not liking my brother is a sin, he's only one, but he's nasty. He scratches and pulls my hair.
>
> (aged 6)

There were many and varied examples, sometimes moving away from relationship with people to a wider awareness of sin against animals and creation. But the children moved quickly to describe how sin made them feel, using much more intuitive language to describe the feelings of guilt: 'If you've done a bad thing you feel small' (aged 10).

This phrase, expressed in different ways by several of the children, echoes adult theological explanations, for example: 'our lives are diminished not only by the outrage but also by the bitter resentment that holds us captive'.[4]

The notion of being 'diminished' by sin is identical to the sense of being made small by doing something wrong, and was an awareness expressed by children across the age range and in both schools.

Children are well aware that sin affects their lives, both outwardly and inwardly, with a clear sense that sin involves emotions as well as actions. The children's view is intuitively sophisticated, and at one point the older group of children became embroiled in a complex discussion about the notion of good sin:

> Logically you could have a good sin – maybe if you did something without thinking about it.
>
> (aged 9)

> It's like when you go shooting (as in the countryside) all day and no one gets anything so everyone is grumpy. Then just at the end someone gets a duck and everyone starts smiling and laughing. That's like a good sin.
>
> (aged 10)

In a follow-up discussion, the children explored this idea further and some of them became very indignant about the issue of killing animals, whereas the child from a farming family was very clear that there were complexities that are not easily resolved. However, when the discussion moved away from the specifics of shooting animals there was a more ambiguous response and an acceptance of contradiction. Initially the conversation roamed around the topic of shooting in self-defence:

> It might be okay to shoot someone if you were going to be shot.
>
> (aged 11)

> Or your Mum was going to be attacked.
>
> (aged 10)

But then the children moved away from shooting to a more general discussion of the notion of a good sin: (referring to a picture of children working) 'This is a good sin. Children shouldn't work but if he's working for his family . . .' (aged 10).

In a similar vein another child picked up a picture of a prison and talked about the idea that keeping people in prison might be bad, but it might be good if it prevented crime, and another child began to think about questions of different beliefs. (Referring to a picture of a person meditating) 'It's a sin because we don't believe it in our religion, but it's good because it's in her religion' (aged 11).

These children are beginning to be aware that a range of frameworks and viewpoints exist and are attempting to place their notions of sin alongside ideas of justice. Interestingly, they don't use the language of shame and blame but are even-handed, accepting the inherent tension in the moral dilemma with tolerance.

Adult responses to ideas such as these can polarize into two directions. First, it is easy for adults to laugh or smile indulgently at the story or at the naivety of the idea being explored. Alternatively adults treat the notion as wrong, and intervene to explain that there is no such thing as good sin. However, instinctively these children have begun to explore a complex ethical and theological issue that exercises theologians everywhere. In her work on gender and moral development, Gilligan[5] asked boys and girls aged around ten years old to ponder the classic moral dilemma of Heinz, his sick wife and the costly drug treatment. (Heinz works for a pharmacist and his wife is very sick and will die without drug treatment. Heinz cannot afford to buy the drugs. Should he steal them from work?) She quotes at length from interviews with two children. The boy was consistently clear that Heinz should steal the drug, arguing that human life is worth more than money. The girl was much more hesitant:

> If he stole the drug, he might save his wife then, but if he did, he might have to go to jail, and then his wife might get sicker again and he couldn't get more of the drug, and it might not be good. So they should really just talk it out and find some other way to make the money.[6]

Although Gilligan was exploring gender differences, her work also shows how children can make sophisticated, nuanced and instinctive exploration of moral and theological dilemmas. But my conversations also show that they also draw on a clear understanding of the world to make absolute judgements. The doctrine of original sin is alive and well for five-year-olds! 'Babies do sins. They are naughty – everybody sins' (aged 5).

Not all the children would have equated the idea of being naughty with sin, but the younger children were retelling stories of family life, switching between the vocabulary of home and playground and the language of faith.

Forgiveness between people

But this chapter is about forgiveness not sin, although classic theologies of forgiveness begin with the notion that to forgive is to name the wrongdoing and to condemn it.[7] Child theology names wrongdoing in various ways: as the experience of being harmed and of harming others and as the causing of unhappiness; yet child theology also questions some definitions of sin, stopping us in our tracks and making us question our boundaries.

Volf goes on to say that the second part of forgiveness is to 'give wrongdoers the gift of not counting their wrongdoing against them'. Child theology does not necessarily explain forgiveness in such a way, although as with the defining of sin, the defining of forgiveness also begins with relationship:

> You have to say sorry.

> You have to play with them again.

Although apparently simple, this notion of taking action to demonstrate forgiveness is something that adults frequently struggle with. Countless self-help and spiritual books give examples of those who profess forgiveness but cannot move on in the relationship. But the children were very clear: unless there is reparation or restitution there can be no forgiveness:

> If you do something bad, do a good thing to undo it.

> (aged 10)

> Saying sorry doesn't work – it's just a word. It doesn't jump out into someone's life, it doesn't make the wrong better – you must do something nice for the person you have sinned against.
>
> (aged 11)

> You would say sorry and maybe make something for your Mum.
>
> (aged 5)

> If you do something really bad, do something better to make people forget about it.
>
> (aged 6)

Forgiveness is expressed in very concrete experiential terms and sometimes clearly reflects things they have seen within their own relational networks: 'If I wanted forgiveness from my Mum I would buy her a handbag' (aged 9).

Although the children are very clear that forgiveness involves some kind of concrete action that in some way compensates for the wrong that has happened, there is some difference in approach depending whether the wronged person is an adult or child. When the children talked about having upset an adult they were more likely to talk in terms of making physical restitution or doing something to make up for what had happened. It may be that this reflects the experience of relationship with adults. Children are normally in the position of being recipients from adults, whether in terms of basic needs such as food or shelter or as those with the capacity to reward. In seeking forgiveness from an adult the child offers something materially significant, either bought or made, which might be a sense of appeasing the one with power or simply a reflection of their daily lives. This is different from the way in which they express forgiveness with their peer group, as we will see.

At one level these kinds of explorations fit perfectly with conventional understandings of child development. Children in this age range are concrete and literal thinkers, draw clear boundaries and like to live within the framework of rules, fair play and justice. Every parent and teacher has heard the cry: 'it's not fair' from children of this age. Yet the talk about forgiveness goes beyond this framework of retribution and punishment as the children explore the idea of reconciliation:

> Children stay friends easily. I fell out with *x* and after a bit we just became good friends again.
>
> (aged 6)

> If you fall out with someone you just become friends again.
>
> (aged 5)

> If my friends hurt me, there is no point getting angry, no point hurting them back, instead we just say sorry and get on with stuff.
>
> (aged 9)

Some of us may have watched as children find their way towards reconciliation, perhaps slowly edging closer, tentatively offering to share, or maybe just simply letting time pass and continuing with the activity in which they are engaged. In an episode of *Eastenders* two children, Ben and Abi, are shown sitting side by side after a falling out. Suddenly one of them says, 'Do you wanna play, then?' and that's it, argument over – for once, a realistic portrayal of relationships![8] What is clear across the age range is that this activity of restoring things is an essential component of children's theology of forgiveness. This becomes increasingly clear when the children talk about what cannot be forgiven:

> If you broke an unfixable thing, say, like in memory of a dead parent, or for example, if you chucked away my dead uncle's present of a watch, that would be unforgivable.
>
> (aged 9)

> Unforgivable sin is an unfixable breakage, something that is in the unchangeable past.
>
> (aged 9)

> Killing somebody that God likes the most. God would never, ever forgive this.
>
> (aged 5)

> God sometimes forgives for killing, but civil war is really bad, with people being killed from the same country, so it's unforgivable.
>
> (aged 6)

> I could never forgive someone for killing my cat. If someone hurt my cat, I would never ever forgive them, even if they said sorry, and that means that person would be sad for ever.
>
> (aged 5)

Almost all the examples of refusing to forgive relate to the impossibility of putting things right. Over and over again the children expressed the idea that reparation is an essential part of forgiveness, whether between people or between people and God. Restitution, reparation and reconciliation are all important in the process of forgiveness, and the children express a sense that some kind of compensation must be made even when it seems impossible. Repentance by itself is not enough. Jones[9] writes about the dynamic relationship between judgement and grace, forgiveness and repentance. Theologians suggest that there is a need to find a balance between these different facets of Christian doctrine. Bonhoeffer argues in his book *The Cost of Discipleship*[10] that without an emphasis on the consequence of sin, we fall into the danger of continuing to sin 'that grace may abound'. Child theology is a powerful voice into these discussions, offering a clear sense of the need to face the consequences of wrongdoing, and also the sense that forgiveness has a price attached to it. This clear sense of cause and effect is reflected when the children talk about consequences, including punishment. For example (after asking the children to focus on a picture of a mother and child, clearly in poverty):

> She was born into being poor – but sin caused the poverty.
>
> (aged 11)

> When my uncle was stabbed by his girlfriend's father the man had to go to jail, and maybe he was sad, but he had to be punished. God might forgive him for it, but it might take a long time.
>
> (aged 9)

> If you do something bad it will repeat on you later in life, so if you sin at 10 then when you are 30 the Devil might come back and repeat it.
>
> (aged 10)

If there is no possibility of reparation or restitution, then there is no possibility of forgiveness. The tendency of adult Christians – and perhaps all moral adults – would be to see this theology as 'wrong' (the clear admonition given in childhood 'two wrongs don't make a right!'), but one of the tasks of child theology is to make us reconsider our ways of understanding God and to see if there are different perspectives. Contemporary theologies of grace easily stray into cosy affirmation, ignoring the fact that sin is wrong and overlooking the notion that God is a God of justice. We can find ourselves uncomfortable with Jesus teaching about judgement as in Matthew 5ff., yet the children's perspective fits well with the Sermon on the Mount, not least with the instruction to go and be reconciled with others (Matthew 5.22). This need to demonstrate forgiveness in concrete ways can be challenging for adults. We come to church week after week and offer a confession of our sins, expressing repentance and regret, but a child theology of forgiveness clearly requires the words to be accompanied by actions.

It is possible to build this into a worship or liturgical experience. One of the most moving things I have been involved with is a time of repentance with young people aged 5–17 on a Christian camp, who were given the opportunity to be concrete in forgiveness. After a time of quiet they were encouraged to go and be reconciled, and the children moved quickly and readily to one another saying sorry, and offering hugs. For all kinds of reasons – inhibition, fear, rationality – adults find this kind of thing much more difficult. But children take at face value Jesus' instruction in the Sermon on the Mount:

> 'So if you are about to place your gift on the altar and remember that someone is angry with you, leave your gift there in front of the altar. Make peace with that person, then come back and offer your gift to God.'
>
> (Matthew 5.23-24).

This gives the children a clear opportunity to act out their theology of forgiveness in which action is necessary.

Forgiveness as received from God

Almost immediately we began to talk with the groups of children in school about sin and forgiveness it became clear that it was intrinsically tied up with spiritual awareness. Most of the children talked about God and about an inner sense of knowing. Adults would name this awareness of wrongdoing as 'conscience' or guilt, and might spend a long time agonizing over where this awareness of wrongdoing comes from. Recent questioning of social behaviours and constructs has revealed them as powerful influences, and cast suspicion on many of the ways in which we have formed our sense of right and wrong. So, for example, questions are now asked about whether widely held gender constructs affect the way we judge women's crimes more harshly. The notion of 'fault' or 'blame' across a whole spectrum of issues has resulted in changing values and practices. The influence of 'postmodernity' has paralleled a growth in individualism in western culture which means that there is a sense in which as long as no one is harmed then any behaviour is acceptable. Child theology makes us question this and returns us to a sense of absolute standards that exist beyond our own decision-making capacity:

> Sin is something wrong inside. It's like what you feel after you do something which will always haunt you.
>
> (aged 10)

> God makes it feel sorry inside you – the feeling of doing
> something bad.
>
> (aged 11)

> It hurts your feelings to make a sin or to have a sin against you.
>
> (aged 9)

> When I was in reception I pushed someone over and made them cry
> and I felt sad and wanted to run away and hide.
>
> (aged 6)

This sense of needing an external guide for behavioural decisions also
extended to wider ethical questions, so a group became involved in a
discussion about euthanasia. This is a good example of a child theological
framework in action. The discussion grew from the children's life experience,
rooted in family relationships. In particular, some of them had encountered the
death of a grandparent, and one girl in particular had recently watched that
person suffer and change as illness took hold. Although she had probably
heard some adult reflections and questions about this issue, she drew on her
own intuition to ask questions:

> Being killed for being ill is better than having pain in life. It is the right
> thing to do, but the person who does it will regret it. God will comfort
> them in this regret.

> Yes. It's better for people to die and be in a better place than suffering
> down here. I get worried about my grandparents – I know they're dead,
> but I still worry.

> Turning the machines off for an ill person – it's okay if God says to do it.
> I was very unhappy when my granddad was dying. I knew he wasn't
> well and that he wasn't happy and my school work went down. It's
> really sad that he's dead, and I miss him, but God cares for him in
> heaven now.
>
> (aged 11)

In some ways this moves beyond a theology of forgiveness and strays into the
territory of ethics, but issues can't always be neatly compartmentalized, and
the children were trying to express the difficulties surrounding sin and
forgiveness as their horizons began to broaden. This group of children were all
aged 10 and 11, and this more nuanced thinking also fits with developmental
models of childhood.[11] Children of this age are beginning to develop the
capacity for abstract thought and their theology reflects this. But their idea of

forgiveness also taps into notions of corporate sin, responsibility and forgiveness:

> *(Looking at picture of woman holding three children)*
>
> The sad woman in the picture. I think her husband has gone to war and died. But her poverty is caused by the government. They caused the sin and the whole government can't be forgiven, it's too big.
>
> An individual in the government could maybe be forgiven, but they could have resigned and campaigned against the issue instead of just going along with it.
>
> People have to do the forgiveness because they do the sin – it's like slavery. It's a human choice.

The issue of corporate forgiveness is very topical, for example in post-apartheid South Africa, and has also been expressed by leading public figures or called for by representatives of harmed groups. So descendants of the slave trade have called for a public apology, but it is not clear how this kind of action is linked to forgiveness. A child theology suggests a more direct connection, and a clear sense that actions need to be evident.

Recent writing on the theology of forgiveness opens up the complexity of the subject, showing how forgiveness is both a spiritual, sometimes specifically Christian concept, and also an intrapersonal human concern.[12] The youngest child interviewed showed an intuitive awareness that some issues might be more complex than others:

> *(She picks up a picture of a girl holding incense sticks and continues talking about forgiveness)*
>
> God does forgive people, this girl is saying 'I forgive you.' She's standing in front of a tomb of someone who had been naughty and was killed, but she is forgiving after death and God forgives people after death. It's the same with God, he forgives people after death, and sometimes it's not easy to understand, so I look at my Bible to make me feel better.
>
> (aged 5)

This child lacked the experiential framework to apply her theology into wider situations, and mostly grounded it in terms of her mother, brother and pets, but she also reached out beyond those boundaries to express something of the eternal nature of forgiveness, an issue also explored more widely in the theology of forgiveness. For Christians forgiveness offers the possibility that the past can be transformed, and the child is intuitively exploring this idea.

Acknowledging the mystical

The spiritual dimension of forgiveness was expressed using both intuitive and mystical language, particularly as the children began to move beyond the specifics of forgiveness in their own world to a more general discussion, often drawing on archetypes of light and dark to discuss the nature of good and evil:

> The devil has the moon and God has the sun, which is why the morning is the best time because it tells us that God is stronger.
>
> (aged 10)

> You might get bad luck if you commit a sin. The devil makes you do a sin, and if you do a bad thing you are possessed by the devil. God takes away this possession. The devil lives near the earth's core while God is up in heaven where it's always light.
>
> (aged 9)

> There is a diamond star in the sky that people see – this is the sign of God's forgiveness for them. They see it and are forgiven.
>
> (aged 5)

> Sin is dark and gloomy.
>
> (aged 10)

Images of dark and light, up and down are used throughout literature, film and art to explore notions of good and bad and even by the age of five the children will have been exposed to such imagery, not least in the Harry Potter books and films).[13] Yet it was startling to hear them drawing on this imagery in the context of forgiveness, almost echoing words from 1 John 1.5ff. with its language about deeds of darkness and living as children of light:

> If we say that we have fellowship with [God] while we are walking in darkness, we lie and do not do what is true; but if we walk in the light as he himself is in the light, we have fellowship with one another . . .
>
> (1 John 1.6-7)

Experientially, this language may link to their imaginative world, but it also seems to speak to instinctive archetypes that humanity has always referred to in exploring the nature of good and evil and our place within this framework.

This language is part of the third dimension of their theological framework – an awareness of mystery, which is explored through stories as well as play that involves the creation of invisible worlds and people. This is also linked to imaginative possibilities and creativity, but implies that child theology can be explored in terms of complex and mystical language, such as the language of liturgy and hymnody, as well as within the concrete experiences of their reality. Practically, this opens up the whole area of liturgies of confession and reconciliation, and as a Roman Catholic one of the children had a clear trust in the role of the priest:

> It's much better when you talk about it. Father x just listens and then tells you how to be right again. It's easy.
>
> (aged 9)

There was a clear confidence in the capacity of God to offer forgiveness:

> If you do a bad thing, you pray to God and ask for forgiveness.
>
> (aged 6)

> If you don't you get trapped. If you do pray you will be free.
>
> (aged 9)

> Forgiveness is saying sorry. I don't know really what kind of forgiveness Jesus had, but he makes the world better when it goes bad.
>
> (aged 6)

This accords with the intuitive understanding of sin as something that affects the whole person and echoes the words of absolution spoken in churches (although generally the children talking were not churchgoing children). It also suggests that being forgiven has positive consequences, which are experienced emotionally and expressed in almost bodily terms. The child quoted above talked of being 'free' and another child spoke of feeling tall again. This connects to the physicality of shame and pride as expressed in everyday speech – we hide our heads in shame and hold them high in pride. For the children, forgiveness, whether from God or another person, has similar consequences.

Yet this positive warm picture is modified by the clear understanding that just as there are unforgivable things between human beings, there are also things that God would not forgive:

> Unforgivable sin is an unfixable breakage, something that is in the past, and can't be changed. God couldn't forgive the killers of Jesus or forgive Judas. Paralysing members of the royal family would be unforgivable.
>
> (aged 9)

> God doesn't forgive everything – the person has to do something
> good.
>
> (aged 10)

This is where child theology can offend our adult ways of understanding God.
We want to correct this kind of understanding, and yet it acts as an antidote
to our culture's emphasis on affirmation without condemnation. We would
like our children to be gentle and kind, yet actually child development
theories[14] tell us that in this age group (7–11 approximately) children are very
literal and concrete thinkers, seeing the world in hard and fast ways. This is
borne out by their experience in family, classroom and playground and their
theology draws on this experience. Their understanding is of a God who
has rules and who needs to see restitution as well as repentance – actions,
not just words.

The challenge of child theology on forgiveness

> We are seeing at present a decoupling of forgiveness and sin; the
> practice of forgiveness is being embraced but the concept of sin is
> being rejected. The sense of sin led people in past generations to
> want to receive forgiveness. In contrast, it seems to be our
> self-pre-occupation that leads us now to want to be able
> to forgive.[15]

There is no doubt that in recent years there has been a shift away from the
presentation of the gospel in terms of the need for forgiveness towards an
emphasis on God as inclusive love. Volf suggests that God is presented within
contemporary western culture in two main guises: as implacable judge or as
doting grandparent. The notion of judge emerges from the idea that we can
negotiate with God, a reflection of the consumer culture in which we live
where everything can be bought or sold – so we try to make a deal with God.
However, the problem is, what happens if we break our arrangement or
renege on the deal? Inevitably we encounter God as judge – and if God is
judge then there will be punishment for wrongdoing. The notion of a
punishing God sits uneasily in a culture where individual choice is valued and
respected and therefore the pendulum has swung towards a God who is the
benevolent dispenser of gifts or doting grandparent. We take seriously Jesus'
words that we should love our neighbour as *ourselves*, and much emphasis is
placed on God as affirming and accepting. 'The world is sinful. That's why God
doesn't affirm it indiscriminately. God loves the world. That's why God doesn't
punish it in justice.'[16]

A child theology of forgiveness speaks to the heart of this dilemma and disturbs us from our comfort zone. The experience of life and relationships gives children a huge awareness of wrongdoing – they live with it every day. They break rules at home and at school, they clash in friendships and become aware of their own guilt. It has never surprised me that God chose a child, Samuel, to deliver a harsh message about sin and its consequences. Children understand this through experience and intuition. I once worked with a group of children praying for schools, and one child went up to another, jabbed him/her in the shoulder and said: 'God says you're a bully and it's got to stop.' An adult would have spent a long time agonizing about how to approach the situation, looked for justification, explored the issues (all of which happened subsequently!), but in the first instance it took another child to name and condemn the sin itself. This should make us think, look again at our own adult lives, where we are used to excusing behaviour, working with self-awareness and justifying ourselves. The child's awareness of sinfulness and its consequences is a reminder that we have all 'fallen short of the glory of God'. For children sin and forgiveness are inextricably linked.

Secondly, the process of forgiveness is clearly understood by children as something that needs to be experienced and is restorative. Much has been written about the need for reconciliation as an end result, but children see reparation as a key component to making forgiveness real. Repentance is expressed by words of apology but made real by actions that restore relationship. This picks up on the idea of forgiveness as a gift offered and then received.[17] If nothing changes as a result, then the act of forgiving hangs in a vacuum, something that the children grasp both intuitively and in the reality of their everyday lives.

Ultimately, a child theology of forgiveness is incredibly simple, yet like most simple ideas is also profound. Jesus took a child and placed her in the centre of his embrace and asked us to both value the child and to become like her. In their approach to forgiveness children give us a model of kingdom behaviour that is consistent with Jesus' teaching. I suspect they would be incredulous at the amount of time adults agonize and argue over forgiving: their clear-cut view of the world encourages us to move on by making good what has gone wrong. For adults this simplicity is overlaid by a thousand other questions and concerns, but listening to the children talking made me think that sometimes we just need to get on and do it. It is this simplicity that made the South African model so powerful[18] – a profound belief that wrongs can and should be put right.

The simplicity of a child theology of forgiveness is not just about behaviour but also about an understanding of God. Child theology challenges our understanding of God in two ways. First, it makes us rethink some of the ways we describe God, perhaps balancing out a contemporary theology that can be one-dimensional, ignoring notions of God as judge. Secondly, as feminist theology opened up the discussion about God as woman, so child theology should make us think about God as child. We may not feel comfortable with where that thinking takes us – although forgiving comes easily, it also comes under clear conditions – but that is the wonder of listening to children talk and accepting it as valid on its own terms. Forgiveness will always be difficult for us to grasp, whether we receive it from God or offer it to those who have hurt us. But child theology offers us new avenues to explore.

I began by suggesting that child theology might use a similar framework to that developed by other contemporary theologies, particularly feminist approaches. The starting point is experience, but whereas for many women a large part of that experience is rooted in oppression, for children the experience is one of imaginative possibility born out of the web of immediate relationships. This means that the theology that emerges will be distinctive and different, although there may be common patterns to be discovered. It will not only be the doctrine of forgiveness that looks different from a child's perspective and experience, but it may be that we are privileged to view new facets of God's amazing eternal nature.

Questions

1. What does the word 'forgiveness' mean to you?

2. 'Saying sorry doesn't work – it's just a word. It doesn't jump out into someone's life, it doesn't make the wrong better. You must do something nice for the person you have sinned against.' What might be the implications of these words and in what ways do they challenge your understanding of forgiveness? Take a specific occasion and outline various actions that might be appropriate in response.

3. Look at any stories about children and young people in today's newspaper. In which stories might acts of forgiveness begin to heal the situation? How might the kinds of forgiveness discussed by the children in this chapter make a difference?

4. Read the story of the woman taken in adultery (John 8.1-11). Try to imagine this kind of situation through the eyes of a child. What do you

think the child would see happening and what would the child make of Jesus' words and actions?

5.   What kinds of activity in your church create opportunities for forgiveness and reconciliation? Can you identify ONE occasion where children and adults could be given the opportunity to say sorry to one another and to hear words or actions of forgiveness?

8

Grace

Angela Shier-Jones

Introduction

God does not ignore us until we become adults. This simple fact is something that I am acutely aware of in my day-to-day engagement with children as a Methodist minister. It prompted my earlier explorations into the theology of childhood[1] and provided the initial idea behind this chapter. In Methodist theology, grace is that unmerited but essential favour without which it is impossible for anyone to live and experience life in all its fullness as God intended. But what does this mean for children? How does grace operate in childhood? In this chapter I will argue from my experience and perspective as a Methodist minister and theologian that children are not exempt from the necessity of grace, indeed I intend to show that they are in some ways more in need and in receipt of grace than most adults will ever be. I will also suggest that, as the author of all grace it is God who ultimately provides and enables grace to be responded to regardless of how it is given. Thus, although we may not always understand either the means or the extent of God's grace, we can be sure it is never accidentally or mistakenly given. I will propose that grace is the gift of a loving, caring and intelligent creator in order that that which is created might become more fully that which it was created to be. As adults, we can believe this; children, however, are dependent upon this being true. There is therefore a special relationship between children and grace which this chapter explicates with the specific help of stories about children and stories that children tell about themselves, in the anticipation that this too may become a means of grace, enabling other lives to flourish. As one child tells us:

> If God is someone then we are someone too. He'll make us someone if we let him. I hope He will – that's what you pray for: that He'll be something for you; if you've given Him a chance, by being mostly good. You can't be all good I know . . . You know I guess the Lord and

us, we're all in this together: us wanting to be saved, and Him wanting to save us.

(Junior – aged 12)[2]

God's gracious design?

Tony has no scars. Neither of his parents was arrested. They came to court voluntarily in a custody battle. They were divorced when Tony was four years old. He is now nine. The father tells Tony his mother is a whore, an evil woman. The mother tells Tony his father will kill him, his stepfather, and his half-brother. Tony twitches and stammers. He has attempted suicide twice. He is failing in school although he is a brighter than average child. Neither parent will consent to his hospitalization and no psychiatrist would give a professional opinion that Tony's mental health was endangered by remaining with his mother and stepfather. Without such evidence, I could not order the institutionalization of Tony. The rights of the family cannot be violated.

I gave Tony a paper and pencil and asked him to write a story while he was waiting in the anteroom during my conference with his parents. Tony wrote: 'Dear God, Please help me.'[3]

What led Tony to believe that God could help, or might want to help? We live in a world where children need 'rights' to protect them from all sorts of abuse, physical, emotional and even political abuse. Belief in a loving, caring and intelligent creator is not easy to reconcile with the vulnerability of certain creatures, humans included, during infancy and childhood. What can be deemed intelligent about designing something so completely and utterly dependent on others in its earliest years, not only for its very survival, but also for its formation? The only immediately obvious suggestions of intelligence seem to lie in the coping strategies that various species have evolved to offset what seems, at first glance at least, to be a rather glaring design flaw. The sheer numbers of tadpoles and turtle hatchlings for example, can be seen to provide a small measure of security for the survival of those particular species: the reproductive cycle of the rabbit and the mole similarly function as guarantor of the stability of those respective populations, the more frequently you reproduce, the more likely it is that some will survive. Human fecundity, however, cannot compare as a means of offsetting the losses incurred as a result of human frailty and dependence in childhood. Human intelligence and engineering skills, of the bio, socio and medical variety have done much to lower infant mortality in the western world, while education and psychology have helped to minimize some of the consequences of poor parenting during a child's formative years. Nonetheless, all too many children still suffer and even die as a direct consequence of being weak and dependent. Long-term scientific observation and the study of genetics have led to the formulation of many mechanistic theories of evolution which exclude even the possibility of external intelligent design. Things simply are as they are, it is claimed; the loss of life among the vulnerable and weak actively ensures the survival of the fittest. While such losses might be deemed acceptable or even inevitable for Professor Richard Dawkins and those who support his 'selfish gene' theory,[4] they pose a fundamental theological question for Christians: How can the basic design of humanity, which begins in the frailty and dependence of children, be reconciled with belief in a loving, intelligent creator God who 'loves all that he has made' and who 'has made nothing in vain'? I would say that there is only one feasible answer that does justice to the complexity of the issue: by grace. Human design is based on God's urgent desire to make available to as many as can receive and respond to it, the grace necessary for salvation, for life in all its fullness.

Such a bold statement requires clarification, not least because of the cost of this grace in terms of the lives of countless thousands of children who die every day of starvation, abuse, neglect or violence. Unfortunately, a full theodicy lies outside of the scope of this chapter, but in what follows I hope to demonstrate that far from being a design flaw, humans are lovingly created to be vulnerable and dependent. Infancy and childhood dependency is a means of grace, a God-given gift with the power to overcome a far more dangerous and costly threat to human life and human flourishing – the independence of human beings when separated and cut off from nurturing mutuality and relationships.

Dependence and grace

The relationship between grace and dependence can be based on the truism that all humans are ultimately dependent on God, regardless of their age, for their life and their salvation, but there is more to this relationship than simple hierarchical dependency. Children are made in the image of God: Scripture defines no upper or lower age limit to this. Although there is considerable dispute over exactly what it means to be made in the image of God, one thing is certain, it is not an exclusive, or merely allegorical or metaphorical state of being, but is something fundamentally inclusive which does not diminish our humanity, or reside in some way separate from it, but rather forms an integral part of it. There is, accordingly, something of the image of God in the risky[5] dependency of infancy and the open vulnerability of childhood. The sociologist Martinson puts it this way: 'If children in all their dependency are recognized as of equal worth with adults, it means that dependency can no longer be seen as something negative but must be taken into the model of what it means to be human.'[6] Christmas is an annual reminder that when the Word became flesh, it was not fully grown, mature, adult flesh, but weak and dependent, swaddled flesh. What is less seldom acknowledged, however, is the relationship between that dependent state and grace, in spite of the fact that John's Gospel states it quite clearly: 'And the Word became flesh and lived among us, and we have seen his glory, the glory as of a father's only son, full of grace and truth' (John 1.14).

Adoptionism was a heresy not simply because it denied the full divinity of Christ; by attempting to bypass the birth narratives and the idea of the 'Christ child', it also denied the full humanity of Christ. It was as a child in a state of total dependence on frail flesh and on human relationships which included a 'foster father' and an immature mother, that Christ entered the world full of grace and truth. Grace and dependency are thus inseparable as the mode and means of God's gift of salvation and reconciliation – of life. By grace we are saved from all that would hinder life – independence, rather than *inter*dependence.

Sin is that which separates: it separates people from God, from others, and from their created nature. The 'original sin', which the Church teaches is inherited from Adam, is not the mythical sin of eating fruit, or even of disobedience (although the originating sinful impulse led eventually to disobedience). The original sin that is described in Genesis and that is repeatedly recorded in the Old and the New Testaments is the sin of separation, the desire for and subsequent insistence upon independence: independent thought, independent action, independent judgement, independent living. Time and again the Old Testament describes the process as a 'turning away' from God. The tendency to sin, to separate, to become independent from God, from others and from their true nature is what humanity needs saving from. An *inter*dependent life with God is what salvation is for.

In spite of, or perhaps in some instances because of, their experience of childhood, most adults have a well-developed aversion to at least one dimension of dependence – namely that of being dependent (the aversion is not so strongly evidenced with regard to being depended upon!). Our society clearly values independence, lauding it as a sign of maturity and even intelligence. Children are therefore repeatedly taught and encouraged to 'stand on their own two feet' and to become independent. Being too clingy, holding on too tightly to the apron strings are all frowned upon. Children must 'come of age', by which is meant assume not only adult responsibilities but assume them independently.[7] All of which is in direct contradiction to the repeated message of the gospel which stresses the importance of interdependence. On the contrary, the warning is given that unless we become as little children we will not enter the kingdom of heaven. Paul's comment: 'When I was a child, I spoke like a child, I thought like a child, I reasoned like a child; when I became an adult, I put an end to childish ways' (1 Corinthians 13.11) is not meant to indicate the partial nature of our earthly life, it is not meant as an injunction against the state of childhood. Rather, as Coles notes:

> All this talk about being 'mature' and growing up and progressing through stages and phases misses the point of how important it is to retain that connection – not to 'the inner child' but to the sense of vulnerability and yearning that childhood is about.[8]

The message of loving dependence, not just on God, but on one another is found repeatedly on the lips of Christ in both parable and direct teaching form, culminating in the great commandment to love God and to love your neighbour as yourself (Mark 12.30-31).

The extent to which desire for independent, separated, maturity is offensive to God is highlighted by Jesus in the parable of the prodigal son. Although most commonly interpreted as a story of God's enduring faithfulness, the parable is also a direct condemnation of human selfishness and individualistic behaviour. To ask for a share of inheritance before the father is dead is tantamount to wishing the father dead in order to be relieved of the burden of keeping the commandment to 'honour your father and your mother'. The parable is at pains to point out that real relationships cannot be bought – neither can they be lost. The sort of selfish independence that leads to separation from community and the family threatens life, identity, honour and integrity to the extent that relational dependence – even that of a slave, is always preferable. The generosity of the father in welcoming the child back into the family is indicative of the extent and the purpose of God's grace. Grace is the gift that is given by God to maintain and sustain the relationships that enable humanity to keep the commandment of Christ and live in loving interdependence. Grace may therefore include an act of forgiveness, but it is always forgiveness with a purpose, namely to restore a relationship. The gospels teach us that childhood is one of the primary means of making that gift of relationship known and of enabling it to be received.

Childhood as a means of grace

Antoine de Saint-Exupéry's preface to *The Little Prince* declares that 'All grown-ups were once children – although few of them remember it.'[9] Children are not adults, adults are failed children. Children only grow up to become independent adults if they have not received sufficient grace to enable them to mature instead into children of God. Karl Rahner is one of many theologians who have argued that the human adventure is to become a child to an ever-increasing extent. His claim is that 'childhood is not a state that only applies to the first phase in our lives in the biological sense. Rather it is a basic condition which is always appropriate to a life that is lived aright.'[10] In particular, the form that childhood takes must include a 'readiness to be controlled by another'.[11] To be a child is to be dependent and without control.

As vulnerable dependents, children enter the world demanding and expecting grace. From the moment of birth, they scream for food, for shelter, for attention, even though they are incapable of doing anything to earn these things other than exist in a relationship with their gracious providers. Children have no control over how graciously, or otherwise, their needs will be met. In most circumstances the relationship on which the child's demands for grace are made is one of loving care. It is also possible, however, for the relationship that binds children to their providers to owe more to societal duty than to filial care: this is irrelevant to the child who remains both needful and expectant of grace. It is, however, this universal expectation of grace that is so revealing of the state of childhood as a deliberately divinely appointed means of grace. There is an unquestionable equality in the expectation of the child: colour, race, gender, even the religious allegiance of the parents, are all irrelevant, as are ability or disability, future sexuality and whether or not the child is born into extreme wealth or extreme poverty. The expectation of children is that their needs will be met graciously: love and attention will be given, food will appear and immediate salvation from all that threatens their lives will be provided, by a community of care.

According to Scripture, childhood *should* provide the opportunity for grace to flow in and through relationships regardless of socio-political boundaries and barriers. Jesus healed the daughters of both a Jewish woman (Luke 8.41-55) and a Gentile woman (Mark 7.25-29). He also makes it clear that God watches over children (Matthew 18.2-10). In the Old Testament, similarly, the Israelites are told repeatedly that the care of children in their society must extend to the orphans. God is declared as the protector and father of orphans, who will respond to their cries if they are abused (e.g. Exodus 22.22-23, Deuteronomy 10.17-18). The writer of the epistle of James encapsulates all this by saying 'Religion that is pure and undefiled before God, the Father, is this: to care for orphans and widows in their distress, and to keep oneself unstained by the world' (James 1.17). Gracious care as modelled in Scripture, however, is more than the provision of food and shelter, it is the provision of those things in and through a nurturing, protective, loving, relationship.

According to psychologists, psychological health is dependent on three main areas of need being met.[12] The first is safety. Children need to be protected from the dangers of the environment into which they have been born. The second is support, defined in terms of the sense of belonging, the close contact and love of others. The third area is self-esteem, which is defined as the worthiness of the individual as conveyed through appreciation and interaction with others. These same three areas are paralleled in terms of the spiritual health and well-being of a child. Children need to be protected from the dangers of religiosity and secularity, supported by belonging to a godly community and enabled to develop the awareness of their intrinsic value as part of God's loving creation. All three areas, whether psychologically or spiritually speaking, are contingent on grace, on the undeserved favour of others with whom trust can be established which will allow the child to experience close, supportive relationships.

Communities fail when they do not respond graciously to the needs of the children placed in their care. One of the things which we do not often think about is that a failure to provide grace as well as sustenance can cause serious harm to a child.

For example, at 18 years of age, the only God that Patience[13] knew was the God of condemnation. Patience was raised in a strict Wesleyan holiness movement in Africa, and weekly church attendance had drummed into her that children are naturally naughty and that God always punishes such naughtiness. Grace was unknown. Religion equated to dutiful obedience. Patience's relationship with God was dominated by the need to 'be good', to beg for forgiveness and to accept the failures and abuse in her life as God's punishment – God, she had been taught, only blesses the good. When she was twelve years old, and her parents were in the process of separating, she experienced a powerful moment of grace which brought her to her knees in tears of joy at the unexpected presence of a loving, caring 'Father God'. The intensity of that moment never left her. It was, however, so contrary to everything else that she had been taught to believe about her own relationship with God in the church that it created almost a split spiritual personality. Within the secular world, Patience is a civil servant who is also studying part-time for higher professional qualifications. In the church setting, however, Patience behaves, and relates to others, in every way more like a child of twelve than a successful young professional. She is unable or unwilling to think interdependently on matters of faith, and remains perpetually afraid of the judgement of the church elders – and of God.

It is already well recognized that 'when a child's basic psychological and physical needs are not met, the result is a stunting of psychological growth and self-esteem, a failure to thrive, and a deprivation of opportunity extending into adult life'.[14] What is true of the physical and psychological would also seem to be true of the spiritual. When a child's spiritual needs are not met, the result is a stunting of spiritual growth and self-awareness, a failure to live fully, and shows a deprivation of grace extending into adult life. The evidence suggests, however, that the Church tends to be frighteningly unaware of the spiritual needs of the children in its care. When a selection of ministers, for example, were asked to prioritize the times in a child's life that they needed the ministry of the church, they listed the following in order of importance:

> Day of baptism
> First day of school
> Day of first communion or confirmation
> Day of departure for college or armed forces
> Wedding
> Death of parents or grandparents.[15]

This should be compared with the answers given by children aged 6 through to 16 when asked to list the times they felt the need to see or speak with a minister:

> The day your best friend moves away
> When you get left back in school or aren't selected for a team
> When parents divorce
> When your dog/cat/pet dies
> When a kid you know dies
> When parents or grandparents die.[16]

The lack of awareness of the spiritual needs of children is most often interpreted by children as a lack of grace precisely because it is indicative of a failed (or non-existent) relationship. A minister in a relationship of grace would know when the child needed gracious care. The pressing question for the Church is: to what extent does this failure affect the child's belief in the possibility of a real relationship with a loving, caring, creator God?

A community of grace?

A child's spiritual growth is evidently in a close symbiotic relationship with social growth. Children borrow images and models from their own life experiences to describe, understand and respond to the grace of God that surrounds them. If a child grows up surrounded by many loving and gracious providers the tendency is to develop an understanding of grace as the unmerited, free and welcome generosity of those in power and authority over the child. Extending the circle of grace to include God is often a case of recognizing the addition of one more generous provider in a position of power and authority. This tends to be so regardless of the wealth or poverty of the family background as is evident in the story of a seven-year-old boy called Cliffe from the South Bronx, one of the largest racially segregated concentrations of poor people in America. His story is told by Jonathon Kozo. Cliffe, he says,

> has an absolutely literal religious faith. When I ask him how he pictures God, he says, 'He has long hair and He can walk on the deep water.' To make sure I understand how unusual this is, he says, 'Nobody else can.' He seems to take the lessons of religion literally also. Speaking of a time his mother sent him to the store 'to get a pizza' – 'three slices, one for my mom, one for my dad, and one for me' – he says he saw a homeless man who told him he was hungry.
>
> 'But he was too cold to move his mouth! He couldn't talk.'
> 'How did you know that he was hungry if he couldn't talk?'
> 'He pointed to my pizza.'
> 'What did you do?'
> 'I gave him some!'
> 'Were your parents mad at you?'
> He looks surprised by this. 'Why would they be mad?' he asks. 'God told us, Share!'[17]

Cliffe's story is a powerful reminder that children know the language of grace and are often puzzled at 'adult' complications over what should come naturally if God's free grace is understood aright. Questions such as cost, worth and value are irrelevant. Who knows better than a child what it is to experience hunger and expect that hunger to be addressed? In such instances, children's theological understanding of grace can seem almost instinctive and, as such, directly challenges the conditional generosity enforced by secular meritocracies or religious rituals. Daniel, for example, enjoyed receiving Holy Communion. He particularly liked the fresh bread that was always given to him on such occasions. Following one very important service of Holy Communion which had been shared with an illustrious preacher, Daniel asked the minister, in the preacher's presence, if he could have some of the 'left-over' bread.[18] The minister turned to the visiting preacher for advice, 'What would you do?' she asked, only to receive the reply, 'I'm not sure what the liturgical protocol is on such an occasion.' 'Well,' said the minister, 'neither am I, but I'm not going to be the one who denies him a second helping at Jesus' table!' Daniel received his extra bread and Jesus remained the gracious host that Daniel knew and expected him to be.

A child's knowledge of the generosity and grace of God is formed in the context of the generosity or otherwise of their parents and the grace shown to them in their familial and other significant relationships, such as with their minister, teacher or pastoral visitor. It is well known, for example, that children often mix together in their understanding of God, real and imagined perceptions of their parents.[19] Research into the correlation between perceptions of parents and images of God has conclusively proven that, 'When children perceived their parents as nurturing and powerful, God too was perceived as nurturing and powerful.'[20] Correspondingly, when a child's experience of gracious relationships has been limited then, regardless of the wealth of the family, there is often a correspondingly stunted appreciation of the potential for grace that is open to it:[21]

> A child who has a history of abuse expects others to be rejecting, hostile, and unavailable. A child who has been neglected (physically, emotionally, or both) expects others to be unresponsive, unavailable, and not willing to meet his or her needs. Maltreated children bring these expectations to relationships, and they respond to others in a fashion consistent with their expectations.[22]

Sometimes, such children struggle to comprehend the possibility even of a God of grace, a God who desires a relationship with them: they are far more at ease with the distant, authoritarian image of God presented in some parts of the Old Testament. For these children, the God of the wilderness wanderings who keeps a safe distance can seem more familiar than the God who reaches out to children and sits them on his knee to bless them.

The tendency in the western world to shrink the community of care for a child to that of the immediate family is therefore not only sociologically and economically dangerous, it poses a real threat to the spiritual formation of children by narrowing the opportunities for gracious relationships to be witnessed and experienced. It is a further example of the pervasive sin of separation. Even in the days of disposable nappies and preprocessed food it is simply not possible for two competent parents to raise a child entirely on their own, cut off from any other kind of help. A whole community committed to the well-being of the child is needed. To quote the African proverb, 'It takes a village to raise a child':

> We call this context a 'village' because people are linked together by mutual need and a common covenant. In such a setting, families are no less responsible for their children, but they rely on one another and the institutions they create and sustain to participate in the process of raising children. The image of the village affirms a fundamental truth about the interdependence of all of life.[23]

In his theology of family living, Anderson examines the increasing diversity of family structures, from the extended family model through to the single-parent model and, although he is able to recognize something God-given and creative about new structures, he remains insistent that, 'The commitment to interdependence is essential both for the family as an organism in the world and for each particular family unit.'[24] The demands that children make and the expectations that they have are a constant reminder that no single person can ever fully satisfy the need for grace in another. Only in community can a child grow and mature from being dependent into being interdependent rather than separated and independent.

The persistence of grace

A community of care is thus the primary means of grace for every child. The knowledge of this is so integral to the human design that children seek out communities of care and/or create imaginary communities as required, populating them with imaginary friends and relatives in an attempt to satisfy their need for grace. Children seek out love and affirmation and will even automatically insinuate themselves deliberately and trustingly into what they perceive to be caring family relationships and groupings. They are opportunists when it comes to affection, and are happy to borrow modes of belonging and dependence from friends and families as the following story from the research of Herbert Anderson and Susan B. W. Johnson illustrates:

> When I was eight, I went on my first overnight to a girlfriend's house. We lived on the same street, and our families were very close. In the morning, after breakfast, I sat watching cartoons with my friend and her two sisters on the sofa in the family room. As their father prepared to leave for work, he came in and kissed them all on the forehead to say goodbye for the day. I was at the end of the line on the sofa and he kissed me too. In my own family there was no kissing or hugging or holding of each other. I held onto that kiss like a treasure, like a tangible sign that families could be places of safe affection.
>
> (Wanda)[25]

Children also seem to be aware that the relationships which they crave are not confined to the so called 'traditional' family of two loving biological parents:

> Children's criteria for family life included: the presence of children; living with at least one parent; a sense of security and a place to belong; and, most important of all, being able to give children unconditional love and care – *'people who never ever don't care about you'*, as one child put it.[26]

Study after study shows that the way family life is lived is more important to children than what family life ought to look like.

The fact that children will repeatedly infringe socially constructed boundaries of race, gender, status and even the nuclear family in pursuit of love and affirmation serves as a constant reminder of how artificial such separations and distinctions really are. They serve only as a barrier to grace and to growth in grace. As with any means of grace, however, childhood can be, and all too often is, abused. Children's trusting expectation of a gracious community of care renders them frighteningly vulnerable to social, physical, emotional and sexual abuse, as Tony's story earlier testifies.

What is remarkable is the persistent confidence in grace that abused children often demonstrate. Children are not easily dissuaded from the search for grace. It is only when the child's need for grace is repeatedly not met that the child ceases automatically to expect grace:

> A child who has been neglected (physically, emotionally, or both) expects others to be unresponsive, unavailable, and not willing to meet his or her needs. Maltreated children bring these expectations to relationships, and they respond to others in a fashion consistent with their expectations.[27]

In spite of such claims, research into the psychological and emotional maturity of children who have been abused has demonstrated that the trust and expectation of loving grace still lingers, providing the potential for reconciliation – or further abuse. 'Despite grave misgivings about and sometimes even fear of their parents, children still love them and want to give their parents freedom to fail.'[28] Children who do not receive grace, or whose expectation of grace has been repeatedly abused, are, it would seem, miraculously often still able and, almost inconceivably still choose, to be gracious in their turn – a powerful testimony to the predominance in human design of grace as that which creates and maintains human relationships.

Law and grace

Throughout the history of the Church, grace has frequently been defined in strict opposition to law: either we are saved by grace, or we are not. The idea that grace and law can collaborate to ensure the proper growth and development of a child is not new, however, in spite of the fact that it was not until the last century that a comprehensive attempt was made to safeguard the child's expectation of grace by law. Legal rights for children are often justified on the basis that they are necessary to prevent children from being abused by families, communities and societies. It is, however, a harsh reality that a significant proportion of those who abuse children are themselves children[29] and any realistic theology of law and grace must take such figures into account.

The cruelty of children is as well known, if not as openly culturally owned, as the innocence of children is. While children's bullying behaviour is often explained away as a 'stage' that a child is passing though or 'cry for attention', the truth is that children are no more exempt from selfish inclinations than adults are. The shock of such crimes as the murder of James Bulger and the school killings in America appear to stand as irrefutable proof of Augustine's belief that children and infants possess an innate depravity: such innocence as can be ascribed to children is, he believed, due to their physical weakness alone.

Although such sentiments might offend the contemporary western romantic idealized view of children as 'little angels', there is strong scriptural warrant for them outside of the narrative of the 'Fall'. God's declares in Genesis, for example, that 'the inclination of the human heart is evil from youth' (Genesis 8.21) and the Psalmist writes: 'Indeed, I was born guilty, a sinner when my mother conceived me' (Psalm 51.5) and 'The wicked go astray from the womb; they err from their birth, speaking lies' (Psalm 58.3). Biblically speaking, children are considered to stand in justifiable need of divine grace for their salvation.

As every parent and child carer knows, children learn very quickly how to use their apparent innocence and vulnerability to serve their own ends. A child might cry, for example, after a fall to try to elicit a hug or some other means of attention even when knowingly neither hurt nor injured. A lack of complete innocence in action, however, does not necessarily imply a deliberate intent to sin. Can such actions be considered 'sins' to the extent that a child needs to be saved from them? The fact that children are not always fully cognizant of their motives or actions prompts the question as to whether, or when, children can be held individually accountable for their 'sins' and hence stand in need of grace. Given a child's dependency on others in the early stages of their life, would it not be more just for the burden of their sin, such as it might be, to be borne by those who bear the responsibility of educating them and keeping them safe from harm?

Responsible grace?

In the legal system of England and Wales children below the age of ten are not deemed criminally responsible. Until fairly recently, a presumption of *doli incapax* was also applied to children of 10 to 13 years of age. Children in this age range were presumed to not know the difference between right and wrong and consequently to be incapable of committing a crime because they lacked the necessary criminal intent. In Judaism, children are held accountable before God for keeping the Torah from 13 years plus one day for boys and 12 plus one day for girls. The responsibility for any contraventions of the law by a child prior to this age lies with the parents – even if the child had been fully aware of what they were doing and the consequences of their actions. Islam likewise recognizes different levels of accountability based on age. A child under seven is held blameless. From the age of seven until puberty, a child can be rewarded in heaven for their good deeds, but their bad deeds are not counted against them. From the age of puberty, however, a child is classed as an adult and is therefore fully accountable before God.

Christianity, however, does not have any universally agreed age or even doctrine of accountability. Some Christian traditions teach that children have only sinned if they have knowingly sinned, while others insist on the letter of the proclamation that 'all have sinned and fall short of the glory of God' (Romans 3.23): every child, accordingly, bears the stain of original sin. In spite of this discrepancy, however, there is now almost universal agreement that baptism is both an acknowledgement of the need for grace, as well as a means of grace for the child, regardless of the age of the person being baptized.[30] In baptism a child is made a member of the Body of Christ, and is enabled to take their place within the loving gracious community which they have been designed to both hunger for, and seek after. The sin of separation is stripped of its power to alienate and limit the grace of God by virtue of the child being known as a child of God and part of God's extended family – the Church. In the Methodist baptismal service, for example, the minister prays that the child who is to be baptized may 'be born to new life in the family of your Church'.[31]

From a child's perspective the question of sin is more troublesome and less easily understood or dealt with, not least because of the conflicting messages children receive from those they turn to as models of gracious and 'good' behaviour. The maxim 'don't do as I do, do as I tell you' often betrays the lie of what is universally 'good' or 'right'. Grace, once understood as the undeserved, but seemingly endless supply of love, affection and everything else that makes life liveable to the child, becomes mixed up, almost without warning, with undeserved forgiveness for as yet unknown, but nonetheless punishable sins:

> Dear God,
>
> How do you decide what is good and what is bad? Sometimes when I want to do something, they say it is good, but sometimes they say it is bad, but I don't know why.
>
> From Cathal[32]

For the children of religious families this confusion is all the more distressing because it is unclear to the child whether the grace of forgiveness that is needed, is the forgiveness of the parent – or of God – or both!

This transformation of grace from the means of living life well, to the means of being forgiven for sins committed, occurs gradually as the child is educated and inculturated. As children grow, they are encouraged by their family and society to move from dependence to independence. At the same time, they are taught to respond to the grace that they receive through such simple requests as 'say please' or 'say thank you'. Consequently, children learn that a positive response to grace often promotes more grace. It is not long, however, before the child begins to realize that that which they were able to take for granted at a younger age as being 'free' and 'gracious' actually comes with a price attached: all grace is costly grace.

Costly grace

At first the cost is negligible: a smile, a please or a thank you, but as the child matures, so gradually grace is replaced with familial, communal and religious 'law' and the child learns the necessity of 'earning' favour through obedience. More importantly, the child learns that disobedience entails the loss of favour – even with those who were previously gracious to them. The love and support that was once offered as grace, that is, as an unconditional gift, is now frequently separated into seemingly unrelated independent components, each of which can be now only be conditionally offered. Parents learn to trade for things within the relationship. A parent's affection is earned by 'good behaviour', food is a reward for good manners and keeping elbows off the table, shelter is deserved by keeping the bedroom clean, a good-night hug is dependent on having washed behind the ears, and so on. Conversely, bad behaviour can be met with punishments which underline the dependency and the harm caused by resisting it. So children are subject to deprivation of grace, whether it is in withholding treats, being 'grounded' or sent to bed. When these things happen the child is subjected to a state of separation which feels horrible and not at all the kind of way to live. Making up and being forgiven affirms love and gracious care once again and feels wonderful. In all this, the child remains dependent, but seemingly now on law, not on grace.

What becomes true in the family is often mirrored in the child's relationship with the Church and with God. From identity and a sense of belonging being given as an act of grace, the child moves to understanding that belonging, being a part of God's family, and religious identity are somehow dependent on certain behaviour patterns and keeping certain rules:

> *Tom* (11-7): How do you become a Catholic? 'You gotta study your religion, study the catechism, receive communion and first confession.'
>
> *Beth* (12-5): How do you become a Protestant? 'Well, you are baptized first and worship in the Protestant way and follow Protestant rules.'[33]

The introduction of 'salvation' and 'damnation' or 'reward' and 'obedience' into what had formerly been understood as a gracious relationship is evidently puzzling to children and can often lead to serious misunderstandings and lasting harm. Children of divorced parents, for example, often blame themselves for their parents' separation out of a mistaken understanding that it was their failure to be obedient that led to the withdrawal of a parent's affection for the other. 'Similarly, the majority of abused children report that they blame/d themselves for the abuse, that they suffer/ed and that in some way not fully understandable, they deserve/d the treatment that they receive/d at the hands of their abusers.'[34]

The idea that children have an innate sense of justice that would enable them to intuitively grasp the principles of obedience and reward as a substitute for grace and favour is highly questionable. Children learn and develop an understanding and appreciation of justice experientially and, as such, their learning is extensively culturally conditioned. The young male child, for example, raised in a country where it is still considered normal to ignore or marginalize the education of girls would see nothing unjust or ungracious in his sister being prevented from learning or attending school. Children do, however, very quickly develop their own sense of what is 'fair'. Abused children, for example, will often admit to behaviour that could prompt disciplinary action while nonetheless rejecting the intensity of the discipline that is administered to them: 'One 14-year-old remarked, "I wasn't no angel neither. I did things wrong, you know . . . they had like 3/4 of the reasons to hit me, but not that hard." '[35]

Children often recognize that the choices they make have consequences, even if they still lack the necessary cognitive or intuitive skills to inform and enable them to make the necessary judgements. This is something that they tend to be well aware of and which they justifiably categorize as unfair. Even when they are aware of the part that retribution can play in making the world a fairer place, however, children are reluctant to favour it. In a fascinating study, children of all ages were asked which of the two endings to the Cinderella story they thought most appropriate, the first ending where everyone lived happily ever after, or the second where the two ugly sisters who had abused Cinderella were punished by having their eyes pecked out by birds. Time and time again, the children repeatedly favoured forgiveness over retribution.[36]

Church and society may value 'free will', but from the child's perspective there is little that is recognizable as 'free' in the limited choices that govern their lives while they remain so dependent on others for their education, information and hence survival. Thus children know best that there is no real choice to be made between grace and human freedom. Grace, from a child's perspective, *is* freedom – freedom from being required to make (probably wrong) individual choices without the wherewithal to make them.

In spite of the educated transition from grace to law, from undeserved favour to rewarded obedience, most children cling tenaciously to an expectation of a community of grace and are exceedingly reluctant to give up the ideal. It is at this point that a community of grace can make the most significant impact on the life of a child. When grace has been replaced by 'laws' and/or expectations that exceed the child's ability to either fully comprehend or comply with them, all that the child is able to do is appeal to the grace of a higher authority. By their baptism, children have the right to make that appeal, and to expect that, contrary to what their parents or society might say, in Christ, their appeal will be heard:

> Dear God,
>
> My grandma got angry with me because I broke her pot. I didn't know we weren't allowed to play with the pot. She didn't tell us not to. Can you tell her it wasn't my fault. Thank you very much.
>
> Hatty.[37]

The way in which children pray and talk about God is very revealing of the particular understanding of grace as God's ability to cut through 'law' to make, repair and restore relationships:

> Our minister told us one day in a church sermon that Jesus knew what it is to feel left out and when he said that, I thought of how you can feel in school – you're alone, and no one gives a damn (that's how my father talks). When he died he knew the score here, and he must remember that – how he felt – while He's in heaven.
>
> (Charlie aged 10)[38]

Charlie's story shows an amazing insight into the understanding of grace as given by the cross in Christ. His words echo those spoken from a neighbouring cross: 'Jesus, remember me when you come into your kingdom' (Luke 23.42). Charlie has discovered that what God gave us in Christ was someone who didn't forget how it feels to be alone somewhere where no one gives a damn. Grace is not just about generous forgiveness where God forgives and forgets our sin – it's about generous remembering too. God remembers what we really need.

Conclusion

Grace does not change according to age: the generosity of God in identifying with us, in knowing, loving, forgiving and remembering us in Christ, is not dependent on how young or how old we are. Our ability to grasp the important consequences of such grace at an intuitive level does, however, seem to have a tendency to diminish with age. Most children seldom question their need for grace until forced to do so – it is, quite simply, the way in which they are made. Children accept their dependence on others and, as a rule, have to be taught and encouraged to value independence. Many, thankfully, do not completely succeed but learn instead to value interdependence and to find their identity within that. The harm that separated independence causes and the extent to which it is contrary to the design of human life is questionably a measure of how much childhood itself can be seen as a means of grace.

'The survival of the human community, and all of creation together, hinges on the belief that interdependence in society, like reconciliation in the family, is a necessary ideal even though it often eludes us.'[39] Global warming, the risk to the planet, has forced humanity to reassess the pride that it places on individuality and independence. The recognition of human childhood as a divinely appointed means of grace provides an opportunity for humanity to own the ideal of reconciliation and to value it above all things.

But all grace is both risky and costly. When viewed from the perspective of children and childhood, grace is recognizable as both the great equalizer that liberates and empowers the weak, giving strength and purpose in dependent vulnerability, and as the risky precursor to abuse and exploitation. All of us begin our lives totally dependent on another human being for life. The first sounds that we recognize are the heartbeats and voices of those entrusted with the means of grace to enable us to live and flourish – or not. We are cut loose from the womb to enter into the world as children, weak and helpless, vulnerable and dependent. But above all this, by grace, we also enter life with the potential to grow, to become more than we once were – to become community.

This is God's gracious gift and the reason why those who mistakenly become adults are enjoined by God to once again become as little children; in order that they might grow in grace and so grow more fully into the image that they bear.

Questions

1. What do you understand by 'grace'?

2. This chapter tells the story of Cliffe, who automatically shared his food with a homeless person. What do you think this tells us about the grace of God towards human beings?

3. Draw a spider diagram with yourself at the centre and all your

important relationships attached. Fill in as many interrelationships as you can. What does this diagram tell you about interdependence between human beings? How significant are children in your diagram?

4. Read one of the accounts of the Nativity. Where is the operation of God's grace in this story? Who are the recipients of God's grace and in what way is the presence of Jesus as a child important as both as focus and mediator of grace to others?

5. This chapter tells us about grace as flowing naturally from a mutually supporting and loving community. Thinking about your own situation, what ONE thing might be changed to put children more firmly at the heart of a loving and supportive community?

9

Salvation

John Pridmore

Through the eyes of a child

What we believe depends on where we are. Theology is necessarily contextual. The context of a Christian understanding of children and salvation is the world as the child finds it. That world is many worlds. The world where this chapter happens to be written – home for two happy and healthy small children – is relatively affluent and, so far as there can be such absolutes, entirely secure. Many children experience a very different world, in deep pockets of dire poverty, in the 'north' as well as in the impoverished 'south'.

In this chapter we aim to explore the issue of salvation 'through the eyes of a child', and not just through the eyes of the toddlers who distract me as I write. Theology will not say exactly the same about the child in prosperous and untroubled circumstances as about the abused child, the orphaned child, or the chronically sick child. It follows that, if a theology of children's salvation is to be authentic, the child's voice must be heard, even if – especially if – that child has 'no language but a cry'.[1] Only as we are attentive to the experience of childhood, so often the endurance of suffering, will our understanding of childhood, and of the salvation of children, rise above sophistry.

We start where the child is. Staying with the child, we turn to the Bible – especially to the teaching of Jesus of Nazareth about children – and to Christian tradition. We study those texts and explore that heritage, with the child alongside us to keep our feet on the often very hard ground of the child's world. We then take what we have learned from Scripture and tradition, as we have tried to see them from the child's perspective, and ask how what we have learned might apply to his or her experience. Then – this above all – we set about what we must do. As we take action, we find ourselves sent back to the Bible and to what we say we believe. And so the circle – theologians call it 'the hermeneutic circle' – goes on.

This approach is, famously, that of 'liberation theology'. Liberation theology is about liberation. It's about how slaves can be set free. Its mission statement is Jesus' sermon in the synagogue in Nazareth with its words about release to the captives and liberty to the oppressed (Luke 4.16-29). But 'liberation theology' is also *about theology*, about how theology itself can be liberated if it is set free from the places where it is usually confined: child-free zones such as universities and, alas, many churches. Liberation theology – and its day is not quite done – has been powerful because it has come, or at least to the extent it has come, not from academic experts but from poor people in poor places, from the marginalized and the powerless. As such, it is a methodology well fitted to help us form a Christian estimate of childhood, the stage of life when we are most vulnerable.

'Lord, give to men who are old and tougher, the things that little children suffer.'[2] The statistics recording the plight of children in our twenty-first-century world are readily available. Each year UNICEF publishes its report, *The State of the World's Children*. These annual reports and UNICEF's other publications are there on the Web.[3] For example, a recent UNICEF report tells us that in sub-Saharan Africa there are over 48 million orphans, 12 million of them orphaned as a result of the AIDS epidemic. The facts and figures are there at the click of a mouse. It is less easy to see in these figures the face of the individual child, still less easy to see *out of* those eyes. But we must seek the grace of a baptized imagination to do just that if our theological reflection on children and salvation is to be more than a gavotte, pleasing to those who take part in it but of no consequence to anyone else.

To help us come alongside the children whose salvation we are presuming to discuss, it will be helpful – rather than once more rehearsing the readily available statistics – to have in our mind's eye some specific images.

I think of the first child I buried. He suffered from severe cerebral palsy. He was totally paraplegic and was wholly dependent on his single mother, who trundled him around on a huge cumbersome gurney. He was unable to speak. He survived until his early teens. My second image is a sharply imprinted memory. The toddler at my feet was treating me like a tree. I was someone fun to climb. Eventually he reached my arms where he settled comfortably in total trust. Only then did I notice that this child, picked out of a Calcutta gutter by Mother Teresa or by one of the sisters of her order, was totally blind. A more recent image – a grinning child, looking about 13, holds a gun at the head of a much younger child who also has a gun in his hand.

This picture on the front page of the *The Guardian* was taken on a street in Baghdad, where, we learn, children like to play at beheading people.[4] A final image recalls us to the poor places in our own society. I am thinking of the child who fell asleep in the assembly I was conducting in the primary school attached to our inner city church. He slept, not from boredom, but from weariness and weakness. No one in his dysfunctional household had cared if or when he went to bed or had bothered to give him any breakfast.

Original sin and original innocence

With such children beside us, we turn to Scripture and tradition. It will be helpful to touch on the tradition first, for we are steeped in our traditions long before we read our Bibles. It is fair to say that the process of reflection that led to the Church's understanding of salvation was rarely distracted by children. Theology has always been an adult activity. It has always been by grown-ups, for grown-ups and about grown-ups. Children, so far as the Church has thought about them, have had to fit into the adult theological schemata as best they can.

The classic understanding of salvation in the Christian West has been that we are saved from sin and from the consequences of sin. The doctrine of sin that has dominated the thinking of the western Church, and which has done so much damage to western children, is largely the construct of two brilliant but troubled individuals, Saul of Tarsus (later St Paul) and Augustine of Hippo. To this day the Christian appraisal of children and young people is conditioned by Augustine's damning judgement on childhood and adolescence, beginning with his own. The tragic legacy of Augustine is to have burdened the West with his own guilt. We belong, he says, to one *massa peccati*, 'mess of sin'. Paul had said 'in Adam all die' (1 Corinthians 15.22). Augustine understood him to mean that, germinally, in the loins of our first father, we each participated in that primal sin, and that the guilt of sin and the taste for it, like the symptom of some sexually transmitted disease, is transmitted from one generation to the next. Hence the urgency of an early baptism to eradicate our 'original sin'. The Protestant Reformation may have redrawn the maps by which we may escape from the abject state from which God turns away his face, but it did not significantly challenge or qualify the Augustinian verdict on our plight or on the futility of supposing that there is the possibility for us in our earliest days of a life wholly human and wholly God's.

Of course, there were always dissentient voices. There were those who spoke with deep Christian faith and feeling, yet who reacted against the pessimistic account of human nature propagated by the doctrine of original sin. Thomas Traherne (1636–74) and Henry Vaughan (1621–95) saw the light of heaven lingering a little longer on children, whose 'original innocence' they celebrated. Traherne saw out of the child's eyes. 'The corn stood orient and immortal wheat, which never should be reaped, nor was ever sown. I thought it had stood from everlasting to everlasting . . .' For Traherne, God keeps the child company. 'He in our childhood with us walks.' So far from being a depraved state, from which the child must swiftly be saved, childhood becomes exemplary of what the adult, who has strayed far from this early Eden, must recover:

> That childhood might alone be said
> My tutor, Teacher, Guide to be,
> Instructed then even by the Deitie. (*Centuries*)

Similarly, for Henry Vaughan childhood was irradiated with the light of heaven:

> Happy those early days!
> When I shin'd in my Angel-infancy. ('The Retreate')

The lyrical voice exalting childhood has not fallen silent. There are those who still talk like this, poets who teach us that childhood, notwithstanding its tantrums and its terrors, notwithstanding the unspeakable suffering of countless children, notwithstanding William Golding's *Lord of the Flies*, is still a time of life to be celebrated. At best, the joy of childhood is only intermittent and it is always fleeting. Yet however momentary are its delights, it seems that images of Eden are alone adequate to evoke them, even if Eden never was. There are echoes of Traherne and Vaughan in Dylan Thomas's 'Fern Hill':

> Now as I was young and easy under the apple boughs
> About the lilting house and happy as the grass was green,
> The night above the dingle starry,
> Time let me hail and climb
> Golden in the heydays of his eyes . . .

Such a childhood recalls how it all once was:

> . . . It was all
> Shining, it was Adam and maiden . . .
> So it must have been after the birth of the simple light
> In the first spinning place . . .

The most powerful refutation of the Augustinian judgement on our sorry state came from a voice the Church sought to silence. 'Let us lay it down as an incontrovertible rule,' wrote Jean-Jacques Rousseau (1712–78), 'that the first impulses of nature are always right; there is no original sin in the human heart.' The child should never be punished 'for he does not know what it is to do wrong'.[5] The child, for Rousseau, is naturally innocent and, left to nature, the child will flourish.

Of those who distanced themselves from the Christian consensus that the child was inherently sinful and must be 'saved' as soon as possible, whether by baptism or by conversion, two nineteenth-century theologians in particular claim our attention. They are wells to which a Church, confused about childhood, needs to return.

For Friedrich Schleiermacher (1768–1834), childhood offers 'eine reine Offenbarung des Göttlichen', 'a pure revelation of the divine'.[6] The child, for Schleiermacher, possesses the gift of living each moment to the full, unburdened by wistfulness for yesterday or by fear of tomorrow. Rather than a fallen state from which the child must be 'saved', childhood is a condition to which the adult must be converted.

If one book has to be identified as the first 'theology of childhood' it must be Horace Bushnell's *Christian Nurture*, published in 1847. Bushnell (1802–76) was an American Congregationalist minister, liberal in his theology, powerful in his preaching, as famous in his day as he is now – almost – forgotten. *Christian Nurture* is a seminal and very great work. In it Bushnell took issue with the 'revivalism' central to the American Protestantism of his day. Revivalist preachers proclaimed that to be saved an individual had to be converted. This doctrine left little children stranded, old enough to go to hell, too young to go to heaven. Bushnell insisted that the child was to grow up as a Christian, never having known a time when he or she was other than a child of God. Bushnell's work is remarkable for its recognition – rare among those who have reflected theologically on childhood – of the pivotal significance of the childhood of Jesus himself for a Christian estimate of the status of children. 'Having been a child Himself,' writes Bushnell, 'who can imagine even for one moment that He has no place in His fold for the fit reception of childhood?'[7] Bushnell also recognized – again noticing what few before him had seen – the theological significance of the child's delight in *play*. 'Play,' he writes, 'is the symbol and interpreter of liberty, that is, Christian liberty.'[8] We are, in short, saved to play. It is the conclusion to which this essay will be drawn.

Broadly speaking, two sharply contrasting images of childhood have shaped Christian attitudes to children and determined how they have been treated and their salvation understood. There is the image of the child as 'lost', the conviction that the child is born a guilty sinner and that his or her spiritual plight is as desperate as that of the unrepentant adult. Every child, on this view, is born at enmity to God. Accordingly, 'the breaking of the child's will betimes', as the Puritans used to say, is seen as a parental duty. Stern discipline is necessary to curb the rebellious and as yet unregenerate spirit of the young child. Such robust discipline claims scriptural sanction, notably in the book of Proverbs. 'Iniquity is bound up in the heart of the child but the cane will thrash it out of him' (Proverbs 22.15, author's translation), a text taken literally and applied ruthlessly in many homes and schools until well into the twentieth century. We think of another innocent who was mercilessly flogged. Never was Christ's identification with children (Mark 9.36-37) more evident than when he was being whipped by Pilate's thugs (Matthew 27.26).

'Iniquity is bound up in the heart of the child.' Alas, this damning judgement on the child and the child's spiritual status is not confined to a closed chapter of Church history. In such a faith terrible things continue to be done to children. How far such an understanding of childhood is fuelled by pathological rather than theological influences, by mischief done to us long ago and deep within, is too complex a question to consider here.

By contrast, there is the image of the innocent child, the view that 'heaven lies about us in our infancy'. The contemporary secular manifestation of this idea is the cult of the 'cute kid'. The modern image of the adorable child is both extremely powerful and deeply dangerous. It is a kind of idolatry. Idols have to be constantly propitiated and pampered. They are lavishly dressed for special feasts. The analogy may be pressed too far, but not before we register just what mischief the commercially driven 'idolizing' of childhood has done to the children of many western households. Cute kids have to be kitted out in designer clothes. Little children put on catwalks are turned into grotesques. Still more seriously, the cult of the child is always the cult of the 'perfect' child. The cult forbids our accommodating – or even seeing – the child as other than we wish him or her to be. The child is the child I want. One day, when the technology is developed, the child will be the child I design. That child is unlikely to be disabled.

Christians drawn to an exalted view of the child have seen Jesus' high estimate of childhood as his recognition of *qualities and attractive attributes* distinctive of childhood. 'The Kingdom', writes one commentator, 'is for the loving, the natural, the unspoiled, the gay, the imaginative, the free-hearted, the happy.'[9] The problem with this position is that not all children are like that, least of all those children through whose eyes we are seeking to look, those whom the world has treated so cruelly. Again we ask whether something more than theology has been at work. We wonder whether this exalted estimate of the nature of the child perhaps owes as much to the romantic elevation of the intuitive and impulsive over the rational, of the heart over the mind, as to scriptural sources of a Christian anthropology.

The vulnerable child

Wise voices in recent years have urged us not to settle for either of these polarized estimates of the nature and status of children. Neither the image of the child as innately sinful, nor that of the child as innocent, do justice to the realities of children's lives in the early twenty-first century or to the radical re-envisioning of childhood in the teaching of Jesus.

Emerging from recent reflection is a Christian understanding of childhood which neither romanticizes childhood nor condemns it, but which recognizes that from birth – indeed from before birth – the child is inescapably bound up in a web of life shot through with sin and tragedy. This 'third way' of seeing the status of the child emphasizes the essentially relational and communal nature of our existence. Theology takes leave of reality when, as often it does, it discusses sin and salvation as if each of us lived as individuals in aseptic isolation from others. The truth is that we are always at the mercy of others, never more so than in our childhood. Sadly, for many of the children through whose eyes we seek to see, the mercy of others has been meagre. That fact must be our point of departure if we are to take our discussion of children and salvation any further. Children may or may not be 'culpable'. It is very difficult to give substantial content to such a concept, as indeed to the idea of original sin – and a child dies of malnutrition every three seconds while we try to do so. What is certain is that children are *vulnerable*. Whether or not they are in any sense the *agents* of sin, they are the indisputably the *victims* of sin.

I write on the day when I read in the paper of an eleven-year-old who has hanged himself because the bullying inflicted on him by his peers had become intolerable. To instance bullying is surely sufficient to dispel any lingering myths of childhood's innocence. But to point to what the bullies did as evidence of their inherent sinfulness is to miss the complexity of what is happening when children do wrong. It is not to minimize the moral seriousness of bullying – or the moral responsibility of bullies – to call attention to the wider context of a world awry, to the violence of which both the bullied and the bullies are victims. A Christian understanding of salvation must engage with the sin that children suffer, as well as the sin with which they are complicit.

According to this 'the third way' of seeing salvation, my salvation – if I am a child – is not from what I have done and its consequences, but from what has been done to me. David Jensen writes, in a book to which the author of this chapter is much indebted, 'Perhaps the classical doctrine of sin is strongest in calling our attention to the fact that brokenness and suffering precede any child's birth: all children, in this manner, are born into sin.'[10]

Jesus and the child

We turn now to our texts. What are we to make of the teaching of Jesus about children and what bearing does that teaching have on the question of children's salvation? We remind ourselves of what happened.

The disciples are debating who is the greatest among them. Jesus says that greatness lies in lowliness and in the service of all. What Jesus then does would have been powerfully eloquent had no further word been said. He sets a child among them. Then – again the telling action – he takes the child in his arms, declaring that in receiving the child they receive him and the one who sent him (Mark 9.35-7).

On a second occasion the acts of Jesus again speak as loudly as his words. Children are brought to Jesus for him to touch. His disciples try to prevent this happening. Jesus is angry that they should assume he shares their estimate of children. (The anger of Jesus is rare, heard only when the divine priorities of his mission are challenged.) He invites the children to him, forbids any hindrance to their coming, and announces that God's kingdom belongs to these children and to those like them. Then – once more it is his action that anchors the event historically – he takes them in his arms and gives them his blessing (Mark 10.13-16).

We start with the events. A theology of childhood and of salvation is not to be constructed, line by line, from propositions. It rests on the works of God on the soil of Palestine. It is not a metaphor in the midst of them, but a flesh and blood child that stuns the disciples into silence. Jesus does not identify himself with the image of the child but with the real child.

The children are invited to Jesus, not so that they may be brought within the realm of God's kingship, but because that is where they already are. When Jesus says 'of such is the kingdom' there is no suggestion that he means some children and not others. Much of the commentary and discussion on these words reveals a reluctance to accept that Jesus' pronouncement was really so simple and all-embracing and unconditional. Some have insisted that the children in the gospel story were all candidates for infant baptism; others have claimed that these children were young converts, examples of saving faith in infancy; others have argued that here are the children of believing parents. And so on. All such interpretations are attempts to force the words of Jesus into an understanding of salvation which the interpreter already holds.

'Of such is the kingdom.' A technical point is worth making. A comparison with other New Testament instances of the Greek grammatical construction used here makes it clear that the reference is to children and not just, as some have asserted, to the childlike. Behind our 'of such' is a Greek 'correlative demonstrative pronoun of quality'. The same form is used, for example, at Acts 22.22 where we are told that those listening to a lengthy testimony from Paul, deciding that they have heard enough, shout, 'Away with such a fellow from the earth!' Clearly it is Paul himself they wish to be rid of, not just those like him! The words are decisive – still more are the unprecedented actions by which Jesus emphasizes what he says.

The implication of the words of Jesus, words accompanied so eloquently by what he does, about the question of the child's salvation is of the first importance. The teaching of Jesus challenges any understanding of salvation which makes the child's status – 'saved' or 'unsaved' – consequent upon compliance with what adults require of the child. There is, for example, what has been perhaps unfairly caricatured as 'beach mission theology', the understanding of salvation which makes the child's relationship with God dependent on a personal commitment to Jesus as saviour. The perceived need for such a commitment has motivated much 'children's evangelism' with its eagerness to 'win children for Christ'. The evangelist may well elicit from some very young children the faith response deemed necessary. But in the youngest child, however slowly you say the long words, such a response is inconceivable.

Where does this leave the child who is too young – or too weak – to grasp what the well-intentioned grown-up is talking about? The peril of any understanding of salvation that makes the child's status in any way conditional or contingent on what the adult requires of the child is that it revives the unlovely doctrine of limbo, the melancholy realm, neither heaven nor hell, that until very recently was supposed by the Roman Catholic Church to be the destiny of the unbaptized who die in infancy. Our new limbo is the spiritual no-man's-land, somewhere neither here nor there, where our unhappy children must wait until they are old enough to understand what is asked of them. The absurdity of any such view of the child's salvation is that it implies a doubt about the standing before God of the very ones about whom Jesus is least equivocal.

As for the status of the unbaptized, it is perhaps sufficient to recall Tess of Thomas Hardy's *Tess of the D'Urbervilles* who baptizes her sick child and worries that the baptism will not be good enough. The insistence that baptism is essential for salvation is a construct of adult males and has more to do with the maintenance of male clerical authority than with either with the words and works of Jesus or the well-being, temporal or eternal, of children. It is not the only example in Christian theology where man-made law – *man*-made law – has prevailed over divinely maternal love.

As we shall see, a theology of salvation that remains agnostic about the status of children is not only incompatible with the teaching of Christ. It is incompatible too with what we say we believe about the *incarnation* of Christ. To that fundamental principle we shall turn shortly. Here we simply register the fact that a view of salvation that accommodates children only so far as they ape adults overlooks both the children we meet in the Bible and the boys and girls we know. We do not have to succumb to the sentimentalizing of the child Samuel to recognize that he was closer to God than the grown-up in the story who, as a priest, was supposed to be the one around the place most alert to presence and interventions of the deity (1 Samuel 3). The child does not have to wait to be 'born again' to be a child of God. Indeed he or she does not even have to wait to be born – at least Jeremiah did not have to. 'Before I formed you in the womb,' says the Lord to his prophet, 'I knew you' (Jeremiah 1.5).

Equally subversive of adult schemata of salvation is all that has become clear to us in recent years about the innate spirituality of children. To be sure, spirituality is not to be confused with religion, the Christian religion or any other. Religion is an expression of spirituality not its source. This chapter is not the place to recapitulate the empirical evidence that our spirituality, our 'awareness of the other and the beyond', is 'hard-wired' into us. That evidence is ably surveyed in David Hay's *Something There: The Biology of the Human Spirit*.[11] Children are 'alive in spirit' long before any they can comply with any confessional blueprint for their salvation drawn by grown-ups. This we know both from Hay's own findings and from the extensive research of others to which he directs us. It is a conclusion that will come as no surprise to those familiar with words about things hidden from the wise and intelligent and revealed to infants (Matthew 11.25).

On what grounds are children affirmed so highly by Jesus? We turn again to the texts, seeking to read them through the child's eyes. Whose is the kingdom? Twice, and only twice, does Jesus directly answer the question. The kingdom, Jesus tells us, belongs to the poor (Luke 6.20) and it belongs to children (Mark 10.14). It is instructive to set those two claims side by side and to allow them to interpret each other. If the context of that comparison was a devotional Bible study in a suburban sitting-room, we might claim that the poor are 'the poor in spirit' (Matthew 5.3) and the children are 'the little ones who believe' (Mark 9.42), adults who have become children at heart (Matthew 18.1-5). These are edifying reflections and there can be no quarrel with them. But the perspective of those who struggle to survive requires a different reading of the texts. 'The poor' are the actual poor, the materially poor, the homeless and hungry, the outcast and oppressed, the victims of war, those who suffer crippling disability and debilitating disease. They are the poor who, so the Lord tells the rich in Israel, are his people (Isaiah 3.15). Equally, the children are flesh and blood children – though those children, through whose eyes we try to look, are often only skin and bone. Like the poor, they are powerless. Left to themselves they will die.

To the poor and to children Jesus promises the kingdom. From the child's perspective, the issue is not their salvation in the sense of their eternal destiny but their immediate need. The promise of the kingdom is not of a place in heaven, though that is assured, but an expression of the divine 'preferential option'. The promise carries a demand, the demand that God's commitment to the poor – and to the children who invariably are the poorest of the poor – be shared by Christ's adult and affluent disciples. Because it's us he's talking to.

Moreover, it is both with children and with the poor that Jesus expressly identifies himself. 'Receive a child and you receive me', he says (Mark 9.37). But also he says, 'What you do to the hungry and homeless you do to me' (Matthew 25.31-46).

The children are one with Christ, and theirs is the kingdom, because, like the poor, they are the vulnerable and the victimized. If we hear the words of Jesus about children addressing us from situations where those children go blind for the lack of the occasional taste of fresh vegetables, or who die of an AIDS-related condition they were born with, we shall recognize that his familiar words have as much to do with the *survival* of children as with their salvation, as salvation has traditionally been understood.

So are the children who succumb to these afflictions – those who do not survive – 'unsaved'? If the fourth Gospel is to be believed then, alas, in a sense they are. At least, it might shock us into a more purposeful awareness of their condition if we thought and talked in those terms. John's Gospel understands salvation as Jesus' gift of 'abundant life'. That abundant life, for the Jesus of John's Gospel, begins here and now. It is 'life before death'. For the evangelist for whom the Word became hungry flesh, Jesus' promise of life has as much to do with the child's present experience – his or her sickness or hunger now – as with his or her future destiny. Evangelical missionaries of an earlier generation went to the ends of the earth because they feared for the eternal destiny of the millions who had never heard the gospel of salvation. Perhaps we should pray for something of that same evangelical spirit, even if we are sure that the child who dies of a preventable disease is safe in the arms of Jesus. The world-wide evangelization of children is still a mission to rescue the perishing.

This principle of hearing the word of the Lord from where children are hurting – of 'seeing through the eyes of the child' – applies equally in the regions where this book is more likely to be read. Children lead impoverished lives on the wildernesses of our bleak British estates as well as in sub-Saharan Africa. A recent UNICEF report concludes that children growing up in Britain suffer greater deprivation, worse relationships with their parents and are exposed to more risks from alcohol, drugs and unsafe sex than those in any other wealthy country in the world. The headline of the *Guardian* on my desk reads, 'Study reveals stressed out 7- to11-year-olds'.[12]

Salvation now

Children's lives unfold in a 'continuous now'. As they grow older they may enjoy looking forward and begin to savour memories, but they always default to the present. For the youngest child the words 'tomorrow' and 'yesterday' are meaningless. 'No thoughts have they of ills to come, nor cares beyond today'.[13] Jesus' command, 'Do not worry about tomorrow' (Matthew 6.34) is contained in his command to his disciples to turn and become as children. If we are to speak of salvation and of children in the same breath, we must interpret salvation so that it relates meaningfully to the continuum of the child's life as it is immediately experienced. The concept of salvation is vacuous unless it makes a difference to the child *now*.

There is a child who will help us do just that. The childhood of Jesus may have been 'hidden', but the facts are that he was a child and that his childhood, as Bushnell but few others have seen, has the greatest bearing on what we believe about the children and salvation. There is also one Church father who saw the significance of that child and who will help us, more than Augustine does, in formulating an understanding of salvation which recognizes that, unless salvation can be apprehended in childhood's 'continuous now', it is not salvation at all.

Christians affirm that at Nazareth the Word took human flesh. The historical Jesus was 'God with us' from his conception. Once upon a time – this is our story – a life was lived in which at every stage the human nature and the divine were 'one person'. The heart of this matter is truth about us as well as truth about Jesus. The truth about us is that there is a potential fullness of life appropriate to each moment of the ongoing 'now' of childhood. To claim otherwise is to deny the Incarnation. Salvation in Christ is the realization at every stage of one's life of that living to God, to others and to oneself which befits each succeeding moments in the sequence of one's days.

There is more about all of this in the New Testament than we have noticed. In Luke's Gospel we move from one familiar episode to the next, like gallery-goers strolling through an exhibition of well-loved pictures. But we need to pause *between* the pictures. The familiar story about the twelve-year-old Jesus in the temple is such a picture. There's a note before it and after it, an introduction and a conclusion which are often overlooked:

> The child grew and became strong, filled with wisdom; and the favour of God was upon him.
>
> (Luke 2.40)

> And Jesus increased in wisdom and in years, and in divine and human favour.
>
> (Luke 2.52)

These comments are far more than editorial seams, far more than dabs of glue sticking together the discrete episodes the gospel-writer records. The word Luke chooses to describe God's disposition to Jesus and his relationship to others is not chosen lightly. It can be translated 'favour', as it is in most modern translations. But the word used is *charis*. God's *grace* was on the child Jesus. Luke does not of course anticipate later controversies about the relationship of the divine and human natures in the person of Jesus. But he does imply that in his childhood Jesus was relating both to other people and to God in ways that were not defective because they were not those of an adult.

There is a pattern of childhood in the incarnation of the growing Jesus. The pattern is not that urged on us by Mrs Alexander in the carol 'Once in royal David's city', that 'Christian children all must be, mild, obedient, good as he'. The childhood of Jesus does not provide a blueprint of how our kids should be. But if Jesus was as much at one with God in childhood as in adulthood then there must be for children too the potential of a wholeness of life, no less 'the finished product', that it is not the same as that of the adult.

In the light of Luke's account of the growing up of Jesus, salvation is to be understood not as an event, but as a continuing process, a making real to the child at every succeeding stage of the child's life that wholeness of life that befits his or her age.

The incarnational model of the salvation of the child has its scriptural foundation in the Lukan commentary on how Jesus grows. The Patristic foundation is in the claim of Irenaeus that Jesus, 'sanctifying every age', made every stage of life his own:

> He therefore passed through every age, becoming an infant for infants, thus sanctifying infants; a child for children, thus sanctifying those who are of this age . . . a youth for youths, becoming an example to youths, and thus sanctifying them to the Lord.[14]

An understanding of salvation that postpones to adulthood any possibility of life that is all that it is meant to be is a denial of the Incarnation. We are not made like kettles on a conveyer belt, bits bolted on along the production line so that only at the end of the line do we emerge as finished products. Timothy, five years, five months and a day, is already 'all there'. Equally, my salvation is the realization at every stage of that living to God, to others and to myself which befits each succeeding moment in the sequence of my early days.

Saved to play

It has often been pointed out that the word 'save' in the New Testament is a rich one. It is the word the gospel writers use, writing in Greek, when they record Jesus as sometimes saying to someone he heals, 'Your faith has *made you well*' or, a much better translation, 'Your faith has *made you whole*' (e.g. Mark 5.34; Luke 8.48). The 'salvation' Jesus offers implies more than the cure of a physical ailment, though for someone afflicted with leprosy that is the 'salvation' he or she cries out for. It certainly means more than an advantageous change of spiritual status. The saving gift of Jesus to those who turn to him is 'wholeness' – becoming all that we are made to be and meant to be. It needs to be stressed that the relationship of faith and healing in the gospels is not that the faith must always come first. Jesus heals ten who suffer from leprosy. Only one shows the faith in him he seeks (Luke 17.11-19). The children whom Jesus heals are not children who have first put their faith in him. The unnamed epileptic boy at the foot of the Mount of Transfiguration was deranged (Mark 9.14-29) and Jairus' twelve-year-old daughter was dead (Mark 5.21-43). Yet Jesus made them whole.

Salvation means wholeness. For the child, living only in the moment, that salvation, that wholeness, must be understood as salvation now. That said, images of the heaven we hope for, visions of the age to be when a little child shall lead us, help us to speak of the salvation we seek for the child in the here and now. Horace Bushnell directs us to the prophetic vision. 'The streets of the city shall be full of boys and girls playing in its streets' (Zechariah 8.5). Bushnell saw play as the expression and the symbol of the liberty of the children of God. Only in our own time, with the work of Jerome Berryman and the approach to children he has developed known as Godly Play, have we begun to recover Bushnell's understanding of the theological significance of play.[15]

According to John's Gospel, Jesus came that we might have life and that we might have it 'abundantly' (John 10.10). In childhood life is never lived more abundantly than in play. The 'saved' child, the whole child, is the child who plays. The malnourished child, whether in sub-Saharan Africa or in a situation of deprivation and neglect in the so-called 'developed' world, is the child who does not play. Often such a child has never learned how to play. There is no sight more harrowing than that of the child who is so weak and listless that he or she can no longer brush the flies from their mouth, let alone get up and run around. Children who have no energy to play have not brought that condition on themselves. As we saw, that is the condition they were born into. Sin is still what children must be saved from, but it is not the sins they have committed from which they must be saved. It is because of what has been done to them, not what they have done, that they must be made whole.

The salvation of the child of God is the health and strength and liberty to play. From the hurting child's perspective, salvation is not some 'spiritual' status on which the child's physical and material condition has no bearing, but the meeting of that child's primary needs, the provision of what he or she requires to able to live life to the full.

There is nothing whimsical or frivolous in claiming that, for the child, salvation is the enjoyment of the fullness of life that overflows in play. Indeed there are scriptural grounds for claiming that to be absorbed in play is to be caught up in the divine nature. The New Testament speaks of Christ as 'the wisdom of God' (1 Corinthians 1.24). For the author of the fourth Gospel, Jesus, the Word 'made flesh', is the embodiment of that divine wisdom (John 1.1-14). The wisdom of God is not an abstract principle but a person, a woman with a name and a voice. She is *Hochmah* in Hebrew. She is *Sophia* in Greek. In a remarkable Old Testament passage she speaks for herself. The force of the original text is much debated but it could be translated, 'Then I was at his side each day, his darling and delight, playing in his presence continually, playing over his whole world, while my delight was in humankind'(Proverbs 8.30-31). According to this extraordinary passage, wisdom is older than all that is, older than the earth and oceans, older than the mountains and hills, older than the springs and streams. Wisdom was already there when it all began. And who is she, this woman more ancient than we can begin to comprehend, there from eternity at God's side and the agent of his creation? She is a child, a little girl who never stops playing. She's *playing*. The same word is used here as in the prophetic text that Bushnell saw as so significant – 'The streets of the city shall be full of boys and girls playing in its streets'.

Jerome Berryman has asked, 'Is God a play-group?' There are other and more familiar ways of speaking of the common life of God – the life we are saved to share – but few of them are more illuminating and suggestive, if it is the salvation of children we are considering. Salvation for the child – as for all of us, for children we must all become – is to be caught up into the joy of our playful God.

But meanwhile someone must brush the flies from the child's face. Someone must answer the child's cry from the cross, 'I thirst'. Someone must comfort the bullied and challenge the bully. Our reflection on the theme of salvation, seen 'through the eyes of the child', turns the question of the child's salvation back on us, on us adults who so lightly speculate about it. After the First World War, the great Christian prophet and poet, G. A. Studdert Kennedy, contemplating the wasteland around him, wrote these words: 'You cannot stop at crying, "What shall I do to be saved?" You must go out into the world crying, "What can I do to save?" '[16]

Questions

1. What do you understand by the concept of 'salvation'?

2. This chapter tells us that 'children are saved to play'. In what ways can it be said that the happily playing child offers us a glimpse of God's salvation and the damaged, withdrawn child shows us a world in need of salvation?

3. Draw a child at the top of a piece of paper. In two columns list on one side issues and events in our society which free the child and offer the child potential for growth and on the other side any issues and events which cause today's children stress and difficulty. Where does the Church stand in this balance?

4. Have a look at Proverbs 8.30-31, which John Pridmore finds so significant. What does the delight and joy spoken of in this passage suggest to you?

5. The chapter reminds us that there are many children in the world who are in need of salvation now. What ONE thing could be done in your situation to raise awareness or help to bring salvation to the suffering children of today's world?

Activities

Sin / Forgiveness / Grace / Salvation

1. **Game**

You will need sheets of paper, pencils, crayons, paints, glitter, etc. and some Post-its™.

With a child or a group of children decide on an event or experience which has something sad or wrong at the heart of it. Draw a picture of the event, or you could use a picture from a newspaper. Now invite the children to suggest how the event could be redeemed, recovered or made better and write or draw on paper or Post-its™ all the suggestions, as well as using colours, glitter or other means of transformation. Reflect on the children's suggestions and actions. This activity could also be used to create get well cards, prayer cards or 'sorry' cards for community or liturgical use. In reflecting on the game you could use the verse, 'Out of the depths I cry to you, O Lord' (Psalm 130.1) as a focus for meditation if you wish.

2. **Create**

You will need ingredients for cake mix with some cake decorations (e.g. chocolate buttons) OR a cardboard or other cross and some rose petals or confetti.

These creative activities are described in Emma Percy's chapter and Sandra Millar's chapter. With a child or some children, make a Simnel cake together and use the decorations to depict the disciples. Invite the children to decide whether Judas Iscariot should be on the cake and note what they decide and why.

Alternatively, invite children to cover the cross with petals or confetti while thinking of all the bad things they would like to be rid of, then remove it to show the empty space left behind. Use this image to discuss with children the cost of what Jesus did on the cross and how Jesus bears our sins.

You can use the verse, 'He was despised and rejected by others; a man of suffering and acquainted with infirmity; and as one from whom others hide their faces he was despised, and we held him of no account' (Isaiah 53.3) as a meditative reflection for both activities if you wish.

3. **Learn from**

You will need a ball and a rope or other indicator of a line and a bag or basket and any other items suggested by the children.

Work together with some children to create a ritual that will help them articulate their understanding of sin. You could use Emma Percy's example of throwing a ball to reach a far away line to signify how we fall short of what God wants. Another variation on this is to designate a person as 'Jesus' to catch the balls and throw them across the line, or carry them in a basket across the line. Invite the children to make other suggestions and let them lead the way in creating the ritual. How does this activity make you feel? You can use the verse, 'a broken and contrite heart, O God, you will not despise' (Psalm 51.17) as a focus for meditation if you wish.

4. **Celebrate**

You will need to arrange a trip or other children's activity.

Organize a fun trip out or another enjoyable activity for a group of children. During the trip or activity spend time with the children but paying special attention to anything you might identify as moments of grace. If this is too difficult to manage you could videotape some of the activity and watch it later. What is it about these moments that make them grace-full? Are moments of grace difficult to identify? How would you describe such moments to another person? You can use the verse, 'the grace of our Lord Jesus Christ be with your spirit' (Galatians 6.18) as an aid to reflection on this activity if you wish.

5.  **Scripture**

Look up Scripture passages which mention grace, such as John 1.14; multiple references in Romans and Galatians 1.15. What do you think the word means in each context and how would you apply those meanings to your experience of children? Does your experience of grace among children go beyond its description in Scripture? How do children invite us to understand more of God's grace towards human beings? Another way of focusing this activity would be for children to create pictures or prayers of blessing, which could be set alongside the biblical passages. How do the pictures illuminate the texts?

10

Death

John Drane and Olive M. Fleming Drane

Personal angles

When we were asked to write on this topic of children and death, our minds immediately turned to two episodes within our own family. The first has probably been the most traumatic and also the most formative experience of our entire life together, when our second child unexpectedly died. To say that this was both devastating and bewildering for us is merely to state the obvious. With the benefit of hindsight, it is possible to realize that it probably changed the course of our respective careers. Olive's work up to that time had been in scientific and medical research, but in the years following that one experience, her life was turned upside down and radically reshaped as she began to explore clowning, and then pursued the study of theology and the arts in the process of seeking the kind of personal integration that can pull together seemingly disparate threads of human experiences into a narrative of meaning.[1] John, for his part, was at the time a relatively young academic, whose career path looked set to follow traditional lines of research and teaching in theology, using the conventional tools of historical and exegetical scholarship that had been well honed by generations before him. As he struggled to come to terms with this unexpected loss, it was inevitable that he too would question much of what he was doing, for the one thing that became clear to both of us was that conventional theological explanations of undeserved suffering simply did not address where we found ourselves. It was not so much that the answers were intrinsically inadequate – more that they began from an entirely different set of questions than the ones we found ourselves asking.

What was true of classical theology was also true in relation to church life. At the time, we were involved in a congregation that, within its own terms of reference, was outgoing and caring. There were many good people in that church, some of whom are still in touch with us, and they did the best they knew – but it simply did not touch us in ways that made a difference. No words that anyone could say ever brought much consolation to us – and, as much for cultural as for theological reasons, words were the only form of communication that were available to them. We found ourselves increasingly frustrated, if not alienated, by this apparent failure of the faith and the church that we had trusted, and without fully appreciating it at the time, we found ourselves forced to ask questions about how to live as faithful disciples of Jesus, how to be church, and how to do theology that took both of us into territory that extended well beyond the boundaries of anything that we might previously have regarded as conventional Christianity. At an intellectual level, we found ourselves questioning the role of reason and rationality, and in terms of pastoral care we wondered how the Church could be so disconnected from the actual needs of people, when training for ministry had for generations been dominated by a concern to equip clergy to deal empathetically with precisely such situations of personal crisis. We were also faced with challenging questions about the nature of community, as it dawned on us intuitively – if not, at that stage, coherently – that we would not be able to continue our journey of faith without asking awkward questions about theology, Church, Bible, spirituality, and much more besides.

At the centre of all this were two children: the daughter who was dead, and our older son (at that time, our only son) who was four and a half years old. He, of course, was inevitably caught up into the distress that we ourselves were experiencing, as a home that had been full of joy and hope was suddenly transformed into a darker space. But whereas the adults around us busied themselves with 'carrying on as normal', he seemed to know that at such a time things could never be 'normal'. Other adults (including our own relatives) kept their distance as if we were contaminated with some contagious disease, but he did what small children always do, sitting on our knees, putting his arms around us, and – crucially in that circumstance – praying with and for us. Long before he was born, we had always believed that children have spiritual insights right from the start, and therefore had been as consciously intentional about nurturing his spiritual development as we had been in attending to his physical needs – and in the midst of tragedy we learned more from his intuitive spirituality than from all the professional attention of clergy, medics and therapists. The teaching of Jesus about children as bearers of the good news took on a new meaning, and affected not only how we came to regard the faith of a child, but how we started to re-imagine our own faith – not (as we had been taught) as a set of absolute propositional truths, but as an experience of the heart and the spirit that would in due course provoke its own reflections, out of which new ways of perceiving God could emerge. At the time, we did not have the vocabulary to know that this was a praxis-reflection way of doing theology. It was just a child's way. For, in Kierkegaard's memorable phrase, children do indeed live life forwards and reflect on it backwards, in ways that are both challenging and life-giving. It is an interesting reflection that our own vulnerabilities actually contributed to our renewed wholeness at this point, for had we not been quite as devastated as we were we might well have fallen into the more usual default position of adults, and hidden our grief in order to protect him from it. Is this an example of what Jesus meant when he emphasized the importance of even adults becoming 'as a little child' in order to inherit the kingdom (Mark 10.13-16)?

The second episode can be described more briefly, because it is in essence a different version of the same story. By the time John's mother died without warning and at the relatively young age of 67, we had another son, who at that point was seven years old. Faced with sudden death, adults easily fall into a sort of disconnected daze, and are often unable to bring themselves to do and say even those things that they might wish to express. This was the case on that occasion, as we all stood around the grave going through the traditional motions of such an event. No doubt we were all deep within our own thoughts, but our seven-year-old did what no one else would (or could) do, walked over to his grandfather, took him by the hand and gave him that all-important physical reassurance that someone cared. Phyllis Rolfe Silverman expresses an important lesson that can be learned here from children's reactions to death: that 'Learning to accept our helplessness is part of learning to accept that death and the sorrow that accompanies it are part of life.'[2] A child will always operate from a position of helplessness and vulnerability, but for that very reason is able to appreciate a more profound reality that is concealed from those who are apparently more sophisticated and secure in their own identity. We will return to this theme later, but before that it will be helpful to place all this in a wider cultural context.

Cultural attitudes

In reflecting on these two episodes from our own experience, two things seem fairly incontrovertible. One is that they both took place within the context of a settled Christian world view, and the other is that this world view was in significant respects different from the Christian world view inherited from previous generations. In our own childhood, Christian children were still being nurtured on the remnants of a Victorian spirituality which had been motivated by an understandable concern for the suffering of children who died young as a result of what were then incurable ailments like diphtheria or polio, and who were assured that death was not the end, but merely an entrance into a grander and, in many ways, more glamorous lifestyle than any living person could possibly imagine. When congregations sang words such as 'There's a Friend for little children above the bright blue sky', it was more than a pious hope.[3] For that generation, it was a reality to be affirmed and sought after, in spite of the fact that it could only be attained by a child being cut adrift from the networks of home and family that gave life its meaning and purpose on a daily basis.

It is easy to dismiss such sentiments as being romanticized and idealistic, if not thoroughly scary – at least for people like us, living in a culture that on the surface shuns any mention of death, still less of any possible afterlife. But one does not need to look far to see that what might now seem simplistic and irrelevant in the countries of the global north is a hope that is still widely embraced by millions of the world's Christians who are faced on a daily basis with high rates of infant mortality and short adult life spans. In relation to western culture, the sort of notions expressed in late nineteenth- and early twentieth-century hymnology reflected the certainty that our forebears felt about many things. It was a period when the British Empire was at the pinnacle of its powers, and western Christians were supremely self-confident not only about their faith, but also about their own lifestyles and ways of understanding the world and its people. Today, that has all gone. Though our politicians occasionally (and disastrously) play with the idea that we have something to teach the rest of the world, our culture more widely has lost confidence in itself, and instead of believing that we deserve some celestial post-mortem future, we are more likely to be overburdened with a sense of our own inadequacy in life, and death as a more or less meaninglessness end that, if it is any better than life, is certainly unknown and unpredictable.

Many explanations can be advanced for this loss of self-confidence. Psychologists like Jean M. Twenge have argued that it is an inevitable consequence of a certain form of political correctness that instils in us unrealistic expectations from a young age, with the inevitable consequence that most of us are bound to be disappointed.[4] More generally, it is clearly not unconnected with the loss of confidence now being experienced by our entire culture, which is partly related to the steady erosion of Christian belief in the West, and partly to our awareness of alternative world views, which has cast doubt on the possibility that there might be any sort of confidence (let alone certainty) on fundamental matters such as life and death.

Though children never talk in terms of world views, all these cultural factors have had a profound effect on the ways they regard death, and we live in a situation where these perceptions are continually changing. An optimistic culture sees a bright future for itself, and instils the same hope in its children – a hope that both survives and lives on beyond death. But a pessimistic culture spawns the opposite. For those who have little sense of hope in this life, it is incredibly difficult to imagine that things could be better (or worse) in some other life. One of the iconic songs of the 1990s was the *Queen* hit, 'Who wants to live forever?' It sums up the experiences of the parents of many of today's children, with its insistence that today is all that counts because it is all we have, and if there is such a thing as eternity, then this is it.[5] Children of the late nineteenth century might well have identified with the aspirations of the sort of hymns referred to earlier. Today, we find no point of reference beyond our immediate experience. For a significant number of young people, hope and identity are no longer vested in God or heaven – still less in the Church – but (at least in the UK) in football teams and gangs. Though parents and the media wring their hands in horror when young people take their own lives, the very possibility of doing so is fuelled by the values of our consumerist culture in which everything becomes a matter of personal choice and preference. Sociologist George Ritzer has been studying this phenomenon for 20 years or more, and uses the concept of 'McDonaldization' to identify the ways in which our lives have become ever more rationalized. Beginning from the way in which fast food is served, he identifies efficiency, calculability, predictability and control as values that on the one hand we resist, while on the other we find to be irresistible. In a culture that is increasingly dominated by this way of being, there is a certain attractiveness in supposing that even matters of life and death can be within our own power to control, and in the most recent edition of his classic *The McDonaldization of Society* he identifies this trend as just one more manifestation of our obsession with pursuing McDonaldized lives.[6] As a consequence, for some individuals suicide is no longer to be regarded as a mark of despair, but as the opposite – as just another lifestyle choice, albeit a somewhat bizarre and self-contradictory one.

In parallel with this, there has also been a shift in the prevailing world view of the West, from a theistic, transcendent outlook to something that is more loosely defined. It is sometimes claimed that the traditional western outlook has been replaced by a more 'eastern' world view, influenced by Hindu and Buddhist views of reincarnation, and it is not hard to find Christians who now openly espouse such beliefs.[7] It is certainly the case that the number of people who say they believe in 'God' has been in steady decline for the past 20 years or more, while the number of people who will say that they believe in a 'soul' is rising all the time. The Christian tradition has conventionally believed in such continued non-bodily existence through the detachment of a soul from the body, though that view is now being subjected to serious questioning on biblical and theological grounds.[8] Not all those who claim priority for the soul will necessarily have a conventional belief in reincarnation, and there is in fact a noticeable tendency to reimagine such views in line with our western individualism, that puts us in control even of cosmic processes.[9] It is not just television programmes like *Buffy the Vampire Slayer*, but also the emphasis on things like recycling, that feed into an assumption that we are the agents in determining our own future. The incidence of online 'suicide clubs', a phenomenon noted particularly in Japan, in which people make pacts to kill themselves with others whom they have never met, or indeed of debates about euthanasia, is more evidence of the fact that death can now be regarded as a lifestyle choice.[10] The understanding of life as a self-contained entity is also mirrored in the development of civil funerals offered through the agency of local registrars' offices in the UK, in which the emphasis is on celebrating the life of the deceased individual, backed up with a legal requirement to avoid anything that might begin to place death in a bigger frame of reference.

Defining death

All this – and more – is reflected in the literature on the subject. Historically, most people would have regarded the nature and definition of death as a matter of simple common sense, and if pressed to be more precise may have made reference to the cessation of a heartbeat or some other readily observable physiological symptom. But with the rapid development of sophisticated medical technologies that can keep heart and lungs going mechanically, and when a relatively simple procedure such as CPR can apparently revive individuals who might otherwise seem to be dead, offering even a straightforward biological definition of death is now a far more complicated matter than would once have been the case. But long before these new questions were being raised about the scientific definition of death, psychologists and others had already evolved their own multidimensional perspectives on the matter.[11] As far back as the 1930s, therapists were developing sophisticated definitions of death in the effort to understand its consequences for their bereaved clients – including children. Over a period of several decades, many theories have come and gone, though there is a generally accepted consensus that death should be thought of as 'not a single, unidimensional concept but is, rather, made up of several relatively distinct subconcepts'.[12] These subconcepts generally include four primary aspects: universality (everyone dies sometime), irreversibility (no one comes back to life again), non-functionality (the dead can't do anything) and causality (there is always some reason for a person's death).

Research suggests that the ways in which an individual might process each of these aspects of death is likely to be age-related to some extent. As a general statement, it may be the case that attitudes to death tend to become more abstract as people grow older, though this developmental view is by no means the whole story, and adults as well as children tend to conceptualize the reality of death in ways that are highly diverse and quite resistant to systematization. It is certainly a mistake to assume that there is a standard adult view of death that is clear enough to be serviceable as a standard against which we might understand (still less judge) the responses of children. In relation to the four aspects of death just mentioned, it is not difficult to find adults who will adopt viewpoints that, on a strictly developmental understanding, they might be assumed to have left behind in childhood. The one possible exception to this could be in relation to the universality of death, as there is some evidence that children see it as an experience that, through luck or ingenuity, might somehow be avoided. At the same time, however, other research suggests that children come to accept their own mortality at an early stage, though naturally projecting it into some remote future rather than anticipating it as an immediate possibility.[13] On the other three aspects of death, however, it is much harder to distinguish between a widely held mature adult view and its supposedly less sophisticated infantile version. For example, in relation to irreversibility, it is often claimed that young children are more likely than older individuals to regard death as temporary and reversible, perhaps like going on a trip, or even going to sleep. This view is by no means always created by children themselves. One person reminisced with us of how she was told as a young child that she would no longer be visiting her grandfather because he had 'gone to Australia'. When she subsequently understood that the dead were buried, and knew that Australia was on the other side of the world to the UK, she concluded that burial must be the preferred mode because it gave more direct access to Australia than other methods of disposal! This sort of fiction is perpetuated in one of the most popular poems for funerals of all sorts (including secular humanist events). Henry Scott-Holland's 'Death is nothing at all' begins by asserting that, 'Death is nothing at all / I have only slipped into the next room' and concludes with

> I am but waiting for you,
> For an interval, somewhere, very near

Just around the corner.[14]

And, of course, adult culture is full of euphemisms that tend to hide, if not deny, the reality of death. We talk, for example, of individuals who are 'pushing up the daisies' who have 'gone away for a long, long time', or who have 'passed away'. Far from helping to inform children, such terminology can itself be a source of confusion, if not amusement. In research carried out for this book, a boy in Year 3 at school (aged 7 or 8) told how

> My mum said she was sad because her friend was Pastor Way. I didn't know . . . who was Pastor Way? I thought Pastor Way was a man, but her friend was a lady. I thought my mum was gone mad!

Something similar can be said on the matter of non-functionality. Here again, it is generally the case that younger children are more likely than adults to imagine that the dead continue to do things, whether eating or drinking or just dreaming and thinking. But that is far from the whole story, and in recent years there has been an explosion of interest among the adult population in connecting with the dead through spiritualism and various forms of channelling, and such connections invariably lead to some sort of description of what the dead are doing, and often detailed information about their current disembodied 'lifestyle' in an extra-terrestrial environment. In March 2003, psychics Craig and Jane Hamilton-Parker made a film entitled *Spirit of Diana* in which they claimed to relay messages from the late Diana, Princess of Wales. When it was screened on television stations around the world, more than 30 million viewers watched it.[15] Even more remarkably, when the public inquest into the princess's death took began in London at the end of 2007, a key witness was Myriah Daniels, a self-described 'minister of natural spiritualism of the real world', who among other things offered real-time accounts of the princess in her now disembodied state.

Similar observations about the responses of adults and children might be offered in relation to causality: while younger children may tend to offer unrealistic, even naive, reasons for someone's death (such as their own bad behaviour), significant numbers of bereaved adults also blame themselves for the death of a loved one, by supposing that if they had noticed signs of illness sooner, or had taken a different route on the occasion of some fatal accident, or been more available with support, the outcome might have been different.

As well as highlighting the difficulty of correlating attitudes to death with neat patterns of psychological and physical development between childhood and adulthood, these factors also draw attention to a weakness in so-called scientific understandings of death, namely that they tend to play down, if not ignore altogether, the possibility of any form of transcendent continuation of the individual person. It can, of course, be argued that such ethereal concerns go well beyond anything that can legitimately be explored through the scientific method. Yet the empirical reality is that a majority of the world's people at all times and places has always held onto belief in some form of continued existence beyond death, which means we ought to take account of this dimension of the subject, regardless of how ridiculous or unlikely it may seem to be.

Adults and children

The American Transcendentalist Ralph Waldo Emerson identified something significant when he claimed that, 'Sorrow makes us all children again'.[16] Not only do adults frequently revert to what might appear to be childlike attitudes in the face of death, but the mention of sorrow might also offer the clue to a more productive way of thinking about the topic of children and death, focusing less on the fact of death itself and more on the diverse ways in which children (and adults) deal with the sorrow that it inevitably entails. Part of the problem in today's world is that death is widely regarded as being anomalous rather than as a natural and inescapable fact of human life. For our Victorian forebears, sex was a taboo subject, while death was everywhere. Today, the reverse is true: we talk endlessly about sex, while death is scrupulously avoided. We began this chapter by referring to our own experience of the death of a child, and noted how even our Christian friends were unable to speak of it in any meaningful sense. Yet even in the earliest days, they were brazen in talking about sex, and repeatedly advised that the sooner we had lots of it (and conceived another child), the better it would be for everyone. Naturally, our own four-and-a-half-year-old never mentioned such a thing, for at that time he had no knowledge of what sex might be, but neither did he ever suggest that another child might be procured by whatever means he imagined might be possible. He lived in the moment, and the moment was one of pain and isolation. Of course, he did not become obsessive about it, as we were tempted to do. This is typical of the way in which most children deal with death, agonizing over serious questions one minute while also doing 'normal' things like playing games, going out with friends, or whatever. Juxtaposing those two approaches, however, may not be the best way of putting it, because such 'ordinary' things can also be agents of healing at a time of great sorrow, just as they can function at other times as key instruments in the nurturing of personal relationships and the building of community. Jesus taught his disciples to question an easy differentiation between what we regard as sacred and what might be secular. Our children challenge the idea that playing and having fun is a less serious way of facing death than morbid personal introspection.

Actually identifying the moment itself is getting harder for adults than it used to be in days gone by, and this will have knock-on effects on children as they come to terms with the nature of death. A major contributory factor is the creeping rationalization of scientific medicine, which has not only introduced enormous ambiguities into the nature and meaning of death, but has also tended to create an environment in which death is regarded as the failure of medical science to keep us alive. Today's physicians regularly have to make decisions about death that would have been meaningless to previous generations, as they wrestle with complex philosophical and ethical questions about the efficacy of keeping patients artificially breathing but in a vegetative state. Are they dead or alive? One can sympathize with a Year 9 student (aged 13 or 14) who went to the hospital where his grandfather lay dying, but was disappointed to discover that:

> when we got there I couldn't see my granddad. We sat in this room and everybody was drinking water and the nurse kept going in and out. We sat there for hours and it was really boring. I thought it was stupid just sitting there. My auntie arrived and my mum went on about how he was OK before and she couldn't believe it. Then the nurse took my mum and my auntie out and left me with some other people who were just sitting there. When they came back they said he was dead and we went home. I couldn't see the point of going there just to sit in a room while he died somewhere else.

At the same time, one can also sympathize with the boy's mother, whose reactions and responses were being managed (some might say manipulated) by a healthcare system that appears to be still dominated by a mechanistic and materialistic attitude to health, in spite of paying lip service to offering care for the whole person that would include spiritual and relational aspects of life and death.

The terms in which debates about the importance of posthumous organ donation are conducted reinforces all these ambiguities, as we are reassured that by making our organs available for transplant after our deaths, we will 'prevent' hundreds of other deaths – as if the 'prevention' of death is either possible or desirable for the long-term flourishing of the human species. At the same time, other debates are taking place about the need to hasten death in the case of individuals with terminal illnesses – another set of choices that would have been meaningless to previous generations, but which now arises as a result of advances in diagnostic procedures that mean we can know for much longer that we are 'dying', knowledge which is bound to induce fear about what it might be like to live for a period as a sort of half-person, not quite dead but certainly not fully alive. When you add to this the reality that the same lack of clarity abounds in a parallel discourse related to how we can know when life begins, it is not hard to understand why adults would rather not talk about any of this at all, and why their children are bemused by it.

The American poet Edna St Vincent Millay wrote in 1937 that 'childhood is the kingdom where nobody dies',[17] and in spite of our openness about many things, most adults tend to try to protect children from death, appearing to think that if it is not spoken about then it will never impinge on their lives. In reality, of course, children can hardly avoid being aware of death. Our television news bulletins carry gruesome images of warfare and famine on a daily basis (and in more recent times, multiple stories about children killing other children in the UK), and when children are not seeing that they might well be playing computer games whose only purpose is to kill virtual people, in graphic images that are so lifelike that the boundaries between fantasy and reality become blurred, and for some non-existent. The result is that we create an environment in which children are exposed to death only in a kind of make-believe way that does little to prepare or equip them for dealing with it in the real world of their own family or wider community. This is a particular challenge for children whose parents serve in the armed forces, and who may well have to face the reality of the death of a mother or father in such circumstances. A Year 8 student (about 12 years old) suffering from leukaemia admitted that the surreal character of the digital world profoundly influenced the way in which he reflected on his own future prospects:

> I started to think about whether I was going to die. But I never really thought I was going to die. I thought about it in my mind like a film, my brother going into my room and me not being there, and about my dog and someone else taking him for a walk, but inside I didn't think I was going to die.

Even when a real death does occur, adults often ignore it when speaking with children, perhaps hoping that if it is never mentioned it will somehow go away, and working on the mistaken assumption that children need to be protected from such a harsh reality.

At a time when, in the UK, two children are bereaved of either an adult or a sibling every hour of every day,[18] preventing children from dealing directly with death in their own way might be regarded as abusive behaviour that will do more harm than any imagined good. No doubt this reticence to include children stems from the fact that most adults themselves live in a state of denial (or at least avoidance) about death. This is perhaps inevitable in a culture that is driven by the belief that we should all have the freedom to choose who we are, and how we will conduct our lives – because death is the one thing that challenges this mindset. It is the one unavoidable point where by definition we are not going to be in control. If we are unable to accept our own helplessness and vulnerability, we will always struggle to accept that death – and the sorrow that goes with it – is a natural part of the human condition. This sense of vulnerability and openness is an intrinsically spiritual characteristic, not least because it naturally evokes a consciousness that, as Shakespeare famously expressed it,

> There are more things in heaven and earth, Horatio,
> Than are dreamt of in your philosophy.[19]

Children processing sorrow

It was noted earlier that any sort of spiritual dimension is the one aspect of death that is routinely ignored by academic studies. David Hay and Rebecca Nye have made a coherent case for the opinion that children are born with a natural spirituality, and that our conventional processes of socialization and education are actually damaging to a child's spiritual perceptions.[20] If this is true, it implies that children (especially young ones) might well have a more authentic understanding of death than most adults, which means that paying attention to the ways in which children deal with death when they encounter it might also inform and expand our adult perceptions. That was certainly the case in our own experience, with which we began this chapter. So how do children cope with loss and the grief that always accompanies it?

As with most questions of human development, there is no one simple answer to this, though there are certain general statements that might be made. The most obvious concerns our definition of 'childhood' and 'children', which are wide categories that can be used to designate all the years from childhood to teenage – years in which we change more rapidly and radically than at any other point in life, not only in terms of physical growth but also in relation to psychological maturity and spiritual perception. The one thing we can say about childhood, therefore, is that it is a time of enormous change. Nothing stays the same for very long, which means that children are often better able than adults to deal with change, because they are experiencing it all the time. Most change, however, is predictable and normative, whereas death is generally unpredictable and unexpected. The death of a grandparent or other older relative – or indeed of a family pet – might well be predictable, and even recognized as such by children as young as five or six years, but such events are never frequent enough to be regarded as part of one's normative life experience. And, though there are common elements, the nature of bereavement (and therefore the consequent grief) is likely to be different in each case. In the final analysis, from the perspective of the living, death is about loss, and the way children (and, indeed, adults) react in any given case will depend on what is lost. By definition, bereavement involves the loss of a meaningful relationship, otherwise it is not a loss.

In this respect, we are probably at a turning point in western culture in relation to family bereavement, as growing numbers of children have only loose attachments even to their own parents (especially fathers), as relationships break up and family structures are rearranged into ever more complicated sets of connections.[21] In the past, the central attachment figures for children would always have been their parents and grandparents, along with aunts and uncles, siblings and then a wider family circle of cousins and so on. They still are for very many children, though with some variation in relation to the ethnic and cultural context. But the inexorable rise of celebrity culture is undoubtedly changing that, and in the not-too-distant future it may not be too far-fetched to contemplate that even the death of what might seem to be close family relatives may be of less significance than the loss of celebrities and other cultural icons from whom growing numbers of young people take their values and role models. Reference has already been made to the death of Princess Diana in a car crash in 1997, which is a classic case of a death that for many people evoked a deeper sense of loss than they had apparently experienced with the death of their own relatives – though some have suggested that it was precisely because of their own inadequate grieving for family members that they felt so profoundly moved at the death of the princess.[22] Whether this was essentially an adult phenomenon is impossible to say. No doubt some children will have felt a sense of empathy with Diana's young sons, though it may have been no more significant than the sense of solidarity that children tend to express to one another over any loss, however trivial.

The question of relationships, and which ones are sufficiently meaningful to call forth a real sense of loss, is not as fixed as it once was. Then there are also what might be called secondary losses, for example when a way of life has to change as a consequence of the primary loss through death. The way children deal with death always depends on which of these typical aspects of loss are most important to them.

Previous research on children and death has tended to concentrate on cognitive aspects, focusing on such questions as whether children are able to acknowledge the reality of the loss, or whether they tend to live in denial, maybe by retreating into some inner fantasy world. But a more useful approach might be to reflect on the ways in which children's reactions and responses to loss differ from those of adults. Recent research identifies several distinctive aspects:[23]

- Pre-school children can often respond to loss with aggressive behaviour that appears to have no obvious cause or reason, though older children's grief reactions at the actual point of death tend to be less intense than those of adults, while also lasting for much longer, albeit at a lower level of intensity.

- A key element in enabling children to deal with the painful elements of bereavement is to have consistently available adult parenting figures to help them process their loss and its resultant feelings.

- A loss during childhood affects a child's identity more deeply because self-development is still in progress. This is particularly the case with children between the ages of about six and ten, who can appear to be in denial about loss, though in reality such behaviour is motivated by a desire to look grown-up to others, or not to appear weird to their peers who have no experience of such things. In private, though, children can become preoccupied with blame and guilt, expressed in diverse ways ranging from a feeling that the death was their fault to becoming obsessed with their own bodily functions, especially in relation to minor ailments.

- Because of the interconnectedness of grief and normal development, it can be difficult to see when mourning ends in the life of a child and 'normal' life takes over again. This can be especially difficult in the case of adolescents, who frequently become withdrawn and depressed, perhaps adopting rebellious behavioural patterns in order to compensate for a loss they cannot articulate. At the same time, however, such behaviour is often characteristic of adolescents who have not been bereaved, and all the evidence is that there is a growing incidence of loneliness among teens more generally.

Some widely held assumptions about children and death should be approached with caution. For example, it has been known for a long time that under-elevens have fewer cognitive resources than either teenagers or adults with which to process and understand death. But this assumes that cognitive and rational understandings play a central role in dealing with death – something that has probably never been wholly true, and which is now rightly being questioned, for adults as well as for children. Arguably, therefore, children who are content to live with intellectual ambiguity might actually have greater insight than adults who assume that there will always be a rational explanation for things. Another widely held notion that ought to be questioned is the supposition that it is only children who are likely to deal with death through fantasy. It is also generally supposed that whereas adults intentionally create distance between themselves and the dead, by focusing more intensely on the living, children have a tendency to form even stronger attachments to the dead than they had when the deceased individual was alive. That may have been the case in the past, especially at a period when a Judaeo-Christian world view was dominant within society. But with the collapse of that consensus, we are seeing a rapid increase in the numbers of adults who hold to different opinions, and regard the dead as still involved in some mystical (and quite often physical) way with the world of the living. At one time, our family spent most summer holidays by a loch in the Scottish highlands, and it was not at all unusual in this remote wilderness to find shrines to the dead, with documentation around them that made it perfectly obvious they were more than just memorials: they were places where the dead could be encountered, and indeed where they were believed to live on, perhaps in the natural world that was now their post-mortem location. The rise of Internet blog culture has only served to heighten this trend among adults, and the sort of comments posted on many of these sites only serves to emphasize the extent to which fantasy is by no means limited to children as a way of dealing with the grief of bereavement. At a less dramatic level, anyone with pastoral experience will be able to identify lone widows or widowers who still use a plural pronoun ('we') to describe their life, even many years after the death of their spouse.

Children leading adults

It is often said that children lack cognitive or linguistic skills in dealing with life's hard questions, with the unspoken assumption either that this therefore makes it harder for them to process the pain of death, or that such processing as they are capable of will always be inadequate and incomplete. There are several reasons why this attitude should be challenged. Given the difficulties that adults experience in the face of death, who can say that the adult way is better or that it offers a standard by which a child's reactions can be judged? It is, of course, reasonable to think that children ought to be able to learn something from adults, because longer life experience should lead to greater wisdom, though that is by no means an assured conclusion, especially in relation to ultimate matters such as life and death. At the very least, we ought to acknowledge that the learning is unlikely to be all one way, and adults might have something to learn from children. Actually, they might learn the most important things from children. That was certainly our experience in the circumstances with which we began this chapter. It goes further than that, though, as we should also be asking why we think that cognitive rational and linguistic skills are the most appropriate ways to process our experiences of life more generally. We know the answer to that: for the last half millennium or so, western culture has been obsessed with understanding the universe by reference to what we regard as rational categories – most famously encapsulated in Descartes' dictum, *cogito ergo sum* (I think, therefore I am). But it is now becoming clear that abstract thinking of the sort that he and his successors valued is not only not the whole story, but might actually be the wrong story when it comes to any deep understanding of our human predicament.

Educationalists have known for a long time that 'there can be no learning that does not begin with experience'[24] and Richard Rohr reminds us that this has its spiritual counterpart because 'Christians do not think their way into a new life; they live their way into a new kind of thinking.'[25] It is no coincidence that in many traditional cultures, people never tried to understand death in a detached analytical way, but by telling stories. Rational analysis tends to close down creativity, because it always claims to offer the 'right' answer to our questions, though according to Walter Ong such analytical 'answers' are themselves likely to end up static and unserviceable in relation to the actual business of life.[26] Stories, on the other hand, embody the very essence of spiritual creativity because they open up new possibilities and prospects, inviting those who hear them to step into a new space in which their personal story can interact with other stories, and in turn all our human stories can somehow connect with that cosmic story that is bigger than any of us.[27]

Children do all these things intuitively. They tell stories of their departed loved ones, whether humans or pets. They paint pictures. They have fun with colours. They play games. They invent what liturgically sophisticated adults might describe as rituals to celebrate both life and death. All this takes us back to where we began: our own story, and the way that the spirituality of a small child dealing with death impacted our own lives. When Olive found herself becoming involved in clowning – especially clowning as a Christian ministry – it challenged everything we thought we knew, about ourselves as well as about theology and God. We were amazed when people all over the world started to share profound things about themselves as a direct result of encountering Olive's clown characters, and it took a while for us to work out what was going on. She regularly invites members of a congregation to take part in painting her face. Adults rarely respond, but children always do – and then it is the adults who are most obviously moved as a result, and more often than not they are taken back to revisit some experience of bereavement or other personal loss. There is a rational explanation for this, as the white face of a clown invokes primal images of a death mask, which is a key reason why many children are afraid of a clown when they meet her in full costume and make-up. But they never back off the opportunity to engage in the process of transformation from 'ordinary' person to clown. By painting the colours of new life on the white face, they not only engage with the reality of death, but point the way to new life and hope for others, even in the midst of tragedy. It must have been something like this that Jesus was thinking about when he took a child, and placed her in the midst to instruct the disciples in spiritual discernment (Mark 9.33-37; 10.13-16). But then, he also was more likely to address life's big questions by telling stories, drawing pictures, and invoking the imagination about the nature of God – all things that seem to come naturally to children.[28]

Questions

1. How has death among your family or friends affected your own Christian life?

2. This chapter says that 'Sorrow makes us all children again.' Can you identify whether and how this is true for you?

3. Make a list of any significant losses you experienced as a child (pets, people, objects, etc.). Try to imagine meeting them again in order to re-encounter them through the eyes of a child. How might they appear to you and how would this be different to your adult relationships and expectations?

4. Read the story of Jairus' daughter (Mark 5.21-24; 35-43). How do Jesus' reactions to the dead child and to the adults in this story help us understand the relationship between God and children? What would

looking at this story through the eyes of Jairus' daughter add to our understanding of Jesus' healing and saving actions?

5.   Identify ONE way in which bereavement visiting in your area might be improved by attending sensitively to the material in this chapter. How might looking through the eyes of a child help the pastoral process after a bereavement in a family with children?

11

Judgement

Paul Butler

Introduction

In their book, *The Bible: A Child's Playground*, Roger and Gertrude Gobbel argue very strongly and cogently that, 'It is not sufficient that they (children) hear about it or hear stories based on some biblical passage or character. Children must have direct access to the biblical content itself.' In their summary they state:

> In broad strokes, to teach children the Bible is to encourage and assist them to engage, act upon, and interact with it *as they are able*. It is to assist them to experience the Bible *as they are able*. It is to encourage and assist them to play and learn to play with the Bible *as they are able* and to assist them in their own process of interpreting and learning to interpret the Bible. It is to assist them to tell, share, and celebrate their own stories of their engagements with the Bible stories. It is to assist them in learning a way of thinking, feeling, and wondering about the Bible and a way of engaging and listening to it.[1]

In approaching the question of the Christian idea of 'judgement' through the eyes of a child I decided to try working from the Gobbels' premise. If given the text of the Bible itself on judgement, what do children make of it?

Many questions obviously follow. This particular project is limited by time and space so the full breadth of judgement in the Bible could not possibly be covered! Hence I had to make a clear decision about working with a limited number of children around a clearly defined part of the Scriptures. I contemplated seeing how they would respond to the story of Noah and the Flood; but this, in its entirety, is a long story for children to read. Additionally, I was keen that for this limited project we worked with Jesus himself in one of the Gospels. After much inner wrestling I finally settled on the parable of the sheep and goats. This parable is found only in Matthew's Gospel (25.31-46). It is also very clear that it has judgement as a theme. How, I wondered, would children respond to it if given it to read? What would they make of it and did it connect to any ideas of judgement that they might already hold?

Then, naturally, there were the questions of the children: how many? From where? What age? I am greatly blessed in being able to visit many schools across the southern half of the Diocese of Winchester. I visit to lead collective worship, answer questions in classes, present certificates, open new buildings, visit breakfast and after-school clubs, and simply spend time with children and staff alike. These schools cover the full range of county, voluntary aided, voluntary controlled and private foundation. My part of South Hampshire includes the city of Southampton, the suburbs of areas like Eastleigh and Chandlers Ford, market towns like Romsey and the villages of the New Forest and Test Valley. I settled on three schools, one (voluntary aided) in an urban priority area which is multi-ethnic and multi-faith in character, a second (voluntary aided) in a small town and a third (county) in a very rural village. I worked with children from Years 2 and 3 and 5 and 6 in small groups of seven or eight children. They talked, they wrote and they drew in response to the parable which we read together from the Contemporary English Version. I am deeply indebted to the 40 children who participated, and to the headteachers, teachers and teaching assistants concerned. It was a thoroughly enjoyable experience. It was also enlightening. I trust that the following summary of the conversations throws light on just how these children view the idea of judgement.

The text reads as follows:

> When the Son of Man comes in his glory with all his angels, he will sit on his royal throne. The people of all nations will be brought before him, and he will separate them, as shepherds separate their sheep from their goats.
>
> He will place the sheep on his right and the goats on his left. Then the king will say to those on his right, 'My father has blessed you! Come and receive the kingdom that was prepared for you before the world was created. When I was hungry, you gave me something to eat, and when I was thirsty, you gave me something to drink. When I was a stranger, you welcomed me, and when I was naked, you gave me clothes to wear. When I was sick, you took care of me, and when I was in jail, you visited me.'
>
> Then the ones who pleased the Lord will ask, 'When did we give you

something to eat or drink? When did we welcome you as a stranger or give you clothes to wear or visit you while you were sick or in jail?'

The king will answer, 'Whenever you did it for any of my people, no matter how unimportant they seemed, you did it for me.'

Then the king will say to those on the left, 'Get away from me! You are under God's curse. Go into the everlasting fire prepared for the devil and his angels! I was hungry, but you did not give me anything to eat, and I was thirsty, but you did not give me anything to drink. I was a stranger, but you did not welcome me, and I was naked, but you did not give me any clothes to wear. I was sick and in jail, but you did not take care of me.'

Then the people will ask, 'Lord, when did we fail to help you when you were hungry or thirsty or a stranger or naked or sick or in jail?'

The king will say to them, 'Whenever you failed to help any of my people, no matter how unimportant they seemed, you failed to do it for me.'

Then Jesus said, 'Those people will be punished for ever. But the ones who pleased God will have eternal life.'

(Matthew 25.31-46, Contemporary English Version)

Now let the children speak for themselves as they respond to this parable of Jesus.

Initial responses to the story

Having made the decision to use this particular parable I had no specific expectations of whether the children would or would not know the story. However, there was a very broad agreement from them on this point; almost every child involved stated that the story of the sheep and the goats was one that they had not heard or read before. Only Emma (10 years 5 months; hereinafter 10.5) said that she thought she had heard the story before at church but that it had sounded a bit different (probably either because a different version was read or because she had been told the story rather than reading the text for herself). The reactions therefore were to a completely new story and text. All the initial responses were spoken ones. In the way that the groups ran we always spoke first. The responses in drawing thus came a little later after some conversation and discussion had taken place. I also sought at this initial stage not to offer any 'help' with understanding the story. This, for example, inevitably meant that these children saw pictures in their minds of sheep and goats as they are found usually in the fields of Hampshire and the television and book images they had seen. Without exception sheep were talked of, and later depicted in the drawings, as the woolly variety. Goats likewise were generally seen as larger, probably with horns. The similarity of sheep and goats found in Israel in Jesus' day (and still today) was therefore 'lost' on these children. But then I suspect it is equally lost on most adults when they read this story, unless someone explains it to them.

During the conversation I did later take the opportunity to explain verbally, but this made little difference to the conversation; indeed all the pictures still depict sheep as the woolly type most had seen locally, in books or on television; likewise the goats. Having not had pictures available for the first group I decided not to change tack at all through the process. Pictures of middle eastern sheep and goats mixed together would, I suspect, aid deeper understanding.

The range of initial responses varied widely. Matt (10.7) summarized the reaction of some, 'I'm surprised Jesus told this story.' When asked to explain why he was surprised he stated simply, 'Because Jesus never curses anyone.' He added later, in writing, 'I'm confused but at the same time know what's going on.' Interestingly Patrick (10.6) was quite quick to dispute Matt's 'surprise' by pointing out that Jesus, when he was in the temple, 'was furious, and he threw them out'. To which point others in the group found themselves siding mainly with Patrick.

Overall the initial response in every group was to speak positively of the story:

> It makes sense; the people that believe didn't get punished.
>
> (Amy 10.7)

> It makes sense. Jesus is trying to teach people a lesson.
>
> (Amy 10.7)

> The story sounded very good; the people were being treated like royals – well treated.
>
> (Jacob 10.7)

> It's interesting. Amusing.
>
> (Sophie 8.3)

> It's quite funny – especially because there's stuff about no clothes.
>
> (Ned 8.5)

Yet alongside this generally positive response there was a willingness to express questions and confusion. This was more noticeable among the younger children:

> I'm getting a little bit mixed up with the goats and the sheep.
>
> (Ben 8.2)

> It's quite hard to understand; it's confusing.
>
> (Henry 10.2)

From among all the children, Sophie's (8.3) summary reaction to the story used many of the words found individually in the response of the others: 'amusing, interesting, OK, confusing, good, brilliant, understandable, weird, disturbing' (see drawing overleaf). Her list contains a mixture of words which on the surface appear to be almost contradictory. But that is an adult logically putting them together; for Sophie there was no contradiction in the story being both confusing and understandable. They were all genuine reactions to what she had read. Adults tend to avoid paradox and contradiction; we want things sorted out, logical and consistent. Children, however, appear to be able to live with paradox and contradiction quite happily. Perhaps this is a key lesson for adults to learn from theology done through the eyes of a child: learn to live with and accept paradox and apparent contradiction, don't always try to work out a neat theological solution.

Having made such initial responses, every group, indeed every child, then engaged happily both in talking about the story together, and, in most cases, even more enthusiastically in drawing a picture in response to the story. They were nearly all then willing to talk about their picture. What they all, perhaps not surprisingly given their age, felt less inclined to do was write very much, or in many cases anything at all. The children were 'doing theology' in the manner that suited them best. The use of conversation was important, but so too was the use of visual expression. As adults we tend to value the place of words, written and spoken, and perhaps undervalue 'doing theology' in other ways, such as art. These children teach us that sometimes exploring the Scriptures and theological ideas through visual expression is a more powerful and helpful way of expressing our ideas and emotions.

The actions of the sheep and the goats

Ben's (8.2) comment that 'the sheep are being nice to God so God's being nice to them. But the goats aren't being fair to God so he's being fair to them' in one way acts as a summary of the actions of visiting the sick, clothing the

naked, feeding the hungry, and so on, given by all the children. 'Fairness' arose regularly in the conversations. It appears to represent something of a reward / punishment view of the world. Being, or doing, good deserves a reward; being, or doing, bad deserves punishment. There appears to be some inbuilt desire for justice, certainly a conviction that wrong deserves punishment of some kind. Certainly in these conversations there was no reference to mercy or forgiveness as options, but then this particular text does not place these on the agenda.

The actions of practical help were all regarded as good things to do for which being rewarded was appropriate:

> If you don't have clothes Mum and Dad buys them and gives them to you.
>
> (Tom 6.11)

The bit about the clothes thing is kind because of giving him food and drink when he hasn't got that stuff.

(Tom 8.2)

There was widespread agreement among the children that caring action for people in need, as expressed in the story, was a good thing to do. Action they themselves would be willing to take.

Many expressed their displeasure with those who failed to take caring action:

It's terrible he was in prison and [they] didn't care for him.

(Grace 8.6)

It's unkind because some of them have nothing at the end.

(Sophie 8.3)

The goats are being nasty. So they get put in the fire.

(Ben 8.2)

The inclusion in the story of reference to people being 'naked' caused some amusement and questioning among the younger children:

It's quite funny, because there's stuff about no clothes.

(Ned 8.5)

It's weird about wearing clothes and not wearing clothes. If it was a man it would be disturbing.

(Grace 8.6)

It appeared that every older child did not see the story as really being about sheep and goats but about the actions of people. This was also true for most of the younger children, although at least a few did appear to take it more literally as being about actual sheep and goats. Here's Ben, 'It's hilarious for the sheep; they're being kind to Jesus and the goats aren't. The sheep are being nice to God, the goats are being nasty', at which point Ieuan piped up, 'so they get put in the fire'. Ieuan appears to have been quite content with the idea that such an action was fair; punishment was appropriate for the goats' behaviour.

In one picture the action of caring for the naked is depicted as Jesus acting. Lizzie (10.1) has a sad-faced naked man (with fig leaf) being handed a package by a man whom she labels 'Jesus'; above this she wrote 'follower'. On the other side she has another naked man (again with fig leaf) on his knees being whipped by a similar figure labelled Jesus; above this she wrote 'non follower'. Thus she appears to have seen Jesus as both the example of a follower and being the one who enacts punishment on the non-followers. Whipping is a fairly violent act to portray, and is not referred to within the original text. Somewhere Lizzie has heard, or more probably seen, whipping as a way of punishment. She apparently had no qualms with the idea of physical violence as a form of punishment. This does not square with her words, which are given below. Perhaps within her picture and words we have another example of a child coping with apparent paradox and contradiction.

The actions of the King

However, there was much greater discussion and disagreement between the children, particularly the older ones, when it came to the action of the King towards the sheep and the goats.

'It's like blackmailing someone to say he will curse you if you don't do something' (Lizzie 10.1). She later added, 'You have a right to believe in who you want to believe in', and, 'I think it's mean to say to someone you shall be cursed if you don't follow me. I think people have a right to choose.' She was joined by Abi (10.0) who asserted strongly, 'It's not up to Jesus to decide.' She then added, 'If Jesus was going to curse them I think more people follow because of encouraging them to do good things.' She also commented, later, that, 'I think it is fair that they get punished but it is not for the whole life. And they should worship the king and his people.' Unfortunately Abi did not spell out why she did not think it was for Jesus to decide on such matters. Patrick (10.6), on the other hand, in a strong three-way debate asserted Jesus' right to judge. He also commented that, 'the story goes with all religions. If they are part of their community, if they don't believe in God in their own religion then it's fair that they are cursed.'

Elena (9.11) stated, 'The story made sense and was fair. On the other hand, Jesus should of gave the people who did *not* believe God another chance.' Emma (10.5) commented, 'I liked the story. People who didn't follow God and Jesus went to the devil and people who followed Jesus stayed with God/Jesus.'

These responses were not, however, confined to the older children. Stephanie (7.6) said, 'Jesus, maybe he told the story because he wants people to, wanted everybody to be kind so they enter God's kingdom. If you disobey you're automatically sent out of God's kingdom and are being in the bad kingdom.' This latter phrase, 'the bad kingdom' suggests some transposing of the idea of kingdom on to eternal punishment. She appears to have thought of two parallel kingdoms: God's and that of those who are sent away.

There was widespread use of talking about Jesus or God as being the King in the story. This seemed almost to be assumed. Nowhere in the text is that connection explicitly made, and nor did I make any such comment. Somewhere in their reading/hearing of the text and what they already knew of Jesus and God they all seemed to make the connection that the King should be so identified. Exactly what the children understood by being King is not clear. They brought to the story kingship images from other backgrounds and stories; these would be a mixture of fairy tales, films like *Shrek*, and television programmes. They certainly saw the King as the person in charge, and having authority to act, but none of them pursued references to kings or kingship in other contexts. King appears to be an image with which they all happily worked. So Henry (10.2) could comment, 'It was very confusing in some places but tells us a lot about how Jesus and God lived.'

Jamie, in his picture with a king's head in the middle, goats and a devil with flames and a pitchfork to one side, and angel and sheep on the other writes 'GOD' above the king with an arrow pointing towards the head. Emma (10.5) wrote, 'I liked the story. People who didn't follow God and Jesus went to the devil and people who followed Jesus stayed with God/Jesus.' Anna (8.1) in her drawing (overleaf) has a sheep, labelled on one side, a goat, also labelled on the other. The sheep is saying 'baa' and the goat 'boo'. Above the sheep she wrote 'good' and above the goat 'bad'. In between them is a Jesus-like figure clearly labelled 'Jesus'. Why the labelling? Was it for her benefit or for mine? Did she regard me as needing help to understand her picture, or did she see the labelling as a way of emphasizing her point? In some other pictures there was also labelling. My instinct is that this is done to make the drawing clear to the viewer. Some specifically expressed their lack of confidence in their drawing abilities. Anna's pictures of the goat and sheep are identical, so the drawing alone does not make it clear which is which. Once she had started labelling then she added a label for Jesus for completeness.

Romy (7.6) in her drawing of sheep in a pen on one side and a pen labelled 'goat left' on the other has a clearly Christlike figure standing between them with a hand outstretched towards the sheep while his hand on the side of the goat hangs down. Jesus has a smile on his face, and is dressed in a bright yellow, knee-length dress, with a green belt and green shoes. The emphasis of the picture seems to be entirely on the positive imagery; that is where Romy wanted to focus.

Finally, we have Lizzie's picture referred to earlier in which Jesus is identified in

one part of the picture as the one enacting the punishment. Somewhere in all of them this connection between the King in the story and God/Jesus is made.

The idea of judgement

Every child found a way of expressing something about their idea of judgement. Here's the range of comments made:

> Judging means that if you're on *The X Factor* and you're singing you get judged which means like having a mark.
>
> (Stephanie 7.6)

> I think that judgement means when people go up to heaven.
>
> (Sam 7.3)

> It means you need to say something out loud to people.
>
> (Chantelle 7.7)

> I think judgement means that someone goes in a grave that's good/bad good goes to heaven bad go to hell.
>
> (Ben 7.9)

> Judgement is saying something about what a person is doing.
>
> (Romy 7.6)

Like when you're in a court and judge who's guilty and not guilty, innocent. [Someone] judged what book you're reading.

(Thomas 8.6)

Describing people who's good and who's bad. In court, in jail, in police station or fire station.

(Anna 8.1)

Judged by team points.

(Thomas 8.6)

Judged if you push someone over on purpose.

(Jack 7.5)

Represented by some scales – if person's good it balances; if bad it gets heavy. Judge is the right person you put on the scales, not in a physical way. If someone is found guilty it goes down, if not guilty it balances.

(Jamie 10.0)

Judgement is sometimes a way of judging somebody or something to restore order.

(Jacob 10.7)

Trying to be fair. Danger of punishment. The final answer . . .

(Elena 9.11)

I think judgement means like making a decision out of two things.

(Luke 9.9)

You judge someone for their appearance.

(Patrick 10.6)

Judgement means the judge has made a decision.

(Abigail 10.0)

Judgement for me means your idea on something like what you think of someone and something.

(Lizzie 10.1)

Get told off, badly told off, for being bad.

(Sasha 10.8)

I think it was right to judge those people and bless the people who worship him and punish the people who did not help him.

(Luke 9.9)

I think it's fair that all the people who didn't believe in God got punished for all eternity.

(Patrick 10.6)

The comments illustrate a broad range of ideas about judgement. Some focus on decision making; some pick up on the idea of good and bad; and some pick up on the idea of blessing or punishment and a final judgement. They use examples and illustrations from their own lives and experiences, alongside using more generalized statements. Interestingly some of the children found it easier to write their response to this privately rather than engage in any conversation. As if, for them, they wanted to keep their own personal opinion to themselves. But others, notably among the older children, happily engaged in quite heated conversation about their different ideas of judgement.

What was clear from them all was that a notion of judgement was accepted by everyone. For some it appeared to be entirely to do with events in the here and now, while for others it extended into thoughts of the whole of life, and the possibility of life hereafter. It included the possibility, even necessity, of punishment, but was also seen as a positive way of recognizing good and achievement.

Other comments

Inevitably there were a variety of other comments made on the story which cannot be left unspoken.

Literary criticism

A few children decided that they wanted to comment on the way that the story was told:

I think that the story was a bit too long. They could have made it a lot shorter and to the point.

(Chloe 11.2)

I think what Jesus said was kind of the same in both of the main parts. Maybe it could have been a bit more different. But the story is OK.

(Heidi 10.1)

It was predictable what he would say in the second half because he was positive about the first group you can expect him to be negative about the second group.

(Josh 11.4, first comment)

It should be noted, I think, that these three literary-critical comments came from the same group. Perhaps Josh's initial comment triggered off a literary thought in the minds of the two girls, who were sat together so perhaps 'copied' one another's idea.

However, one younger child from a different group entirely did offer something of a literary critique. 'The story is clever. The reason why it is clever is because of how they use the words over and again' (Grace 8.6).

On another occasion it might have been interesting to ask the children to look at it as a piece of literature first to see whether it made a difference to the response.

A story with a lesson

A few of the children wanted to make it clear that they saw the parable as a general lesson from Jesus for us all today:

> A Christian story that I would say the messages are if you believe God will always be with you.
>
> (Jacob 10.7)

> Jesus is trying to teach people a lesson.
>
> (Amy 10.7)

The drawings

Every single younger child happily spent time producing a drawing, even though some protested that they were not very good at drawing. However, a few of the older children who professed either a dislike of art, or that they were not very good at it, chose to draw nothing; they preferred to talk. This would appear to be simply a matter of greater confidence in older children to stick with their own preference. I had made it clear that no one had to do any of the suggested activities (though no one opted out completely).

All the pictures drawn, bar one, were to illustrate part, or all, of the parable. The one exception, however, was by Tom (6.11), who chose to produce a picture of Jesus telling the story to a group of people rather than a picture of the story itself (overleaf). He added verbally that, 'all the people were concentrating on listening to Jesus'. For him, it would appear the most significant thing about the story was not the content at all but rather who told it and that people listened to it. His comment acted as an intriguing critique of the chosen methodology. Tom managed to imagine the setting without being offered it either by the text or by my own introduction. How often do we encourage children to imagine, and dream, the setting of the stories of Scripture? How much might have been added to this exercise for all the children with just a little more scene setting by me? But how quickly would such scene setting become my laying down of a narrower agenda for understanding?

For the rest, the common images were largely as one would probably expect. A good number produced a picture that had a clear divide of a group to the right and a group to the left. The clarity, or sharpness, of the divide was accentuated in several cases by the children drawing a line down the middle of the page (see, for example, Grace's picture opposite). Mostly these were pictures of sheep and goats but some chose to depict people rather than animals. These certainly had grasped that the story was intended to be understood as being about people. Smiles and sad faces were in abundance on the faces of the people depicted.

In the middle of the pictures came a variety of a king sat on a throne, or wearing a crown (or both) or simply a central figure with arms outstretched in both directions.

Fire appeared regularly for the goats' destiny. Swirling colours of red, orange and yellow with figures mingled inside it, or stepping into it. Fire holds huge fascination for children, and adults. My many years of running children's camps at which every evening we held a campfire taught me just how much children love a fire, and how they wonder at it. They enjoy its colours, its warmth and the way one can 'play' with it. But this is not simply true of children; every adult leader was also observed enjoying real fire, and wondering at it. Fire is a fantastic shared event for adults and children together. Given this highly positive experience of fire it is perhaps surprising that fire as judgement is accepted so readily.

Intriguingly, those who chose to depict something of the deeds of the sheep and the goats favoured two matters in particular. The first of these was showing someone, or a group of people, inside a prison. This image was used both negatively (sad person clearly alone) and positively, the person being visited and smiling. The second image was that connected with clothing. Several children chose to draw people well clothed, poorly clothed or naked. A pile of clothes, carefully selected to show different types of clothing, also featured in some, such as the drawing below by Ben. Why these two images, of prison and clothing should be given prominence over the others is an intriguing question. The clothing reference is understandable because of its immediate connection with the child's everyday life. The fascination, and giggles, about the naked people fits entirely with children's intrigue about the human body. But why 'prison' rather than hunger or thirst? It is probably easier to draw, so that may have attracted some of them; they may simply have copied each other, but I saw little evidence of this. Perhaps it is a fear they have for themselves, which they do not have of going hungry or thirsty, both of which are not realities for the children with whom I was dealing. I'm sure all factors came into play, but given the evidence that at all stages the children

made connections between the story and their own immediate world I think the ease of drawing and likelihood of their greater fear were both significant in this emphasis on prison.

There were those who attempted something more like a storyboard effect of this part of the parable, showing all the different ways in which help had been offered by the sheep, such as the drawing below by Sam, but the majority chose just one or two aspects of this part of the parable.

One or two made the decision to draw something that did not appear to be immediately connected with this story. So among the collection I have a couple of pictures of the crucifixion. It is perhaps worth noting that in one of these, which depicts three crosses, the large central cross of Jesus has one of the other crosses underneath his outstretched arm while the other is at a distance from him. There are tears of rain and a sad sun over the top of the whole picture. But has Ieuan (7.11)(see drawing overleaf) somehow linked the divide between the sheep and the goats of the parable with a divide at the cross? Has he depicted Jesus' death being shelter for one but loss for another? Or is that an adult trying to see more in this young child's drawing than the child himself intended? He gave no indication either way verbally, although he did say that 'The sun's crying because of what's happening; the clouds are crying.' Ieuan, I should add, was among the quietest of all the children who took part.

One final point to make about the drawings. Several of the least vocal children in the group conversations produced the most detailed and colourful drawings. Olivia (7.2), who hardly said a word, produced the most colourful

picture of anyone. Her picture has a large central smiling figure dressed in yellow with arms outstretched to both sides. On one side is a group of happy people, on the other a group of sad, crying people, several with their hair standing on end. Olivia also wrote no words. Being given the opportunity to draw, however, she burst into life and expression. Her contribution speaks volumes about the importance of art and visual expression for some children; this is the way they think and express themselves. We happily and readily encourage this in children. Does not this way of their doing theology challenge adults to keep doing the same? This surely is why Christian art, icons and the like have always been valued in worship and prayer. Somehow at least some sections of the Church seem to have underplayed or undervalued this.

Joshua (11.40), another quieter child, produced one of the most complex and detailed pictures (see p. 241) entirely in lead pencil. On the bottom right, shaded figures in a group; on the bottom left, another group but not shaded. Between them is a wide jagged line thickly shaded leading to an angel figure in the middle of the page inside a kind of bubble. To the right and above the angel are flames; to the left and above, a picture of a palm tree and another tree with an animal walking between the two and what appears to be sea in the distance and clouds above. Above this is written HEVEN.

Tabitha (7.10) also produced a highly colourful picture with a multicoloured coated figure in the middle with a halo and a sheep and a goat to either side. Above, across the whole picture, is a bright red sky.

For these three, at least, drawing helped them express their response to the story in a way that words, either spoken or written, had failed to do. This is drawing for expression. How often have adults in church used drawing as a way of keeping children quiet rather than as a positive means of engagement and expression? How often as adults have we dismissed the child's drawing too quickly, not noticing what the child may be trying to communicate to us as adults? If we paid more attention, what fresh insights might we have into the child's own life? And what fresh insights into God and his ways might we find the child expressing to us?

Reflections on the context

Ideally I would have conducted all the group sessions in the same week, but diary constraints of a bishop meant that this was not possible. This led to an interesting change in responses. In the first two schools that I visited, when it came to conversations about the children's understanding of 'judgement' and offering examples there were a number of references to the television programme *The X Factor*. Among these comments were:

> Judgement is like lots of things, like *The X Factor*; lots of judges who decide how good or bad they are.

> (Ben 8.2)

> 'Judge – like in *The X Factor*. 9 out of 10 would be judging and someone
> would win. If you judge you're giving a person a score out of 10,
> something like that.
>
> (Stephanie 7.6)

The X Factor offered a frame of reference for judging which involved success
and failure, joy and sorrow. Interestingly, the children made little reference to
any particular acts, nor to specific judges; they were content to make general
references to the programme as an example of judgement in action. Perhaps
they are better at moving from specifics to general ideas than they are often
given credit for doing.

However, the third school visit produced no references at all to *The X Factor*.
On the other hand, references were made to Harry Potter, particularly around
Harry, and his friends, having to make decisions on how to act in lots of
situations. I was intrigued by the difference. The context, however, may
contain the explanation. The first two schools were visited towards the end of
The X Factor series and many of the children were avid watchers of the
programme. By the time of the third school visit, the series had been finished
for two or three weeks. On the wall of the library where we worked in this
third school, though, was a poster of Harry Potter and the media hype around
the launch of the seventh and final Potter book was well under way.

In all three settings therefore I suggest that the responses to the Bible story
were partly influenced by the immediate circumstances of the children's lives
at the time. Their world interacted with the world of the Bible story and helped
them reach an understanding of it. This is, I believe, further seen in the range
of other illustrations that the children used to express their understanding of
judgement. In every conversation illustrations were drawn from family life, the
school setting and police or judges and law courts.

As examples of these three, here are Chloe (11.2), Bethany (7.8) and Thomas
(8.6):

> When Mum says, 'I will reserve my judgement', she hasn't blamed me
> yet but she is sort of suspecting me.
>
> (Chloe)

> When I'm at home my Mum does things wrong sometimes and I have
> to correct her. That's what I call judging things.
>
> (Bethany)

> We're judged who's best by team points.
>
> (Thomas)

Judging is like when you're in court and judge who's guilty and who's not guilty, who's innocent.

(Thomas)

Around all three settings, home/family life, school and the law, every group talked about examples of where and how judgement takes place in their, and others', daily lives. In this way judgement was virtually always seen as something that happens in life here and now. Regularly as part of the process children cited people who had an authority to exercise judgement – parents, judges, the police and teachers being the key figures. Indeed, if we reflect on some of the comments quoted above it appears that authority residing in specific authority figures seems to be central, rather than some abstract notion of 'judgement'. Judgement is connected with a person having the authority to act as judge. Yet alongside this they happily talked of and drew a separation of people into heaven and hell. As Ben (7.9) put it, 'Judgement is the day when someone goes to hell and someone to heaven. St Valentine was good so he went up to heaven.' (We weren't meeting anywhere near St Valentine's Day and Ben couldn't explain why he particularly thought of him.) Alongside him, however, Sam (7.2) simply said, 'A wrestling ring is called Judgement Day', with no further comment. Only later did someone explain to me that there is a television wrestling event called Judgement Day. He was clearly again using his own world for reference – one lost on me.

All of this leads me to ponder once again the significance of context for how children understand and respond to the Bible, and all it contains. There are ongoing wider contexts that shape their thinking and responses, like the family and community, plus wider society. But this experience also highlighted the way that their response was influenced by more immediate contextual factors, like current television programmes, posters on the wall and advertising campaigns. It ought to make us all reflect on the total context of the children with whom we work, and the immediate surroundings within which we work. All of this context will affect how they understand and respond to the story(ies) of the Scriptures.

Reflections on the methodology

This was a small sample of children in a limited period. However, their openness and willingness to engage with the actual text of a Bible story being given to them certainly highlighted for me the key point that the Gobbels were making. We need to allow children to explore the Bible itself, for themselves. Certainly we can offer help and support to strengthen this. But perhaps we need to do this as a response to their response, rather than deciding beforehand what help they might need. Every time we tell and retell a Bible story we do so in an interpretative way, however carefully we seek to stick to the text and its context. We should encourage children to engage in imagining the context themselves, as happens so helpfully with Godly Play's 'I wonder . . .' This is perfectly proper but as we tell and retell the stories, and as we encourage godly imagination, we should be encouraging adults and children alike to check this out against the Bible text itself, and the clues it offers about context. The Gobbels' work needs really to feed into our work with children. Let them have the text of the Bible and discover that it really is 'a child's playground'.

The mix of words in conversation and writing, and the opportunity to draw created a range of options for the children to respond. I noted in the section on the drawings how for at least three of the children the drawing came as a great release. This simply acts as a reminder once again that different children learn, and communicate, in different ways. In all work with children, this reminds us, we need to ensure that we do employ a wide variety of methods and encourage the full range of learning styles that we know exist in all people.

The doctrine of judgement

It is clear that children do work with ideas of judgement. For all the children involved in these conversations there was an immediacy about judgement taking place in daily life. It happens in the home, at school and in our wider society through the police and the law courts, and in the media. It is this daily process of judgement which formed the largest bulk of comment and thought from the children's conversations.

But there is also some idea of a final judgement undertaken by God. This does involve thoughts around being judged on our behaviour and our beliefs in this life. For most of them, responding to this particular story, there was an acceptance, even endorsement, that such a judgement would lead to 'God, Jesus and heaven' for some and 'the devil and hell' for others. For most of the children this judgement was also on the basis of God being 'fair'. However, among the older children in particular there was a willingness to question whether or not people should be given a second chance, or even if Jesus/God had the right to act as judge in this way. There was not time to explore these children's understanding of what they might understand by 'heaven' or 'hell', although the image of fire as punishment, drawn straight from the parable itself, was used consistently in the children's drawings. The consistent image for 'heaven' was of happy people together being with God and Jesus. Interestingly these images were not about 'doing' anything but were entirely about 'being' with God.

Not one single child expressed concern for themselves and any judgement on their own lives. They all appeared sure that if they lived good lives, expressed in caring for other people, then they would be in heaven. There was no evidence of any great personal fear of hell or punishment; it would happen to some people but not to any of them; nor indeed any of their family or friends. They all accept that they do and say wrong things but somehow feel punishment is only for the really wicked.

In conclusion

The scope of this exploration into how children think of and understand the Christian doctrine of judgement has been limited. It leaves me wanting to spend more time with children encouraging them to explore this, and other doctrines. Yet limited though it is, I believe it does reveal that judgement is an idea of which children do have some grasp. They see it as an ongoing part of life, including their own lives. Yet they are also open to the idea that there might be some kind of final judgement in the future which will be undertaken by God/Jesus. In this they all see themselves as 'safe' because, in the light of the particular parable, they seek to live good lives. Most of the children expect that in any such judgement there will be those who are sent to hell and will be punished.

But perhaps even more than these reflections on judgement, for the author this piece of work makes me want to encourage the giving of the text of the Bible to children for them to explore and seek to understand for themselves. Our general failure to do so may be denying them joy in a playground of discovery; and in so doing also denying the older generations the freshness and insight that these young lives can bring.

Questions

1. What does the word 'judgement' mean to you?

2. How do the children's reflections in this chapter match up with your ideas of both day-to-day judgements and final judgement?

3. In two columns headed 'sheep' and 'goats' list any characteristics, behaviour or attitudes that might deserve a sheep or goat label. What

might the children see as 'sheep' or 'goat' behaviour and how might it contrast with your own view?

4. Re-read the passage about the sheep and the goats in Matthew 25.31-46. What is clear and what seems baffling or paradoxical for you? In what ways do the children's comments throw light on the passage? In what ways do they challenge the passage?

5. What kinds of events or activities in your church allow discussion or exploration of moral questions? Can you think of ONE such activity which might benefit from feeding in children's thoughts and ideas?

12

Angels

Howard Worsley

In this chapter I will argue that it is far easier to have a conversation about angels with children than with adults. Until recently, many Christian adults (who are not New Age or secular seekers) would feel concerned about being considered eccentric, fundamentalist or mad, even to talk about angels, but children are far more relaxed . . . up to a certain age.

This chapter also discusses how angels are understood by children, using insights from current classroom research. Before considering this research, and looking at the implications of its findings for the twenty-first-century adult, the broader topic of angels, as understood and mediated by adults, is discussed.

Why consider angels?

In the more 'spiritually open' discourse of the twenty-first century, angels are re-emerging as part of the climate of spirituality, but they are doing so in vastly different ways. On the one hand, a New Age type of exploration allows people to perceive angels, especially guardian angels, and to discern them at work in their lives, while on the other hand, it also opens up opportunities for a more poetic or metaphoric language that alludes to angelic beings. Angel workshops and angel healing are just two forms of 'angel spirituality' which are supposed to create links between human beings and the angelic beings of the heavenly realm. Access to angel therapies and practices is readily available through web sites on the Internet as any casual search of the word 'angel' will show.

For example, the contemporary interest in angels is reflected in the works of Theolyn Cortens, whose writings detail a developed research into angels from 'Discovering Angels' written in 1996, through 'Angels' Script' written in 1997 to 'Living with Angels' in 2005 and finally 'Working with your Guardian Angel' in 2006. This latter work is a twelve-week programme which has the aim of harnessing the help of a guardian angel. Her evangelistic attitude with regard to angels leads her to suggest that 'working with angels' benefits any kind of spiritual practice.[1]

Contemporary interest in angels

Yet angels are not a new phenomenon, but are evident in the ancient scriptural texts and certainly a part of both Jewish and Christian tradition. While they have always existed within the boundaries of more speculative theology, of late they are discussed far beyond the cloister. Most recently, and of note to this study, the experience of angels has been the topic of a doctoral research (*Seeing Angels*) conducted by Emma Heathcote-James in 2001.[2] This researcher interviewed over 800 people who claimed to have experienced visions of angels and recorded the data of the first 350 accounts. These people emerge as ordinary members of the British public whose experiences are presented to us analytically by the researcher. The findings of this study indicate that angels appear to be alive and well in ordinary life.

In my article entitled 'Has secularism emptied the world of angels?',[3] I argued that these researchers, such as Cortens and Heathcote-James, tend only to chart the reappearance of angels in the experience of British people and offer little analysis of the psychological profile of those interviewed and only brief insights into the cultural contexts in which renewed interest in angels is now emerging.

What are we then to make of people who claim to have seen or encountered angels? One perspective is that people who believe in the presence of angels are more likely to have a simplistic world view and to believe in fantastical events whereby spiritual reality merges with physical objects. Understood positively, such perceptions and descriptions may be seen to be poetic; in neutral terms they may be seen to be literalist; and in negative terms such perceptions may be seen to be mentally disordered.[4]

Some people, then, would find their spirituality enhanced by reference to angelic help, beneficence or intercession. Such people would not necessarily attest to having seen or encountered an angel, but would talk about angels as part of the divine life or the spiritual world. A literalist world view would be one that understands spiritual beings to be operating in physical ways, such as that portrayed in the book *Angels* by the twentieth-century evangelist Billy Graham recording instances of actual angel sightings.[5] This results in a different kind of discourse, in which angels directly act on the world and are available to the physical senses.

Examples of fantastical world views are found frequently in children's fiction, such as the works of Philip Pullman, whose trilogy *His Dark Materials* (1997)[6] offers multiple worlds living next to each other, inhabited by angels and daemons. It is interesting to note that these books are often debated by Christian 'occult-realists', who are Christians who apply a literal belief to the physical embodiment of evil in demonic beings. Such believers would be concerned about the damaging effects of atheistic writers (like Pullman) or more agnostic writers (like J. K. Rowling) who portray the presence of evil within demons or wizards. For some such Christians, there is concern about the effects of works like these on children, yet at the same time this concern is sometimes linked to a belief in the actuality of guardian angels or a view that the angelic host is on hand to wrestle with the powers of evil. For such people, angels are not to be treated lightly or manipulated by human whimsy.

Such thinking is offered in the novels of Frank Peretti, whose books *This Present Darkness* (1986) and Piercing *the Darkness* (1989)[7] describe an 'occult-realist' world in which angels of light are empowered by prayer. Although these books are clearly fictitious and fantasy literature, they nonetheless represent a world view that is lived by many Christians and which perceives a struggle between 'good' powers of light which come from God and 'evil' powers of darkness which attempt to subvert, corrupt and enslave human beings.

This contemporary scene then, creates one of the contexts through which children can encounter the idea of angels. However, there are also other important contexts through which information and evidence about angels can be offered to children. For example, children are often exposed to angel images and angel ideas through visual images and through historic literature.

Artistic interest in angels

If the scriptural texts on angels are relatively sparse, the same cannot be said of art, which after the early Church heresy of angel-worship (when prohibition of angelic representation was made), has seen a proliferation of images of angels from the mosaics of Ravenna (AD 400) through the Byzantine influences and the Renaissance (Correggio, Michelangelo, Botticelli, Fra Angelico, Fra Filippo Lippi, Raphael and Titian) to modern times.[8]

To offer comment on such a development in art is wider than the scope of this text, though it needs to be noted if we are to look at the artwork of children drawing angels, which we shall do shortly.

Artists such as William Blake[9] and Stanley Spencer not only depicted angels in their paintings but saw angels coming and going in ordinary human life and experience. Such art suggests that angels are natural go-betweens in communication between earth and heaven and that we can notice them around us if only we pay attention in the right way. The 'Angel of the North', situated by the A1 at Newcastle, is probably the most well-known contemporary icon of an angel, with a wingspan of 54 metres and a height of 20 metres. The sculptor, Anthony Gormley, said in an interview: 'It is important to me that the angel is rooted in the ground – the complete antithesis of what an angel is, floating about in the ether.'[10]

In saying this, Gormley had a sense of integrating the historical roots of mining in the North East to the spiritual world. Clearly he sensed that this was a revolutionary creation and a radical statement, but it is in fact merely a traditional representation of what an angel is – the interface between God and the human, between the spiritual and the material.

This is why angels are beloved by poets, theologians and artists. The visionary artist Cecil Collins has used the image of angels to symbolize the relationship between the divine world and the physical world. In his lecture entitled 'Angels' (2004) he connects this interest in angels to children. He said, childhood is the period of our lives 'when we experience virginity of consciousness before it is obscured by the conditional mind'. It is my observation that he then goes on to speak of childhood as the time when angels are seen, for, in his words,

> like sees like, like attracts like . . . The angels are a wind; they are winged because they belong to the open skies of the spirit. They live in the oxygen of God. The angels are a wind force of divine mind. They are the spiritual intelligence that connects all worlds; they unify and they help transform our consciousness and our awareness. They are infused with the beauty of the divine world from which they come – Angels are essentially a being of the universality of the spiritual life; they redeem us from our selfish provincialism, our narrow tribal view of life.[11]

Such poetic and artistic thinking links with the concept that the child's fresh vision can be seen again if adults look out for it. It is a timely caution to any notion of development that sees a later stage as being qualitatively advanced on a former stage since this suggests that in the process of growing up, some insights are forgotten.

Theological interest in angels

Finally, another important context for Christian children in particular, is how the Church itself speaks about angels.

In the introduction to their work *Angels*, a popular overview of angels within Christian thought, the husband and wife team Robert and Ro Willoughby write:

> Sadly very few Protestant theologians or commentators give them [angels] much space. Maybe it's the remnants of anxiety about the rather exotic miracles and visions of angels which were very prominent in the late Middle Ages in Europe. Or perhaps theologians today are concerned not to give too much space to what might be mistaken for New Age Spirituality. It seems a pity that so few thinkers have given them the attention they deserve.
>
> Even more sadly, many Christians dismiss the whole idea of the existence of angels out of hand. Some rank them alongside goblins, fairies or elves – as fantasy or the product of a Tolkienesque imagination. Some people can't imagine why God would need to create them or make use of them.[12]

The Willoughbys offer four different categories of angel: angels of power, angels of protection, angels of praise and angels of proclamation. In considering angels of power they examine the story of Peter being rescued by an angel (Acts 12.1-19), whereas angels of protection are exemplified by the angels seen by Elisha as those who protect Israel from the enemy (2 Kings 6.8-23). Angels of praise are seen in John's vision of heaven (Revelation 4 and 5) and angels of proclamation are the messengers of God appearing in the Nativity stories of Matthew and Luke.

However, the Willoughbys' straightforward classification of angelology has not always been how angels have been understood. For example, in the sixteenth century, John Calvin showed his wariness at offering too much respect or adulation for angels. In *The Institutes of the Christian Religion* (1599) he wrote, 'Surely, since the splendour of the divine majesty shines in them, nothing is easier for us than to fall down, stupefied, in adoration of them, and then to attribute to them that which is owed to God alone.'[13]

Another major figure within Protestantism, the twentieth-century theologian Karl Barth devoted a great deal of text in his influential *Church Dogmatics* (1932–68)[14] to indicate his thinking that angels were a key contact between this world and eternity. He wrote:

> Where God is, there the angels of God are . . . where there are not angels, there is no God . . . We know nothing of their essential being and its particular nature. We know nothing of their mutual relationship and distinction. We know nothing of the way in which they are a totality yet distinct. But we do know that even in the mystery of their being, they exist in and with the kingdom of God coming and revealed to us . . . They are in the service of God.[15]

Since then, mainstream theological works (both Catholic and Protestant) have tended not to discuss angelic beings, though children's Christian fiction has continued to keep angels alive. As well as the books by Frank Peretti, the trilogy by Robert Harrison needs to be mentioned. These books, *Oriel's Diary* (2002), *Oriel's Travels* (2003) and *Oriel in the Desert* (2004),[16] more closely reflect the biblical narrative, recounting the life of Jesus (*Oriel's Diary*), then of Paul and finally of Moses from the imagined viewpoint of an archangel. Although these works are fictional, they are included in a discussion of theology because they influence how angels are perceived within believing world views. It can be argued that such folk stories about biblical images (alongside hymnology) have been some of the greatest sources of religious influence in the ways people believe and how then such images and ideas are transmitted to children.

A look at the actual biblical record explains why so much writing is speculative or imaginary because relatively little descriptive material about angels exists in Scripture. Indeed, most Christian references to angels appear in hymns, appearing particularly at Christmas or at Eastertime and sometimes in the more popular hymns like John Wade's 'O come all ye faithful' or 'Hark the herald' or Moultrie's 'Let all mortal flesh keep silence'.

Much of the biblical terminology relating to angels and heavenly creatures can be directly connected to the culture in which the biblical writers lived. There are various sorts of angelic hosts (the cherubim, seraphim, archangels and fallen angels), as well as those who appear as messengers. The cherubim are winged creatures with human features who protect what is holy, the tree of life (Genesis 3.24), the ark of the covenant (Exodus 25.18) and the throne of God (Ezekiel 10). The seraphim are pure guardians of God's throne (only mentioned in Isaiah 6). The archangels are senior angels found more in apocalyptic literature and in apocryphal writings. Fallen angels are hinted at in various places (Job 4.18; Isaiah 14.12; Matthew 25.41; 2 Peter 2.4; Revelation 12.9) but never given the dualistic prominence of influential fictitious works like Milton's *Paradise Lost*.

Indeed, the biblical records offer a more fluid understanding of angels as the Old Testament signifies that since human beings cannot encounter God directly, it must be done via an intermediary. Hence there is the appearance of the three travellers at Abraham's tent, which he understands as an encounter with God in Genesis 18.2. Similarly there is the story of Jacob's wrestling match in which he struggles with an angel throughout the night before being overthrown in Genesis 32.24.

This in turn gives birth within the Scriptures to the notion of angels of the presence who signify the presence of God, messenger angels who offer God's voice, angels of death who bring God's righteous anger and guardian angels who epitomize the protection of God. Often, it is angels who make it possible for humans to understand what God is doing, as occurs at the empty tomb in Matthew 28.5-8.

The angelic messengers of the Bible have been variously categorized over time. A 1906 compilation entitled *A Book of Angels* included 15 contributions on topics such as 'the angel of the presence', 'the angels round the throne', 'visitants and messengers', 'guardian angels', 'angels of good tidings and joy' and 'angels of victory', as well as those already mentioned.[17]

Bringing a much-needed note of academic theological rigour to the field, Walter Wink offers a wider definition of angels as being found amid the powers that determine human existence. His literary juices were unlocked by reading Wesley Carr's *Angels and Principalities* (1981),[18] a book that argued for the increasingly populist notion that the New Testament was a world that did not recognize the presence of evil spirits.[19] Fired by these thoughts, he set about researching the terms for power in the New Testament. His conclusion was to state firmly that the seven terms for spiritual power in the New Testament (namely, (i) demons, (ii) Satan, (iii) angels of the churches, (iv) angels of the nations, (v) angels of nature, (vi) gods and (vii) the elements of the universe) were all very present in the thought-world of the New Testament writers and point to a world view that allows us to identify powers that foster institutional evil. The books in his *Powers* trilogy[20] are essentially about power manifested in its superhuman or corporate manifestations. This has direct significance for how many Christians have come to process thinking of the powers at work in the twenty-first century and creates another perspective through which the action and character of angels can be understood.

It could be that the language of angels has been pushed into particularized language zones because spiritual insights operate on the boundaries of cognition and on the edges of consciousness. As such, angelic thinking may be being relegated by adults to a more private place, less accessible to the conscious or the rational mind. However, within children, not yet controlled by societal norms, these insights of original vision may still be operating.

Theology, fictions and art therefore provide further contexts from which the concept of angels can enter the lives of children. We need to understand how this happens, because children may be able to offer us a fresh insight and understanding about angels. In order to see if, and how, this is so, we need to disentangle cultural referencing from what children give us.

In order to do this, we can look at a research project which aimed to examine what children think about angels.

The Bible Story Project's method to unearth children's understanding of angels

For this current enquiry, to consider a Bible story with angels, the BSP went to two different primary schools to find out the views of children in Years 5 and 6 (i.e. aged between 9 and 11 years of age).[21] Both schools were voluntary aided Church of England primary schools where there existed a faith ethos in which Bible stories were familiar. One of the schools (school A) was situated in an inner city and had an open admissions policy, attracting pupils from several world faiths and from across the Christian denominations. The other school (school B) was situated in a market town on the outskirts of a rural area. It had a very inclusive intake of children from some of the less advantaged parts of the community, but had no children from other faith backgrounds.

In each school, the BSP research involved a four-stage lesson plan. The first stage was introductory, in which the children met the researcher and were told the reasons for the lesson on angels. At this point it was made clear that there were no right or wrong answers and that the children's insights were important.

The second stage was the telling of a Bible story involving an angel. In each instance the Godly Play method[22] was used to tell the story of Daniel in the lion's den. This method involves the researcher sitting on the floor in a circle with the children and drawing objects from a box in order to develop the story. The main value in this methodology is that it encourages wonder and endeavours to tell a story by employing the imagination of those to whom it is told.

In selecting Daniel in the lion's den from the large choice of angel stories in the Bible, the BSP was looking for a story that engaged the particular interest of both boys and girls at Key Stage 2. This story had imaginative appeal for its use of animals, a distant land long ago ruled over by a powerful king, the victory of the righteous over the less virtuous and of course it involved an angel (something that many versions of the story omit from the original telling in Daniel 6, where it is an angel that accompanies Daniel through the long watches of the night and keeps the lions from harming him).

The BSP also considered other angel stories, namely the expulsion from Eden (Genesis 3), the killing of the firstborn (Exodus 12), the fight over Babylon (Daniel 10), Balaam's donkey (Numbers 22), the call of Gideon (Judges 6), the birth of Jesus (Matthew 1) and the resurrection of Jesus (John 20). All these stories had potential currency in terms of being of interest to this age group, but the story chosen and the story of Balaam's donkey stood out as being of particular interest because of the presence of animals as well as angels. Daniel in the lions' den was finally selected as being a story that is easier to understand as a single standing story event.

The actual text referred to is Daniel 6.1-24, a text that details Daniel's rise to power while maintaining a faithful devotion to prayer three times a day. In this he incurred the jealousy of other officials who incited King Darius to issue an edict that anyone praying to any God other than the king should be thrown to the lions. Aware of this edict, Daniel continued to pray and was arrested by the jealous officials and brought to the king. King Darius was greatly distressed at seeing Daniel charged and tried to release him but was held to the 'law of Medes and Persians'. Daniel was thrown into the den of lions and a stone was placed over the den. King Darius sat up all night fasting and hurried down to the lions' den in the morning to find Daniel safe and well because God had sent an angel to shut the lions' mouths. Daniel was released unharmed and given a top job, whereas his accusers were thrown into the lions' den and instantly devoured. This story was told dramatically using different objects to signify the various characters and the angel and lions in the story.

The third stage was the individual class work when children returned to their desks to complete a threefold worksheet that requested them to draw a picture of the story involving the angel, to describe the angel and then answer two questions. The first question was simply, 'What do you think that angels do?' and the second was, 'Do you think that angels are found in [the area of their school] and how do you know?'

The fourth stage was the corporate class discussion when the children were given the opportunity to share their reflections and their work in public. The researcher and class teacher had spent the previous time being available to the children for help and encouragement (but not for advice or consultation on the subject of angels) and had been able to identify some patterns or ideas that could be discussed.

Findings about angels from the two primary schools

School A

The 20 children from Year 5 (aged 9–10) offered a wide range of insights in their artwork. Generally, the angels were drawn to match the child's gender, as is apparent from page 257, where the male angel was drawn by a boy, whereas the angel on page 258 is female and was drawn by a girl. However, in many cases the angels were given wings. Of all the objects depicted, the angels were drawn with greatest detail, matched only by the care given to the lions. Most angels were depicted as being larger and more powerful than the human and looked as though they were in control and happy to be there.

Of particular note were several pictures that showed Daniel to be comfortable and sound asleep while the angel stood by. Below is an example of this, drawn by a boy whose angel figure hovers above the ground with his hand placed authoritatively in front of the roaring mouth of a lion (p. 257). This depiction is remarkable for its insights into trust, in that it emphasizes Daniel's total ease and relaxation, leaving the angel to handle the lions. Such is the state of his faith that the lions are almost an afterthought – simply hungry mouths held at bay on the edges of consciousness.

A similar example by a girl shows Daniel asleep on his back, feet tucked in while the angel figure domesticates the lion and seems to be patting it on the head (p. 258).

This picture suggests that the artist not only identifies with the angel but with the sleeping Daniel – both of whom have longer hair. Daniel appears totally relaxed, asleep on his back as the zzzzs float upwards. Etched in the background of the picture, it almost looks as though he floats above the threat.

Indeed, the lion is no danger at all but smiles serenely like a house cat as the angel maintains control. The angel is wearing make-up on her eyes and lips and is evidently seen to be a beautiful woman dressed in stylish, gossamer clothing.

Of all the words used by this class to describe the angel the most common was 'helpful', followed by 'caring' and 'loving'. Several boys used the word 'strong' or 'powerful' and girls used the word 'beautiful' or 'pretty', which may denote

gender-specific attributes of value. Many children used the words 'glowing', 'white', 'shining', 'bright' or 'invisible' to detail the conventional depictions of angels. Unusual words were 'heart saver', 'rubbish' (which was taken to be a statement of his picture's inadequacy), 'sensitive' and 'genius'.

In terms of what angels do, a huge 13 out of the 20 children said that angels help you if you are in trouble by protecting you from danger or evil. This perception clearly fitted with the actions of the angel in the story being discussed. Two children said that angels did 'everything that is good' and two others explained that they did God's will, 'like sending messages'. One child said that angels brought peace. Another was quite clear that angels helped only those who prayed to God or worshipped him. Another specified that angels catalogued good deeds and bad deeds and were ultimately responsible for sending you to heaven or hell. Both these last responses were examples of particular interpretations from religious contexts, one emerging from a Christian evangelical background and the other from an Islamic culture.

It is of wider interest to observe the different emphasis placed on the same Old Testament stories told from different faith perspectives. The BSP noted[23] that the story of Noah's ark told to children in churches emphasized details about

animals and rainbows, whereas when told to children in mosques, it emphasized details about God's judgement, a more accurate if less palatable rendition of the story.

In terms of whether angels are to be found in the area in which the school is situated, thirteen said that angels were present, six said that they were not and one declined to answer. Of the children who said that angels were not present near the school, two said that this was because they were only to be found with God in heaven and four said that this was because they could not be seen.

Of the children who said that the angels were present, the answers were based on authority ('my religion says so', 'it says so in a book', etc.) or reason ('otherwise we'd have bad luck', 'they care for us') or on imagination ('they live in our brains'). Without doing further individual background work on these children, the BSP was not able to offer particular reasons for these comments.

The wider class discussion drew attention to the different faith backgrounds of the children. The differences were articulated and noted with interest rather than being causes for dissent and showed encouraging signs for interfaith dialogue between children. In this, children at this age often show not only a greater spiritual openness than adults, but also a firmer ability to entertain diversity of viewpoint, if given a safe environment. It seemed that with a focus such as angels, where the closer definition is less apparent, wider perspectives are more readily welcomed.

School B

The 19 children from Year 6 (aged 10–11) offered a wide range of insights in their artwork. Over half of the angels were depicted with wings and nearly all of them had a halo. Another regional variation for this school was that the lions' dens were normally drawn with bars. As with school A, most angels matched the child's gender and were larger than the nearby figure of Daniel.

Several pictures showed the angel standing as a buffer between a large lion and a perplexed Daniel. By means of contrast, one boy's picture (depicted below) showed an angel muzzling the lions while Daniel looks on nervously.

This picture is somewhat in contrast to the two earlier pictures (pp. 257, 258), in that it shows a very small and frightened Daniel standing with arms wrapped around himself as the angel harnesses the wild animals. The angel is experiencing the situation quite differently to Daniel as he hovers on extended wings, a broad grin on his face as he controls the lions by long leashes, as if they were dogs. The lions are clearly not likely to get out of hand as they stand muzzled with drooped tails in a passive pose. Above this scene the crescent moon rises, reminding us that it is night-time.

On the other hand, one girl's picture (below) showed an angel calming the lions by magical power.

This picture mirrors the emotions of the previous picture closely, in that it also depicts a very frightened Daniel actually crying for help while a dominant angelic figure flies triumphantly aloft, smiling and superior as she keeps the lions submissive by a form of angelic ray. The effect of these magical powers upon the lions is to reduce them to cowering creatures, their startled faces

expressing fear and their tails snaking out behind them. These two pictures are remarkably similar to each other (and dissimilar to the two on pp. 257, 258) in the way in which Daniel is depicted. In all four pictures the angel is supreme but only in the first two does this bring about a sense of calm. All four pictures show the gender of the artist reflected in the gender of the angel who is in fact the hero of the story.

Another artist had rubbed out the drawing of the angel and then gone over it again in very fine pencil to emphasize the fact that the angel was almost invisible or ghostly. This picture shows the angel to be almost identical to Daniel but again standing between him and the beast.

When I have reflected on this research project it is this picture that has most frequently returned to my mind. I am astounded by the level of reflection in this ten-year-old boy who has had the insight to perceive the angel as being a transitional being between form and matter and who has been able to draw him with such creativity. It is the fact that the child has drawn an angel, been unsatisfied with his depiction, rubbed it out and then realized that the faint outline left most clearly depicts his thoughts, that most impresses me. The result is quite startling.

To the right of the picture a very large and virile lion, complete with tusks and teeth, prances in the direction of Daniel. To the left of the picture Daniel stands at ease with a smile. In between, the faint outline of an angel is the powerful but invisible barrier between pain and fear.

Another interesting idea was offered by a boy who drew his angel without hair to identify it to be neither male nor female. One girl stated that her angel did not need legs because it floated.

Of all the words used to describe the angel, the most common was 'powerful'. Many children commented on the angelic qualities of being 'warm', 'friendly', 'kind', 'helpful' or 'caring'. Again many described the physical nature of the angel as 'drifting', 'floating', 'ghostly', 'yellow', 'pink and white'. Two girls sitting on different tables described the angel as both 'skinny' and 'beautiful'. Unusual words were 'magical', 'gorgeous', 'a good listener' and 'cheerful'.

In terms of what angels do, every child mentioned that angels existed to help people, normally by bringing peace or calm when danger was nearby. An example of this from one girl was,

> they are God's messengers. They help us in difficult situations. They are caring people who are kind and caring in different ways. They're honest people who help us, for example if we were ill, they could help us.

It is interesting to notice the way in which this description has made the angel more like the portrayal of a decent and immanent human being than a more distant and spiritual figure from heaven.

> By contrast, another girl offered a more transcendent view – God looks over us and then when we feel sad, he sends down an angel from heaven to make us happy again.

These interpretations offer strong insights into the bipolar ways in which Key Stage two children (aged 8–11) understand the relationship between earth and heaven. They will often see them as one thing or the other, as earthly or heavenly, as being about humans or about God.

In terms of whether angels are to be found in the area in which the school was situated, twelve said that angels were present, two said they were not and five were unsure. The five agnostics were uncertain whether angels were actual people or messengers from heaven. They felt that the only source for them was the Bible.

The two who believed angels were not present based their reasons on sight, but one concluded that they might be seen by people in hospital. The majority who believed angels to be on hand had a variety of comments, one saying she identified their presence when she would get 'funny feelings'. Two others said that everyone had their own angel. Another mentioned that anyone could be an angel if they were helpful. One particularly reflective girl wrote:

> I think there is an angel in everyone somewhere because people who are kind are angels. You don't have to see angels to believe in them. They are in the Bible. They look down on us like God so they can care for us.

The wider class discussion wanted to hold a belief vote, which turned out to be slightly different to what they had written, with ten believing angels to be present in the school, nine being uncertain and none being unbelieving. Some children commented that they were impressed by the artist who had drawn a faint picture of the angel to depict ghostliness and would have used this idea had they drawn another angel.

This suggests that the class discussion had enabled the children to move on from their more bipolar thinking to a more symbolic or metaphorical way of expression. This shows a development in the use of language and a need to begin to use artistic expression more creatively, moving from literal depiction of pencil on paper to a more abstract form of art.

How the angelic world of the Bible is understood in schools in twenty-first-century Britain

The BSP is not the only project to be interested in the Bible and its use of angelic language within the world of school. Another project, also funded by the Bible Society, is the Biblos Project with researchers working from the University of Exeter. They have offered us the concept that insights into angels are 'splashes of God light'.[24]

Working in schools towards the end of the twentieth century and at the beginning of the twenty-first century, the Biblos Project published three reports, each referring to angels. They are *Echo of Angels* (1998), *Where Angels Fear to Tread* (2001) and *On the Side of the Angels* (2004).[25] In the introduction to *Echo of Angels*, Terence Copley wrote:

> If there are angels, can they create an echo? The Bible is quite clear that there are angels and that whether they are human or whether they are a type of heavenly being, they act as messengers of God. They are not passive, like the recumbent stone figures over graves.[26]

It goes on to note that the three revealed religions that have most interest in the characters and events described within the Bible also share a belief in angels and angelic intervention. The Jewish and Christian Scriptures speak about meeting angels unaware (Genesis 18 and Hebrews 13.2) and the Qur'ān states that angels are never sent without good reason (Sura 5.8).

Maybe because of such references and world views that do not easily fit in with a more reductionist secular world view, the Biblos team wanted to test whether the Bible was disappearing from RE or whether it was being relegated for use only for nurture and worship. Their aim was to reclaim the Bible's place within narrative, allowing for late modern readers to be 'sceptical believers, credulous sceptics, fundamentalist atheists, biblical literalists etc.' but noting that whatever the reader's personal script, they will have been affected by the influence of a former biblical world view. Of particular value for this discussion of angels is their stated intention to reclaim the Bible as narrative and to allow for the indescribable to be articulated by the incomplete media of symbols, metaphors, similes, parables, riddles, analogies and stories, all of which offer 'splashes of God light'.[27]

Three years later, the second report of the Biblos project, *Where Angels Fear to Tread* (2001) offered findings after research had been conducted on how the Bible was taught in different stages of schooling. The third and final report of the Biblos Project was entitled *On the Side of the Angels* (2004) and this endeavoured to get closer to the problems of the Bible in British culture and was careful in research to listen to the insights of children in Years 6, 9 and 12, checking how attitudes vary with age, gender or religious affiliation.

What is helpful to the present discussion is that the Biblos project believes it is writing into a late modern culture that has become ambivalent towards religion and yet which still has not abandoned many religious beliefs and values. Within an ongoing process of secularization in which many people have become estranged from institutional religion, beliefs are becoming increasingly personalized.

G. K. Chesterton is attributed to have said that when people stop believing in God they do not believe in nothing, they believe in anything. In this he is interpreted to be commenting on the more bizarre ways of belief that spring up after orthodox creeds are abandoned. Maybe this is what is beginning to be recorded by more secular researchers into angel lore such as Heathcote-James (in *Seeing Angels*), who note the huge range of references to angels that exist in the experience of people.

If this is true, as the Biblos project suggests, it might be worth asking what has happened to the belief in angels. Maybe they have not been slain but reborn. Maybe there is a 'return of the repressed' when the more demonic beings of Halloween have emerged when the feast of All Saints is forgotten. This could be a reason to explain the contemporary rise in interest in Halloween merchandise or the popularity of magical children's television such as *Buffy the Vampire Slayer* or *Heroes*, where characters operate with extraordinary powers. Similarly, the films *Underworld* and *Blade* detailing worlds where vampires fight against werewolves (lycans) or against mortals are hugely popular with teenagers.[28]

How children's thinking can impact on adult thinking

We can see from the drawings and comments from the children that children's ideas about angels contain the birth of a new age and the redemption of a former one. My contention in this chapter is that their voices offer a way back into a more imaginative understanding of faith and the means for adults to grow up as they listen to them and reclaim a former simplicity. This paradox is that of Ricoeur's second naiveté: the mark of a fully integrated adult who can embrace their inner child as well as their previous childhood experiences. It is a means of allowing religious spirituality to be explored without the scorn of inappropriate analysis at every stage, as has become the case with emergent secularism. The children lead us into forms of religious truth which have become distorted by current influences and processes in our society.

Late modern world views in the West tend towards secularism or towards non-credal spiritual world views, and are beginning to pervade culture in a way that was once true of Christianity. Any articulated belief in God and of spiritual worlds requires caution in communicating to this new age. David Hay's research[29] has shown that increased care with religious language has driven the vocabulary of spiritual experience deep into the public psyche so that many people will not actually own up to such experiences until they are sure that they are safe to do so.

One wonders if it is true that to express a belief in God in secular society requires the dredging of a dusty vocabulary; even more whether it is true that 'religious language' in the public church arena will be increasingly unused to speaking about angelic hosts or demonic legions. Faced with this dilemma, angelic language faces the danger of being driven underground or of being reinvented in personal constructs that may appear bizarre to other people.

It seems to me that the time is ripe to draw deliberately upon the insights of children as they engage with spiritual reality. This enquiry would be to empower the notion of the child as prophet, first flagged by the prophet Isaiah who spoke of 'a little child' leading others through a world of danger (Isaiah 11.6).

Writing in the sixth century BC, shortly before the Israelites were taken into captivity, Isaiah was offering a rich insight to a nation that had forgotten God. These words have been taken up and reworked by the singer-songwriter Adrian Snell who applies them into the present day context:[30]

> 'A Little Child Shall Lead Them'
>
> And a child shall find them, free them, lead them
> from the lonely prison of the heart.
> There the breath of God is blowing, burning
> all that death and hatred tears apart.
>
> And the child shall take them, hand outstretched to
> guide them in the way of beauty through the night.
> There the power of God is moving, healing,
> turning blindness into sight.
>
> The wolf and the lamb, together are dwelling

The calf and the lion, asleep they lie.
The bear and the kid together are feeding
Their young are at play, side by side.

And a child shall lead them to a land of freedom
where darkness is forever turned to day.
Where a world was broken, wounded, weeping
then a child will kiss the tears away.

And a little child will call them, softly
bless them, hold them tenderly.
The earth shall be filled with the glory of the Lord
as the waters cover the mighty sea.

The world shall follow, humble, forgiven
no more sorrow, nor more sword.
And all creation, that once was groaning
now shall rejoice in the way of the Lord.

And a child shall lead them to a land of freedom
where darkness is forever turned to day.
Where the world was broken, wounded, weeping
then a child will kiss the tears away.

Where the world was broken, wounded, weeping
then a child will kiss the tears away.

Through applying these ancient words to the twenty-first century, we consciously draw on the historic Christ's injunction to his adult followers that they must become like little children if they are to enter the kingdom of God (Luke 18.17).

To reclaim the child's insights might connect with the romanticism of the eighteenth century in which William Blake began to write and draw. However, if this is so, the same potential misunderstanding is also true, in that Blake's angelic visions were not universally viewed as rich insights.

If we are to return to the insights offered by the children's artwork of angels, the same question remains true to us encountering children. Do we see their perceptions, as merely developmental insights that need education or, conversely, are we fed by an original vision teaching us that we might be entertaining angels unaware? If we strip off our own cultural perceptions about angels, how might the children's drawings and thoughts challenge us and challenge our faith?

Personally, I perceive the original vision of the child to be an aspect of research that is extremely fruitful. A brief reflection upon angels that has drawn upon the insights of children has opened up for us the complexities and subtleties of spiritual experience. Although we may note that the children superimpose themselves on to their angelic superheroes, they empower their angels with the ability to make a difference in a world of danger. The angels may be pretty or grandiose but they have the ability to change a frightening situation into a place of peace.

To draw a few lessons from the selection of artwork by children of this research sample, we may learn that:

- Angels stand between Daniel (us) and danger.

- The presence of the angel brings calm in which it is possible to relax.

- The angel is comfortable in situations that are complex.

- Angels are not universally perceived as being male, female or even visible but they make a positive difference.

In fact, a brief look at the simple four angel figures depicted here (which are only a small fraction of a larger sample) already offers us new ideas and fresh ways of thinking.

This enquiry not only allows for research into developmental understanding of symbols in a child's culture, but it reminds the researcher of what has been forgotten in adult culture. In this way, the child's insight can serve as a reminder of a previous developmental stage in the observing adult. Maybe this idea will re-energize us to consider angels afresh, empowered by what we once knew.

Questions

1. What does the word 'angel' mean to you?

2. This chapter suggests that there is a resurgence of angel imagery and ideas in contemporary culture. What examples of television, film or music can you think of which might influence how children think about angels?

3. Make a list of all the angels in the Bible you can think of. What function and purpose do these different angels have? How might this chapter help elucidate the meaning and importance of angels in Scripture and Christian tradition?

4. Look yourself at the story of Daniel in the lions' den (Daniel 6.15-28). How do the children's drawings change the way you understand this story?

5. Identify ONE time during the year (e.g. St Michael and All Angels or Christmas) at which children can be invited to explore the angels of the Bible in story, drawing or other creative ways.

13

Heaven and Hell

Philip Fryar

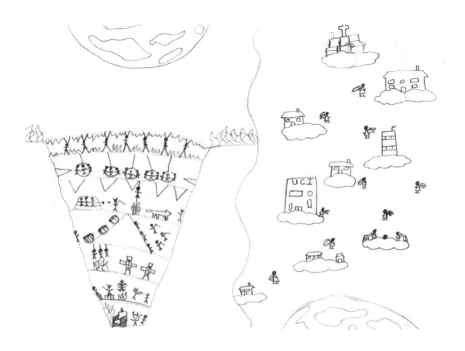

This chapter deals with issues of heaven and hell as seen through the eyes of a child. The child in this case is myself. I am 15 years old and I have been thinking back about my childhood and reflecting on how my ideas have changed since I was very small. I like to spend time writing and drawing and over my childhood I have produced a lot of material on spiritual themes. What I did was to look back through the stories I wrote and pictures I drew and use them to remember what I was thinking and feeling about heaven and hell at the time. I start with the sort of ideas I had before I went to school and then look at what difference going to school made to my thoughts. Church has also had a big influence, but often in a way which convinces me that adults don't like to look through the eyes of a child very much.

Heaven

When I was a very small child, before I went to school, I wondered about heaven and found it hard to imagine. I didn't worry about that, because heaven was not something that children needed to be bothered with. Heaven was something that you had to think about later on; it was enough to know that it was there. Eventually, I picked up ideas from other people and put them together in my mind. My picture of heaven was like something in a painting – white, cloudy, above, beyond, not of this world. I remember feeling very small in the face of heaven, but I was pretty clear it was out of reach. I wondered about where it was. Mostly I thought that heaven must be just out of sight, not in the universe but somehow alongside the universe. I thought that if you just suddenly turned a corner, or looked out of the corners of your eyes, you could just see it, whipping out of sight.

I remember wondering what was in heaven. I saw it as being the same as I know now but better. So it was very beautiful, with houses, sunshine and acres of waving grassland that I could run on forever, being happy and having fun. Then I had to decide who else would be in heaven besides me and at that time in my idea of heaven I believed that everyone you ever knew or came into contact with was there and would be there. But I could only imagine that there would be people I loved or liked – close friends, family, the people I would never be able to get enough of and whose love would be around me forever. I could not imagine that anyone I was afraid of, or disliked, could be a part of my heaven. I thought of it for a long time as a second life with continuity with life on earth. It would be a perfect earth-like world, earth as it was meant to be, and I would have a part in it. Animals, birds and plants, grass and seas were part of the reality of it. Although I was certain that there was day and night in heaven, I could not imagine heaven at night-time, in my mind it was always perpetual day.

Although I assumed there must be day and night and things happening, I never imagined time passing in heaven. As I imagined it, the people there were complete. Life in heaven meant no worries, no rushing about in a panic, no one would be concerned about material things, there would be no stress, just fun and happiness. Heaven allows people to stop and be, perhaps for the first time. Then you would never stop wondering at it and playing in it, and that would fill up all time and space. Time would be as you experience it as a small child: you would be totally absorbed in the moment and never be bothered about what came next.

Different heavens for different people?

As I got older and went to primary school I quickly discovered holes in my ideal of heaven. The biggest hole was the matter of who you would be in heaven with. I assumed that I would be in heaven with everyone I had known and loved, but no one else; I wouldn't need any other relationships. But then I worked out that the people who love me, love others that I don't know, so their heaven would look different and have different relationships. How could every single person have a different heaven? I couldn't work out how heaven could be the end of life for every person with all their loved ones around them and all their relationships intact. Were there overlapping heavens, or different communities of loving and loved ones? I was aware that my picture of heaven was selfish and centred around me, but I couldn't make it work any other way. Jesus said that in his father's house there were many mansions and so maybe there were many collections of people gathered together by love.

Another hole was the way we experience change. My picture of heaven as a little child was fixed but as I got older I realized that who we are changes very quickly. Even love itself changes. Some things which you think are good and you want to have them forever change so that you don't like them any more. This is part of being human. So how is that part of being human a part of heaven? I remember drawing picture after picture of worlds beyond this one, being pleased with each one, but always trying to produce another one that contained just a bit more of the goodness and joy of being alive. I drew pictures of angels and heavenly beings, but I was always thinking that there was more to their story. The way I understood it, a person's story ends when they get to heaven, but that has never made much sense to me. Perhaps heaven is always being reinvented.

What are people like in heaven?

I also started to worry about how I would recognize people. I knew my grandmother as an old lady, but in heaven she could be a young woman that I could not recognize. She died when I was six years old – how would she know me as a grown man? It wouldn't work if we were all children, or all adults, or all the same. The quality of my love for her was that I was a child with a granny, what would happen to that relationship, unique and special, if it could not be part of heaven? The matter of knowing, recognizing and finding each other began to bother me. I thought about how the disciples didn't recognize Jesus at first after his resurrection, but they came to be sure in their hearts that it was him, and I supposed that that might answer my problem.

When my granny died I believed that she was not alone in heaven waiting for me but that we were both there together, so she would not be sad or incomplete. I thought that in terms of the way we understand things now, she was on the 'fast track' and I was on the 'slow track', but in heaven that would not make any difference. I didn't have any words for it at the time, but I imagined it in my mind. I imagined that out of the time line of human lives a glow appears when we leave our life on earth. Her glow emerged before my glow in the line of history, but from heaven's point of view above the line, they both come out at the same time. No one could be missed in heaven. When my granddad died, I felt comforted because he had lost so much that he loved and I felt he had got back all that he loved, his wife, his parents, his friends. It comforted me to think that he got away from the hardship of his life, he had become young again. He did not have to deal with old age and illness any more, or continue to watch his children live their lives, while his was over. This could only be true if heaven was there to receive him. At that time, when I was six, I probably did think that going to heaven was like going home. We all came from there and we all go back there. It is where we belong.

Who is not allowed into heaven?

It was not until I went to primary school that I learned about the possibility of some people not being 'allowed' into heaven. It never occurred to me that anybody could be refused heaven. We were taught that heaven was there to sort out the good from the bad, the good sheep from the bad goats, and I believed it. When I was younger I had a clear sense of right and wrong and so I could say that when someone died you weighed up their acts and deeds and a judgement was made upon them. What I was being taught made sense in terms of what I saw around me. At school I was rewarded for being good, punished for being naughty. But I couldn't help feeling that the bad people got a raw deal. As far as I was concerned, the people I loved, even if God said they had done bad things, were in my eyes still perfect. I could not see them as being eternally banished because of wrongdoing. Whatever they might be to others, I loved and forgave them.

I think that when we are little children we understand that better than when we are older. One minute there is unkindness and tears, the next everything is forgotten as though it had never been. When I was first taught that Jesus forgives sins that is how I imagined it. First two children are brawling in the playground and one goes off crying. The next minute they are running around with their arms round each other shouting with the pleasure of being friends, the best feeling in the world. I remember one incredibly badly behaved boy who was the despair of my teacher, putting his arm round my shoulder and asking me if he could help when I was crying. He was rude, aggressive, out of control and a bully, but he was also part of my heaven. If I had had to draw up a list of people who would be in heaven, he would be there too, though definitely not in my teacher's heaven . . . We were all encouraged to be good children and to do good in the world and this would help us become fit for heaven. I remember being asked in school to write about what people would say about me after I died and I wrote that I hoped that I would become a saint and that in the eyes of God I would become a perfect being. I thought all of us were saints in the making. I imagined myself as Saint Philip looking down on the world and helping to look after it, listening to the prayers people were saying to God and everyone remembering me.

I am now 15 years old. I no longer believe in the pretty heaven of my childhood, although I feel nostalgic for it. I don't believe in the sheep and the goats any more; in fact I can't work out why human actions should qualify you in any way for life beyond life. I worry instead about people finding out who they truly are, who they were meant to be. This means that I feel ever more strongly about doing the right thing for the world, the planet, for other people, because doing those things teaches us about ourselves. I have strong feelings about the future of the planet, the future of human beings, the conservation of animals and plants. I prefer Jesus' version of the commandments to the Law of Moses. I am clear that heaven is a mystery and I am not ready to understand it right now. Perhaps it is still just round the corner.

God

When I was much younger I did not associate God with heaven. Heaven was a place like earth, only perfect and beautiful and God was somewhere else. I could have relationships with others in heaven, but I did not think I could have any kind of relationship with God, who was too big, too far away and far too great and mighty. When I was younger I believed God to be an authority figure, an almighty omnipotent being. He set the rules and made people abide by the rules. He decided who went to heaven, but he was not in heaven himself. I believed that God was human, so to speak, or, of human form. I imagined God in human form. The reason I believed this was my church, Bible stories, parents and teachers always referred to God as 'He' so that helped form the picture in my mind. So I never thought of God as animal or a creature, although I did not really see why God could not be some other kind of being altogether.

A royal family in heaven

Once I went to school, I learned that God was in heaven, which is something that I had not assumed before. So now I had to put my ideas of God and my ideas of heaven together. I then imagined heaven as having a royal family. This made sense because we sang songs in church and school about God as king and Mary as queen of heaven. I believed that Mary was a queen, so to speak, and was ruling over heaven. In my royal family, Jesus was the prince, as God's son and Mary's son and the Holy Spirit was around them all. This royal family looked after all the subjects in heaven and on earth. I believed that Mary helped people on earth while God ruled and kept everything in balance. Mary would ask God to help people in their suffering, because she herself was human and knew what it was like to suffer. She had seen her son die. When I heard stories about Mary appearing to people or giving them messages, I believed them because it made sense to me that Mary would reach into people's minds and hearts in that way. When I was little I prayed to Mary when I was scared or lonely or woke from a nightmare. I believed she would take pity on me because she knew what it was like to feel like me, and praying to her helped. I never thought that she was God, or the same as God. What I wanted from her was her human understanding and being a mother, like my mother. I needed the Mother of God.

In my mind Jesus was God's knowledge. He has the knowledge of what it is to be human like me, he experienced humanity and has the knowledge of humanity. Mary was the sweet side of God's will for the world. Jesus was the omniscient side of God and God himself was the omnipotent side of God. The Holy Spirit was God's influence on human beings, the activity of God on earth.

As he was the king, I believed that God cared about every single one of us as a whole, the whole creation. I believed Mary cared about the individual person. I believed that God weeps for the tragedies of the world as a whole. Mary grieved for the suffering experienced by human beings, because that was deeply rooted in her own experience – she had watched her son suffer. In my primary school we had statues of Mary on tables, on the walls we had Jesus on the cross and we had Bibles. We put flowers on the tables, remembered how Jesus suffered when we looked at the cross and read about what God had done. All these things seeped into my imagination and got into the way I thought about heaven.

I don't believe in much of this stuff any more either. I think I put it together from what I was taught in school, but I think it was just a way of making sense of things that adults didn't often understand. What I think it did for me though was to make me certain of the value of prayer. I am sure that no matter what I think about how heaven is organized, or the life of God, in need or trouble, or in times of happiness I would pray and believe that prayer went right to the heart of wherever and whoever God is.

Hell

For me, hell was actually always more real, near and rooted in human experience than heaven. When I was very small I thought of hell as dark, wet and cold. I always believed that hell wasn't fiery, but damp and dismal like a cellar or a lonely dripping cave. A place where you shiver and you are scared, you don't know anything. I believed that you are completely in a place where everything is wrong, the worst of everything, filled with evil, sin and people who wanted to hurt you. Hell was a place where every sort of pain could exist, emotional, physical. It was therefore a place you wanted to avoid at all costs. A place of wolves, a cave, a chasm, wet and dark. When I was little I was afraid of the dark. The thing that scared me most about the dark was not being able to see properly, anything could be there and I could not make it out, especially someone who was trying to hurt me. The fear and terror I had of the dark was like a foretaste of hell. That was how I understood it. In the same way I had nightmares which felt to me like foretastes of hell. I had nightmares about death. I feared dying and the hell that was out there waiting for me. I was convinced someone was trying to kill me and that I would be pursued into the hell world.

Hell as nightmares

If I woke up in terror from a nightmare in the dark I would get rid of the fear by praying. Praying calmed my mind and allowed me to put the fear away so that I could go back to sleep. Things have changed. Gradually these nightmares of murderous strangers and faceless killers went away to be replaced with nightmares based on evil, like being trapped. I have a recurrent nightmare about a little girl with dark hair and I come across her at the side of a road. There is just fog all around and I ask her where her parents are and she just smiles and laughs and says everyone is gone. I say we have to escape because it is not safe and as we walk away, she says she killed everyone she was with because it was fun. She is quite calm but she will not allow me to go back, I have to go with her. I keep trying to refuse and get back but she will not allow it. She enjoys the fact that I suffer and I panic. A little girl should be innocent, but she is corrupt, disgusting. She is in a place where everything is wrong. When I try to run she is everywhere and won't let me get back to reality. When we get to a town it is burning, everything is wrecked. This is how I imagine the journey to hell. One of the worst things about the nightmare is the sense of no redemption, no escape and no forgiveness. It is a place where God cannot reach.

Hell as hurting people

I also have hell dreams in which I lose control and hurt someone. I would end up in hell because I would be cut off from the people who love me, or I might kill them. I also dream that people kill my family and me, or that members of my family kill me. This is a hell world in which everyone I rely on is wrecked. I sense the possibility of evil in me and I am very frightened of it and it emerges in dreams. I carry this hell around with me. I think hell is more present and real to me now than it used to be. I no longer pray when I wake from a nightmare. I am clear that if a monster should ever be in my room trying to hurt me I would have to fight the monster with physical weapons. I am also clear that the fear of evil in me has to come under my control. If I am to escape hell then I have to do this for myself. I have a baseball bat at the end of my bed. It means two things to me. One: I *could* defend myself against someone who broke in and tried to hurt me. Two: I *would* never use it to hurt someone, even though I could.

I now feel that the hell people talk about in the church is an absence of love, of God, not a punishment. I think that if you don't believe in God, God won't force himself upon you. Yet without God you cannot know love and this becomes absence, misery. It would be terrible to be someone who could not love.

Satan

When I was younger I didn't believe in Satan, Lucifer or the fallen angels, but I believed in the devil, not a being but a monster who inspired terror, awe. A monster that was terrifying, but I thought about the terrifying part of it in a visual sense – big, flaming, flared nostrils, large sharp teeth, a bit like a Balrog (the fiery demon creature who takes Gandalf into the abyss in *The Lord of the Rings*), a huge wild animal, vile, but still just an animal. That was just about the worst I could imagine, so that was the devil. I wasn't bothered much by the idea of a devil. I couldn't see why a devil would want anything to do with little children at all.

It changed and I began to believe in Satan, a being with intelligence, still monstrous, evil and horrifying, but worse because it knows what it's doing. Finally I heard the story that Satan was once an angel, Lucifer, fallen from heaven and that caught hold of my imagination. The creature which keeps hell has knowledge and memory of God's ways and so the most terrifying thing about this creature is that it is a shapeshifter. Lucifer is a monster of evil, not a dragon or a Balrog, but intelligent evil, which enjoys suffering – everything God is not. Satan takes pleasure in human suffering and pain, intentional evil. He needs no motive or reason, he takes pleasure in suffering because it amuses him to see people cower and squirm in fear. I believed he knows what we fear the most and can use it against us. I believed that he is temptation. He will tempt people to do something wrong because it amuses him to see people turn aside from goodness and become unlike themselves, and be corrupted, lost to who they really are. I don't really believe that Satan is a ruler of hell. He is the most damaged of all who could be in God, but not in control of the world of such beings. He has power over human beings because evil is part of the world and his power is bound up with it. They say the world is a balance, so Satan works hard to balance out the good that God pours into the world. Satan fears his world of darkness, and does not sit on a mighty throne: his rule is subtle.

'Satan' as the ills of the world

I no longer believe literally in Satan, but I believe what 'Satan' stands for is all around us. I believe that in our present days and times 'Satan' is becoming more powerful. 'Satan' is selfish and people in our world are selfish, they don't want to give money to others, or take care of others, or listen to people who are trying to say what harm human beings are doing to the world and the people and creatures in it. He stands for resisting authority and anarchy – so he tempts people away from God, demanding proofs. So you get people writing about how stupid and pointless it is to be religious and then people listen to them.

I think that people find the idea of Satan is attractive, because it suggests that you can live life fully, without wasting time on God. Satan is cool. Drawings and interpretations of Satan look really cool. The evil people in comic books and films often have a sort of dazzling attractiveness, even if they get defeated in the end. God just doesn't get a look in. Satan can appear in so many ways – handsome, intelligent, persuasive and seductive but all the same evil, like the young Lord Voldemort in Harry Potter. That made sense to me and I thought it made sense of how people get into bad things, they are attracted by the look of the person who tempts them and the things they say.

Today I think that all we mean by the devil is the bad acts in life, the evil and corruption in the world today. People don't associate Satan with resisting God any more because doing what you want is the natural state for people. People are not interested in what the old order says is right or wrong, personal views are the most important, more important than any religious law. This bothers me a lot because I care a great deal more about the future, about the environment and the world that others will inherit. But I don't think too many people around me care like I do.

Good and evil

Towards the end of primary school I believed that the child lived under protection from heaven, but also lived in fear of heaven, in fear of God. I thought it meant that if you broke a line you would be punished for all eternity. I began to worry about the difficulties of being good all the time. If you put even a toe out of line you would be heading for punishment. I felt that you couldn't be free because you would be in trouble. The Ten Commandments covered everything and I started to worry that everyone was going to hell, because the commandments were impossible to keep. I saw that there were people who lied, who stole things, who were envious and covetous and I started to worry that all these people around me were going to hell and would be banished from God's sight. I began to think that if this was true then God probably didn't give a damn about human beings after all, just the stupid laws. It bothered me a lot. I was told that if you said you were sorry you would be OK, but I began to think about cases where you would fall into sin and could not make yourself be sorry. If you stole bread because your children were starving you could not be really sorry and promise not to do it again. Life and actions were not simple and so the easy pictures of heaven I had lived with during most of my early years became clouded and started to fall away. I missed them.

Problems with right and wrong

When I was younger it was simple. There was right and wrong and heaven and hell. People would then be divided simply into how they behaved and where they ended up. You couldn't escape because God was watching you in a creepy, Big Brother sort of way. But it quickly occurred to me that life is not that simple because there is not such a thing as just right or just wrong. This started as soon as I began to learn some history. People went on crusades and killed others who came from other countries and followed other religions. It bothered me about people such as Nazis who thought it was right to kill Jews.

How on earth could anyone see rightness in behaving like that? And yet they did. Slave masters often thought it was right to keep slaves to look after them, give them work, clothe and shelter them. It is clear that life and its decisions are extremely complex and that you can't merit heaven or hell just on the simple basis of what we say has been inescapably right or wrong throughout the history of time. So now I think that you have to look at all the things you have done with hindsight and with learning. Life chucks us difficult decisions, we struggle with them, make mistakes and God will know the difference. Who ultimately decides what is right and wrong if not God who has all of history to work with? As a child in primary school, though, these questions troubled me a lot. We were taught by our teachers that we had to think of what we had done wrong and say sorry to God and to know that we were forgiven, but I couldn't help thinking that that was just a bit of the story. The story of our forgiveness by God extends over our whole lives and so thinking about what you have done wrong is just as much making decisions about the future as it is dwelling on the past. How could I say sorry for kicking my friend when he annoyed me when I knew perfectly well that if he annoyed me again I would kick him again, and probably harder? I wasn't really sorry about kicking my friend, even though he cried, it had something to do with my friend being my friend no matter how much we annoyed each other and that being true no matter how often he kicked me back. There was a limit on kicking which saying sorry to God or to teachers didn't cover and you would *know*, you would absolutely *know*, if you ever went past that limit.

I think that all normal human beings are born with the capacity to know instinctively what is right, and what your heart tells you helps you to negotiate the difficult decisions. You know in your soul if you did what you could. If you feel content with how you acted, in your conscience, God too will be content. If you know in your heart that you did not do all you could, you will want to ask for forgiveness and God will take away your discontent and make you fit for heaven. Something about your soul is the ultimate decision maker of how you act and what you try to do. I believe that Jesus is right when he says the two most important things are loving God with all you've got and loving other people as yourself.

Influences

School

Since I have been very small I have had different influences on the way I think about heaven and hell. One obvious set of influences includes my parents, my church primary school and going to church generally. The other set of influences includes the books I have read and films I have seen. The books and films seem to get into my imagination and help me to think more widely, creatively. People in school and church have told me what to think and I have problems with that because they just smile indulgently, or ignore me, if I start going outside the box with some of this stuff. In secondary school, I am supposed to be 'good at' RE, but I reckon I get more impatient sighs than anybody when I make suggestions or ask questions. In general I have been very disappointed with RE. For me, it's been very boring and like Sunday school. We learn arguments, rather than imagine or explore. Sometimes you get chucked a little rope and we start discussing something that sounds like we're about to get somewhere, think new things, then we get reeled in again and end up with having to learn the 'right' stuff to get the marks in the exams. It's very frustrating. Heaven and hell are now just givens. We deal with things like evil and suffering, but not in terms of where you are supposed to end up and why you do. I don't think Jesus would do very well in RE, actually.

Church

For example, when I was younger I believed what the adults told me because I trusted them. I trusted what the adults at church told me. Heaven is all good, hell is sinful. You do good things you go to heaven. You do bad things you will go to hell. Yet it was clear that kids were still naughty and did bad things, but did not seem too bothered about what that meant in terms of heaven and hell. To small children those kinds of matters were a very long way off and were something to be reckoned with as adults not as children. I decided very early on that we were learning about grown-up matters that affected them and not me. These were things that were true in the 'big' world. For children, the issues were more about finding out about things that were just out of sight but ready to be discovered, like my heaven that was always there but not quite visible. I also got the idea from church that the adults had to be very serious and grave about religion, whereas the children went down into the parish room and did other things, so there was a difference between being grown up and worshipping God and being a child and making pictures or playing games. I got confirmed recently and it was put to us in my group that we were moving away from the child's view of Christianity and ready to take on the official adult view of Church and Christian truth. I noticed very quickly that that made us feel more strongly that we were starting off as 'us' and 'them', and *we* were supposed to end up on the other side. I got told off for asking questions and 'mucking about', but I felt that with all my friends in the confirmation group we were really getting somewhere. When we went on retreat we stayed up talking and having fun and when we talked about heaven and hell I found that others my age have the same thoughts and dreams as me. It was great. Lots of friends from the confirmation group are on MSN and we're always texting and emailing each other, and so many of the things we share come from our thoughts about the Christian faith. But it's cool, not like sitting in rows and being talked at.

Adults

As I got older I started to find things out about the Church which made me less likely to trust the adults. The Church always says that it is right and there is only one way to live. The Church has made mistakes in the past and this makes it more difficult to trust implicitly in what it says about heaven and hell. As I have made friends with people in other religions I have begun to worry about the Church's insistence on rightness and the only way to heaven. I have worried about the Church's actions in history and begun to worry that it is difficult to see clearly what the Church is for. The Church acts like it is God himself instead of an instrument of God. For me the pictures of heaven and hell are no longer straightforward. Things were easier when I was a little child and everything was straightforward, but I would not want to go back to it. I would rather have the puzzle and the difficulty, even though I now have a strained relationship with the Church.

Secrets and different stories

I think that there are truths about heaven and hell which the Church does not offer us. For example, I think the Church doesn't want to think about the possibility that maybe sin and judgement are not part of God's plan. Maybe the world is better and more beautiful than the Church seems to think. Maybe there is more goodness than wrongdoing. It bothers me that the Church doesn't want to think outside the box and adapt or grow. I have seen a number of films and programmes which include ideas of heaven and hell and they have affected me and the views that I have.

Films

For example, one film that has made a big impression on me is the film *Donnie Darko*. A lot of people think the film is incredibly difficult to understand and full of weird pseudo-science. Perhaps it is, but to me it brings together a lot of what

I think about heaven and hell. In the film, Donnie, who is a troubled American teenager with mental health problems, sees strange visions of a monster rabbit, who is either friend or evil hallucination or a bit of both. Donnie himself does all kinds of bad things. There are all kinds of evil people. Donnie is facing the end of the world: heaven and hell are on his doorstep. Yet love makes all the difference in the world. Donnie changes time by finding out about the secrets of time and space, making it possible for him to go back and change the past and sacrifices his life, giving everyone, including the evil people, a second chance. Donnie Darko saves the world and makes a sacrifice which no one knows about. As he lies down in his bed before the jet engine crashes into his bedroom and kills him, he gives a little smile. I think I understand a lot more about what God did in sending Jesus to die for us from watching *Donnie Darko*, which moved me so much. It's a complicated film but has given me so much to talk about with my friends on spiritual matters.

Books

Similarly, I stayed up all night reading Philip Pullman's *The Amber Spyglass* because I was captivated by the world of the *His Dark Materials* trilogy. I know people say that Philip Pullman doesn't like the Church very much, but in his books the remaking of the garden of Eden story appealed to me a lot. I was devastated when Will and Lyra discovered that they had to live in different universes to allow people to get out of the land of the dead, but that is another sacrifice which makes sense to me in terms of heaven and hell. I believe that Philip Pullman really knows what it is like to be a child and their thoughts and feelings about religion and stories of good and evil, and this comes across in the presence of angels, witches and talking bears and in the daemons which are like souls or personalities, a combination of pet and best friend who will stay with you always. I like the idea that you can make friends with your death and that telling your story with all its complexities is the path to complete freedom. That makes sense to me.

Issues to do with heaven and hell are still with me, but the way I think about them is more intricate and complicated these days. However, the way in which I thought about heaven and hell, good and evil, when I was a very small child, is important to me and I hope will not fade away completely when I am an adult. Those thoughts and pictures are the foundations for other things I am waiting to learn and I hope when I have children myself I will not forget them. Perhaps I will laugh with surprise when I die. I have not ruled that out.

Questions

1.   How do you imagine heaven and/or hell?

2.   Philip highlights some of the things that hindered his perceptions and reflections. Are you aware of any such hindrances in your own spiritual growth and development? If so, what were they and how did you deal with them?

3.   Make a list in two columns of anything in our culture (film, television, pop music, etc.) that alludes to ideas of heaven and ideas of hell. What effects do you think the media has on our ideas about our ultimate destiny?

4.   John 14.3 says 'I go and prepare a place for you'. What do you think is involved in that promise and how should we respond to it? In what ways might children help us think about this more creatively?

5.   It is sometimes said that people outside the Church look especially to Christians for the hope that is in us. Can you think of ONE thing in your church that could offer children's insights about the hope of heaven to other people?

Activities

Death / Judgement / Angels / Heaven and Hell

1. **Game**

You will need crayons, pencils, paints, glitter, paper and Post-its™.

Together with a group of children let your imagination run wild. What might an angel really look like? Draw the angel with the children and colour and decorate it. Play a game in which you reflect with the children what difference the angel could make in the world. From what dangers might it protect you? What gifts does it bring? Write or draw suggestions on the Post-its™ and arrange these around the angel. What insights might this reveal about yourself and God? You can reflect on the verse, 'Then an angel of the Lord stood before them, and the glory of the Lord shone around them' (Luke 2.9) as an aid to reflection if you wish.

2. **Create**

You will need stiff card or paper, string, pens, crayons, paints, glitter, or other decorations, ribbons or transfers.

Use a mask template (you can download these from the Internet) on stiff card or paper to create some masks that represent moments of sadness, loss or death. It may be possible to do this in a mixed group of adults and children. Use the masks to talk about the feelings and emotions behind them. Respect anyone who does not want to talk about the mask. Another way of encountering the masks is to swap finished masks and talk about how another mask makes you feel. Spend some time considering what you learn from the mask-making activity and how this might enable you to see death, sadness and loss through the eyes of a child. You may like to reflect on the verse, 'Death will be no more; mourning and crying and pain will be no more, for the first things have passed away' (Revelation 21.4) as an aid to meditation.

3. **Learn from**

You will need a wastepaper basket containing some small objects, some of which have no obvious use or are broken.

Re-read the passage about the sheep and the goats referred to in the chapter on 'Judgement' in Matthew 25.31-46. What is clear? What is paradoxical for you? In what ways do the children's comments throw light on the passage? In what ways do they challenge the passage? You can also offer a group of children a waste bin containing a number of objects. Some of the objects can be 'useless' or broken. Ask the children to decide if the objects are so useless that they must be thrown away or whether they could be reused, used for something else or mended. What would it take to change the objects? Is there anything in the bin which cannot be redeemed? Does God ever 'waste' human beings? Is any person beyond redemption?

4. **Celebrate**

You will need items for a children's party.

Invite some children to help you plan a 'heaven' party, with food, drink, dancing and games. Who will be invited? Invite the children to consider what would be involved in a 'heaven' party, whether there should be guests of honour, special dress code, particular foods, drink, music or decoration. When the party takes place, pay careful attention to the way the children enjoy the party, how they relate to one another, how they play the games and how they express themselves. How does this activity give insight into Christian understandings of heaven? You might like to use the verse, 'Go therefore into the main streets, and invite everyone you find to the wedding banquet' (Matthew 22.9) as an aid to reflection if you wish.

5.  **Scripture**

Work slowly through the Gospel of Matthew noting the various references to 'heaven'. What does each reference mean and why is it there? Compare this exercise with what you have learned from children about heaven. How does this add to your understanding or challenge your perceptions?

Resources

Recommended reading

H. U. von Balthazar, *Unless You Become Like This Child*, Ignatius, 1991.

I. Beckwith, *Postmodern Children's Ministry*, Zondervan, 2004.

J. Berryman, *Godly Play: An Imaginative Approach to Religious Education*, Augsburg Fortress, 1995.

J. Berryman, *The Complete Guide to Godly Play* (especially vol. 1), Living the Good News, 2002.

M. Bunge (ed.), *The Child in Christian Thought*, Eerdmans, 2001.

M. Bunge (ed.), *The Child in the Bible*, Eerdmans, 2008.

S. Cavalletti, *The Religious Potential of the Child*, Paulist Press, 1983.

R. Coles, *The Spiritual Life of Children*, HarperCollins, 1990.

K. Copsey, *From the Ground Up*, Barnabas BRF, 2005.

C. Erriker, et al., *The Education of the Whole Child*, Cassell, 1997.

D. Hay, D. and R. Nye, *The Spirit of the Child*, Fount, 1998; 2nd edn, Jessica Kingsley, 2006.

K. Herzog, *Children and our Global Future*, Pilgrim Press, 2005.

B. Hyde, *Children and Spirituality: A Theology of Childhood*, Jessica Kingsley, 2008.

D. H. Jensen, *Graced Vulnerability*, Pilgrim Press, 2005.

M. Kopelman, 'Varieties of false memory', *Cognitive Neuropsychology* 16.3–5, 1 May 1999.

J. A. Mercer, *Welcoming Children: A Practical Theology of Childhood*, Chalice Press, 2005.

G. Miles, and J. J. Wright (eds), *Celebrating Children*, Paternoster Press, 2003.

B. Miller-McLemore, *Let the Children Come*, Jossey-Bass, 2003.

J. Moltmann, *The Church in the Power of the Spirit: A Contribution to Messianic Ecclesiology*, Harper & Row, 1977.

E. Robinson, *The Original Vision*, Religious Experience Research Unit, 1977.

H. R. Weber, *Jesus and the Children*, World Council of Churches, 1979 (now available from Treehaus Communications Inc.).

R. Williams, *Lost Icons* (especially ch. 1), T&T Clark, 2000.

D. W. Winnicott, *Playing and Reality*, Brunner–Routledge, 2002.

G. Wolff Pritchard, *Offering the Gospel to Children*, Cowley Publications, 1992.

K. M. Yust, *Real Kids, Real Faith*, Jossey-Bass, 2004.

International Journal of Children's Spirituality, Carfax Publishing, from 1996. Available from PO Box 25, Abingdon, Oxford, OX14 3JU.

Some useful web sites

http://childfaith.net/experience/experiencewithpics.pdf

http://www.childtheology.org/new/

http://childtheology.net/

http://www.godlyplay.org/

http://www.godlyplay.org.uk/

http://www.goodchildhood.org.uk

http://www.yearofthechild2009.co.uk

http://www.cctheo.blogspot.com/

Works cited in the text

R. Alves, *Tomorrow's Children: Imagination Creativity and Rebirth of Culture*, Harper & Row, 1972.

Herbert Anderson, *The Family and Pastoral Care*, Fortress Press, 1984.

Herbert Anderson and Susan B.W. Johnson, *Regarding Children: A New Respect for Childhood and Families*, 1st edn, Westminster/John Knox Press, 1994.

M. Argyle, 'State of the art – religion', *The Psychologist* 15, 2002, pp. 22–6.

J. C. Arnold, *A Little Child Shall Lead Them*, Plough Publishing, 1997.

John E. Baker and Mary Anne Sedney, 'How bereaved children cope with loss: an overview', in Charles A. Corr and Donna M. Corr (eds), *Handbook of Childhood Death and Bereavement*, Springer, 1996.

Iain M. Banks, *The Player of Games*, HarperCollins, 1997.

J. Barr, *The Scope and Authority of the Bible*, Westminster Press, 1980.

K. Barth, *Church Dogmatics*, T&T Clark, 1932/1975, paperback edition, 2004. ET of *Die Kirchliche Dogmatic*.

K. Barth, *Homiletics*, Westminster/John Knox Press, 1966/1991.

K. Barth, *The Word of God and the Word of Man*, Harper & Brothers, 1928/1957.

J. Barton, 'The Messiah in Old Testament Theology', in J. Day (ed.), *King and Messiah in the Ancient Near East*, Sheffield Academic Press, 1998.

William J. Bausch, *Storytelling, Imagination and Faith*, Twenty-Third Publications, 1984.

R. Benthall, *Madness Explained*, Penguin, 2004.

J. Berryman, 'Children and mature spirituality', Godly Play web site, http://www.godlyplay.org.uk, accessed 2005.

J. Berryman, *Godly Play: An Imaginative Approach to Religious Education*, Augsburg Fortress, 1995.

J. Berryman, *Godly Play: A Way of Religious Education*, Harper, 1991.

J. Berryman, *The Complete Guide to Godly Play*, vol. 1, Living the Good News, 2002.

Ron Best (ed.), *Education Spirituality and the Whole Child*, Continuum, 1996.

W. Blake, *Songs of Innocence and Experience* (1794). Facsimile reproductions and text transcript © 1991 The Tate Gallery and William Blake Trust Introductions.

Dietrich Bonhoeffer, *Creation and Fall*, Fortress Press, 2004.

Dietrich Bonhoeffer, *The Cost of Discipleship*, SCM Press, 2001.

John Bowlby, *A Secure Base*, Routledge, 1988.

J. Branne, E. Heptinstall and K. Bhopal, *Connecting Children: Care and Family Life in Later Childhood*, Routledge, 2000.

Marcus Braybrooke, *Thoughts on Forgiveness*, Braybrooke Press, 2003.

Libby Brooks, *The Story of Childhood*, Bloomsbury, 2006.

F. Brown, *Play Theories and the Value of Play*, Library and Information Service, National Children's Bureau, 2006.

F. Brown and S. Webb, 'Children without play', *Journal of Education* 35, 2005.

W. Brueggemann, *The Book That Breathes New Life*, Fortress Press, 2005.

E. Brunner, *Truth as Encounter*, SCM Press, 1964.

Marcia Bunge (ed.), *The Child in the Bible*, Eerdmans, 2008.

Marcia Bunge (ed.), *The Child in Christian Thought*, Eerdmans, 2001.

Horace Bushnell, *Christian Nurture*, Alexander Strahan, 1866.

J. Calvin, *Institutes of the Christian Religion*, Arnold Hatfield, 1599.

Colin Campbell, 'The Easternisation of the West', in Bryan Wilson and Jamie Cresswell (eds), *New Religious Movements: Challenge and Response*, Routledge, 1999.

W. Carr, *Angels and Principalities*, Cambridge University Press, 1981.

Philip Carrington, *According to Mark: A Running Commentary on the Oldest Gospel*, Cambridge University Press, 1960.

S. Cavaletti, *The Religious Potential of the Child*, Paulist Press, 1992.

P. Cawson et al., *Child Maltreatment in the United Kingdom: A Study of the Prevalence of Child Abuse and Neglect*, NSPCC, 2000.

Childhood under Threat: The State of the World's Children, UNICEF, 2005.

Child Poverty in Perspective: An Overview of Child Well-being in Rich Countries, UNICEF Innocenti research centre, Florence, 2007.

Children and their Primary Schools, The Plowden Report, of the Central Advisory Council for Education (England), HMSO, 1967.

Paul de Clerck, 'Baptism', in Jean-Yves Lacoste (ed.), *Encyclopedia of Christian Theology*, vol. 1, Routledge, 2004, pp. 149–52.

Robert Coles, *The Spiritual Lives of Children*, HarperCollins, 1990.

Robert Coles, 'Struggling toward childhood: an interview with Robert Coles', *Second Opinion* 18.4, April 1993, pp. 58–71.

J. Collicutt, 'Post-traumatic growth and the origins of early Christianity', *Mental Health, Religion and Culture* 9, 2006.

C. Collins, *Angels*, Fool's Press, London, 2004.

T. Copley, *Echo of Angels*, the first report of the Biblos Project, School of Education, University of Exeter, 1998.

C. Copley and T. Copley, *On the Side of the Angels*, the third report of the Biblos Project, School of Education, University of Exeter, 2004

T. Copley and S. Lane, *Where Angels Fear to Tread*, the second report of the Biblos Project, School of Education, University of Exeter, 2001.

T. Copley, J. Priestley, D. Wadman and V. Coddington, *Forms of Religious Assessment in Religious Education*, the FARE Report, University of Exeter, 1991.

Kathryn Copsey, *From the Ground Up*, Barnabas, BRF, 2005.

Kathryn Copsey, 'From the ground up . . .', in D. Ratcliff (ed.), *Christian Perspectives on Children's Spirituality*, Cascade Books, 2004.

J. D. Crossan, *Cliffs of Fall: Paradox and Polyvalence in the Parables of Jesus*, Seabury Press, 1980.

M. Csikszentmihalyi, *Flow, the Psychology of Optimal Experience*, Rider, 1992/2002.

W. Damon and R. M. Lerner (eds), *Handbook of Child Psychology*, vol. 1, *Theoretical Models of Human Development*, 6th edn, Wiley, 2006.

Richard Dawkins, *The Selfish Gene*, Oxford University Press, 1976.

T. Dennis, *Imagining God*, SPCK, 1989.

DES, *The Education Reform Act 1988. The School Curriculum and Assessment*, HMSO, 1988.

J. Dewey, *Experience and Nature*, Dover, 1929/1958.

C. H. Dodd, *The Parables of the Kingdom*, Fontana, 1961.

M. Donald, *Origins of the Modern Mind*, Harvard University Press, 1991.

John Drane, *After McDonaldization: Mission, Ministry and Christian Discipleship in an Age of Uncertainty*, Darton, Longman & Todd, 2008.

John Drane, *Cultural Change and Biblical Faith*, Paternoster Press, 2000.

John Drane, *Do Christians Know How to be Spiritual?* Darton, Longman & Todd, 2005.

John Drane, *The McDonaldization of the Church*, Darton, Longman & Todd, 2000.

John Drane and Olive M. Fleming Drane, *Family Fortunes: Faith-full Caring for Today's Families*, Darton, Longman & Todd, 2004.

Olive M. Fleming Drane, *Clowns, Storytellers, Disciples*, Augsburg, 2004.

J. Duff and J. Collicutt, *Meeting Jesus: Human Responses to a Yearning God*, SPCK, 2006.

L. Dupré and D. Saliers (eds), *Christian Spirituality: Post-Reformation and Modern*, SCM Press, 1990.

B. Egeland, 'A history of abuse is a major risk factor for abusing the next generation', in R. J. Gelles and D. R. Loseke (eds), *Current Controversies on Family Violence*, Sage Publications, 1993.

David Elkind, *The Child's Reality: Three Developmental Themes*, Lawrence Erlbaum Associates, 1978.

Encyclopaedia of the Bible and Christianity, 2nd edn, Lion CD ROM, 1998.

C. Erricker and J. Erricker, *Reconstructing Religious, Spiritual and Moral Education*, Routledge Falmer, 2000.

C. Erricker, J. Erricker and C. Ota (eds), *Spiritual Education*, Sussex Academic Press, 2001.

C. Erricker, et al., *The Education of the Whole Child*, Cassell, 1997.

D. Ford, *The Shape of Living*, Fount, 1997.

Lois G. Forer, 'Bring back the orphanage: an answer for today's abused children', *Washington Monthly*, April 1988.

James Fowler, *Stages of Faith*, Harper & Row, 1981; HarperCollins, 1995.

F. Furedi. and J. Bristow, *Licensed to Hug?* Civitas, 2008.

C. Garvey, *Play*, Harvard University Press, 1974.

Sue Gerhardt, *Why Love Matters*, Routledge, 2004.

Carol Gilligan, *In a Different Voice*, Harvard University Press, 1993.

W. H. Gilman and J. E. Parsons (eds), *The Journals & Miscellaneous Notebooks of Ralph Waldo Emerson*, vol. 8, *1841–1843*, Belknap Press, 1970.

H. Gleitman, Alan Fridlund and Daniel Reisberg, *Psychology*, 6th edn, Norton, 2004.

Roger Gobbel and Gertrude Gobbel, *The Bible: A Child's Playground*, Fortress Press/SCM Press, 1986.

Godly Play UK, *Launch Brochure*, Westminster Abbey, 2007. Also available at http://www.godlyplay.org.uk/

Golden Bells: Hymns for Young People, CSSM, 1925.

William Golding, *Lord of the Flies*, Faber, 1954.

R. Goldman, *Readiness for Religion*, Routledge & Kegan Paul, 1965.

R. Goldman, *Religious Thinking from Childhood to Adolescence*, Routledge & Kegan Paul, 1964.

S. J. Gould, *Ontogeny and Phylogeny*, Belknap Press, 1977.

B. Graham, *Angels, God's Secret Agents*, Hodder Headline, 1981.

M. Green and C. Christian, *Accompanying Young People on their Spiritual Quest*, a Report to the Church of England General Synod, National Society/ Church House Publishing, 1998.

Joel B. Green, Stuart L. Palmer and Kevin Corcoran (eds), *In Search of the Soul*, InterVarsity, 2005.

Stanley Grenz, *Theology for the Community of God*, Eerdmans, 2000.

Colin E. Gunton (ed.), *The Doctrine of Creation*, T&T Clark, 1997.

Stuart Hample and Eric Marshall (eds), *Children's Letters to God*, Kyle Cathie, 1992.

S. Hardman Moore, 'Such perfecting of praise out of the mouth of a babe: Sarah Wright as child prophet', in D. Wood (ed.), *The Church and Childhood*, Blackwell, 1994.

Thomas Hardy, *Tess of the d'Urbervilles*, Penguin Classics, 1891/2003.

M. Harris, *Teaching and Religious Imagination: An Essay on the Theology of Culture*, Harper & Row, 1987.

R. Harrison, *Oriel's Diary*, Scripture Union, 2002.

R. Harrison, *Oriel in the Desert*, Scripture Union, 2004.

R. Harrison, *Oriel's Travels*, Scripture Union, 2003.

David Hay, *Something There: The Biology of the Human Spirit*, Darton, Longman & Todd, 2006.

D. Hay and K. Hunt, *Understanding the Spirituality of People Who Don't Go to Church*, University of Nottingham, 2000.

David Hay and Rebecca Nye, *The Spirit of the Child*, Fount, 1998; 2nd edn, Jessica Kingsley, 2006.

E. Heathcote-James, *Seeing Angels*, John Blake, 2001.

Sharon D. Herzberger and Howard Tennen, 'Coping with abuse: children's perspectives on their abusive treatment', in Richard D. Ashmore and David M. Brodzinsky (eds), *Thinking about the Family: Views of Parents and Children*, Lawrence Erlbaum Associates, 1986.

Kristin Herzog, *Children and our Global Future*, Pilgrim Press, 2005.

Johan Huizinga, *Homo Ludens* (1938), Beacon Press, 1971.

John M. Hull, *God-Talk with Young Children: Notes for Parents and Teachers*, Trinity Press International, 1991.

S. Hurley, *Consciousness in Action*, Harvard University Press, 1998.

J. R. Ickie et al., 'Parent–child relationships and children's images of God', *Journal for the Scientific Study of Religion* 36.1, March 1997, pp. 25–43.

R. Janoff-Bulman, *Shattered Assumptions: Towards a New Psychology of Trauma*, The Free Press, 1992.

Peter Jarvis, *Adult and Continuing Education: Theory and Practice*, Routledge, 1995.

David H. Jensen, *Graced Vulnerability: A Theology of Childhood*, Pilgrim Press, 2005.

L. Gregory Jones, *Embodying Forgiveness*, Eerdmans, 1995.

S. Jones and P. Lakeland (eds), *Constructive Theology: A Contemporary Approach to Classical Themes*, Fortress Press, 2005.

Journal for Children's Spirituality 9.2, August 2004.

P. Kane, *The Play Ethic: A Manifesto for a Different Way of Living*, Macmillan, 2004.

R. Kay, *Saul*, St Martin's Press, 2000.

N. Kazantzakis, *Zorba the Greek*, Faber, 1961.

S. Keen, *Apology for Wonder*, Harper & Row, 1969.

S. Keen, 'Hope in a posthuman era', *The Christian Century*, 25 January 1967.

S. Keen, *To a Dancing God*, Harper & Row, 1972.

D. Kelsey, *The Uses of Scripture in Recent Theology*, Fortress Press, 1975.

D. Keltner and J. Haidt, 'Approaching awe: a moral, spiritual and aesthetic emotion', *Cognition and Emotion* 17, 2003, pp. 297–314.

F. Kermode, *The Genesis of Secrecy*, Harvard University Press, 1979.

A. Kirkpatrick and P. R. Shaver, 'Attachment theory and religion: childhood attachment, religious beliefs and conversion', *Journal for the Scientific Study of Religion* 29, 1990, pp. 315–34.

June D. Knafle and Alice Legenza Wescott, 'Public, private, and home school: children's views of forgiveness and retribution in "Cinderella" ', available at http://www.eric.ed.gov/ERICWebPortal/custom/portlets/recordDetails/detailmini.jsp?_nfpb=true&_&ERICExtSearch_SearchValue_0=ED422592&ERICExtSearch_SearchType_0=no&accno=ED422592

Jonathan Kozol, 'Poverty's children: growing up in the South Bronx', *The Progressive* 59.10, October 1995.

L. Krasnor and D. Pepler, 'The study of children's play: some suggested future directions', in K. Rubin (ed.), *Children's Play*, Jossey Bass, 1980, pp. 85–96.

Harold S. Kushner, *How Good Do We Have To Be?* Little, Brown & Co., 1996.

A. J. Learner and F. Loewe, *My Fair Lady*, Max Reinhardt & Constable, 1958.

Eileen W. Lindner, 'Children as theologians', in Peter B. Pufall and Richard P. Unsworth (eds), *Rethinking Childhood*, Rutgers University Press, 2004, ch. 3.

Long, T. *The Witness of Preaching*, John Knox Press, 1989.

I. Loudon, 'Maternal mortality in the past and its relevance to developing countries today', *American Journal of Clinical Nutrition* 72.1241s–246s, July 2000.

'LP', *Book of Angels*, Longman Green & Co, 1906.

J. Martin Soskice, *Metaphor and Religious Language*, Clarendon Press, 1985.

Floyd M. Martinson, *Growing Up in Norway, 800 to 1990*, Southern Illinois University Press, 1992.

Martin Marty, *The Mystery of the Child*, Eerdmans, 2007.

A. Maslow, *The Farther Reaches of Human Nature*, Penguin Books, 1973.

Scottie May, Beth Posterski, Catherine Stonehouse and Linda Cannell, *Children Matter*, Eerdmans, 2005.

F. McCourt, *Angela and the Baby Jesus*, Simon & Schuster, 2007.

S. McFague, *Metaphorical Theology: Models of God in Religious Language*, SCM Press, 1983.

A. McGrath, *Christian Spirituality*, Blackwell, 1999.

Methodist Church, *The Methodist Worship Book*, Methodist Publishing House, 1999.

David L. Miller, 'The *bricoleur* in the tennis court: pedagogy in postmodern context', 1996 paper for conference on Values in Higher Education. available at http://web.utk.edu/-unistudy/ethics96/dlm1.html

G. Miller, 'The magical number seven, plus or minus two: some limits on our capacity for processing information', *Psychological Review* 63, 1956, pp. 81–97.

W. Miller and J. C'deBaca, 'Quantum change: toward a psychology of transformation', in T. Heatherton and J. Weinberger (eds), *Can Personality Change?* American Psychological Association, 1994, pp. 253–81.

Bonnie J. Miller-McLemore, *Let the Children Come*, Jossey-Bass, 2003.

Mission-shaped Church: Church Planting and Fresh Expressions of Church in a Changing Context, Church House Publishing, 2004.

J. Moltmann, 'The first liberated men in creation', in *Theology of Play*, responses by Robert E. Neale, Sam Keen and David L. Miller, Harper & Row, 1972.

J. Moltmann, *God in Creation: An Ecological Doctrine of Creation*, SCM Press, 1985.

Nancey Murphy, *Bodies and Souls, or Spirited Bodies?*, Cambridge University Press, 2006.

R. Nye, 'Psychological perspectives on children's spirituality', unpublished PhD thesis, University of Nottingham, 1998.

Walter Ong, *Orality and Literacy*, rev. edn, Routledge, 2002.

S. Palmer, *Toxic Childhood: How the Modern World is Damaging Our Children and What We Can Do About It*, Orion, 2006.

F. Peretti, *Piercing the Darkness*, Kingsway, 1989.

F. Peretti, *This Present Darkness*, Kingsway, 1986.

J. Piaget, *A Child's Conception of the World*, Rowman & Littlefield, 1975.

J. Piaget, *Play, Dreams and Imitation*, transl. C. Gattegno and F. M. Hodson, Norton, 1962.

J. Piaget, 'Response to Brian Sutton-Smith', *Psychological Review* 73, 1966, pp. 111–12.

J. Piaget, *The Child's Construction of Reality*, Routledge & Kegan Paul, 1937/ 1955.

J. Piaget, *The Origins of Intelligence in the Child*, Routledge & Kegan Paul, 1936/1952.

N. Postman, *The Disappearance of Childhood*, Vintage Books, 1994.

P. J. Privett, *Living in a Fragile World*, BRF, 2003.

P. J. Privett (ed.), *The Marches Chronicles*, Hereford Diocese, 2000.

Philip Pullman, *Northern Lights*, Scholastic, 1995.

Philip Pullman, *The Amber Spyglass*, Scholastic, 2000.

Philip Pullman, *The Subtle Knife*, Scholastic, 1997.

Gerhard von Rad, *Genesis*, Old Testament Library, Westminster/John Knox Press, 1972.

Karl Rahner, *Foundations of Christian Faith*, Darton, Longman & Todd, 1976/1978.

Karl Rahner, 'Ideas for a theology of childhood', in *Theological Investigations*, vol. 8, *Further Theology of Spiritual Life*, translated D. Bourke, Herder & Herder, 1971.

H. Räisänen, *Jesus, Paul and Torah*, Sheffield Academic Press, 1992.

S. Rajagopal, 'Suicide pacts and the internet', *British Medical Journal* 329, 4 December 2004, pp. 1298–9.

P. Ranwez, 'Discernment of children's religious experience', in A. Godin (ed.), *From Religious Experience to Religious Attitude*, Lumen Vitae Press, 1964.

K. Raschke, 'On rereading Romans 1–6, or overcoming the hermeneutics of suspicion', *Ex Auditu* 1, 1985.

Carmel Reilly, *Dear God: Children's Letters to God from around the World*, Silverdale Books, 2007,

A. Richards, 'A short piece for virginal', *New Fire* 8.65, Winter 1985, pp. 489–90.

P. Ricoeur, *Essays in Biblical Interpretation*, Fortress Press, 1980.

G. Ritzer, *The McDonaldization of Society 5*, Sage, 2007.

R. Roberts, *Self-esteem and Successful Learning*, Hodder & Stoughton, 1995.

Eugene C. Roehlkepartain, Pamela Ebstyne King, Linda M. Wagener and Peter L. Benson (eds), *Handbook of Spiritual Development in Childhood and Adolescence*, Sage, 2005.

Richard Rohr, *Simplicity: The Art of Living*, Crossroad, 1991.

G. Rosen, *Madness in Society*, Routledge & Kegan Paul, 1968.

Jean-Jacques Rousseau, *Emile*, Dent, Everyman's Library, 1762/1963.

J. K. Rowling, *Harry Potter and the Deathly Hallows*, Bloomsbury, 2007.

J. K. Rowling, *Harry Potter and the Goblet of Fire*, Bloomsbury, 2000.

Antoine de Saint-Exupéry, *The Little Prince*, trans. Richard Howard, Harcourt, 1943/2000.

D. E. Saliers, 'Spirituality', in D. Musser and J. Price (eds), *A New Handbook of Christian Theology*, Abingdon, 1992.

Tex Sample, *Ministry in an Oral Culture*, Westminster/John Knox Press, 1994.

D. Schachter, *Searching for Memory*, Basic Books, 1996.

E. Schillebeeckx, *Christ the Sacrament of the Encounter with God*, Sheed & Ward, 1995.

Friedrich Schleiermacher, *Christmas Eve: a Dialogue on the Celebration of Christmas*, translated and with an introduction and notes by N. Tice, John Knox Press, 1967. Also published as F. Scheiermacher, *Christmas Eve: Dialogues on the Incarnation*, Edwin Mellen, 1991.

P. Sheldrake (ed.), *The New SCM Dictionary of Christian Spirituality*, SCM Press, 2005.

A. Shier-Jones, *Children of God: Towards a Theology of Childhood*, Epworth Press, 2007.

Phyllis Rolfe Silverman, *Never Too Young to Know: Death in Children's Lives*, Oxford University Press, 2000.

P. Smith, H. Cowie and M. Blades, *Understanding Children's Development*, Blackwell, 2003.

A. Snell, *I Dream of Peace*, produced by A. Verlek, Serious Music, The Music Works, Netherlands, 2001.

Mark W. Speece and Sandor B. Brent, 'Children's understanding of death: a review of three components of a death concept', *Child Development* 55.5, 1984, pp. 1671–86.

Mark W. Speece and Sandor B. Brent, 'The development of children's understanding of death', in Charles A. Corr, and Donna M. Corr (eds), *Handbook of Childhood Death and Bereavement*, Springer, 1996.

The State of the World's Children, UNICEF, 2008.

Elizabeth-Anne Stewart, *Jesus the Holy Fool*, Sheed & Ward, 1999.

C. Stonehouse, *Joining Children on the Spiritual Journey*, Baker Books, 1998.

G. A. Studdert Kennedy, *The Word and the Work*, Longmans, Green & Co., 1925.

Edna St Vincent Millay, *Collected Poems*, Harper, 1956.

R. Tedeschi and L. Calhoun, *Trauma and Transformation: Growing in the Aftermath of Suffering*, Sage, 1995.

Desmond Tutu, *No Future without Forgiveness*, Doubleday, 1999.

Jean M. Twenge, *Generation Me*, Free Press, 2006.

F. Varela, E. Thompson and E. Rosch, *The Embodied Mind: Cognition, Science and Human Experience*, MIT Press, 1991.

S. Verney, *Water into Wine*, Fount, 1985.

Miroslav Volf, *Free of Charge*, Zondervan, 2005.

A. Walsham, 'Out of the mouths of babes and sucklings: prophecy, Puritanism and childhood in Elizabethan Suffolk', in Diana Wood (ed.), *The Church and Childhood*, Studies in Church History 31, Blackwell, 1995, pp. 285–99.

Fraser Watts and Liz Gulliford (eds), *Forgiveness in Context*, T&T Clark, 2004.

H. R. Weber, *Jesus and the Children*, World Council of Churches, 1979.

J. Westerhoff, *Will Our Children Have Faith?*, Seabury Press, 1976.

R. Williams, 'Does it make sense to speak of pre-Nicene orthodoxy?' in R. Williams (ed.), *The Making of Orthodoxy: Essays in Honour of Henry Chadwick*, Cambridge University Press, 1989.

R. Williams, *Lost Icons*, T&T Clark, 2000.

R. Willoughby and R. Willoughby, *Angels*, Scripture Union, 2006.

W. Wink, *Engaging the Powers*, Fortress Press, 1992.

W. Wink, *Naming the Powers*, Fortress Press, 1984.

W. Wink, *Unmasking the Powers*, Fortress Press, 1986.

M. Withers, *Mission-shaped Children: Moving Towards a Child-centred Church*, Church House Publishing, 2006.

Diana Wood (ed.), *The Church and Childhood*, Studies in Church History 31, Blackwell, 1995.

R. I. Woods, P. A. Watterson and J. H. Woodward, 'The causes of rapid infant mortality decline in England and Wales, 1861–1921, part 2', *Population Studies* 43.1, March 1989, pp. 113–32.

H. Worsley, 'Has secularism emptied the world of angels?' *Journal of Modern Believing* 49.2, 2008, pp. 46–53.

H. Worsley, 'How children understand Bible stories', *International Journal for Children's Spirituality* 9.2, August 2004, pp. 203–17.

H. Worsley, 'Insights from children's perspectives in interpreting the wisdom of the biblical creation narrative', *British Journal of Religious Education* 28.3, 2006, pp. 249–59.

Notes

Prologue

1 For more information see http://www.yearofthechild2009.co.uk

2 In August 1963 the then Minister of Education, Sir Edward Boyle, asked the Central Advisory Council for Education (England) 'to consider primary education in all its aspects and the transition to secondary education'. The Council, under the Chairmanship of Bridget Plowden, presented its report to the Secretary of State for Education and Science, Rt Hon. Anthony Crosland, in October 1966. Published as *Children and their Primary Schools*, 1967.

3 *Child Poverty in Perspective: An Overview of Child Well-being in Rich Countries*, UNICEF Innocenti research centre, Florence, 2007.

4 Hans Ruedi Weber, *Jesus and the Children: Biblical Resources for Study and Preaching*, World Council of Churches, 1979.

5 'Children in the Midst', GSMisc 781, 2005; 'Children Included', GSMisc 804, 2005; 'Sharing the Good News with Children', GS 1515, 2003.

6 James W. Fowler, *Stages of Faith: The Psychology of Human Development and the Quest for Meaning*, Harper and Row, 1981; John Westerhoff, *Will Our Children Have Faith?*, Seabury Press, 1976.

7 See, for example, the reports cited above in footnote 5 and for a twenty-first-century example, see Margaret Withers, *Mission-shaped Children: Moving Towards a Child-centred Church*, Church House Publishing, 2006.

8 See D. Hay and R. Nye, *The Spirit of the Child*, Fount, 1998; 2nd edn, Jessica Kingsley, 2006.

9 For more on Godly Play, see www.godlyplay.org.uk

10 See www.childtheology.org and references in Keith White's chapter in this book (Ch. 2).

11 David Jensen, *Graced Vulnerability: A Theology of Childhood*, Pilgrim Press, 2005.

Introduction

1 For more on Godly Play, see Peter Privett's Prologue.

2 For example, Lawrence Kohlberg's and Carol Gillgan's respective work on children's moral development is challenged by a number of the findings from the chapter on sin.

What is a child?

1 It was Freud, most notably who made this connection, see S. Freud, 'The archaic features and infantilism of dreams', in *Introductory Lectures on Psychoanalysis*, ed. J. Strachey, Norton, 1916/1966.

2 See, for example, M. Kopelman, 'Varieties of false memory', *Cognitive Neuropsychology* 16.3–5, 1 May 1999.

3 H. Gleitman, Alan Fridlund and Daniel Reisberg, *Psychology*, 6th edn, Norton, 2004.

4 At the time of writing there is interest in changing the restriction to age 21 in some cases, such as purchase from supermarkets.

5 S. J. Gould, *Ontogeny and Phylogeny*, Belknap Press, 1977.

6 Neotony, or paedomorphism, refers to the retention in animals of juvenile physical features into maturity. It is seen in the wild in a number of amphibians and also in some domesticated animals as a result of selective breeding for particular traits. Some scientists, such as Stephen J. Gould in *Ontogeny and Phylogeny*, argue that it is present in humans as evidenced by the flattened face, short jaw and late arrival of teeth, continuing brain growth and bulbous forehead compared to other adult primates.

7 Gould, *Ontogeny and Phylogeny*, ch. 5.

8 For example, Richard Dawkins, *The Selfish Gene*, Oxford University Press, 1976. The principal argument of selfish gene theory is that evolutionary selection acts on genes rather than on individual organisms. Dawkins himself draws on the work of John Maynard Smith and J. S. Haldane, among others.

9 For explorations of these see Marcia Bunge, *The Child in Christian Thought*, Eerdmans, 2001.

10 *Childhood under Threat: The State of the World's Children*, UNICEF, 2005.

11 S. Palmer, *Toxic Childhood: How the Modern World is Damaging Our Children and What We Can Do About It*, Orion, 2006.

12 N. Postman, *The Disappearance of Childhood*, Vintage Books, 1994.

13 R. I. Woods, P. A. Watterson and J. H. Woodward, 'The causes of rapid infant mortality decline in England and Wales, 1861–1921, part 2', *Population Studies* 43.1, March 1989, pp. 113–32.

14 John Calvin, *Institutes of the Christian Religion*, ed. John T. McNeill, Westminster, 1960.

15 F. Schleiermacher, *Christmas Eve: Dialogues on the Incarnation*, Edwin Mellen, 1991, p. 36.

16 Office of Health Economics Statistics: Royal College of Obstetrics and Gynaecology.

17 WHO Statistical Information System (WHOSIS).

18 I. Loudon, 'Maternal mortality in the past and its relevance to developing countries today', *American Journal of Clinical Nutrition* 72.1241s–246s, July 2000.

19 Office of Health Economics Statistics: Royal College of Obstetrics and Gynaecology.

20 Office for National Statistics, *The UK in Figures*, Office for National Statistics, 2007.

21 UNICEF, *The State of the World's Children*, UNICEF, 2008.

22 Statistics from the Ecomonic and Social Research Council.

23 P. Cawson et al., *Child Maltreatment in the United Kingdom: A Study of the Prevalence of Child Abuse and Neglect*, NSPCC, 2000.

24 *Time*, 12 February 2008.

25 Available from the Good Childhood Inquiry web site at http://www.goodchildhood.org.uk

26 *Mission-shaped Church: Church Planting and Fresh Expressions of Church in a Changing Context*, Church House Publishing, 2004.

Chapter 1 Nakedness and vulnerability

1 In March 2008, it was widely reported that the celebrity actress and singer Jennifer Lopez spent $1.4 million on a birthing suite for her twins, including leather furniture, plasma screens, computers and a kitchen.

2 So advertisements for lavatory paper and other such products not only include children and puppies, but images of adults pillow fighting, etc.

3 Rosemary Kay, *Saul*, St Martin's Press, 2000, p. 12.

4 Kay, *Saul*, p. 9.

5 Children often empathize powerfully with the child Jesus in the Christmas crib. Fr John McKeon, of St Thomas of Canterbury Roman Catholic church, Grays, tells the story of how one Christmas the adults were frantic after the baby Jesus went missing from the crib. A boy who got a wheelbarrow for Christmas was found giving the Christchild a ride in it. He said that he had promised that if he got his wheelbarrow as he had wanted, he would give Jesus the first ride in it. Also see, Frank Mc Court, *Angela and the Baby Jesus*, Simon & Schuster, 2007.

6 Known as the *Von der Ropp Madonna* c.1502 in the Staatliche Museum in Berlin.

7 Robert Campin, *Virgin and Child before a Firescreen*; Jehan Fouquet, *Madonna and Child*; Filippino Lippi, *Virgin and Child with Saints*; Massaccio, *Madonna and Child*.

8 'See Amid the Winter's Snow'.

9 'Coventry Carol'.

10 'Once in Royal David's City'.

11 Charles Wesley, 'Gentle Jesus Meek and Mild'.

12 'Once in Royal David's City'.

13 A painting illustrating this stroppiness is Simone Martini's *Christ Discovered in the Temple*, Walker Gallery, Liverpool, where Jesus stands before his remonstrating parents with his arms folded.

14 'Praise to the Holiest in the Height'.

15 In the Roman Catholic Church Mary is understood to have been called 'full of grace' by the angel because she was herself free from sin from the moment of her conception, the Immaculate Conception.

16 I have looked at the irony of this teaching in relation to the human experience of birth in 'A short piece for virginal', *New Fire* 8.65, Winter 1985, pp. 489–90.

17 Such as Piero della Francesca, *The Baptism of Jesus*, c.1449, National Gallery, London; Andrea del Verrocchio, *The Baptism of Christ*, c.1472–5, Uffizi Gallery, Florence; *The Baptism of Christ*, centre panel of a triptych by Gerard David, c.1502–7, at the Groenigemuseum, Bruges; Giovan Battista Caracciolo known as Battistello, *Baptism of Christ*, 1610, Girolamini Picture Gallery; El Greco, *Baptism of Christ*, 1608–14, Hospital de San Juan Bautista de Afuera, Toledo. The scrap of cloth Jesus wears is for modesty.

18 J. K. Rowling, *Harry Potter and the Deathly Hallows*, Bloomsbury, 2007, p. 566.

19 Frank Kermode, in *The Genesis of Secrecy*, Harvard University Press, 1979, ch. 3 'The Man in the Mackintosh, the Boy in the Shirt', discusses the significance of the mysterious young man in the shirt in the Garden of Gethsemane who runs away naked. One argument is that the young man has come for baptism (see above), but Kermode looks more closely at Farrer's suggestion of a symbolic link between this incident and the young man disovered at the tomb by the women, especially as his garment is described with the same word as a winding sheet. A young naked person flees from the garden, but is recovered, reclothed, accompanying the resurrection (Mark 16.5). There are a number of interpretations, but on one level then, this can be seen as a soul's journey, fleeing as a naked child into the darkness where its story is not known, but discovered again as a witness to the story of the the reality of resurrection.

20 At the time of writing, the campaign, even 'movement' to find Madeleine McCann has dominated the media for months.

21 Redmond O'Hanlon, *In Trouble Again*, Penguin, 1989, p. 312.

22 Philip Pullman, *Northern Lights*, Scholastic, 1995; *The Subtle Knife*, Scholastic, 1997; *The Amber Spyglass*, Scholastic, 2000.

23 So there are calls for a 'Sarah's Law' after the murdered child Sarah Payne, to emulate 'Megan's Law' in the United States.

24 This research is published as Frank Furedi and Jennie Bristow, *Licensed to Hug?*, Civitas, 2008, and generated a large amount of media coverage, discussion and comment. See http://www.frankfuredi.com/index.php/news/article/219/

25 http://artmarketblog.com/2007/10/31/when-pornography-is-pornography-and-not-fine-art/

26 The photo by Associated Press photographer Nick Ut of nine-year-old Kim Phuc running out of Trang Bang village, about 25 miles west of Saigon, emerged as one of the most compelling images of the war and its impact on civilians. It won the Pulitzer Prize in 1972. There were also problems at first about the publication of the photo, as the depiction of Kim Phuc's frontal nudity was felt to be unacceptable.

Chapter 2 Creation

1 From Peter Privett (ed.), *The Marches Chronicles*, Diocese of Hereford, 2000. These contain a number of reflections on the natural world by children and were suggested for inclusion in this chapter by Peter himself.

2 The name of the house in South Woodford, East London, where we live is Mill Grove. It's something of a cross between a foster family and a residential community. Some of its rather unique nature and dynamics stem from the fact that it is the home of five generations of a family called White and that as a Christian family it lives by simple faith.

3 It is important to note that the person speaking was a teenager, rather than a little child. It is the argument of this chapter that little children do not reflect on creation in this way. The teenager had helped me to begin to see and understand the natural world in a way that opened my eyes to ways in which younger children were interacting with it.

4 I am using the term 'secure base' in the way Dr John Bowlby describes it in his book by the same name, *A Secure Base*, Routledge, 1988.

5 I am aware that the Gobbels have described the Bible as a playground and this has seemed to me a glorious insight into a truth hidden from many of the wise and learned commentators, theologians, pastors and adults engaged in traditional forms of children's ministry. Roger Gobbel and Gertrude Gobbel, *The Bible: A Child's Playground*, Fortress; SCM Press, 1986.

6 Stanley Grenz, *Theology for the Community of God*, Eerdmans, 2000.

7 Gerhard von Rad (1901–71) applied form criticism in his work on the Old Testament, for example, in his commentary on *Genesis*, The Old Testament Library, Westminster/John Knox Press, 1972.

8 This is not contested by those who have been exploring this matter in recent years. Children have been studied in a variety of ways, by a number of significant theologians, but they have not figured in mainstream theological discourse and enquiry either as the subject of theological anthropology, or as a substantive element of theological orientation. For example, see Kristin Herzog, *Children and our Global Future*, Pilgrim Press, 2005, ch. 1: 'Theology's historic neglect and recent interest in the child'.

9 Colin E. Gunton (ed.), *The Doctrine of Creation*, T&T Clark, 1997.

10 Dietrich Bonhoeffer, *Creation and Fall*, Fortress, 2004.

11 There is in my view a synchronicity between the elusive nature of childhood and the mystery of the kingdom of heaven.

12 'It is not death that is the final goal of our life, but being born', Kristin Herzog, *Children and our Global Future*, p. 18.

13 See 'Quotations', *Encyclopaedia of the Bible and Christianity*, 2nd edn, Lion Publishing, CD-ROM, 1998.

14 Stuart Hample and Eric Marshall (eds), *Children's Letters to God*, Kyle Cathie, 1992. (The pages of this book are not numbered, so in the text I have referred to which of the 60 letters is being quoted.) For the record I have mostly stayed with the original spelling and grammar unless I felt it obfuscated what the children were trying to say.

15 http:// www.froebel.org.uk/elements.html

16 From Peter Privett (ed.), *The Marches Chronicles*, Hereford Diocese, 2000.

17 From Privett (ed.), *Marches Chronicles*.

18 Quoted by Martin Marty, *The Mystery of the Child*, Eerdmans, 2007, p. 102.

19 Quoted by Marty, *The Mystery of the Child*, p. 103.

20 From Privett (ed.), *Marches Chronicles*.

21 From Privett (ed.), *Marches Chronicles*.

22 I am grateful to Professor William Brown for pointing this out to a group of theologians at a conference in Chicago in 2005 as part of the process leading to the forthcoming book edited by Marcia Bunge and others, *The Child in the Bible*, Eerdmans, 2008.

23 J. Moltmann, *God in Creation: An Ecological Doctrine of Creation*, SCM Press, 1985.

24 Jane Clements, reproduced in J. C. Arnold, *A Little Child Shall Lead Them*, Plough, 1997, pp. 29–30. Reproduced with kind permission of Plough Publishing.

25 See http://www.childtheology.org and the Child Theology Movement
reports: *Penang One: Report of Consultation (2002)*; *Cape Town: Report of Consultation (2004)*; *Houston: Report of Consultation (2004)*; *Penang Two: Report of Consultation (2004)*; *Cambridge: Report of Consultation (2004)*; *Prague (Praha): Report of Consultation (2005)*; *Penang Three: Report of Consultation (2006)*; *Sao Paulo: Report of Consultation (2006)* (Portuguese and English); *Addis Ababa: Report of Consultation (2006)*; *Australasia: Report of Consultation (2007)*. Also the Child Theology Movement booklet series: Haddon Willmer & Keith J. White, *Introducing Child Theology* (no. 1); Haddon Willmer, *Experimenting Together* (no. 2); Sunny Tan, *Child Theology for the Churches in Asia: an Invitation* (no. 3).

26 For example, Exodus 12.26, 'When your children ask you "What do you mean by this observance?" you shall say, "It is the passover sacrifice to the Lord . . ." ' Also Joshua 4.6, 'When your children ask in time to come, "What do those stones mean to you?" then you shall tell them that the waters of the Jordan were cut off in front of the ark of the covenant of the Lord.'

Chapter 3 Spirituality

1 Quoted in Rebecca Nye, *Psychological Perspectives on Children's Spirituality*, Unpublished PhD Thesis, University of Nottingham, 1998.

2 E.g. *The International Journal of Children's Spirituality*, Carfax, 1996-present; Eugene C. Roehlkepartain et al. (eds), *The Handbook of Spiritual Development in Childhood and Adolescence*, Sage, 2005; David Hay and Rebecca Nye, *The Spirit of the Child*, Jessica Kingsley, 2006 (first published 1998); R. Best (ed.), *Education, Spirituality and the Whole Child*, Continuum, 1996; and J. Erricker, C. Erricker and C. Ota (eds), *Spiritual Education*, Sussex Academic Press, 2001.

3 DES, *The Education Reform Act 1988: The School Curriculum and Assessment*, HMSO, 1989, p. 7.

4 K. Copsey, 'From the ground up . . .', in D. Ratcliff (ed.), *Christian Perspectives on Children's Spirituality*, Cascade Books, 2004.

5 J. Berryman, The *Complete Guide to Godly Play*, vols 1–7, Living the Good News, 2002; J. Berryman, *Godly Play: An Imaginative Approach to Religious Education*, Augsburg Fortress, 1995.

6 See http://www.natsoc.org.uk/schools/gp/intro.html; also P. Privett, *Living in a Fragile World*, BRF, 2003.

7 Especially based on Hay and Nye, *The Spirit of the Child*; Nye, *Psychological Perspectives on Children's Spirituality*.

8 John M. Hull, *God-Talk with Young Children: Notes for Parents and Teachers*, Trinity Press International, 1991.

9 Hay and Nye, *The Spirit of the Child*.

10 David Ford, *The Shape of Living*, Fount, 1997, p. 104.

11 For example, the rather adult-centric, religious-knowledge-dependent definition given in A. McGrath's *Christian Spirituality*, Blackwell, 1999: 'Spirituality concerns the quest for a fulfilled and authentic religious life, involving the bringing together of the ideas distinctive to that religion and the whole experience of living on the basis of and within the scope of that religion' (p. 2); or that of Don E. Saliers (also quoted by McGrath): 'Spirituality refers to a lived experiences and a disciplined life of prayer and action, but it cannot be conceived apart from the specific theological beliefs that are ingredients in the forms of life that manifest in authentic Christian faith' (p. 460) (D. E. Saliers, 'Spirituality', in D. Musser and J. Price (eds), *A New Handbook of Christian Theology*, Abingdon, 1992).

12 Ronald Goldman, *Readiness for Religion*, Routledge & Kegan Paul, 1965, p. 49. It is hard to imagine how someone who worked with children did not recognize that the experiences in this list are indeed essential experiences of childhood (as others in this volume pursue), nor understood the condescension that adjudicates the experiences of others such that only some problems are deemed 'real' problems of the human condition.

13 R. Goldman, *Religious Thinking from Childhood to Adolescence*, Routledge & Kegan Paul, 1964, p. 14.

14 M. Bunge (ed.), *The Child in Christian Thought*, Eerdmans, 2001.

15 P. Ranwez, 'Discernment of Children's Religious Experience', in A. Godin (ed.), *From Religious Experience to Religious Attitude*, Lumen Vitae Press, 1964.

16 Ranwez, 'Discernment of Children's Religious Experience', p. 64.

17 Ranwez, 'Discernment of Children's Religious Experience', p. 66.

18 P. Sheldrake (ed.), *The New SCM Dictionary of Christian Spirituality*, SCM Press, 2005.

19 W. Damon and R.M. Lerner (eds), *Handbook of Child Psychology*, vol. 1, *Theoretical Models of Human Development*, 6th edn, 2006.

20 See L. Dupré's 'Introduction', in L. Dupré and D. Saliers, *Christian Spirituality: Post Reformation and Modern*, SCM Press, 1990.

21 T. Copley, J. Priestley, D. Wadman and V. Coddington, *Forms of Religious Assessment in Religious Education*, The FARE Report, University of Exeter School of Education, 1991, p. 23.

22 Fascinating historical studies of children in this period can be found in A. Walsham, 'Out of the mouths of babes and sucklings: prophecy, Puritanism and childhood in Elizabethan Suffolk' and in S. Hardman Moore, 'Such perfecting of praise out of the mouth of a babe: Sarah Wright as child prophet', in D. Wood (ed.), *The Church and Childhood*, Blackwell, 1994.

23 This may be both a strength and weakness. See, for example, the treatment of the child's vulnerability as a kind of inverted power in D. Jensen, *Graced Vulnerability: A Theology of Childhood*, Pilgrim Press, 2005.

24 K. Rahner, 'Ideas for a theology of childhood', in *Theological Investigations 8: Further Theology of Spiritual Life*, trans. D. Bourke, Herder & Herder, 1971.

Chapter 4 Word

1 P. Ricoeur, *Essays in Biblical Interpretation*, Fortress Press, 1980.

2 See J. Duff and J. Collicutt, *Meeting Jesus: Human Responses to a Yearning God*, SPCK, 2006, pp. 26–7 for an example of the response of children to the story of the lost sheep.

3 J. Berryman, *Complete Guide to Godly Play*, vol. 3, Living the Good News, 2002, pp. 102–8.

4 Jerome, *Commentaris in Ecclesiastem*, 3, 13, in *Corpus Christianorum Series Latina*, vol. 72, Brepols 1959, p. 278.

5 E. Schillebeeckx, *Christ the Sacrament of the Encounter with God*, Lanham, Sheed & Ward, 1995.

6 K. Barth, *Homiletics*, Westminster/John Knox Press, 1966/1991; D. Kelsey, *The Uses of Scripture in Recent Theology*, Fortress Press, 1975.

7 J. Barr, *The Scope and Authority of the Bible*, Westminster Press, 1980, p. 55.

8 K. Raschke, 'On rereading Romans 1–6 or overcoming the hermeneutics of suspicion', *Ex Auditu* 1, 1985, pp.147–55.

9 R. Williams, 'Does it make sense to speak of pre-Nicene orthodoxy?', in R. Williams (ed.), *The Making of Orthodoxy: Essays in Honour of Henry Chadwick*, Cambridge University Press, 1989, p. 15.

10 W. Brueggemann, *The Book that Breathes New Life*, Fortress Press, 2005, p. 25.

11 Brueggemann, *The Book that Breathes New Life*, p. 25.

12 Barth, *Homiletics*, p. 41.

13 T. Long, *The Witness of Preaching*, John Knox Press 1989, p. 20.

14 K. Barth, *Church Dogmatics* 1.1, T&T Clark, 1932/1975, pp. 193–4.

15 Barth, *Homiletics*, p. 33.

16 E. Brunner, *Truth as Encounter*, SCM Press, 1964.

17 J. Dewey, *Experience and Nature*, Dover, 1929/1958.

18 K. Rahner, *Foundations of Christian Faith*, Darton, Longman & Todd, 1976/1978; Brueggemann, *The Book that Breathes New Life*.

19 M. Argyle, 'State of the art – religion', *The Psychologist*, 15, 2002, pp. 22–6.

20 F. Varela, E. Thompson and E. Rosch, *The Embodied Mind: Cognition, Science and Human Experience*, MIT Press, 1991; S. Hurley, *Consciousness in Action*, Harvard University Press, 1998.

21 Long, *The Witness of Preaching*.

22 J. Piaget, *The Origins of Intelligence in the Child*, Routledge & Kegan Paul, 1936/1952. J. Piaget, *The Child's Construction of Reality*, Routledge & Kegan Paul 1937/1955. For a critical historical consideration, see P. Smith, H. Cowie and M. Blades, *Understanding Children's Development*, Blackwell, 2003.

23 R. Benthall, *Madness Explained*, Penguin, 2004, pp. 293ff; pp. 23, 387.

24 R. Janoff-Bulman, *Shattered Assumptions: Towards a New Psychology of Trauma*, The Free Press, 1992; R. Tedeschi and L. Calhoun, *Trauma and Transformation: Growing in the Aftermath of Suffering*, Sage, 1995.

25 W. Miller and J. C'deBaca, 'Quantum change: toward a psychology of transformation', in T. Heatherton and J. Weinberger (eds), *Can Personality Change?*, American Psychological Association, 1994, pp. 253–81.

26 D. Schachter, *Searching for Memory*, Basic Books, 1966.

27 Brueggemann, *The Book that Breathes New Life*, p. 5.

28 L. Krasnor and D. Pepler, 'The study of children's play: some suggested future directions', in K. Rubin (ed.), *Children's Play*, Jossey Bass, 1980, pp. 85–96.

29 J. Berryman, *Godly Play: A Way of Religious* Education, Harper, 1991.

30 J. Piaget, 'Response to Brian Sutton-Smith', *Psychological Review*, 73, 1966, pp. 111–12

31 D. Keltner and J. Haidt, 'Approaching awe: a moral, spiritual and aesthetic emotion', *Cognition and Emotion*, 17, 2003, pp. 297–314.

32 T. Dennis, *Imagining God*, SPCK, 1989, pp. 3–7.

33 K. Barth, *The Word of God and the Word of Man*, Harper & Brothers, 1928/1957.

34 J. Barton, 'The Messiah in Old Testament Theology', in J. Day (ed.), *King and Messiah in the Ancient Near East*, Sheffield Academic Press, 1998, pp. 365–79.

35 H. Räisänen, *Jesus, Paul and Torah*, Sheffield Academic Press, 1992, pp. 69–94.

36 Brueggemann, *The Book that Breathes New Life*, p. 28.

37 Brueggemann, *The Book that Breathes New Life*, p. 27.

38 J. D. Crossan, *Cliffs of Fall: Paradox and Polyvalence in the Parables of Jesus*, Seabury Press, 1980.

39 Berryman, *Godly Play: A Way of Religious Education*, pp. 149–54.

40 C. H. Dodd, *The Parables of the Kingdom*, Fontana, 1961, p. 16.

41 S. McFague, *Metaphorical Theology: Models of God in Religious Language*, SCM Press, 1983; J. Martin Soskice, *Metaphor and Religious Language*, Clarendon Press, 1985.

42 G. Miller, 'The magical number seven, plus or minus two: some limits on our capacity for processing information', *Psychological Review*, 63, 1956, pp. 81–97.

Chapter 5 Play

1 David Miller, 'The *bricoleur* in the tennis court: pedagogy in postmodern context', 1996 Paper for Conference on Values in Higher Education, http://web.utk.edu/-unistudy/ethics96/dlm1.html

2 Fraser Brown and Sophie Webb, 'Children without play', *Journal of Education*, 35, 2005, pp. 139–58. Available at http://www.ukzn.ac.za/joe/JoEPDFs/joe%2035%20brown%20and%20webb.pdf

3 Jürgen Moltmann, 'The first liberated men in creation', in *Theology of Play*, responses by Robert E. Neale, Sam Keen, and David L. Miller, Harper & Row, 1972, p. 112.

4 Peter J. Privett (ed.), *The Marches Chronicles*, Diocese of Hereford, 2000. For more information on these reflections on life and faith in Hereford diocese contact the diocesan office, diooffice@hereford.anglican.org

5 Johan Huizinga, *Homo Ludens* (1938), ET Beacon Press, 1955/repr. 1971, p. 7.

6 Jean Piaget, *Play, Dreams and Imitation*, trans. C. Gattegno and F. M. Hodson, Norton, 1962.

7 Catherine Garvey, *Play*, Harvard University Press, 1974.

8 Jerome Berryman, *The Complete Guide to Godly Play*, vol. 1, Living the Good News, 2002.

9 Quoted by Berryman, *The Complete Guide to Godly Play*, vol. 1, p. 42.

10 Huizinga, *Homo Ludens*, p. 206.

11 Mihaly Csikszentmihalyi, *Flow, the Psychology of Optimal Experience*, Rider, 1992/2002.

12 Brown and Webb, 'Children without play', p. 144 (Reflective Diary, 6 February 2000).

13 Serene Jones and Paul Lakeland (eds), *Constructive Theology : A Contemporary Approach to Classical Themes*, Fortress Press, 2005. Contributors to the chapter on 'Sin and Evil' include Margaret Kamitsuka, Kris Kvan, Sally McFague, Linda Merchant, Darby Kathleen Ray, Stephen Ray, John E. Thiel and Tatha Wiley.

14 Fraser Brown, *Play Theories and the Value of Play*, Library and Information Service, National Children's Bureau, 2006.

15 See Jones and Lakeland, *Constructive Theology*.

16 Jones and Lakeland, *Constructive Theology*, p. 197.

17 Jones and Lakeland, *Constructive Theology*, p. 199.

18 David Hay and Rebecca Nye, *The Spirit of the Child*, Fount, 1998.

19 Hay and Nye, *The Spirit of the Child*, p. 127.

20 Privett (ed.), *The Marches Chronicles*, 2000.

21 Privett (ed.), *The Marches Chronicles*, 2000.

22 Csikszentmihalyi, *Flow*, p. 20.

23 Stephen Verney, *Water into Wine*, Fount, 1985.

24 David Jensen, *Graced Vulnerability: A Theology of Childhood*, Pilgrim Press, 2005.

25 Jensen, *Graced Vulnerability*, Foreword, p. viii.

26 Jensen, *Graced Vulnerability*, p. 16.

27 Rowan Williams, *Lost Icons*, T&T Clark, 2000.

28 *Godly Play UK*, Alison Summerskills in brochure (p. 5) for the launch of *Godly Play UK* in Westminster Abbey 2007. Available at www.godlyplay.org.uk/about

29 *Godly Play* launch brochure, p. 5.

30 Maria Harris, *Teaching and Religious Imagination: An Essay on the Theology of Teaching*, Harper & Row, 1987.

31 Maxine Green and Chandu Christian, *Accompanying Young People on Their Spiritual Quest*, A Report to the Church of England General Synod, The National Society/Church House Publishing, 1998.

32 N. Kazantzakis, *Zorba The Greek*, Faber, 1961.

33 M. Donald, *Origins of the Modern Mind*, Harvard University Press, 1991, p. 169, quoted by Brown and Webb, 'Children without Play', p. 152.

34 R. Roberts, *Self-esteem and Successful Learning*, Hodder & Stoughton, 1995, quoted by Brown and Webb, 'Children without play'.

35 Iain M. Banks, *The Player of Games*, HarperCollins, 1997.

36 Pat Kane, *The Play Ethic: A Manifesto for a Different Way of Living*, Macmillan, 2004.

37 Kane, *The Play Ethic*, p. 352.

38 *Delia*, BBC Radio 2, 14 April 2008, 8.30 p.m.

39 Berryman, *The Complete Guide to Godly Play*, vol. 1, p. 132.

40 A. J. Lerner and F. Loewe, *My Fair Lady*, Max Reinhardt & Constable, 1958, p. 100.

41 Berryman, *The Complete Guide to Godly Play*, vol. 1, p. 139.

42 Hans Ruedi Weber, *Jesus and the Children*, World Council of Churches, 1979, p. 35.

43 Weber, *Jesus and the Children*, p. 19.

44 R. Alves, *Tomorrow's Children: Imagination, Creativity and Rebirth of Culture*, Harper & Row, 1972.

45 Sam Keen, *To a Dancing God*, Harper & Row, 1972.

46 Sam Keen, *Apology for Wonder*, Harper & Row, 1969.

47 Sam Keen, 'Hope in a posthuman era', *The Christian Century*, 25 January 1967.

48 Moltmann, 'The first liberated men in creation', pp. 33–4.

Chapter 6 Sin

1 These were choc ices in the Magnum range and each was named after one of the sins.

2 Usury is still considered a sin for Muslims and special arrangements are made to make buying houses and investing money possible under sharia law.

3 Bonnie J. Miller-McLemore, *Let the Children Come*, Jossey-Bass, 2003, p. 22.

4 Sue Gerhardt, *Why Love Matters*, Brunner Routledge, 2004.

Chapter 7 Forgiveness

1 Libby Brooks, *The Story of Childhood*, Bloomsbury, 2006; Kathryn Copsey, *From the Ground Up*, Barnabas, 2005.

2 Sophia Cavaletti, *The Religious Potential of the Child*, Paulist Press, 1992, p. 45.

3 Jerome Berryman, 'Children and mature spirituality', Godly Play web site, http://www.godlyplay.org.uk, accessed 2005.

4 Marcus Braybrooke, *Thoughts on Forgiveness*, Braybrooke Press, 2003, p. 2.

5 Carol Gilligan, *In a Different Voice*, Harvard University Press, 1993.

6 Gilligan, *In a Different Voice*, p. 28.

7 Miroslav Volf, *Free of Charge*, Zondervan, 2005.

8 *Eastenders*, BBC1, 16 July 2007.

9 L. Gregory Jones, *Embodying Forgiveness*, Eerdmans, 1995.

10 Dietrich Bonhoeffer, *The Cost of Discipleship*, SCM Press, 2001 (1966).

11 J. Piaget *A Child's Conception of the World*, Rowman & Littlefield, 1975; Copsey, *From the Ground Up*, BRF, 2005.

12 For example, Fraser Watts and Liz Gulliford (eds), *Forgiveness in Context*, T&T Clark, 2004; Volf, *Free of Charge*.

13 For example, when the boy wizard Harry Potter encounters his nemesis, the evil Voldemort in the dark graveyard which contains the grave of Voldemort's murdered father. The evil Voldemort works within death and darkness; Harry is surrounded by figures of light, protecting him and willing the good in him to triumph. J. K. Rowling, *Harry Potter and the Goblet of Fire*, Bloomsbury, 2000.

14 For example, Piaget, *A Child's Conception of the World*; James Fowler, *Stages of Faith*, HarperCollins, 1995.

15 Watts and Gulliford (eds), *Forgiveness in Context*, p. 186.

16 Volf, *Free of Charge*, p. 140.

17 Volf, *Free of Charge*; Braybrooke, *Thoughts on Forgiveness*.

18 Desmond Tutu, *No Future without Forgiveness*, Doubleday, 1999.

Chapter 8 Grace

1 Angela Shier-Jones (ed.), *Children of God: Towards a Theology of Childhood*, Epworth Press, 2007.

2 As quoted in Robert Coles, *The Spiritual lives of Children*, Houghton Mifflin, 1990, p. 224.

3 Lois G. Forer, 'Bring back the orphanage: an answer for today's abused children', *Washington Monthly*, April 1988.

4 In his book entitled *The Selfish Gene*, Richard Dawkins defined 'selfishness' as behaviour that increases the chances of survival (e.g. increases the number of copies) of genes in one individual at the expense of another. Dawkins argues that 'the fundamental unit of selection, and therefore of self-interest, is not the species, nor the group, nor even, strictly, the individual. It is the gene, the unit of heredity.' Richard Dawkins, *The Selfish Gene*, Oxford University Press, 1976, p. 11.

5 Adoptionism was a minority belief held by some in the early Church that Christ was not born divine, but was 'adopted' by God as the Messiah some time later in his life (most commonly thought to be at his baptism). It was declared to be heresy at various times in the history of the Church, but most emphatically at the first council at Nicea.

6 Floyd M. Martinson, *Growing Up in Norway, 800 to 1990*, Southern Illinois University Press, 1992, p. 11.

7 So when a young person has their own front door key, no one has to wait up; learning to drive means no one has to make sure the young person arrives safely; opening a student bank account means taking control of their own money and financial responsibility and so on.

8 Robert Coles, 'Struggling toward childhood: an interview with Robert Coles', *Second Opinion* 18.4 (April 1993), pp. 58–71, p. 71.

9 Antoine de Saint-Exupery, *The Little Prince*, trans. Richard Howard, Harcourt, 2000, p. 1.

10 Karl Rahner, *Theological Investigations* 8, Darton, Longman & Todd, 1971, p. 47.

11 Rahner, *Theological Investigations* 8, p. 47.

12 See, for example, A Maslow, *The Farther Reaches of Human Nature*, Penguin, 1973.

13 Told with permission, but the person's name has been changed to protect their identity.

14 B. Egeland, 'A history of abuse is a major risk factor for abusing the next generation', in R. J. Gelles and D. R. Loseke (eds), *Current Controversies on Family Violence*, Sage, p. 206.

15 Eileen W. Lindner, 'Children as theologians', ch. 3 in Peter B. Pufall and Richard P. Unsworth (eds), *Rethinking Childhood*, Rutgers University Press, 2004, p. 60.

16 Lindner, 'Children as theologians', p. 60.

17 Jonathan Kozol, 'Poverty's children: growing up in the South Bronx', *The Progressive* 59.10, October 1995, pp. 22f.

18 The practice of consuming the elements is not universal throughout the Church.

19 See Catherine Stonehouse, *Joining Children on the Spiritual Journey*, Baker Books, 1998, pp. 129ff.

20 Jane R. Dickie et al., 'Parent–child relationships and children's images of God', *Journal for the Scientific Study of Religion* 36.1, March 1997, pp. 25–43.

21 Some research has suggested that in instances of neglect or abuse by the father, there is a direct transference of attachment to 'God'. L. A. Kirkpatrick and P. R. Shaver, 'Attachment theory and religion: childhood attachment, religious beliefs, and conversion', *Journal for the Scientific Study of Religion* 29, 1990, pp. 315–34.

22 Egeland, 'A history of abuse', pp. 197–208, p. 206.

23 Herbert Anderson, and Susan B. W. Johnson, *Regarding Children: A New Respect for Childhood and Families*, 1st edn, Westminster/John Knox Press, 1994, p. 91.

24 Herbert Anderson, *The Family and Pastoral Care*, Fortress Press, 1984, pp. 21–79.

25 Anderson and Johnson, *Regarding Children*, p. 60.

26 J. Branne, E. Heptinstall and K. Bhopal, *Connecting Children: Care and Family Life in Later Childhood*, Routledge, 2000, p. 205.

27 Egeland, 'A history of abuse', p. 206.

28 Anderson and Johnson, *Regarding Children*, p. 60.

29 Some reports suggest that over 25 per cent of those on the violent and sexual offenders register are under 18 years of age. E.g. Joyce Plotnikoff and Richard Woolfson, *Where Are They Now?: An Evaluation of Sex Offender Registration in England and Wales*, Police Research Series Paper 126, HMSO, 2000, p. 6.

30 For a fuller exploration of infant baptism and the development of its practice from the time of the early Church, see Paul de Clerck, 'Baptism' in Jean-Yves Lacoste (ed.), *Encyclopedia of Christian Theology*, vol. 1, Routledge, 2004, pp. 149–52.

31 The Methodist Church, *The Methodist Worship Book*, Methodist Publishing House, 1999, p. 66.

✗ 32 Carmel Reilly, *Dear God: Children's Letters to God from around the World*, Silverdale Books, 2007, p. 88.

33 David Elkind, *The Child's Reality: Three Developmental Themes*, Lawrence Erlbaum Associates, 1978, p. 24.

34 The use of dual tense is a means of honouring the continued suffering and pain caused by abuse. For a comprehensive exploration of children's responses to abuse, see Sharon D. Herzberger and Howard Tennen, 'Coping with abuse: children's perspectives on their abusive treatment', in Richard D. Ashmore and David M. Brodzinsky (eds), *Thinking about the Family: Views of Parents and Children*, Lawrence Erlbaum Associates, 1986, pp. 277–96.

35 Herzberger and Tennen, 'Coping with abuse', p. 283.

36 June D. Knafle and Alice Legenza Wescott, 'Public, private, and home: school children's views of forgiveness and retribution in "Cinderella" ', at http://www.eric.ed.gov/ERICWebPortal/custom/portlets/recordDetails/ detailmini.jsp?_nfpb=true&_&ERICExtSearch_SearchValue_0=ED422592& ERICExtSearch_SearchType_0=no&accno=ED422592

37 Reilly, *Dear God*, p. 184.

38 As quoted in Coles, *The Spiritual Lives of Children*, p. 211.

39 Anderson and Johnson, *Regarding Children*, p. 93.

Chapter 9 Salvation

1 Alfred Tennyson, *In Memoriam*, LIV.

2 John Masefield, *The Everlasting Mercy* (1911).

3 http://www.unicef.org

4 *The Guardian*, 6 February 2007, p. 1.

5 Jean-Jacques Rousseau, *Emile*, Everyman's Library, Dent, 1963, p. 56.

6 Friedrich Schleiermacher, *Christmas Eve: A Dialogue on the Incarnation*,

translated and with an introduction and notes by Terrence N. Tice, John Knox Press, 1967.

7 Horace Bushnell, *Christian Nurture*, Alexander Strahan, 1866, p. 52.

8 Bushnell, *Christian Nurture*, p. 221.

9 Philip Carrington, *According to Mark: A Running Commentary on the Oldest Gospel*, Cambridge University Press, 1960.

10 David H. Jensen, *Graced Vulnerability: A Theology of Childhood*, Pilgrim Press, 2005, p. 89.

11 David Hay, *Something There: The Biology of the Human Spirit*, Darton, Longman & Todd, 2006.

12 *The Guardian*, 12 October 2007.

13 Thomas Gray, 'Ode on a Distant Prospect of Eton College' (1742).

14 Irenaeus, *Against Heresies*, 2.22.4.

15 Further information about Godly Play resources and training in the United Kingdom is available at http://www.godlyplay.org.uk

16 G. A. Studdert Kennedy, *The Word and the Work*, Longmans, Green & Co., 1925, p. 5.

Chapter 10 Death

1 This part of the story is told in greater detail in Olive Fleming Drane, *Clowns, Storytellers, Disciples*, Augsburg, 2004.

2 Phyllis Rolfe Silverman, *Never Too Young to Know: Death in Children's Lives*, Oxford University Press, 2000, p. 4.

3 Subsequent verses of this hymn speak of a home, a crown, a song and a robe – all of them 'for little children, above the bright blue sky'. In at least one popular hymn book of the early twentieth century, this hymn was listed in the section of 'Hymns for the Younger Children', no doubt reflecting the high mortality rate of the day: *Golden Bells: Hymns for Young People*, London: CSSM, 1925, hymn 640. Its origins, though, were in the Victorian era, written by Albert Midlane (a businessman on the Isle of Wight) in 1859, and most often sung to a tune composed by the eminent Sir John Stainer.

4 Jean M. Twenge, *Generation Me*, Free Press, 2006.

5 The final lines of the song answer the question with the statement that 'Forever is our today'.

6 George Ritzer, *The McDonaldization of Society 5*, Sage, 2007, ch. 6. For an application of this theory to the ministry and mission of the Church, see John Drane, *The McDonaldization of the Church*, Darton, Longman & Todd, 2000, and *After McDonaldization: Mission, Ministry and Christian Discipleship in an Age of Uncertainty*, Darton, Longman & Todd, 2008.

7 Cf. Colin Campbell, 'The Easternisation of the West', in Bryan Wilson and Jamie Cresswell (eds), *New Religious Movements: Challenge and Response*, Routledge, 1999, pp. 33–48.

8 Cf. Joel B. Green, Stuart L. Palmer and Kevin Corcoran (eds), *In Search of the Soul*, InterVarsity, 2005; Nancey Murphy, *Bodies and Souls, or Spirited Bodies?*, Cambridge University Press, 2006.

9 For more on this, see John Drane, *Do Christians Know How to be Spiritual?*, Darton Longman & Todd, 2005, pp. 147–51.

10 Sundararajan Rajagopal has identified 'a new disturbing trend in suicide pacts, with more such incidents, involving strangers meeting over the internet, becoming increasingly common'. He also speculates that as a consequence 'the epidemiology of suicide pacts is likely to change, with more young people living on their own, who may have otherwise committed suicide alone, joining with like minded suicidal persons to die together' 'Suicide pacts and the internet', *British Medical Journal* 329, 4 December 2004, pp. 1298–9. Quotes are from p. 1299. See also, http://www.bmj.com/cgi/content/full/329/7478/1298

11 On this and what follows, see Mark W. Speece and Sandor B. Brent, 'The development of children's understanding of death', in Charles A. Corr and Donna M. Corr (eds), *Handbook of Childhood Death and Bereavement*, Springer, 1996, pp. 29–50.

12 Speece and Brent, 'The development of children's understanding of death', p. 31. For more on this, see also their article, 'Children's understanding of death: a review of three components of a death concept', *Child Development* 55.5, 1984, pp. 1671–86.

13 Speece and Brent, 'The development of children's understanding of death'.

14 This poem was originally part of a sermon entitled 'The King of Terrors' preached by Scott-Holland (who was an Anglican clergyman) in St Paul's Cathedral in 1910, while the body of King Edward VII was lying in state at Westminster. In that context, he used the words to indicate how people would like death to be, rather than the reality that it actually is. The fact that so many people apparently embrace them as reflecting reality says something about our inability to deal with death on a purely scientific basis. Significantly, http://www.poeticexpressions.co.uk identifies it as the most frequently visited poem on that web site.

15 http://www.spiritofdiana.com

16 W. H. Gilman and J. E. Parsons (eds), *The Journals & Miscellaneous Notebooks of Ralph Waldo Emerson*, vol. 8, *1841–1843*, Belknap Press, 1970, p. 165.

17 Edna St Vincent Millay, *Collected Poems*, Harper, 1956, p. 286.

18 NCB Childhood Bereavement Network, Briefing on Childhood bereavement suggests that around 1 in 25 children and young people

currently aged 5–16 have experienced the death of a parent or sibling. Every 30 minutes in the UK a child is bereaved of a parent. This equates to 53 children a day, 20,000 children every year. Many more children are bereaved of a grandparent, school friend, other relative or another significant person such as a teacher. http://www.childhoodbereavementnetwork.org.uk/documents/GriefmatterspolicypaperOct07_000.pdf

19 William Shakespeare, *Hamlet*, I.v.166–7.

20 David Hay and Rebecca Nye, *The Spirit of the Child*, 2nd edn, Jessica Kingsley, 2006.

21 The impact of this goes much wider than just death, of course, see John Drane and Olive M. Fleming Drane, *Family Fortunes: Faith-full Caring for Today's Families*, Darton, Longman & Todd, 2004, pp. 21–79.

22 For more extensive theological reflections on the death of Princess Diana, see John Drane, *Cultural Change and Biblical Faith*, Paternoster Press, 2000, pp. 78–103.

23 On this, see extensively John E. Baker and Mary Anne Sedney, 'How bereaved children cope with loss: an overview', in Charles A. Corr and Donna M. Corr (eds), *Handbook of Childhood Death and Bereavement*, Springer, 1996, pp. 109–29.

24 Peter Jarvis, *Adult and Continuing Education: Theory and Practice*, Routledge 1995, p. 6.

25 Richard Rohr, *Simplicity: The Art of Living*, Crossroad, 1991, p. 59.

26 Cf. Walter Ong, *Orality and Literacy*, rev. edn, Routledge, 2002.

27 Cf. William J. Bausch, *Storytelling, Imagination and Faith*, Twenty-Third Publications, 1984; Tex Sample, *Ministry in an Oral Culture*, Westminster/John Knox Press, 1994.

28 Jesus has also frequently been depicted as a clown, see Elizabeth-Anne Stewart, *Jesus the Holy Fool*, Sheed & Ward, 1999.

Chapter 11 Judgement

1 Roger and Gertrude Gobbel, *The Bible: A Child's Playground*, Fortress Press, SCM Press, 1986, p. 34; p. 151 (their italics).

Chapter 12 Angels

1 See http://www.soulschool.co.uk/index2.html

2 E. Heathcote-James, *Seeing Angels*, John Blake Publishing Ltd, 2001.

3 H. Worsley, 'Has secularism emptied the world of angels?', *Journal of Modern Believing* 49.2, April 2008, pp. 46–53; Worsley, 'Insights from children's perspectives in interpreting the wisdom of the biblical creation narrative', *British Journal of Religious Education* 28.3, 2006, pp. 249–59.

4 G. Rosen, *Madness in Society*, Routledge & Kegan Paul, 1968.

5 B. Graham, *Angels, God's Secret Agents*, Hodder Headline, 1981.

6 P. Pullman, *His Dark Materials* trilogy: *Northern Lights*, Scholastic, 1995; The *Subtle Knife*, Scholastic, 1997; *The Amber Spyglass*, Scholastic, 2000.

7 F. Peretti, *This Present Darkness*, Kingsway, 1986; Peretti, *Piercing the Darkness*, Kingsway, 1989.

8 Some of the most famous paintings of angels are readily available for viewing on the Internet, e.g. http://www.christusrex.org/www2/art/angels.htm

9 William Blake, *Songs of Innocence and Experience* (1794). Facsimile reproductions and text transcript © 1991 The Tate Gallery and William Blake Trust Introductions © The Folio Society Limited 1992.

10 *The Guardian*, Saturday, 10 January 1998.

11 C. Collins, *Angels*, Fool's Press, 2004, p. 40, pp. 42–3.

12 R. Willoughby and R. Willoughby *Angels*, Scripture Union, 2006, p. 5.

13 J. Calvin, *Institutes of the Christian Religion*, Arnold Hatfield, 1599, 19.10; 22.8,9.

14 K. Barth, *Church Dogmatics*, trans. *Die Kirchliche Dogmatic*, ed. G. W. Bromiley and T. F. Torrance, T&T Clark, 1956–77, 2004 edn.

15 K. Barth, *Church Dogmatics* 3.3, T&T Clark, 1960, p. 451.

16 R. Harrison, *Oriel's Diary*, Scripture Union, 2002; Harrison, *Oriel's Travels*, Scripture Union, 2003; Harrison, *Oriel in the Desert*, Scripture Union, 2004.

17 'LP' (ed. Canon), *Book of Angels*, Longman Green & Co, 1906.

18 W. Carr, *Angels and Principalities*, Cambridge University Press, 1981.

19 W. Wink, *Naming the Powers*, Fortress Press, 1984, pp. 23ff.

20 W. Wink, *Naming the Powers*, Fortress Press, 1984; *Unmasking the Powers*, Fortress Press, 1986; *Engaging the Powers*, Fortress Press, 1992.

21 The BSP is a project that has been interested to find out how Bible stories are used in the various contexts of home, school or church and how children at different ages access meaning. In 2004 it published some initial research on the meanings offered to Bible stories by children aged 10 to 11; see H. Worsley, 'How children understand Bible stories', *International Journal for Children's Spirituality* 9.2, August 2004, pp. 203–17. In 2005 the same journal published a hermeneutical method used by the BSP for interpreting data from within a child's personal world view; Worsley, 'Insights'. The BSP is currently conducting a wider national research project, sponsored by the Queen's Foundation in Birmingham and the Diocese of Southwell and Nottingham, collecting original case material on

conversations between children and their parents after reading Bible stories.

22 J. Berryman, *Godly Play: An Imaginative Approach to Religious Imagination*, Augsburg Fortress, 1991.

23 Worsley, 'How children understand Bible stories'.

24 T. Copley, *Echo of Angels*, The first report of the Biblos Project, School of Education, University of Exeter, 1998.

25 Copley, *Echo of Angels*; T. Copley and S. Lane, *Where Angels Fear to Tread*, The second report of the H. Savini and K. Walsh Biblos Project, School of Education, University of Exeter, 2001; C. Copley and T. Copley, *On the Side of the Angels*, The third report of the R. Freathy and S. Lane Biblos Project, School of Education, University of Exeter, 2004.

26 Copley, *On the Side of Angels*, p. 5.

27 Copley, *On the Side of Angels*, p. 80; p. 33.

28 *Underworld*, dir. Len Wiseman, Lakeshore Entertainment, 2003; *Blade*, dir. David S. Goyer, New Line Cinema, 2004.

29 D. Hay and R. Nye, *The Spirituality of the Child*, Fount, 1998; D. Hay and K. Hunt, *Understanding the Spirituality of Those Who Don't Go to Church*, unpublished paper, University of Nottingham, 2000.

30 A. Snell, 'A Little Child Shall Lead Them', taken from 'The Cry, A Requiem for the Lost Child', composed by Adrian Snell with Murray Watts, published by Serious Music UK Ltd. Reproduced by permission.

General index

Note: Page references in *italics* indicate illustrations. Where the notes for more than one chapter occur on the same page, notes with the same number are differentiated by the addition of 'a' and 'b'.

abortion 12, 26
abuse xvi, 16–17, 39, 166, 176–7,
    180–81
  and touch 120
accommodation, and cognitive
    development 93, 95–6, *97*
adolescents, and grief 218
adoptionism 168
adulthood, as loss 37–43
adults:
  and angels 264–7
  and play 101, 124
  and reactions to death 219–20
  trustworthiness xvi, 35, 281
  vulnerability 112–13
age of consent 3–4
agency of children 16, 18
Alves, R. 121, 315 n.44
Anderson, Herbert and Johnson,
    Susan B. W. 175–6, 317 n.23
The Angel of the North 250
angels 247–68
  artistic interest in 249–50
  contemporary interest in 248–9
  fallen 252, 276
  guardian 247–8, 249
  and primary children 256–67
  theological interest in 251–4
animals, and sensory experience 57
Arnold, Matthew 7
art:
  Christian 240
  and depiction of angels 349–50
  as secondary creation 51, 59–60

assimilation:
  and cognitive development 93,
    97, 98
  and play 95–6, *97*
attunement, affective 116, 117
Augustine of Hippo:
  and childhood innocence 7, 177
  and salvation 197
  and sin 188–9
authority, parental 4–5

Banks, Iain M., *The Player of Games*
    118
baptism 7, 34
  as means of grace 179, 182
  preparation for 80
  and salvation 194
Barth, Karl:
  and angels 251–2
  and preaching of the word 89–90
  and reception of the word 90–91
Berryman, Jerome xviii, 71, 95–6,
    105–6, 107, 120–21, 123, 149,
    199–200
Bible:
  and angels 252–3
  and children and creation 60–61
  and judgement 223–45
  and play 85, 96–7
  in Religious Education 263–4
  see also word of God
Bible Story Project 254–6, 257–8,
    263
Biblos Project 263–4

birth 22–37
  as blessing 22–3
  and creation 49–50, 51
  and death 24
  and incarnation 27–32
  and memory 23–4
  premature 26–7
  and re-birth 32–4, 50
  and relationship 23
birthdays 23
Blake, William 58, 78, 250, 266
blessing 119–21
Bonhoeffer, Dietrich 48, 155
Bowlby, John 307 n.4
Branne, J. et al. 176, 317 n.26
Braybrooke, Marcus 150, 315 n.4b
bricolage 102–3
Brown, Fraser and Webb, Sophie
    102, 107–8, 109, 113
Brown, William 60
Brueggemann, Walter 89, 91, 95
Bunge, Marcia 79
Bushnell, Horace 79, 189–90, 197,
    199, 200

Calvin, John 7, 9–10, 17, 47, 251
capabilities, negative 112
Carr, Wesley 253
Carrington, Philip 191, 319 n.9
Cavalletti, Sofia xviii, 55–6, 148–9
Chesterton, G. K. 264
The Child in the Church xvii
child development theory, literal
    stage 161
child evangelism xvii
child labour 14–15
child protection 5, 16, 166
child theology xix–xx, 146
  and angels 254–62
  and creation 62–3
  and forgiveness 146–63
  and grace 165–6, 173–4, 182
  and heaven and hell 269–83
  and intuition 148–9, 150, 157–60,
    162, 182, 206
  and judgement 225–43
  and sin 130–45
  and the word 88–90, 92
  see also play; spirituality of children

Child Theology Movement 62
childhood:
  constructs 7–8
  contemporary models 16–17
  and death 8–9
  definitions 2–4
  as experienced 17–18
  and human biology 6–7
  idolization 190–91
  as means of grace 170–73, 176,
    183
children:
  ambivalent attitudes to xvi–xvii, 4
  birth 22–37
  as choice 11–12
  and the Church xvii, 19–20
  cognitive development 93–4, 117,
    144
  definitions 1–20
  doing theology xix–xx, xxii, 20
  influence of Church on 280–81
  influence of school on 279–80
  processing of sorrow 216–19
  as prophets 265
  rights xv, 16, 166, 177
  seen as sinful 9, 130–31
  sexualization 10, 38–41
  and sin 130–32
  and society 14–15
  in teaching of Jesus 192–6
  unborn child 25–6
  well-being 16
Children in the Way xvii
Children's Letters to God 51–3
children's literature
  and angels 249, 252
  and evil 249
Children's Society, Good Childhood
    Inquiry 17–18
choice, and child-bearing 12
christology, and creation 48
Church, and children xvii, 7, 19–20
Churches' Year of the Child xv, xx
circumcision 32–3
Clements, Jane 61–2
cognitive development 93–4, 117,
    144, 219
Coles, Robert 169
Collins, Cecil 250

communication, mutual 117
conscience 156
consciousness, and spirituality 80
consent, age of 3–4
Constructive Theology 108–10
contemplation, in play 114–15
contraception 12–13
Copley, T. 81, 263
Cortens, Theolyn 247–8
covenant, and vulnerability 112–13
creation 44–67
    Asian theologies 50–51
    and birth 49–50, 51
    children's interaction with 54–9,
        60, 61–2
    and death 52
    and eschatology 44, 47–8, 49,
        62–3, 64
    identification with 57–9
    interaction with 54–9
    and play 44–6, 53, 61, 115
    secondary 51, 59–60
    and sensory experience 55–9
    stewardship 62, 63
    and the Trinity 46, 47–8
    and wonder 51, 53, 56, 57
crucifixion, and sin 138–9, 142,
    202–3
cruelty, of children 177
Csikszentmihalyi, Mihaly 107, 112

Daniel in the lions' den 254–6, 268
Daniels, Myriah 212
darkness *see* light and dark
Dawkins, Richard 167, 304 n.8
death 205–22
    and birth 24
    of children 8–9
    and children's processing of
        sorrow 216–19
    in creation 52
    cultural attitudes to 207–10
    definition 210–13
    and hell 275
    and loss 217–18
    and trust 36
decision-making, informed 3
Dennis, Trevor 96
dependence, and grace 167–70, 183

development, cognitive 93–4, 117,
    144
devil 276–8
difference, and play 110
discipline 9–10, 17, 190
    religious 134–5
Donald, M. 117, 314 n.33
drawings:
    and angels 256–61, *257–60*
    and judgement *228, 232,* 235–41,
        236–41, 244
Dupré, L. 81–2
duty 134–5

education:
    changes in xvi
    and gender 14
    school-leaving age 15–16
    and spirituality xviii
Education Reform Act 1988 70
Egeland, B. 172, 174, 176, 318 n.14
Emerson, Ralph Waldo 213
empathy 116–17
emptiness:
    and letting go 112–13
    and play 105–6
    and sin 107–8, 112
entropy, and flow 107, 109, 112
Erikson, Erik 5
eschatology, and creation 44, 47–8,
    49, 62–3, 64
ethics, and play 118–19
eucharist, and children xvii
euthanasia 157, 210
evangelism *see* child evangelism
evil:
    in children's literature 249
    and hell 275–8
expectations of children 30, 72,
    77–8
experience:
    and forgiveness 161–3
    sensory 55–9
exploitation, sexual 10

Fabbriano, Gentile da, *Adoration of
    the Magi* 27–8
fairness 18, 153, 181
Fall of humanity 30–31, 141

families 11–13
  and bereavement 217
  and experience of grace 174–5,
    176
  size 13
Farrer, A. 306 n.19
feminist theology 20, 147, 163
flexibility, compound 109–10
flow, and entropy 107, 112
Ford, David 76
Forer, Lois G. 166, 316 n.3
forgiveness 139–40, 142, 144,
    146–64, 272–3, 279
  corporate 158
  and grace 169, 179
  as received from God 156–9
  and relationships 152–6, 163
  and repentance 155–6, 161–2
  and restitution 152–5, 161–2
  and sin 139–40, 149–52, 162
  spiritual dimension 159–61
  and unforgivable sin 154, 160–61
Fowler, James W. xvii
free will 140–41, 181
Freud, Sigmund 6, 304 n.1b
Froebel, Friedrich 53
Furedi, Frank 401

Garvey, Catherine 105, 106, 121
Gerhardt, Sue 144
Gilligan, Carol 151–2, 304 n.2a
Gobbel, Roger and Gobbel, Gertrude
    223, 243–4, 307 n.5
Godly Play xviii, xix, xxii, 71, 85–7,
    111, 123, 199, 254
  and cognitive development 95,
    109
  and silence 113–14
  and wondering 69, 74, 85–7, 92,
    95, 244
  see also spirituality of children
Goldin, Nan 41
Golding, William, *Lord of the Flies*
    106, 188
Goldman, Ronald 77–8, 80
Good Childhood Inquiry 17–18
Good Friday 138–9, 142
Gormley, Anthony, *The Angel of the
    North* 250

Gould, Stephen J. 304 n.6
grace 165–84
  childhood as means of 79, 82,
    170–73, 176, 183
  costly 167, 180–82, 183
  and dependence 167–70, 183
  and forgiveness 169, 179
  and law 177–8
  persistence 175–7
  and relationships 169–70
  and salvation 167
  and sin 155
Graham, Billy 248
Gray, Thomas 197, 319 n.13
Green, Maxine and Christian,
    Chandu 115
Grenz, Stanley 46–7, 52
grief, and adolescents 218
guilt 150, 156, 162
Gunton, Colin E. 48

Hamilton-Parker, Craig and
    Hamilton-Parker, Jane 212
Hample, S. and Marshall, E.,
    Children's Letters to God 51–3
Hardy, Thomas, *Tess of the
    D'Urbervilles* 194
Harris, Maria 114–15
Harrison, Robert 252
Harry Potter series 34–5, 159, 242,
    277
Hay, David 195, 265
Hay, David and Nye, Rebecca xviii,
    75, 110, 216
Heathcote-James, Emma 248, 264
heaven and hell 269–83
  and God 273, 274
  heaven 262, 269–75, 278
  hell 275–8
  influences on children's views
    279–82
  and judgement 272–3
  and relationships 271–2
Herzog, Kristin 308 n.12
Huizinga, Johan 104–5, 106
Hull, John M. 73

I-Thou relationships 114–16
ignorance, and sin 136

:hildren xviii, xxii, 20,

iirituality 75–7, 83
247–8
erstandings 70–75,

rstandings 77–80
ed 75
3, 80
195, 216
d 73
206
tions of 77–8
care 172–3
1–2
experience 56–7
on-verbal 72, 73–5,

lly Play
creation 62, 63
edy, G. A. 201
–41, 144, 188, 205
isia 157
style choice 209, 210
Alison 113–14
olay 107–8

ed Lord 185, 318 n.1

xix–xx, 7, 9, 19–20,
189–90
108–10
185

tion
, 'Fern Hill' 189
59
ince of 36–7, 54, 120
mas 78, 188
e of:
46, 47–8
3

M. 208

UNICEF, Innocenti report 16

Vaier, Jean 76
Vaughan, Henry 188
Verney, Stephen 112
Virgin Mary, and original sin 32
voice of the child xv–xvi, 51, 80
  in the Church xvii, xix
Volf, Miroslav 152, 161
Von Rad, Gerhard 46
vulnerability:
  of adults 112–13
  of children xxii, 3, 21–43, 115,
    166–9, 170, 178, 191–2

Wade, John 252
Watts, Fraser and Gulliford, Liz
  161
weakness, and sin 136–7
Weber, Hans Ruedi xvii, xx, 121
Wesley, John 79
Westerhoff, John xvii, 73
White, Keith xix
wholeness, and salvation 199
Williams, Rowan 113
Willoughby, Robert and Willoughby,
  Ro 251
Wink, Walter 253
Wisdom, as child 60–61, 200
Wittgenstein, Ludwig 57
wonder:
  and creation 51, 53, 56, 57
  and play 95–6, 98
wondering 93–4, 96
  and Godly Play xviii, 69, 74, 85–7,
    92, 95, 244
word of God 85–100
  nature of 88–90
  and nurture 87–8
  and play 95–6, 98–9
  and preaching 87–8, 89–90, 98–9
  reception 90–92
Wordsworth, William 78
wrath of God 132, 137, 140

Year of the Child (2009) xv, xx

image of God, in children 167–8
imagination 95, 148–9, 244, 254–5
incarnation:
  and creation 60
  and dependence 168
  and difference 110
  and the naked child 27–32
  as play 116, 118
  and salvation 197–8
innocence:
  childhood 10, 16, 30–32, 132,
    177–8, 190–92
  original 188
intelligence, emotional 144
International Rights of the Child xv
International Year of the Child (1979)
  xv, xvii, 121
intuition, and child theology 148–9,
  150, 157–60, 162, 182, 206
Irenaeus of Lyons 141, 198

Jensen, David H. xix, 110, 112–13,
  192
Jesus Christ
  baptism 34
  childhood 197–9
  circumcision 32–3
  humanity and divinity 28–9, 31,
    274
  incarnation 27–8, 31–2
  innocence 30, 32
  and second Adam 31–2
  sinlessness 30–31
  and virgin birth 31–2
Jones, L. Gregory 155
Jones, Serene and Lakeland, Paul 108
Joyce, James 101–2
judgement 223–46
  and children's drawings *228, 232,*
    235–41, *236–41,* 244
  and children's experience 242–3,
    244, *272*
  doctrine 244–5
  fire as 237, 244
  and punishment 228–32, 234
justice, child's sense of 181

Kane, Pat 118–19, 123
Kay, Rosemary 25, 26–7, 305 n.3

Keen, Sam 122
Kermode, Frank 306 n.19
Kierkegaard, Søren 207
kingdom of God 48–9, 50, 60, 61,
  69, 193, 195, 266
  and parable of the sower 85–99
Kohlberg, Lawrence 304 n.2a
Kozol, Jonathon 173

law:
  child protection 5, 40
  and childhood 2–4, 14
  and grace 177–8
Leibowitz, Annie 40
liberation theology 20, 147–8,
  185–6
light and dark, ideas of 159, 249
Lippi, Fra Filippo, *Madonna in a
  Wood* 27
Little Miss Sunshine (film) 38–9
Long, Richard 60
Luther, Martin 79

McGrath, A. 310 n.11
McKeon, John 305 n.5
Marcel, Gabriel 57
The Marches Chronicles 44–5, 55,
  57–8, 103–4, 111
Martini, Simone, *Christ Discovered in
  the Temple* 306 n.13
Martinson, Floyd M. 168
Masefield, John 186, 318 n.2
maturity, and age 3–4
media, influences on children's views
  59, 281–2
memory:
  and birth 23–4
  of childhood 1–2
Millay, Edna St Vincent 215
Miller, David 102
Miller-McLemore, Bonnie J. 131
Milton, John, *Paradise Lost* 252
mimesis 116–17
mission, and children xvii
Moltmann, Jürgen 61, 103, 122–3
Montessori, Maria xviii, 56
mortality:
  child 8–9, 24, 166, 208
  maternal 11–12

My Fair Lady 120

naked child:
  adult perspectives on 21, 37–43
  and baptism 34
  and exploration 36
  and God's purposes 21, 28–9
  and incarnation 27–33
  in non-western cultures 36–7
  and the soul 34–5
  and suffering 42–3
  and trust 35–6
nakedness, and shame 30–31, 37–8
nature, and sensory experience 55–7
Nazir-Ali, Michael 76
neoteny 6
New Age thought 247, 251
Newman, John Henry 31–2
nurture:
  and word of God 87–8
  see also Godly Play
Nye, Rebecca xviii, 75, 110

occult-realism 249
O'Hanlon, Redmond 36
Ong, Walter 220
organ donation 214

paedomorphism 304 n.6
paedophilia 38–9
pain and suffering 140–41, 144
parables:
  Good Shepherd 111
  sheep and goats 223–43, 272, 285
  sower 85–99
parents 4–5
  and child's understanding of God
    138, 141, 174, 279
  and criminal responsibility 178
  and discipline 9–10, 17, 144
  and forgiveness and restitution
    153
  and grace 174
participation projects xv
Paul, St:
  and sin 188
  and word play 96–7, *97*
Peretti, Frank 249, 252
Piaget, J. 5, 77, 93, 95–6, 105

play xxii–xxiii, 95–6, 101–127
  and adults 101, 124
  and alternative realities 121–3
  assimilative 95–6, *97*
  and biblical text 96–7
  and creation 44–6, 53–5, 59–60,
    115
  creation as 61
  definition 102–3, 104–5, 123
  ethical dimensions 118–19
  and heaven 270
  as I-Thou activity 114–16
  and negative capability 112
  and pseudo-play 105–6, 122
  and salvation 107, 109, 190,
    199–201
  and synergy 107–8
  therapeutic 113
  and wonder 95–6, 98
  and word of God 95–6
play-work theory 111–19
pornography, child 10, 39, 41
prayer 275
preaching:
  and play 98–9
  and word 87–8, 89–90, 98–9
Pridmore, David xix
Pullman, Philip, *His Dark Materials*
  37, 249, 282
punishment 140, 155, 161
  and judgement 228–32, 234,
    244–5, 272, 278

Rahner, Karl 7, 20, 79, 83, 91, 170
Rajagopal, Sundararajan 320 n.10
Ranwez, Pierre 79–80
Raphael, *Madonna with the Christ
  Child Blessing* 28
reconciliation 153–5, 156, 162, 183
reincarnation 209–10
relationships:
  and birth 23
  with creation 61, 62–3
  and emotional intelligence 144
  and family 11, 13, 18, 148
  and forgiveness 152–6, 163
  with God 25, 35, 273
  and grace 169–70
  and heaven 270, 271–2

I-Thou 114–16
  parent-child 4–5
  and sin 131, 132, 133–8, 143,
    149–50, 168
  teacher–child 61–2
  and vulnerability 112–13
repentance, and forgiveness 155–6,
  161–2
respect 18
responsibility, criminal 4, 178
restitution, and forgiveness 153–5,
  161–2
Ricoeur, Paul 85, 264
rights of children xv, 16, 166, 177
risk, elimination 5
Ritzer, George 209
Roberts, R. 117
Rohr, Richard 220
Romanticism:
  and angels 266
  and creation 56
Rousseau, Jean-Jacques 189
Rowling, J. K. 34–5, 159, 249
Ruskin, John 55

Saint-Exupéry, Antoine de, *The Little
  Prince* 170
Saliers, Don E. 310 n.11
salvation 185–201
  and baptism 194
  and beach mission theology 193–4
  cost 138–9, 142, 144
  and creation 48
  and liberation theology 185–6
  as life 196, 200
  and play 107, 109, 190, 199–201
  in the present 197–9
  and sin 187–91
  see also grace
Satan 276–8
schema, and cognitive development
  93–4, 95, 96–9
Schleiermacher, F. E. D. 10, 189
science, and childhood 6–7
Scott-Holland, Henry 211–12
seed imagery 88–92
self-esteem:
  as human need 171–2
  and play 117

spiritualit
  27, 6
  and ad
  and an
  current
    81–2
  depth
  earlier
  as enda
  as errat
  innate
  as integ
  as intuit
  low exp
  and pas
  as priva
  and sen
  verbal a
    80
  see also
stewardshi
Studdert K
suffering 1
  and eut
suicide, as
Summerski
synergy, ar

Tennyson,
theology:
  Asian 50
  of childh
    46–7, 7
  Construc
  and conte
  of play 1
  see also c
Thomas, Dy
Tolkien, J. R.
touch, impo
Traherne, Th
Trinity, doct
  and creati
  and play
trust 35–6
Twenge, Jea

Index of biblical references

Old Testament

Genesis
  1 88
  1.27 67
  1.31 66
  2.7 54
  2.25 31
  3 255
  3.6–8 31
  3.19 54
  3.24 252
  4.1 31
  8.21 9, 177
  17.10ff. 33
  18 263
  18.1–15 100
  18.2 253
  18.16–33 145
  21.1–20 67
  32.24 253

Exodus
  3.7–8 115
  12 255
  12.26 309 n.26
  22.22–23 171
  25.18 252

Leviticus
  12 33
  27 5

Numbers
  22 255

Deuteronomy
  6.7 9
  8.3 87

  10.17–18 171
  11.18–19
  14.28, 29 67

Joshua
  4.6 309 n.26

Judges
  6 255

1 Samuel
  3.1–21 84, 94, 194

1 Kings
  19.12 88

2 Kings
  6.8–23 251

Job
  1.21 24
  4.18 252
  10.8–11 25
  10.18 25
  38.28–29 50
  39.4 67

Psalms
  8 64
  8.2 50
  51.5 9, 177
  51.17 203
  58.3 178
  65 51
  93 51
  96 51
  98 51
  104 51

104.12–13 54
118.22 125
130.1 202
131.2 34
139.13 66
148 51

Proverbs
3.19–20 50
8.30–31 200, 201
8.30 60
13.24 9
22.15 9, 67, 190

Ecclesiastes
5.15 24

Isaiah
3.15 195
6 252
11 61, 63
11.6 265–6
14.12 252
38.19 67
47.3 30
53.3 203
55.10 90
55.11 90, 125
64.8 54
66.2 49
66.7ff. 49

Jeremiah
1.4, 5 25
1.5 194

Ezekiel
10 252
34 96

Daniel
6.1–24 254–6
6.25–28 268
10 255

Jonah
4.6–11 127

Zechariah
8.5 127, 199

Apocrypha
Sirach
7.23 9
30.1–13 9

New Testament
Matthew
1 255
2.16–18 29
4.3–4 87
5.3 195
5.22 155
5.23–24 156
6.34 197
11.25 195
11.26 61
13.1–23 100
18.1–14 19
18.1–5 195
18.2–19 170
18.2–5 67
18.6–9 120
19.13–15 19
21.15–16 88
22.9 286
25.31–46 196, 223–46, 285
25.41 252
27.26 190
28.5–8 253

Mark
2.18–22 97
3.20–30 106
4.1–9 85–92
4.14 88
4.26–29 89
4.30–32 88
5.21–43 199
5.21–24 221
5.34 199
5.35–43 36, 221
7.25–29 170
9.14–29 199
9.33–37 221
9.35–37 19, 192
9.36–37 190

9.36 121
9.37 196
9.42–48 120
9.42 195
10.13–16 19, 20, 120, 193, 206, 221
10.14 195
10.15 94, 110
12.30–31 169
16.5 306 n.19
16.6–7 110

Luke
1.41–45 25
2.7 27, 65
2.9 284
2.40 197
2.52 198
4.3–4 87
4.16–29 186
6.20 195
8.41–55 170
8.48 199
9.46–48 19
11.13 126
13.8–9 90
15.3–7 96, 124
15.11–32 100
17.1, 2 120
17.11–19 199
18.15–17 19
18.17 266
23.42 182
24.32 94

John
1.1–14 200
1.2 48
1.4 87
1.14 88, 168, 204
1.21, 23 97
3.3–8 33–4
3.8 124, 127
6.25–40 87
6.35 88
8.1–11 163–4
8.3–11 145
10.10 199
12.23–24 89

13.34 112
14.3 283
20 255

Acts
4.11 125
12.1–19 251
22.22 193

Romans
3.23 128, 178
4 33
5.12 32
6.7–23 145
7.15–20 106–7
8.22 29, 49

1 Corinthians
1.24 200
3.6–7 91
9.20–23 91
13.11 169
15.22 32, 188

Galatians
1.15 204
5.3, 4 97
5.12 97
5.22–23 88
6.18 204

Ephesians
4.15–17 87
5.9 88
6.12 144

Colossians
1.16–17 48

Hebrews
1.2–3 88
13.2 263

James
1.17 171

2 Peter
2.4 252

1 John
  1.6–7 159

Revelation
  3.18 38–9
  4 251

5 251
12.9 252
16.15 38
21 50
21.4 285
21.6 48

image of God, in children 167–8
imagination 95, 148–9, 244, 254–5
incarnation:
  and creation 60
  and dependence 168
  and difference 110
  and the naked child 27–32
  as play 116, 118
  and salvation 197–8
innocence:
  childhood 10, 16, 30–32, 132,
    177–8, 190–92
  original 188
intelligence, emotional 144
International Rights of the Child xv
International Year of the Child (1979)
    xv, xvii, 121
intuition, and child theology 148–9,
    150, 157–60, 162, 182, 206
Irenaeus of Lyons 141, 198

Jensen, David H. xix, 110, 112–13,
    192
Jesus Christ
  baptism 34
  childhood 197–9
  circumcision 32–3
  humanity and divinity 28–9, 31,
    274
  incarnation 27–8, 31–2
  innocence 30, 32
  and second Adam 31–2
  sinlessness 30–31
  and virgin birth 31–2
Jones, L. Gregory 155
Jones, Serene and Lakeland, Paul 108
Joyce, James 101–2
judgement 223–46
  and children's drawings 228, 232,
    235–41, 236–41, 244
  and children's experience 242–3,
    244, 272
  doctrine 244–5
  fire as 237, 244
  and punishment 228–32, 234
justice, child's sense of 181

Kane, Pat 118–19, 123
Kay, Rosemary 25, 26–7, 305 n.3

Keen, Sam 122
Kermode, Frank 306 n.19
Kierkegaard, Søren 207
kingdom of God 48–9, 50, 60, 61,
    69, 193, 195, 266
  and parable of the sower 85–99
Kohlberg, Lawrence 304 n.2a
Kozol, Jonathon 173

law:
  child protection 5, 40
  and childhood 2–4, 14
  and grace 177–8
Leibowitz, Annie 40
liberation theology 20, 147–8,
    185–6
light and dark, ideas of 159, 249
Lippi, Fra Filippo, *Madonna in a
    Wood* 27
Little Miss Sunshine (film) 38–9
Long, Richard 60
Luther, Martin 79

McGrath, A. 310 n.11
McKeon, John 305 n.5
Marcel, Gabriel 57
The Marches Chronicles 44–5, 55,
    57–8, 103–4, 111
Martini, Simone, *Christ Discovered in
    the Temple* 306 n.13
Martinson, Floyd M. 168
Masefield, John 186, 318 n.2
maturity, and age 3–4
media, influences on children's views
    59, 281–2
memory:
  and birth 23–4
  of childhood 1–2
Millay, Edna St Vincent 215
Miller, David 102
Miller-McLemore, Bonnie J. 131
Milton, John, *Paradise Lost* 252
mimesis 116–17
mission, and children xvii
Moltmann, Jürgen 61, 103, 122–3
Montessori, Maria xviii, 56
mortality:
  child 8–9, 24, 166, 208
  maternal 11–12

My Fair Lady 120

naked child:
    adult perspectives on 21, 37–43
    and baptism 34
    and exploration 36
    and God's purposes 21, 28–9
    and incarnation 27–33
    in non-western cultures 36–7
    and the soul 34–5
    and suffering 42–3
    and trust 35–6
nakedness, and shame 30–31, 37–8
nature, and sensory experience 55–7
Nazir-Ali, Michael 76
neoteny 6
New Age thought 247, 251
Newman, John Henry 31–2
nurture:
    and word of God 87–8
    see also Godly Play
Nye, Rebecca xviii, 75, 110

occult-realism 249
O'Hanlon, Redmond 36
Ong, Walter 220
organ donation 214

paedomorphism 304 n.6
paedophilia 38–9
pain and suffering 140–41, 144
parables:
    Good Shepherd 111
    sheep and goats 223–43, 272, 285
    sower 85–99
parents 4–5
    and child's understanding of God
        138, 141, 174, 279
    and criminal responsibility 178
    and discipline 9–10, 17, 144
    and forgiveness and restitution
        153
    and grace 174
participation projects xv
Paul, St:
    and sin 188
    and word play 96–7, *97*
Peretti, Frank 249, 252
Piaget, J. 5, 77, 93, 95–6, 105

play xxii–xxiii, 95–6, 101–127
    and adults 101, 124
    and alternative realities 121–3
    assimilative 95–6, *97*
    and biblical text 96–7
    and creation 44–6, 53–5, 59–60,
        115
    creation as 61
    definition 102–3, 104–5, 123
    ethical dimensions 118–19
    and heaven 270
    as I-Thou activity 114–16
    and negative capability 112
    and pseudo-play 105–6, 122
    and salvation 107, 109, 190,
        199–201
    and synergy 107–8
    therapeutic 113
    and wonder 95–6, 98
    and word of God 95–6
play-work theory 111–19
pornography, child 10, 39, 41
prayer 275
preaching:
    and play 98–9
    and word 87–8, 89–90, 98–9
Pridmore, David xix
Pullman, Philip, *His Dark Materials*
        37, 249, 282
punishment 140, 155, 161
    and judgement 228–32, 234,
        244–5, 272, 278

Rahner, Karl 7, 20, 79, 83, 91, 170
Rajagopal, Sundararajan 320 n.10
Ranwez, Pierre 79–80
Raphael, *Madonna with the Christ
        Child Blessing* 28
reconciliation 153–5, 156, 162, 183
reincarnation 209–10
relationships:
    and birth 23
    with creation 61, 62–3
    and emotional intelligence 144
    and family 11, 13, 18, 148
    and forgiveness 152–6, 163
    with God 25, 35, 273
    and grace 169–70
    and heaven 270, 271–2

I–Thou 114–16
parent-child 4–5
and sin 131, 132, 133–8, 143,
  149–50, 168
teacher–child 61–2
and vulnerability 112–13
repentance, and forgiveness 155–6,
  161–2
respect 18
responsibility, criminal 4, 178
restitution, and forgiveness 153–5,
  161–2
Ricoeur, Paul 85, 264
rights of children xv, 16, 166, 177
risk, elimination 5
Ritzer, George 209
Roberts, R. 117
Rohr, Richard 220
Romanticism:
  and angels 266
  and creation 56
Rousseau, Jean-Jacques 189
Rowling, J. K. 34–5, 159, 249
Ruskin, John 55

Saint-Exupéry, Antoine de, *The Little
  Prince* 170
Saliers, Don E. 310 n.11
salvation 185–201
  and baptism 194
  and beach mission theology 193–4
  cost 138–9, 142, 144
  and creation 48
  and liberation theology 185–6
  as life 196, 200
  and play 107, 109, 190, 199–201
  in the present 197–9
  and sin 187–91
  see also grace
Satan 276–8
schema, and cognitive development
  93–4, 95, 96–9
Schleiermacher, F. E. D. 10, 189
science, and childhood 6–7
Scott-Holland, Henry 211–12
seed imagery 88–92
self-esteem:
  as human need 171–2
  and play 117

selfish gene theory 6, 167
senses, and spirituality 56–7
sexuality:
  and age of consent 3
  sexualization of children 10,
    38–41
shame, and nakedness 30–31,
  37–8
sheep and goats, parable of 223–43,
  272, 285
  children's drawings *228, 232,*
    235–41, *236–41,* 244
  initial responses to 225–7
  and judgement 232–4
  literary criticism 234–5
Silverman, Phyllis Rolfe 207
  actions of the King 230–32
  actions of sheep and goats
    227–30
sin 53, 128–45
  and accountability 178–9
  children's definitions 130–32
  collective 128, 142, 158
  and emptiness 107–8, 112
  as fracturing of relationships
    131, 132, 133–8, 143, 149–50,
    168
  and freedom of choice 140–41
  good sin xxiii, 150–52
  and guilt 150, 156, 162
  and human development
    140–41
  and innocence 30–31, 132,
    177–8
  of omission 138
  original sin 9–10, 32, 152, 168,
    178–9, 187–9, 192
  and play 108
  and salvation 187–91
  unforgivable 154, 160–61
  and views of God 138–42
  see also forgiveness; judgement
skin contact 36–7
Smith, Delia 119
Snell, Adrian 265–6
society, and children 14–15
Song, Choan-Seng 50–51
soul 34–5, 210
Spencer, Stanley 250

spirituality of children xviii, xxii, 20, 27, 68–84
  and adult spirituality 75–7, 83
  and angels 247–8
  current understandings 70–75, 81–2
  depth 72–3
  earlier understandings 77–80
  as endangered 75
  as erratic 73, 80
  innate xvii, 195, 216
  as integrated 73
  as intuitive 206
  low expectations of 77–8
  and pastoral care 172–3
  as private 81–2
  and sensory experience 56–7
  verbal and non-verbal 72, 73–5, 80
  see also Godly Play
stewardship of creation 62, 63
Studdert Kennedy, G. A. 201
suffering 140–41, 144, 188, 205
  and euthanasia 157
suicide, as lifestyle choice 209, 210
Summerskills, Alison 113–14
synergy, and play 107–8

Tennyson, Alfred Lord 185, 318 n.1
theology:
  Asian 50–51
  of childhood xix–xx, 7, 9, 19–20, 46–7, 79, 189–90
  Constructive 108–10
  and context 185
  of play 123
  see also creation
Thomas, Dylan, 'Fern Hill' 189
Tolkien, J. R. R. 59
touch, importance of 36–7, 54, 120
Traherne, Thomas 78, 188
Trinity, doctrine of:
  and creation 46, 47–8
  and play 103
trust 35–6
Twenge, Jean M. 208

UNICEF, Innocenti report 16

Vaier, Jean 76
Vaughan, Henry 188
Verney, Stephen 112
Virgin Mary, and original sin 32
voice of the child xv–xvi, 51, 80
  in the Church xvii, xix
Volf, Miroslav 152, 161
Von Rad, Gerhard 46
vulnerability:
  of adults 112–13
  of children xxii, 3, 21–43, 115, 166–9, 170, 178, 191–2

Wade, John 252
Watts, Fraser and Gulliford, Liz 161
weakness, and sin 136–7
Weber, Hans Ruedi xvii, xx, 121
Wesley, John 79
Westerhoff, John xvii, 73
White, Keith xix
wholeness, and salvation 199
Williams, Rowan 113
Willoughby, Robert and Willoughby, Ro 251
Wink, Walter 253
Wisdom, as child 60–61, 200
Wittgenstein, Ludwig 57
wonder:
  and creation 51, 53, 56, 57
  and play 95–6, 98
wondering 93–4, 96
  and Godly Play xviii, 69, 74, 85–7, 92, 95, 244
word of God 85–100
  nature of 88–90
  and nurture 87–8
  and play 95–6, 98–9
  and preaching 87–8, 89–90, 98–9
  reception 90–92
Wordsworth, William 78
wrath of God 132, 137, 140

Year of the Child (2009) xv, xx